How to Do *Everything* with Your

Pocket PC
Second Edition

About the Author

Frank McPherson is an avid user of handheld computers, starting with the Newton MessagePad in 1993 and later the Windows CE Handheld PC. Since 1993 he has been helping Newton, Handheld, and Pocket PC users online with Compuserve, the Microsoft Network, and Internet newsgroups. He developed and maintains the PocketPCHow2 website (http://www .pocketpchow2.com), which is visited by people from around the world seeking help using their Pocket PCs. Microsoft has recognized him as a Most Value Professional for his contributions to the mobile device community.

Frank has been a sports columnist and reporter for the Norway Current, a weekly newspaper in Norway, Michigan, and has also covered high school sports for the Iron Mountain Daily News in Iron Mountain, Michigan. Articles written by Frank about Pocket PC's have appeared in *Pocket PC Magazine*, *Brighthand.com*, and *PocketPC.com*.

A 1989 graduate of Michigan Technological University with a BS degree in Computer Science, Frank is also a Microsoft Certified Systems Engineer and Senior Information Specialist at EDS, where he has been employed for over ten years. Originally from Norway, Michigan, located in Michigan's beautiful Upper Peninsula, this Yooper now lives in West Bloomfield, Michigan with his wife, Ruth.

How to Do *Everything* with Your

Pocket PC
Second Edition

Frank McPherson

McGraw-Hill/Osborne

New York   Chicago   San Francisco
Lisbon   London   Madrid   Mexico City
Milan   New Delhi   San Juan
Seoul   Singapore   Sydney   Toronto

McGraw-Hill/Osborne
2600 Tenth Street
Berkeley, California 94710
U.S.A.

To arrange bulk purchase discounts for sales promotions, premiums, or fund-raisers, please contact **McGraw-Hill/**Osborne at the above address. For information on translations or book distributors outside the U.S.A., please see the International Contact Information page immediately following the index of this book.

How to Do Everything with Your Pocket PC, Second Edition

ISBN 0-07-219414-6

Publisher:	Brandon A. Nordin
Vice President &	
AssociatePublisher:	Scott Rogers
Acquisitions Editor:	Megg Bonar
Project Editor:	Julie M. Smith
Acquisitions Coordinator:	Tana Diminyatz
Technical Editor:	Todd Ogasawara
Copy Editor:	Linda Marousek
Proofreaders:	Paul Medoff, Linda Medoff
Indexer:	David Heiret
Computer Designers:	Lauren McCarthy, Elizabeth Jang
Illustrators:	Michael Mueller, Lyssa Wald
Series Design:	Mickey Galicia
Cover Series Design:	Dodie Shoemaker

This book was composed with Corel VENTURA ™ Publisher.

Dedication

I was nearly halfway through writing this book on September 11, 2001. It was hard to write anything as the horror of that day's events, and the suffering of so many people, made writing books and Pocket PCs seem unimportant. Like many other Americans, I struggled with fear and uncertainty.

As the days passed with images of New York, Washington DC, and Pennsylvania constantly on television, I wondered what it is that I could do. All the people who died on that day did so enjoying the freedom the United States provides. Americans are free to travel anywhere within this great country, and earn a living doing work that provides personal satisfaction. In the United States everyone is free to practice any religion, go to any school, and voice their own opinions. Writing this book is one way that I enjoy my freedom, and in so doing bring honor to those who died on September 11, 2001.

This book is dedicated to those died on the planes, in the buildings, and on the ground in New York, Washington DC, and Pennsylvania. It is dedicated to our real heroes, the men and women of our fire and police departments, doctors, nurses, and emergency technicians, and members of our armed forces.

Let us never forget how precious all life is, and how truly blessed we are to live in a country in which we are free to seek out and fulfill our dreams.

Contents at a Glance

Contents

Acknowledgments

Reading is one of my most cherished activities, and writing a book has always been a dream. Megg Bonar of Osborne/McGraw-Hill presented me the opportunity to fulfill that dream, and for that I am eternally grateful. The time I have spent writing this book has been very rewarding because of the team of people pulled together to make it happen. Without Megg Bonar, Julie Smith, and Tana Diminyatz this book simply would not exist. Thank you, Megg, for asking me, and thank you all for teaching me, and for being so patient and understanding.

Todd Ogasawara is the first person in the Windows CE community that I met online at MSN and he quickly earned my respect. I am very grateful to Todd for being the technical reviewer of this book. Todd, a big part of this book is yours, thank you.

Special thanks goes to Derek Brown and Beth Goza at Microsoft. Much of what is written here occurred while Pocket PC 2002 was still being tested and finished. Without the assistance that Derek and Beth provided I simply would not have had the information I needed to write this book.

For securing the images seen on this book's cover, thanks go out to Chantal Borromeo and Ellen Maly at Compaq, to Heather M. Wagner at Hewlett-Packard Company, and to Shelly Greenhalgh at NEC. Thanks to Crown Logic Corporation, CNetX, Biohazard Software, DDH Software, IA Style, Inc., Idruna Software, Applian Technologies Inc., and Conduit Technologies Inc. for providing permission to include screen shots of their products in this book. Their quick turnaround and efforts are much appreciated.

Thanks to Jason Dunn, Chris De Herrera, Brad Adrian, Ed Hansberry, Michael Gordon, Andreas Sjorstrom, and Dale Coffing, all who helped by answering questions as I wrote this book.

Thanks to my friends, mentors, and co-workers including: Ray Anderson, Scott Van Wolvelaere, Amy Dulan, Bob Naglich, Brad Gee, Bill Weber, Marshall Haney, Mark North, Matt Anderson, Kevin Klott, Keith Muir, Dawn Pfaff, and Rhonda Beline. Thank you for your friendship and support.

Thanks to my grandmother, Dorothy McPherson, and my mother, Sharon McPherson for their love and support. And last but not least, thanks to my wife Ruth. Your love, patience, understanding, and support are what made this book happen. This has been great, but the best is yet to come and I look forward to sharing it all with you.

Introduction

When Microsoft launched the Pocket PC on April 19, 2000, few knew how successful it would be. There was some nervous excitement because the Pocket PC sported a more efficient user interface and performance improvements, but previous handheld operating systems from Microsoft achieved little market success.

Time has shown that there was good reason to be excited, as the Pocket PC became the most successful handheld running Microsoft software to date. By the Pocket PC 2002 launch in October, 2001, the Pocket PC gained significant share of the consumer and enterprise handheld markets. The Pocket PC is now the choice for people who want the most versatile handheld to manage their personal information.

The Pocket PC is the latest in a series of hardware devices that run the Microsoft Windows CE operating system and application software. Also included in the series are the Handheld PC, Auto PC, and embedded devices. Microsoft calls the series Windows Powered devices. The combination of Windows CE and application software is known as Windows for Pocket PCs.

Pocket PCs help you interact in different ways with a variety of information. Think about all of the information that is important to you. It might be appointments, addresses, bank account balances, or documents. It might even be voice recordings, web pages, video clips, or music.

Many people have turned to personal computers to help them keep track of all this different information. But, there is a problem with personal computers. Most sit on tables and desks at home, while we need the information they contain when we are sitting in meetings or out shopping. With a Pocket PC that information can be taken out of the computer so that it is with you at any time, and anywhere. And when you return home that information can be easily updated to your personal computer.

These are incredibly powerful little devices that you can use for work and play. In *How To Do Everything With Your Pocket PC, Second Edition* I show you how to use the latest Pocket PC software to create documents and spreadsheets, check off those items on your task list, and then relax to the sounds of your favorite musician. If there is something that you want to do with a Pocket PC, this book will show you how to do it.

Part I of this book provides the information that you need to get started with your Pocket PC. Chapter 1 provides an overview of the devices that make up the Windows Powered platform to help you decide which is right for you. Then starting in Chapter 2, I walk you through the experience of setting up your Pocket PC, followed by Chapter 3 where you will learn how to personalize your Pocket PC.

One of the first things you will want to do is move information from your personal computer into the device. Chapter 5 shows you how to connect Pocket PCs with personal computers, and in Chapter 6 you learn how to use the ActiveSync software to synchronize data so that what is stored in Microsoft Outlook on your PC, also appears in Pocket Outlook on your device. As that information changes synchronization ensures that it is the same on both the PC and Pocket PC.

Part II, called "Make The Most of Your Pocket PC" focuses on how you will use your Pocket or PC every day. You will use Pocket Outlook to manage your appointments, addresses, and tasks, and Pocket Office to create documents and spreadsheets. I also provide tips for using your Pocket PC at the office, and when you are traveling. And when you are ready for a break you can install and play one of the many games available for Pocket PCs.

The Internet has become a very important tool for retrieving and exchanging information, and Part III, "Go Online with Your Pocket PC" provides all the instructions you need to connect to and use the Internet. Pocket PCs can connect to the Internet using landline and wireless modems, and directly via local area networks. Once the connection is made you can send and receive e-mail, chat with friends using instant messaging, and browse any web site. You can download Web pages to your device so that they can be read any time, even when you are not connected to the Internet.

Part IV, "Customize Your Pocket PC" shows you how to tailor your device to suit your tastes. You can expand the storage space on Pocket PC to install software from a library of thousands of programs available on the Internet. In Chapter 23 you will learn about some of my favorite programs that you can use to expand the functionality of your Pocket PC.

A number of special elements have been added to help you get the most out of this book:

- **How to**   These special boxes explain, in a nutshell, how to accomplish certain tasks that use the skills that you learn in this book.

- **Did You Know**   These special boxes provide additional information about topics relating to Pocket PCs.

- **Notes**   These provide extra information or important things that you need to watch out for in certain situations.

- **Tips**   These tell you how to do something better, faster, or in a smarter way.

Within the text you will find words in special formatting. New or defined terms are in *italic*. If there is a hyphen between two different keys, such as CTRL-B, that's a keyboard combination, and you should press each key while holding down the others, then release them simultaneously. Some instructions involve tapping on different buttons or menu items in sequence. An I-beam separates each step in the sequence, for example File | Open means tap the File and then Open menu options.

Technology changes at a break-neck pace, and undoubtedly you will have a question, or encounter a problem not covered in this book. One good source for information is the microsoft.public.windowsce Internet newsgroup, which is monitored by myself and my fellow Microsoft Mobile Device MVPs. You can also reach me through my web site, PocketPCHow2.com, at http://www.pocketpchow2.com, or via the e-mail address, feedback@ fmcpherson.com.

Part I

Getting Started

Chapter 1

Welcome to Windows for Pocket PCs

How To...

- Recognize the different Windows Powered platforms
- Know what Windows Powered devices include
- Know the different parts of Windows for Pocket and Handheld PCs

In 1996, several companies—including Hewlett-Packard, Casio, Sharp, and Compaq—began selling a brand new device called a Handheld PC. Handheld PCs run Microsoft software that includes the Windows CE operating system and other programs for managing personal information and creating documents and spreadsheets.

The Handheld PC was only the first of a variety of different types of what Microsoft now calls Windows Powered devices. The devices continue to evolve and include the Pocket PC, which is the subject of this book. Each device is designed so that you can work with the information important to you, wherever it is needed, and in the manner you find most comfortable.

Windows Powered devices do more than just manage appointments, addresses, and task lists, though they do that very well. With a Windows Powered device, you can read your e-mail and surf the Web. You can write a letter, balance your checkbook, make voice recordings, read books, and listen to music. In the case of the Pocket PC, all these things are possible in a device that can rest in your hand and fit in your pocket.

Everyone's information needs are different, and the Windows software for Pocket PCs provides you with all the tools to meet your needs. This book is about how to use this software to make your Pocket PC your own personal information appliance.

Each component of Windows for Pocket PCs is covered in depth in the chapters of this book. It focuses on the current versions of the software that run on Pocket PCs. While older versions continue to exist, and much of what is contained in this book applies to those versions, the focus is on the newest software for this platform.

We begin here by laying the foundation—learning about all the different hardware platforms that, when combined, are the Windows Powered devices. This chapter also includes an introduction to Windows for Pocket PCs, all of which is explained in more detail in the remaining chapters of this book.

Information Appliances

In the 70 years since it was introduced, the television set has undergone a number of changes. From black-and-white to color images, and from simple 19-inch round displays to 35-inch flat panels, the television set has been improved and re-invented. Through it all, one thing has remained constant: each television set has a button; and when you press that button, the screen springs to life to display what we commonly call TV.

It is true of all consumer electronic devices that we expect them to work the instant we turn them on. Radios and CD players immediately start playing music and Gameboys start playing games. What about your personal computer? What happened the last time you turned it on? Did it spring to life and start computing?

In offices all around the world, the following ritual is played out every morning (you might even find yourself doing it): After fighting through traffic and dragging yourself and the work you brought home into your cube or office, you hang up your coat, turn on your computer, grab your coffee mug, and head for the coffee machine. Sound familiar? This ritual has come about because of what is known as the *booting process* of personal computers. The booting process includes all steps that computers take from when they are first turned on until the computer is ready for you to use.

Perhaps your boss has heard that notebook computers can make employees more productive, so he or she buys you one. Despite the fact that you are now expected to work 14-hour days, that seems to be a small price to pay as you open the box of your brand new notebook computer. Who cares how much you are now expected to work? Your notebook is cool and nobody else in your department has one.

Over time, you stumble across the Outlook icon on the desktop and discover that it can store appointments, contacts, and tasks. In fact, you learn that it can be used for all of the same functions as the planner you carry constantly. You realize that if you use Outlook to manage your time, rather than your planner, you would have one fewer item to carry home every night. Plus, carrying it into meetings gives you a chance to show off your notebook to your envious coworkers.

So, you begin the task of entering all of the appointments, tasks, and contacts from your planner into Outlook. This works splendidly during the day, as everything is right there at your fingertips as you work on your computer. Then comes your business trip. As you enter the airport, your pager goes off. You seek out the nearest telephone booth to call your boss, who wants to know whether you are available the day you get back to attend an important meeting with a potential client. With one hand on the telephone, you unzip the bag that contains your notebook computer, fumble around to turn it on, and then wait for what seems an eternity while your boss grows impatient and you watch your PC boot-up. You wish you had the planner that you left on your dresser at home.

Wouldn't it be great if your computer were as easy to use as a television set and functioned from the moment you turned it on? That is the promise of information appliances. In his book *The Invisible Computer* (MIT Press, 1998), author Donald A. Norman defines the information appliance as "an appliance specializing in information: knowledge, facts, graphics, images, video, or sound. An information appliance is designed to perform a specific activity, such as music, photography, or writing. A distinguishing feature of information appliances is the ability to share information among themselves."

Information appliances have recently begun to receive a lot of attention, mostly from computer magazines writing about low-cost devices that connect to the Internet and replace personal computers. Most of these articles would have you believe that information appliances are new; but in reality, only the attention is new. The term was created in 1978 and trademarked by Jef Raskin, who was the creator of the Macintosh computer project at Apple Computer.

A newer form of an information appliance is the *personal digital assistant (PDA)*. During a speech at the 1992 Consumer Electronics Show in Las Vegas, former Apple Computer CEO John Sculley defined the PDA and announced Apple's intention to develop such a device. PDAs are information appliances that use computer technology to help manage personal information and assist with mundane tasks. Later in 1992, Sculley introduced Apple's PDA, the Newton MessagePad, at the Spring Consumer Electronics Show (CES) in Chicago.

The Newton MessagePad may not have been the first information appliance, but it can be credited for being the first to draw attention to the concept. Its introduction at the CES captured the imagination of the press, who saw a demonstration of the device that performed handwriting recognition. From that point on, much was expected from this new device that was going to re-establish Apple as a technology leader.

From the time of its introduction in 1992 to its launch at the 1993 MacWorld Expo in Boston, a tremendous amount of hype was generated about the Newton MessagePad. Competitors also weighed in with their devices. Tandy and Casio jointly created their PDA, called Zoomer; General Magic created MagicCap; and Microsoft was rumored to be developing a Newton-killer called WinPad.

Unfortunately, the hype was short-lived; and during the life span of the Newton MessagePad from 1993 to 1998, sales never reached Apple's projected levels. Sadly, despite the technology of the Newton MessagePad, it may be best known in computing history for a series of Doonesbury comic strips that made fun of the results of Newton's handwriting recognition.

With the benefit of hindsight, one can look back at the Newton MessagePad and see its shortcomings. The handwriting recognition was not complete when it was first released, which resulted in the PDA being branded a failure. Even during the existence of the Newton MessagePad, Apple started referring to the device as a Personal Communications Assistant; and, even today, Palm Computing and Microsoft do not refer to their devices as PDAs. During its five years, Newton MessagePads grew larger in size and increased in price, conflicting with a market that wanted smaller devices at a lower cost. Finally, exchanging information between a MessagePad and a desktop computer was too difficult.

Despite these shortcomings, the Newton MessagePad leaves a legacy of creating the PDA market, and furthering the cause of information appliances. Lessons learned from the Newton MessagePad were applied to both Palm Computing devices and Microsoft PC Companions.

Microsoft PC Companions

During the summer of 1992, Microsoft began its version of the Newton MessagePad, which it called WinPad. At the same time, another project—Pulsar—was underway to develop a pager-like device. In 1994, senior management at Microsoft reviewed both projects and decided to combine the two into a new project that was given the code name Pegasus, which became Windows CE.

WinPad was designed to be a companion for business users and was based on Windows 3.1. Pulsar was to include an entirely new object-oriented operating system, completely unlike any other Microsoft product. In the end, Pegasus did not include the technology from either of these projects, but it did inherit the WinPad vision of being a companion for Windows desktop computers. That vision became known as the *PC Companion.*

A PC Companion is a small device that fits in the palm of your hand and is designed to exchange information with programs running on personal computers. A PC Companion enables you to carry all of the information you create on a personal computer, wherever it may be needed. And, equally important as its size and ability to communicate with personal computers, PC Companions use an operating system stored on a computer chip that runs continuously, eliminating the booting process. A PC Companion functions immediately when it is turned on, just like a television set.

> **NOTE** *PC Companion is the old terminology for what Microsoft now calls Windows Powered devices.*

The PC Companion changes the scenario described at the beginning of this chapter. All of the information is still entered into Outlook from a planner; but instead of carrying the notebook computer everywhere, you download the information to a PC Companion. If all you need is the information contained in Outlook, you can leave the notebook computer behind and only pack the PC Companion when traveling.

Now, when your boss pages you to ask whether you can attend a meeting, all you need to do is take out your PC Companion, turn it on, and look up the information—in no more time than it takes to retrieve and look up the same information in a planner. After you determine that you are available on the date and time of the meeting, you create the appointment on the PC Companion. When you return to the office, you connect the PC Companion to the notebook computer; the new appointment uploads to Outlook, eliminating the need to re-enter information, as might be the case if you were using a planner and Outlook together.

The process of exchanging information between a PC Companion and a desktop computer is called *synchronization*. Synchronization is actually a bit more sophisticated than simply uploading and downloading information because it has the ability to determine what has been added to both devices and to ensure that the information is the same on both, all in one step.

One can debate whether or not the Microsoft PC Companion is an information appliance. It specializes in information, yet it can perform multiple activities, rather than just one. Because there are many different ways for information to be expressed and used, PC Companions not only manage personal information like your appointments and addresses, but also documents, spreadsheets, web pages, voice recordings, and music.

Nor is information the only variable; how each person wishes to interact with that information is also different. Some people prefer using small devices with small keyboards, while others are comfortable with a stylus and handwriting recognition. Others prefer a larger device, closer in size to a notebook computer; and some prefer to have that information available in their car, which they can retrieve by using voice commands.

Over the years since 1996, when the first PC Companion was introduced, Microsoft has made changes to the Windows CE operating system and the software that it includes to continually support a wide range of information types. At the same time, new hardware has been introduced, targeted at the variety of different ways users want to interact with the device.

The results are subtle differences between operating system versions and application software, five different hardware platforms, and a confused market. Microsoft discovered that part of the confusion is all of the different hardware and software names. Therefore, in the fall of 1999, Microsoft introduced Windows Powered devices, and Windows for Pocket and Handheld PCs. These two terms are defined in the remainder of this chapter.

Windows Powered Devices

Ever since Microsoft launched the first Handheld PC, several different Original Equipment Manufacturers (OEMs)—such as Philips, Casio, Hewlett-Packard, and Compaq—have made the hardware while Microsoft creates the software. Included in the software is a new operating system and pocket versions of some Microsoft desktop software, such as Pocket Outlook (Calendar, Contacts, and Tasks) and Pocket Office (Pocket Word and Excel).

Unlike a personal computer, the software of the Handheld PC is stored on computer chips. Windows for Handheld and Pocket PCs is only available on Read-Only Memory (ROM) chips. It was necessary to use a ROM chip to store all of the software in a very small amount of space and to eliminate the booting process. The combination of the operating system, Pocket Outlook, and Pocket Office became known as Windows CE, even though Windows CE is really just the operating system. Today, Microsoft calls this combination of software on a ROM chip for Windows for Handheld PCs or Pocket PCs, and the hardware is Windows Powered.

> **NOTE** *There have now been two releases of Windows for Pocket PCs using Windows CE. To distinguish between the two, we refer to the first release as Pocket PC 2000 and the current release as Pocket PC 2002.*

The Handheld PC is only the first Windows Powered hardware platform; and since 1996, Microsoft has introduced four additional platforms: Palm-size PCs, Auto PCs, Handheld PC 2000, and Pocket PCs.

Handheld PCs

Handheld PCs are the result of the Pegasus project, which began in 1994. The device included the first versions of the Windows CE operating system, Pocket Outlook, and Pocket Office. The first version of Pocket Office only included Word and Excel. Microsoft also included a copy of their first Personal Information Manager (PIM), Schedule +, and Handheld PC Explorer, which provided synchronization between Schedule + and the Handheld PC.

A few months later, Microsoft released an upgraded version of the Handheld PC Explorer, which provided synchronization between Handheld PCs and Outlook. Even now, if you have a Handheld PC with Windows CE Version 1, you must use Handheld PC Explorer because the latest version of the software, called *ActiveSync,* does not work with your device.

> **TIP** *You can find Handheld PC Explorer Version 1 at http://www.microsoft.com/mobile/ handheldpc/downloads/hpcexplorer/hpcexp.asp*

Along with the software, the following hardware specifications were typical for Handheld PCs:

- *Clamshell* design, approximately 3.5"W×7"H and weighing approximately 13 ounces.
- Powered by Alkaline batteries.
- 480×240 resolution monochrome display.
- Keyboard for data input and a stylus instead of a mouse.
- At least 2MB of RAM for program execution and storage space. Many OEMs created 4MB devices. Casio also created a 6MB version of their device and Philips had an 8MB device.

- At least a 4MB ROM chip to store Windows CE and other software programs. The software could be upgraded by replacing the ROM chip.

- One of several different RISC processors, of which the Hitachi SH3 was most commonly used, though NEC and Philips used MIPS-based RISC processors. The average processor speed was 40MHz.

- One PCMCIA, or PC card slot. Hewlett-Packard also included a CompactFlash slot, and Philips included a proprietary storage expansion slot called VModule.

- One serial port and cable to connect the Handheld PC to desktop computers.

- An IRDA-compliant infrared port to exchange information with other Handheld PCs.

In addition to these basic requirements, OEMs tried to differentiate their products by adding one or more of the following features to their device:

- Larger ROM chips with more application software. Many of the OEMs made deals with software developers to bundle additional programs with their hardware. Some of the software was included in ROM, while other software was provided on CD-ROM for installation onto the device.

- Backlighting for the screen that the user could turn on or off.

- An indicator LED for alarms.

- Cradles for connecting the Handheld PC with a desktop computer.

- Support for rechargeable NiMH or NiCAD batteries.

NOTE   *Examples of the first Handheld PCs include the Casio Cassiopeia A10, the Compaq Companion C120, the HP 320LX, the NEC MobilePro 400, and the Philips Velo 1.*

The Philips Velo was the only Handheld PC that included an integrated 19.2 modem and a microphone for voice recordings. LG Electronics and Hitachi provided modem and headset options for their devices.

TIP   *For more details about the hardware specifications of Handheld PCs, and a listing of the different OEMs and devices, go to http://www.cewindows.net/wce/wcetech.htm.*

Nearly one year after the first Handheld PCs began selling, Microsoft upgraded Windows CE and the application software. Windows CE Version 2 added support for color displays, direct printing, Ethernet networking, an improved web browser, and video output to external monitors. Pocket PowerPoint was added to the suite of application software.

NOTE   *Examples of the color Handheld PCs include the Compaq 2010C, the HP 620LX, the NEC MobilePro 750C, and the Sharp Mobilon HC-4500.*

Most of the OEMs sold ROM upgrades for their original Handheld PCs, which were installed by replacing the old chip with the new chip. At the same time, new hardware was introduced that had color displays, video output, faster processors, CompactFlash slots, and more RAM.

Palm-size PCs

In 1998, Microsoft introduced two more Windows Powered platforms: Palm-size PCs and Auto PCs. Palm-size PCs are approximately 3"W×5"H and weigh around six ounces. The Palm-size PC screen has a portrait layout and the device does not include a keyboard. Instead, to input data, you use a stylus to either write on the screen using a character recognizer or tap on an onscreen keyboard.

> NOTE
> *Originally, Microsoft wanted to call these devices Palm PCs, but Palm Computing filed a lawsuit against Microsoft. In an agreement with Palm Computing, Microsoft changed the name to Palm-size PC, which is a mouthful and is often abbreviated as P/PC.*

Windows CE remained at Version 2, but the user interface was slightly altered to support the different screen layout and size. Significant changes were made to the software that Microsoft included with the P/PC. Pocket Outlook remained, as did Inbox and Solitaire, but Pocket Office, Windows Explorer, and Pocket Internet Explorer were not included. These applications cannot be installed separately; fortunately, several third-party developers have written programs to provide the functionality that was lost.

Microsoft added software to P/PCs that was not available for Handheld PCs. Included was the Mobile Channel Viewer, which replaced Pocket Internet Explorer. Mobile Channel Viewer is designed for viewing content that you download to your PC using Internet Explorer and then download to the device. Notetaker provides the ability to create files that can contain text, writing in digital ink, or drawings. The files can be synchronized to a PC and opened with Microsoft Word. Voice Recorder enables you to create, play back, and organize recordings made using the microphone of the P/PC.

Windows CE Services replaced Handheld PC Explorer and added support for mobile channels, Notetaker files, and synchronization across an Ethernet network. The hardware specifications for a typical P/PC include the following:

- RISC-based processors with a speed of about 75 MHz. P/PCs continue the support for MIPS and SH3 versions of the processor, though this time the majority of the OEMs chose MIPS for their devices.

- A monochrome screen with a 320×240 resolution and diagonal size of about 4"

- At least 2MB of RAM, though most OEMs created 4MB and 8MB devices, and some even sold 16MB devices

- An alarm LED that flashes to notify you of an alarm

- Microphones to make voice recordings, and headphone jacks to listen to the recording play back

- IRDA-compliant infrared ports for exchanging information with Handheld and P/PCs

- A CompactFlash slot for storage cards and peripherals such as modems and Ethernet cards

- A serial cable and a cradle to connect the device to desktop computers

NOTE *Examples of the first P/PCs include the Casio E-11, the Philips Nino 320, and the Everex Freestyle Associate.*

In February 1999, Microsoft announced a color version of the P/PC. Besides support for color screens, little was changed in Windows CE other than a version number change to 2.11. The hardware for these devices retained basically the same physical size, but some included faster processors and more RAM.

The most distinguishing feature between the different brands of color P/PCs is the technology used in the display. There are two types of color LCD (liquid crystal display) screens: *active* and *passive*. Active displays, such as thin film transistor (TFT), provide a sharper, clearer image by refreshing the screen more frequently than passive displays.

NOTE *Today's Pocket PCs are really the current version of P/PCs. The display technologies discussed here still apply to Pocket PCs.*

An individual transistor controls each pixel of an active display, making it more expensive to make than passive displays that use a grid of horizontal and vertical wires. Because passive displays are cheaper, companies continue to research ways to make them better. Double-layer super-twisted nematic (DSTN) is a passive display that uses two display layers. Color super-twisted nematic (CSTN) is another passive display developed by Sharp that rivals TFT displays at about half the cost.

Another display issue is lighting, and again there are two types: *transmissive* and *reflective*. Transmissive lighting provides backlighting from a light source behind the screen. This type of lighting makes the screens very readable indoors, but virtually unusable outdoors. Reflective screens use external light, such as ambient light around the device, or a front-lighting system. Reflective screens are easier to read outdoors, but are not as bright indoors or under poor lighting conditions. The major benefit of reflective screens, however, is that they use much less power than transmissive screens.

NOTE *The Casio E-100 was the most stunning of the P/PCs, with its TFT screen supporting 65,536 colors and stereo sound. Casio sold the E-100 and later the E-105, which has 32MB of RAM, as multimedia P/PCs.*

While the TFT screens are beautiful indoors, they are practically unusable outdoors. Hybrid transflective TFT screens reflect ambient light but also use a backlight. This makes the screen easier to read outdoors, but also tends to make the screen darker indoors. Older Hewlett-Packard devices used a transmissive CSTN color screen, and Philips used a transmissive DSTN screen.

NOTE *All the manufacturers of Pocket PC 2002 devices use hybrid transflective TFT screens.*

Auto PCs

At the same time that Microsoft announced the P/PC, they also announced the Auto PC. An Auto PC replaces your car radio with a Windows Powered information appliance. The device is voice-activated, enabling you to retrieve information, such as driving directions, using spoken commands. Addresses that you have in the Contacts program on other Windows Powered devices can be transferred to the Auto PC by using infrared.

An optional component of the Auto PC is a wireless receiver with which you can receive traffic conditions, weather, news, stock quotes, and e-mail. The Auto PC voice synthesizer reads all of that information to you.

At the heart of the Auto PC is the Windows CE operating system—the same operating system that runs all other Windows Powered devices. The Auto PC demonstrates the modular design of Windows CE, which allows Microsoft to remove components, like the Pocket PC user interface, and replace it with other interfaces, such as the Auto PC voice recognizer.

Not many people bought Auto PCs; and today, this platform is no longer supported by Microsoft. However, all of the major automobile manufacturers are developing products similar to the Auto PC, and today these types of products are called *telematics*. For more information about telematics, read the Motorola FAQ at http://www.motorola.com/ies/telematics/htmls/faq.html.

Handheld PC 2000

In the fall of 1998, Microsoft announced the Handheld PC Professional. This platform retains the screen and keyboard combination introduced with the Handheld PC, but in a larger size. In the fall of 2000, Microsoft released the current version of this platform, called Handheld PC 2000. The largest Handheld PC 2000 device is 10"W×8"H, and the smallest is nearly 4"W and a little over 7"H.

> **NOTE** *Handheld PC 2000 is the current release of Windows for Handheld PCs, and we will refer to the devices that run this software as Handheld PCs.*

As you can tell from the physical dimensions, Handheld PCs can approach the size of subnotebook computers. With that size and a price hovering around $900.00, you might wonder why you should buy a Handheld PC rather than a notebook computer. If you find yourself facing this question, consider the following:

- Handheld PCs turn on instantly and are immediately functional, unlike notebook computers that use a booting process like desktop computers.

- Battery life can be as long as 12 hours on a Handheld PC, whereas battery life on a notebook computer is usually only half as long, and sometimes shorter.

- The smallest Handheld PC weighs a little over one pound, while the largest is just under three pounds. Subnotebook computers tend to be in the three- to four-pound range, and notebook computers tend to be in the four- to six-pound range.

- Handheld PCs have no moving parts to break, whereas notebook computers have hard disks that can fail.

- Handheld PC 2000—and in particular, Pocket Office—does not support all of the features available in Microsoft Office. For some people, this is a major shortcoming; while for others, the simplicity provided by Handheld PCs is a plus.

- Handheld PC 2000 includes Windows CE Version 3, and Version 3 of Pocket Outlook and Pocket Office. Also included are Pocket Access and InkWriter.

- The hardware specifications of Handheld PCs vary much more than any other Windows Powered device. Here are some highlights:

  - Screen resolutions vary between 640×240 and 640×480, and some even support a resolution of 800×600.

  - Diagonal screen sizes range from 6.5" to 10".

  - Monochrome, grayscale, and color displays. Color displays range from 256 colors to 65,536 colors.

  - Backlight displays

  - RISC processors running as fast as 206MHz

  - Either 16MB or 32MB of RAM

  - PC card, CompactFlash, and SmartCard slots

  - Integrated modems

  - IRDA-compliant infrared ports

  - Microphone for making voice recordings

  - Built-in speakers for playing back voice recordings

  - Rechargeable lithium ion batteries

NOTE   *Examples of Handheld PC 2000 devices include the HP Jornada 720, the NEC MobilePro 790, and the Intermec 6651.*

Did you know?

Handhelds Now Sold To Vertical Markets

Handheld PCs were first sold to consumers, but it never sold as successfully as originally anticipated. Today Microsoft and the manufacturers of Handheld PCs target the devices at the corporate market, where it has had its greatest success. Companies use Handheld PCs for specific functions, like inventory control, or customer relationship management. Such functions require the larger screens and keyboards that are part of Handheld PCs. Consumers can still buy Handheld PCs from online sources such as MobilePlanet at http://mobileplanet.com.

Pocket PCs

The newest addition to the stable of Windows Powered devices is the Pocket PC. In April 2000, Microsoft released the first version of Pocket PCs, which is now called Pocket PC 2000. The most recent version of the Pocket PC software was released in October 2001, and is called Pocket PC 2002. Pocket PC 2002 refers to Windows Powered devices running Windows CE Version 3, Pocket Outlook, and Pocket Office.

Pocket PCs have the same physical specifications as P/PCs, but include faster processors, more memory, and better battery life. Casio, Compaq, Hewlett-Packard, Toshiba, Audiovox, and NEC manufacture Pocket PC 2002 devices.

There are hardware features that make Pocket PC 2002 devices different from Pocket PC 2000. These features are the following:

- The same Intel StrongARM processor in all devices
- A 32MB FlashROM chip for storing the Pocket PC 2002 software
- A minimum of 32MB of RAM
- A color transflective TFT display
- Some devices include multiple storage card slots

Did you know?

FlashROM Enables Device Upgrades

Like ROM chips, software written on FlashROM chips is not erased even when the batteries in the device are completely drained. However, while software can only be written once on ROM chips, software can be erased and rewritten on FlashROM chips. FlashROM chips are more expensive, but they enable the hardware manufacturers to upgrade the Pocket PC software without having to replace the chip.

Only two Pocket PC 2000 device manufacturers, Compaq and UR There, sold Pocket PCs that use FlashROM chips. Consequently, only the Pocket PCs from these manufacturers can be upgraded to Pocket PC 2002. Both companies provide the upgrade on CD-ROM, however, because since these devices only have 16MB FlashROM chips, they cannot store all of Pocket PC 2002 in FlashROM.

Many updated programs of Pocket PC 2002, such as Microsoft Reader and Windows Media Player, can only be installed in RAM on upgraded Pocket PCs. The upgrade CD-ROM will include these programs or include instructions for downloading the programs, which you can install separately. The spell checker included in Pocket Word and Inbox with Pocket PC 2002 cannot be installed on upgraded Pocket PCs.

The requirement for FlashROM in all Pocket PC 2002 devices ensures that they can be upgraded. Pocket PC 2002 uses only 24MB of the 32MB available on the FlashROM chip; so if the size of the Pocket PC software expands, the Pocket PC 2002 devices might be able to store all of the new software. In the meantime, some of the device manufacturers provide a utility that allows the extra 8MB of space on the FlashROM chip to be used as a storage card.

Pocket PC 2002 includes a feature Microsoft calls Update Execute in Place, or XIP. It allows them to provide updates to Pocket PC 2002 on the FlashROM chip, which you can download and execute directly from a web site. On previous devices, these types of updates have to be stored in RAM, taking away storage space that you would use for programs and data.

Looking to the Future

The Microsoft vision for mobile computing is that no one device will be the best fit for every person. As you have seen in this chapter, Handheld PCs meet the needs for vertical applications requiring larger screens and keyboards, while Pocket PCs meet the needs for people who want a portable information appliance. Smart Phones and Tablet PCs are two new mobile computing platforms that Microsoft plans to bring to market in 2002.

The Microsoft Smart Phone platform, which has the code name of Stinger, has been in development for two years. The goal of Stinger is to combine Pocket PCs with mobile phones and to create a device that appeals to people who prefer to use a small device in the form of a mobile phone. Stinger will have some of the functionality of Pocket PCs. For example, Stinger will have an Inbox and a version of Internet Explorer, along with Pocket Outlook, but it will not support stylus input like Pocket PCs.

Tablet PCs appear to be a big brother to Handheld and Pocket PCs, but they are in fact totally different devices. A Tablet PC is a fully functional personal computer that runs Windows XP Professional Tablet PC Edition, and full Windows applications. The key features the Tablet PC provides is handwriting recognition, long battery life, high-resolution displays, and wireless connectivity. The Microsoft vision for Tablet PCs is that they will be used to take notes like pen and paper, to annotate and read digital documents, as well as be used easily during meetings.

Windows for Pocket PCs

Windows for Pocket PCs includes the Windows CE operating system and application software (such as Pocket Outlook and Pocket Office) that run on Pocket PCs. All Windows Powered devices will include the Windows CE operating system, but some may have different combinations of the application software. For example, some devices may include all the software, while others may only include Pocket Outlook.

This section provides an introduction to the different components that make up Windows for Pocket PCs.

Windows CE

In the simplest of terms, an *operating system* manages the interaction between application software and the hardware on which it runs. As a user, you should not be concerned about how the operating system works, only that it can run software at acceptable performance levels and remain stable.

One may be tempted to look at Windows CE and decide that Microsoft simply transferred Windows 95 to handheld devices. The truth is that Windows CE is a completely new 32-bit operating system, built from the ground up to run on embedded devices. The following are things that you need to know about Windows CE that affect you as a user:

- Windows CE implements a subset of the Win32 API, which was completely rewritten for embedded devices. This makes it easier for software developers to write programs using familiar tools, which speeds up the software development process.

- Windows CE is portable and can run on a variety of different processor types. That means that OEMs have a variety of processor manufacturers to choose from, enabling them to implement the latest processor technology at a lower price.

- Windows CE is a real-time operating system, which means that certain actions performed by the operating system occur within bounded times. To you, this means that the operating system should run faster.

- Windows CE is modular, so a system can be built using only the components needed for a particular platform. This means that a variety of different devices, such as the Pocket PC and the Auto PC, can be built from the same core operating system, decreasing product development life cycles.

The Windows CE user interface, or what is called the *shell,* is also a separate component. As such, Microsoft can create separate shells for the different hardware platforms that run the operating system. Separate shells have been created for the Handheld and Pocket PC platforms, resulting in a different look between the two devices. The Auto PC shell is not graphic based, but instead uses a voice command system.

The Windows CE modular design means that it can be used in a wide range of devices. In fact, you might be surprised to know that Windows CE is also used in devices such as gas pumps and point-of-sale terminals.

ActiveSync

It is important that information appliances easily exchange information with other devices; otherwise, the information is on a virtual island and not accessible everywhere it is needed. All Windows Powered devices come with infrared ports that can be used to exchange information with other devices, but they also communicate with PCs running ActiveSync.

ActiveSync runs on PCs that use the Windows 98, Windows NT, Windows 2000, or Windows XP operating systems. It synchronizes information between Windows Powered devices and Outlook. During synchronization, the software compares information between the device and the PC, determining what has been added to both. Then, the two are updated so that the information is consistent on both devices.

The primary purpose for ActiveSync is to synchronize appointments, contacts, and tasks, but it also synchronizes Outlook Notes, Mobile Favorites, and AvantGo content. Synchronization can be done using infrared, serial, USB, and Ethernet networks for communication. You also use ActiveSync to install programs on the device and to back up and restore the device. Chapters 5, 6, and 7 provide all the details for using this important program.

Pocket Outlook

There are many ways to make a Windows Powered device your personal information appliance, but chances are good you will start by using the Pocket Outlook programs to manage your personal information. You use the Calendar program to schedule appointments and all-day events; you use Contacts to store addresses; you use Tasks to manage your projects; and you use Inbox to send and receive e-mail.

ActiveSync synchronizes the information in each of these programs with their counterpart folders in Outlook. When you read Chapter 8, you will learn how to use Calendar, Contacts, and Tasks on Handheld and Pocket PCs. Chapter 20 shows you how to use Inbox.

Pocket Office

When you are traveling about with your Pocket PC, you may need to write a letter, read a report, or determine how much it will cost to remodel your kitchen. Chapter 10 shows you how to create documents using Pocket Word. Included in Chapter 13 are instructions for creating written and verbal notes using the Pocket PC Notes program. In Chapter 11, you'll learn how to use Pocket Excel to crunch numbers and how to use the Calculator program to make quick calculations.

NOTE *Pocket Office does not include versions of Microsoft Access or PowerPoint. Several different software developers have written database programs for Pocket PCs, which you will learn about in Chapter 15. Likewise, there are also several programs for viewing and giving PowerPoint presentations, which are presented in Chapter 14.*

Microsoft Money

Quicken and Microsoft Money are two very popular financial programs that run on desktop computers. In Chapter 12, you'll learn how to synchronize financial information in Money 2002 on a PC and with Microsoft Money on Pocket PCs. Microsoft Money also provides you with the ability to download stock quotes to your Pocket PC by using an Internet connection.

Play Music and Games

The Internet is becoming a popular way for distributing music in the MP3 (MPEG Audio Layer 3) or WMA (Windows Media Audio) file formats. You can download these files to a Pocket PC and play them using the Windows Media Player introduced in Chapter 18.

A beautiful color display and stereo sound make Pocket PCs great for playing games. Included with all Windows Powered devices is that hallmark of Microsoft game software, Solitaire. Other game software is available, including the Microsoft Entertainment Pack and several games that you can download from the Internet. All of this information about games for Windows Powered devices is also provided in Chapter 18.

Read Books

Windows for Pocket PCs is the first Microsoft product to include Microsoft Reader, which uses their ClearType display technology. This technology significantly improves font resolution on LCD screens, making it easier to read text on the device. Microsoft Reader provides tools for bookmarking, highlighting, and annotating books that you purchase and download from the Internet. Chapter 18 provides the instructions for using this program.

Connect to the Internet

The English poet John Donne wrote in *Devotions Upon Emergent Occasions (Meditation XVII)*, "No man is an Island, entire of itself; every man is a piece of the Continent, a part of the main. . ." Today the Internet connects people from all walks of life around the world, reinforcing the idea that no man, or woman, is an island.

Connecting to the Internet is no longer optional for computers because people expect them to connect. And for many, the Internet has become very personal; with it they grow, develop relationships, share a few laughs, and buy their favorite author's book. The Internet has become the location for much personal information, to which a personal information appliance must provide access.

Microsoft Windows for Pocket PCs includes the software needed to connect to the Internet, and Chapter 19 provides instructions to help you get connected. Once online, you can use Pocket

Internet Explorer to view your favorite web site, use Inbox to send and receive e-mail, and use MSN Messenger to send and receive instant messages. You learn how to use Pocket Internet Explorer in Chapter 22, Inbox in Chapter 20, and MSN Messenger in Chapter 21.

Wrapping Up

Windows Powered devices provide a fast and simple way to manage all types of information. Over the course of six years, Microsoft has improved their software for Windows Powered devices, which results in products with many features and integration with Windows desktop software. Today, the Microsoft mobile device strategy recognizes that no one device will meet all the needs for handheld computing: Companies need devices with larger screens and keyboards, which Handheld PCs provide. Consumers want devices for storing personal information, for entertainment, and for connecting to the Internet, which Pocket PCs provide. The remaining chapters of this book provide all that you need to make the most of your Pocket PC. In the next chapter, you'll get acquainted with all of the Pocket PC hardware and software features.

Chapter 2

Get Acquainted with Your Pocket PC

How To...

- ■ Identify hardware components
- ■ Set up your Pocket PC
- ■ Find information
- ■ Use the Start menu
- ■ Use common program elements
- ■ Use Online Help
- ■ Configure storage and program memory
- ■ Organize files and folders

All great athletes master the fundamentals of their sport. They have tremendous physical and mental gifts that set them apart; but if you analyze their performances, you often find that the fundamentals are performed flawlessly. This mastery does not come by chance; it is the result of years of practice and coaching. By the time an athlete becomes a professional, the fundamentals have become habit.

To master your Pocket PC, you need to learn the fundamentals of how they work. This chapter provides the coaching you need to understand and use these skills. First is a review of the hardware components that come with the Pocket PC. Second is a review of the setup procedure for Pocket PCs.

After the device is set up, the first thing you'll see on the Pocket PC is the Today screen. The Today screen is covered before moving on to the Start menu, common application components, organization of files, and Online Help. This chapter finishes with an overview of a very important part of your device—the memory used for storing files and running programs.

Meet Your Pocket PC

Your Pocket PC is a powerful little device that is capable of meeting your needs for an information appliance in a number of different ways. Throughout this book, you'll learn how to make a Pocket PC your own appointment book or checkbook; but to best use the device, you need to understand its fundamental parts.

Each Pocket PC looks slightly different, but has options found on every device. The Today screen is the closest thing to a desktop on the Pocket PC, and provides a summary for appointments, e-mail, and tasks. You enter information using the onscreen keyboard; character recognizer; or handwriting recognition, which let's you write anywhere on the screen. Like your desktop computer, information is stored in files, which you manage using File Explorer.

You will use all of these items, which are covered in this section, as you use your Pocket PC. If you have difficulty, remember that Online Help is available, which you can access by tapping Start | Help.

Review the Pocket PC

In this section, we take a tour of a typical Pocket PC, starting with the front of the device and ending with the back of the device. Along each stop of the tour, I will point out parts commonly found in each location; but keep in mind that there may be slight variations between Pocket PC brands. Some parts will be used more often than others, but all parts are important to know when using the device.

Review the Front

Our first stop is at the front of the device. Chapter 1 describes the typical Pocket PC that is 3 by 5 inches and weighs 6 ounces. The biggest part of the Pocket PC is its screen. The 4-inch diagonal LCD (liquid crystal display) Touch screen has a portrait layout, and is used for viewing and entering information.

To help understand the difference between portrait and landscape, think of a standard 8.5-by-11-inch sheet of paper. The portrait layout of that sheet has the 8.5-inch sides at the top and bottom, and a landscape layout has the 11-inch sides at the top and bottom.

As you can see in Figure 2-1, the buttons below the screen are assigned to different programs. If the Pocket PC is off, you can press one of these buttons to turn it on and start the assigned program in one step.

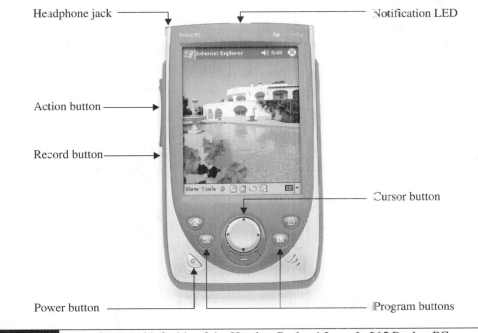

FIGURE 2-1   The front and left side of the Hewlett-Packard Jornada 565 Pocket PC. Other Pocket PCs look different but have many of the same parts.

Usually, two of the buttons are assigned to Calendar and Contacts, with the third and fourth buttons assigned to Tasks, Inbox, or other programs provided by the hardware company. The assignments of each of these programs can be changed using the Buttons icon in the Pocket PC settings; Chapter 3 provides these instructions.

Casio was the first company to place a Navigational button on the front of their Pocket PCs; and since then, all Pocket PC brands include this feature. The Navigational button provides a way for you to scroll through screens and menu options without using a stylus.

> **TIP** *Many Pocket PC games use the Program and Navigation buttons for controlling game play. Older Compaq iPAQ Pocket PCs have problems recognizing two button presses at the same time, which can cause problems when playing some games.*

Some Pocket PCs have the Power button and microphone on the front. It is important for you to know the location of the microphone on your Pocket PC to make the best voice recordings. When you make a recording, the microphone should be placed as close to the source as possible.

> **TIP** *So far, only Hewlett-Packard has designed Pocket PCs that have a flip-top cover to protect the screen. The cover makes it easier to carry the device in your pocket because it takes up less space than the case provided by other manufacturers.*

Review the Bottom

Our next stop is at the bottom of the Pocket PC, which is where the Pocket PC serial port is located. The port does not look like the serial ports that you find on desktop computers, and, unfortunately, each Pocket PC brand has a different port style. Because the ports are different, you cannot share peripherals, such as cradles, between different Pocket PC brands.

> **NOTE** *Do not confuse the serial port at the bottom of a Pocket PC with the USB port that is available with some Pocket PC cradles. USB and serial ports are different, and it is not possible to connect USB devices, like keyboards and mice, to a Pocket PC.*

How to ... Clean Your Pocket PC Screen

The Pocket PC screen can get dirty very quickly through daily use, and some dirt particles can even scratch the screen when they come in contact with the stylus. In my experience, products designed to clean the lenses of glasses work well.

Fellowes sells a PDA Screen Clean kit that includes a soft leather cloth for cleaning the screen throughout the day, and packets of wet-dry cleaning cloths for more intensive cleaning. They also sell the WriteRight screen protectors, which are clear plastic overlays that fit right on top of the Pocket PC screen. You can find more information about both of these products at http://www.fellowes.com.

How to ...   Connect Your Pocket PC to Devices Using a Serial Cable

The serial cable that comes with some Pocket PCs is a special version of a cable, sometimes called a *null modem cable*. These types of cables are designed to communicate with other personal computers rather than peripherals, such as modems. To use the serial cable to connect to a serial peripheral device like a modem, you will need a *null modem adapter*. The adapter will convert the cable into a standard RS-232 cable that provides communication with serial devices.

You can find null modem adapters at your local RadioShack; you will need a DB9 femaile-to-male DB9 adapter, part number 26-264B. Most peripherals have female ports, so if the peripheral you are connecting to has a 9-pin female port, you will also need a DB9 male-to-male DB9 serial gender changer, RadioShack part number 26-280B.

The serial ports are designed to plug the Pocket PC into a cradle, which has a cable that connects to the serial port of a desktop computer. The port may also be used to provide power to the Pocket PC, and is also used to recharge the battery. Some Pocket PCs also include a port for plugging in an AC power adapter, which can be useful for recharging the device without having to carry the Pocket PC cradle.

Review the Left Side

We move next to the left side of the Pocket PC, which, next to the front, is the second most important location on your Pocket PC. Along the left side are buttons designed for using the Pocket PC with one hand. The buttons that you'll find on the left are Action Control and Voice Recorder.

Action Control is used in two ways: Rotating the button up or down performs operations similar to the up and down arrows on a computer keyboard. Pressing the button performs an operation similar to ENTER on a computer keyboard. One way to use Action Control is to scroll through the Start menu items by rotating the button up or down, and then pressing the button to start the program that you select.

> NOTE   *Some Pocket PCs have Action Control on the left side and a Navigational button on the front. On these Pocket PCs, you can use both buttons to scroll up and down.*

To make voice recordings on your Pocket PC, press-and-hold Voice Recorder and begin speaking after the device beeps. Use the Notes program, as explained in Chapter 13, to play back and manage voice recordings. You can configure Voice Recorder in Notes to also switch to the Notes program and start recording, or to stay in the current program and start recording.

Review the Top

Our next stop is at the top of the Pocket PC. Here, you will find the alarm notification LED and either a CompactFlash or Secure Digital card slot. The LED will flash whenever an alarm occurs, unless you turn the LED notification off in the Pocket PC settings. This same LED may be used to indicate that the device is charging (the user manual includes information about how the LED is used).

Most Pocket PCs have slots that support Type II CompactFlash cards. Type II cards are made a little thicker than most so that they can support additional functions. In Chapter 23, you'll find information about a number of different cards that work in these slots. The newest Compaq iPAQ Pocket PCs have Secure Digital card slots. Secure Digital cards are significantly smaller and thinner than CompactFlash cards, and have built-in support for encryption.

> **NOTE**   *@migo Pocket PC from UR There is unique because it is the only Pocket PC that provides a PC Card slot rather than a CompactFlash or Secure Digital slot. More information about this Pocket PC is available at http://www.urthere.com.*

The final item that you will find at the top of some Pocket PCs is an infrared port compliant with the Infrared Data Association (IrDA) standard. Infrared is a form of light, or radiation, beyond red light that cannot be seen. An infrared transmitter sends data to a receiver using pulses of infrared light. Every Pocket PC has software that is capable of using the infrared port as either a transmitter or a receiver; and in order for communication to work, the ports must be lined up with each other. As Chapter 5 shows, the infrared port can also be used with a desktop computer for synchronization.

Review the Right Side

The right side of a Pocket PC houses the stylus, which you use to interact with the Pocket PC. Some Pocket PCs also place a speaker along this side of the device.

Review the Back

Our final stop on our tour of the Pocket PC is at the back of the device. The most important item that you'll find on the back of the device is the Soft Reset button, which is recessed so that it is not accidentally pressed. A soft reset is similar to rebooting a desktop computer because it restarts the Windows CE operating system, and data in the program memory is lost. However, any data in storage memory and all settings are retained. An explanation of program and storage memory is provided in the "File Storage and Program Memory" section later in this chapter.

The back of some Pocket PCs may include covers for the main and backup batteries, and possibly a cover for a memory expansion slot. Because the back of each device varies, consult the user manual for details about your Pocket PC.

Set Up Your Pocket PC

When you turn on your Pocket PC for the very first time, a series of steps are initiated to set up your device, which Microsoft calls the Welcome wizard.

Before turning on your Pocket PC, it is very important that you charge its main battery so that settings and data are not lost. When you charge the batteries on most Pocket PCs, an LED either blinks or illuminates a certain color. The Pocket PC is fully charged when the light stops blinking or stops changing colors. The first charge of the Pocket PC battery may take several hours. Consult the user manual of your Pocket PC for specific instructions on charging the battery.

The first screen that you see is shown in the image on the right. Tap anywhere on the screen to continue.

On the next screen, you align the Touch screen so that it properly recognizes any text or taps that you enter on the screen. Use the stylus to tap the center of the cross as it moves around the screen.

welcome

Tap the screen to set up your Pocket PC.

Microsoft **Windows**

For Pocket PCs

Align the screen at any time by tapping Start | Settings. Tap the System tab and then tap the Align Screen icon. Some Pocket PCs also provide a series of hardware buttons that you can press to start the Align Screen program; consult the user manual for instructions on how to use buttons for this purpose.

The next two screens introduce you to the tap-and-hold process, which is new on the Pocket PC. Tap-and-hold is used throughout the Pocket PC user interface, and is similar to right-clicking on a Windows desktop. It opens a pop-up list of commands that can be executed on the object you select with tap-and-hold.

On the first screen, as shown in the image on the left, you are instructed on how to use tap-and-hold.

The second screen, as shown next, provides an opportunity to try the tap-and-hold procedure:

stylus

You can use your stylus two ways:
· **Single-tap**
· **Tap and hold**

☑   Buy stamps
☐ ! Call Andy
■   Reschedule dental appt.
☐   Write   **Create Copy**
          Delete
          Select All

When you tap and hold an item with your stylus, a pop-up menu containing a list of actions appears.

Next

pop-up menus

Use pop-up menus to reschedule the following appointment:

Tap and hold the 9 A.M. dental appointment, and then tap Cut on the pop-up menu.

8
9   Dr. Johnson's office
10   Cut   nt
11   Copy
12   Paste
1
2   Delete

location

Select your city and time zone:

City: Detroit, MI (USA) ▼

Time zone: GMT-5 Eastern US ▼

Next

After you tap Cut, the third screen automatically appears. Tap-and-hold on the 11 A.M. time slot and then tap Paste on the pop-up list.

After you successfully complete the tap-and-hold procedure, a Congratulations screen appears. Tap Next to move on to the Location screen, as shown in the image on the left.

On this screen, specify your local time zone by selecting a time zone or location in the drop-down lists. If you are in the United States, select a time zone; otherwise, select a city. If the city that you live in is not in the list, select the name of a city in the same time zone. When a city is selected, the Time Zone field is automatically set; but in case the entry is not correct, you can select another time zone from the Time Zone drop-down list.

After you specify a location for your Pocket PC and tap Next, the final screen displays, as shown on the right.

Tap anywhere on the screen to end the Welcome wizard and display the Today screen.

The Welcome wizard sets the basic information for your Pocket PC, but you should perform some additional steps to complete the setup of your device. To set the date and time, tap Start | Settings, tap the System tab, and then tap the Clock icon. Follow the instructions provided in Chapter 3 for changing the date and time using the Clock settings.

complete

Setup is complete. Tap the screen to begin using your device.

Settings 　◀€ 8:40 ok

About

Your device uses this information to identify itself to other computers. Enter a name that starts with a letter and contains the characters _, A-Z, or 0-9

Device name: Pocket_PC

Description:

Version | Device ID | Copyrights

If you synchronize multiple Windows Powered devices with the same desktop computer, each device must have a unique name. To change the name of your Pocket PC, tap Start | Settings, tap the System tab, and then tap the About icon to display the Settings dialog box, as shown in the lower-left image.

Tap the Device ID tab, enter a name and description for the device, and tap OK.

Each Pocket PC can store information about you, such as your name and address, which you enter on the Owner Information screen, as shown in the lower-right image.

Settings 　◀€ 8:40 ok

Owner Information

Name: Frank McPherson

Company: Freelance Writer

Address:

Telephone:

E-mail:

☐ Show information when device is turned on

Identification | Notes

If you want the information to be displayed every time the Pocket PC turns on, tap Show Information When Device Is Turned On. Additional information can be stored on the Notes tab.

One of the first things you'll want to do after becoming familiar with your Pocket PC is synchronize it with your desktop computer. During the first synchronization, you establish a partnership between the device and the desktop computer, and you download data in Outlook to the Pocket PC. The entire synchronization process is explained in Chapter 6.

Meet the Today Screen

When the Welcome wizard completes, you end up at the Today screen, as shown in the following image:

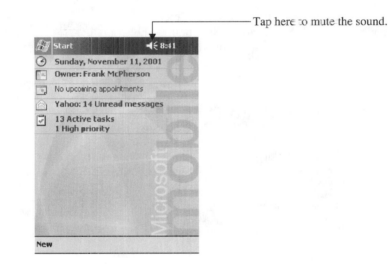

Tap here to mute the sound.

The Today screen serves a purpose similar to the Outlook Today folder in Outlook 2000. It provides a summary overview of personal information, including the owner's name and telephone number, upcoming appointments, the number of unread and unsent e-mail messages, and the number of active tasks.

When you tap a section of the Today screen, the associated program starts. For example, tap the appointments section to start the Calendar program. The Owner Information settings display when you tap the owner name on the screen. You can also start Inbox and Tasks from the Today screen.

TIP *To change the date and time from the Today screen, tap the date to open the Clock Settings dialog box.*

The Today screen displays System Tray icons, and the Today screen is the only part of the Pocket PC that displays these icons. Tap the icon on the System Tray to execute a particular function; for example, when you tap Mute, you turn the Pocket PC sound on or off.

You can select different themes that change the appearance of the Today screen, as well as select which items should display on the screen, by changing the Today screen settings. Chapter 4 provides the instructions for changing these settings.

Use the Pocket PC Start Menu

One change that has been made to the Pocket PC user interface is the location of the Start button. All prior versions of the user interface followed the approach defined by Windows 95, which placed the Start button in the lower left-hand corner of the screen. That same interface is still used on Handheld PCs, where tapping the button expands the Start menu from the bottom up.

Three things are different about the Start button on Pocket PCs. First, as you can see in the image on the right, the title changes to display the name of the current program visible on the screen.

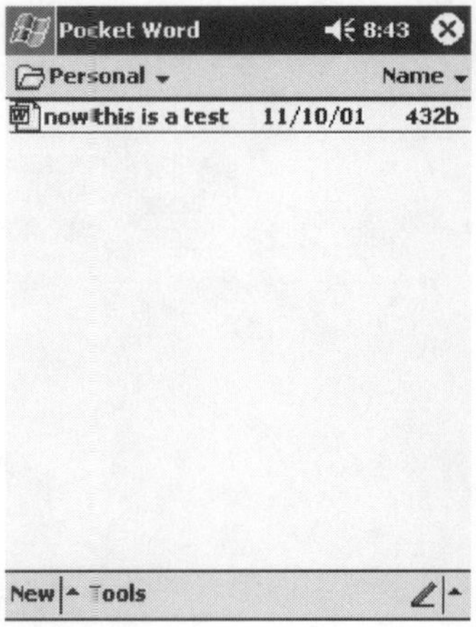

The second change is that when you tap the Start button, the menu expands from the top down, as shown in the following image:

This is the ——→ Shortcut bar.

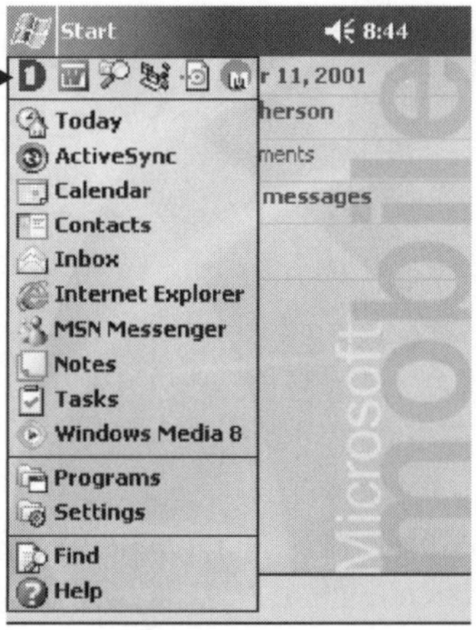

When the menu expands, the title also changes to Start.

The third new item on the Pocket PC Start menu is the Shortcut bar. The Shortcut bar provides an easy way to switch between frequently used programs. Each time you run a program on the Pocket PC, its icon is added to the Shortcut bar, which displays icons for the last six programs you started. After six icons are added to the bar, the next time you run a program that is not on the bar, the oldest icon is removed.

Pocket PC 2000 allows you to add every single program to the Start menu. When more than 11 applications are added to the Start menu, it moves to the middle of the screen and arrows appear at the top and bottom of the menu. Pocket PC 2002 limits the number of programs on the Start menu to nine.

TIP *While it is nice that Pocket PC 2000 does not have this limitation, adding too many programs to the Start menu slows things down. I recommend placing no more than eight programs on the Start menu, and not to put any programs assigned to hardware buttons on the Start menu.*

Another change made to the Start menu is that the Programs and Settings menus do not cascade as they do in Windows. Instead, when you tap either item, a separate program window displays, such as the Programs window, shown at right.

If a program shortcut is not on the Start menu, it will be found in the Programs window. Start a program by tapping its icon.

To change the location of a shortcut between the Start menu or the Programs window, tap Start | Settings | Menus to display the dialog box shown in the image on the left.

Tap the check box next to the items that you want on the Start menu. The items not selected will appear in Programs.

TIP *One of the shortcomings of Pocket PCs is that you cannot create a shortcut on the device unless you use a third-party program. You can use Explorer from ActiveSync to add a shortcut to the \Windows\Start Menu\Programs folder on the device. One third-party program that you can use to create shortcuts on Pocket PCs is Scott Seligman's NewShortcut, which you can find at http://www.scotandmichelle.net/scott/cestuff.html.*

Launching a program from the Start menu on a Pocket PC uses the same process as all other versions of Windows. Tap Start, and then tap the shortcut of the program that you want to run.

Search for Information Using Find

On a Pocket PC, you can perform a search on a word or phrase that is stored in any of the Pocket Outlook and Pocket Office data files, as well as Notes. To search for information, tap Start | Find to open the following dialog box:

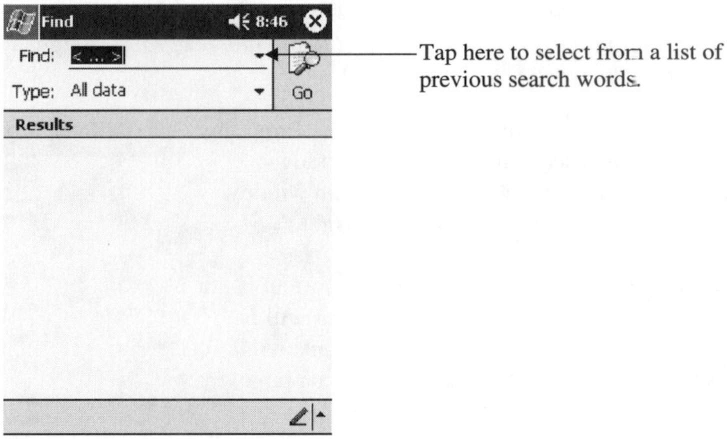

Tap here to select from a list of previous search words.

Enter the word or phrase in the Find field, and select the type of search from the Type drop-down list. Previous search words or phrases are saved and available in the Find drop-down list.

You can narrow the search to a specific program by selecting the program name from the Type drop-down list. The default is All Data, which will search through all Pocket Outlook, Pocket Office, and Notes files on the device.

After you enter the item to find and select the Type, tap Go to begin the search. The search results display in the middle of the screen, as shown in the following image:

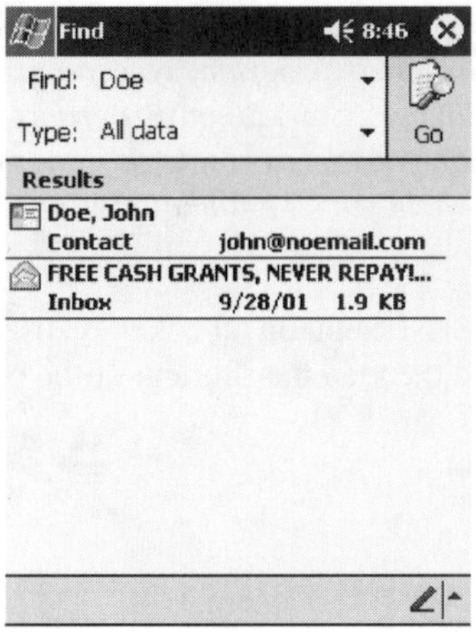

How to ...   **Search for Files**

The Pocket PC search functionality is designed to search for information stored in Pocket Outlook, Online Help, Pocket Word, and Pocket Excel. It does not search for other file types or for files on storage cards. If you want to expand searches to include files on storage cards, you will need to download and install a third-party program. Two programs that provide this functionality are Pocket File Finder at http://www.portable-software.com/ and Kilmist File Quest at http://www.kilmist.com.

The search was on the word Doe, which returned a John Doe contact and an e-mail message.

You can tap any entry in the Results list to open it. When you tap OK to close the item, you return to the results listed in Find.

Work with Applications

The Pocket PC user interface has a flat design that is simple and easy to navigate. At the top of the screen is the Navigation bar, which displays the name of the active program and the current time. Tap the Start icon on the bar to switch the name on the Navigation bar to Start, and to expand the Start menu.

Pocket PC programs display on the entire screen, and do not appear in separate windows like on desktop computers. At the far top-right corner, you'll see a round button with either OK or an X. OK appears within dialog boxes or screens of a program. For example, when you start Contacts and display a contact, you will see an OK button, as shown in the following image:

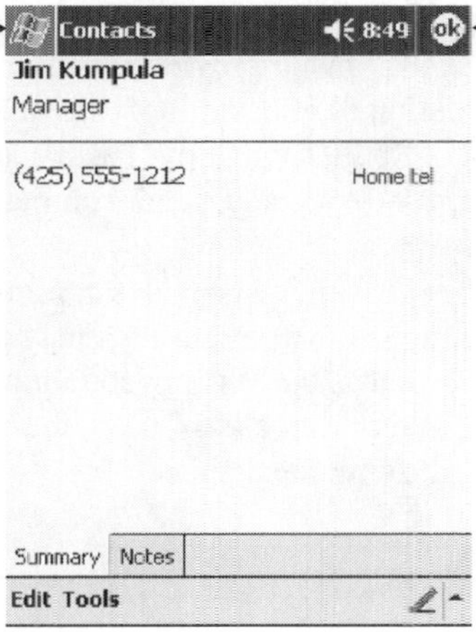

The Navigation bar ⟶
Tap here to close the dialog box.

Contacts   8:49   ok

Jim Kumpula
Manager

(425) 555-1212   Home tel

Summary | Notes

Edit Tools

When you tap OK, the Contact screen closes, but you remain within the Contacts program IN the Contacts list view.

From the Contacts list view, you see an X, such as shown in the image to the right.

When you tap X, the Contacts program disappears, and you see the program started prior to running Contacts. The X appears to exit programs, but instead it simply closes the program screen. The program is still running in memory, which makes it faster to switch between programs.

NOTE *The Windows CE operating system manages the memory on Pocket PCs, and automatically shuts down programs if it starts to run out of program memory. You may prefer to shut down programs manually like you do on a personal computer, which you can do using the Memory setting on your Pocket PC, or by using a program task manager. Chapter 3 has instructions for using program task managers to shut down programs.*

Use the Start menu to switch between programs running on the Pocket PC. At the very top of the Start menu is the Shortcut bar that displays the icons of the last six programs you ran, and it makes the process of switching between these programs a matter of tapping Start and then the icon on the Shortcut bar.

The Command bar.

Located at the bottom of the screen is the Command bar, which has menus and buttons that provide commands for programs. The Command bar in the image on the left shows menu items that you commonly find with Pocket PC programs:

Every program that creates something, such as a document or an appointment, has a New button on the far left side of the Command bar. To create an item, tap New on the Command bar.

The Edit menu provides commands used to edit data that you enter on the Pocket PC. It usually includes commands such as Undo, Redo, Cut, Copy, Paste, Clear, and Select All. Certain programs provide additional commands, such as Format in Pocket Word.

The View menu provides commands that change the appearance of the screen. This may include different input modes, such as the Writing and Drawing modes found in Pocket Word, as well as Zoom, found in many programs, for magnifying the display.

2

The Tools menu provides additional commands available in the program, such as Insert Date and Beam Document, which you find in Pocket Word. If a program includes an Options dialog box, which is used to configure the program settings, open it by tapping Tools | Options.

View List Views

Programs that create files, such as Notes and Pocket Word, have a List view that displays all of the files you created using the program. When you start the program, the first screen displayed is the List view, such as you see in the following image for Notes:

Tap here to open different folders. ──→

Notes	◀€ 8:50 ✕
All Folders ▾	Name ▾
Note1	9/30/01	2k
Note2	9/30/01	1k
Note3	9/30/01	6k
Note4	9/30/01	5k
Personal1	9/30/01	1k
Recording1	9/28/01	0.8s
Recording1(1)	9/30/01	4.8s
woman-demo	4/17/01	3.0s
New ▲ Tools 🖾	✎ ▴

←── Tap here to sort items in List view.

From List view, you can navigate through different folders on the Pocket PC, and sort the items in the list. Tap an item name in the list to open that item in the program, or tap New to create a new file.

NOTE *List view will only display when a file associated with the starting program is found on the device. If no file is found, the Program window opens, rather than List view.*

View Pop-Up Lists

The Pocket PC has a feature that provides the same function as right-clicking an object in Windows on desktop computers. When you tap-and-hold the stylus on an item on the screen, a pop-up list appears with commands that vary depending on the program.

After the menu appears on the screen, lift the stylus and tap the command on the menu that you want performed. For example, to create a copy of a note, tap-and-hold the stylus on the item to be copied in the Notes List view to open the pop-up list, as shown in the image on the right.

Then tap Create Copy to create a new copy of the note you selected.

Create Copy
Delete
Select All
Send via E-mail...
Beam File...
Rename/Move...

Get Help

Online Help is available directly on your Pocket PC; to open Online Help, tap Start | Help. The information that appears on the screen, as shown in the following image, will relate to the program window currently open:

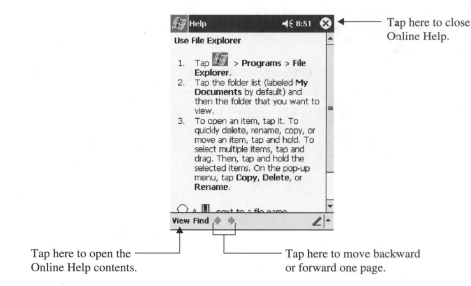

Tap here to close Online Help.

Tap here to open the Online Help contents.

Tap here to move backward or forward one page.

Use Online Help

The Online Help Command bar has a View menu item and buttons for navigating through the help pages. View has two options: Contents and All Installed Help. Tap Contents to display a Table of Contents of Online Help for the current program, or tap All Installed Help to display all Online Help for the device.

Some help pages include hyperlinks, which you can tap to open another page of information. To return to the previous page, tap Back on the Command bar. Tap OK to close the Online Help window.

Receive Help on the Internet

Online Help is a great source of information on your device, but it may not provide an answer to your question. While this book provides enough information to answer the majority of questions, technology changes at a blinding rate and only the Internet seems able to keep up.

On the Internet, you can find pages of frequently asked questions (FAQs) that provide answers for a variety of topics. Over the last four years, I have created and maintained the

PocketPCHow2 website at http://www.pocketpchow2.com, which provides hundreds of links to information that answer many questions about Windows CE and Pocket PCs.

The website is organized into three areas: How, What, and Where. How provides links to information about how to do things with Pocket PCs, such as *How do I display Adobe PDF files on my Pocket PC?* What provides definitions, such as *What is Windows CE?* Where provides links to locations for more information or files, such as *Where can I find the Mobile Channel wizard?*

My website is only one of several websites on the Internet that are dedicated to Pocket PCs. Included on my website are several pages of links to other websites that provide FAQs, News, Forums, Reviews, and Software.

Print Documents

Windows for Pocket PCs does not have the ability to print documents. Fortunately, Field Software Products sells PrintPocketCE, which is a program you can install to print on Hewlett-Packard- and Canon-compatible printers. You will find this program at http://www.fieldsoftware.com.

File Storage and Program Memory

Pocket PCs do not have built-in hard drives like desktop computers. Instead, Random Access Memory (RAM) is used for built-in file storage. However, like desktop computers, your Pocket PC also uses RAM for running programs. Every Pocket PC comes with a certain amount of RAM that is used for file storage and program memory, and it includes a setting for configuring the amount of memory allocated to each.

Using storage cards can increase the total storage space of a device. Storage cards are available in the CompactFlash, Multimedia Card, Secure Digital, and PC Card formats, and come in a variety of different sizes. IBM even sells a microdrive that uses the same type of technology as your PC hard drive, but it is in the CompactFlash size and holds up to 1GB of files.

TIP   *See Chapter 23 for an explanation of how CompactFlash, Multimedia, Secure Digital, and PC cards differ.*

Storage memory is differentiated between internal storage memory and storage cards. Internal storage uses the RAM installed inside your device. Storage cards are cards that you insert into the Secure Digital card or CompactFlash slots.

How to ... Add More Program Memory

Storage cards cannot increase program memory; until recently, program memory could not be increased at all. However, three companies now sell internal memory upgrades for Compaq iPAQ Pocket PCs. Times2 Tech at http://www.times2tech.com/ and PCE2000 at http://www.pce2000.com/ sell 64MB and 128MB upgrades. LearLogiX Corporation sells a 64MB upgrade. Due to limitations in how the iPAQ uses memory, only 64MB of the 128MB upgrade is available for program memory. Times2 Tech and PCE2000 provide a special driver that allows you to use the remaining 64MB as an extra internal storage card.

Configure Memory

To configure memory, tap Start | Settings, the System tab, and the Memory icon to open the dialog box shown on the right.

The left side of the slider represents internal storage memory, and the right side of the slider represents program memory. To adjust the amount of memory allocated to either, move the slider left or right.

At the bottom of the screen, you see the amount of memory Allocated, In Use, and Free for storage and program memory. Tap the Storage Card tab of the Memory Settings dialog box to see the size of the storage card and the amount of space in use and free.

How to ... Conserve Storage Space

Internal storage in Pocket PCs is finite, and it can be important to use a strategy that conserves internal storage space while installing programs. It helps, therefore, to know what must be stored internally, and what can be placed on storage cards.

All data in Calendar, Contacts, Tasks, and Inbox is in databases that are in internal storage. These databases are part of what is called the *object store*, which is limited to 16MB. Over time, you'll want to remove items in these programs, and the best way is to configure

Outlook on your PC to automatically archive data. The auto-archive process removes items from the main Outlook folders; and during the next synchronization, those items will be removed from the Pocket PC.

Data files, such as Pocket Word documents and Pocket Excel spreadsheets, can be easily stored on storage cards or internally. Both programs automatically check the storage cards for files to display in the File List view. However, files on storage cards are not backed up by ActiveSync or by any of the backup programs provided with Pocket PCs. You may want to only store noncritical files on storage cards, or use Windows Explorer to manually copy files from storage cards to the hard drive on a PC.

You can install most Pocket PC programs on storage cards. The instructions for installing software to storage cards are in Chapter 7. Some programs execute immediately when the Pocket PC turns on, and you may have problems running those programs from storage cards. The reason for this is that there is a slight period of time when the Pocket PC first turns on when cards are not available. Most programs include README files that specify whether the program must be installed to internal storage.

I recommend installing system files to internal storage. If your Pocket PC only has one slot, you will need to install programs internally that you would use while peripherals, such as modems, are in the slot.

Manage Files with File Explorer

With File Explorer, you can browse the contents of folders on the Pocket PC to locate, open, copy, move, and delete files. You also use this program to create new folders on the Pocket PC, and to transfer files to other devices using infrared.

The My Documents folder is particularly important on Pocket PCs because it is the storage location for data files. If you synchronize files between a Pocket PC and a desktop computer, the entire contents of the My Documents folder will appear on the desktop computer. Most Pocket PC programs, such as Pocket Word and Pocket Excel, only work with the My Documents folder or its subfolders, while files stored in any other folder on the device will not appear in the program List view.

If you create a My Documents folder on a storage card, the contents of that folder are combined with the contents of the My Documents folder on the device by programs that have a List view. This feature is particularly important for Windows Media Player, which plays music stored in large files that you will want to keep on storage cards. Chapter 18 provides instructions for playing music using Windows Media Player.

Locate Files

To start File Explorer, tap Start | Programs | File Explorer—
and the program will open, as shown in the image on the right.

When File Explorer starts, it opens the My Documents
folder, and lists the files and subfolders stored in My
Documents. The contents of a Folder view can be sorted by
Name, Date, Size, or Type by tapping an option in the Sort
drop-down list located at the top-right side of the Folder view.

Expand the drop-down list on the top-left side of the Folder
view to open a parent folder. The Pocket PC root folder is called
My Device and contains the My Documents, Program Files,
Temp, and Windows folders. If a storage card is in the device,
it appears in the My Device Folder view, as shown next on
the right:

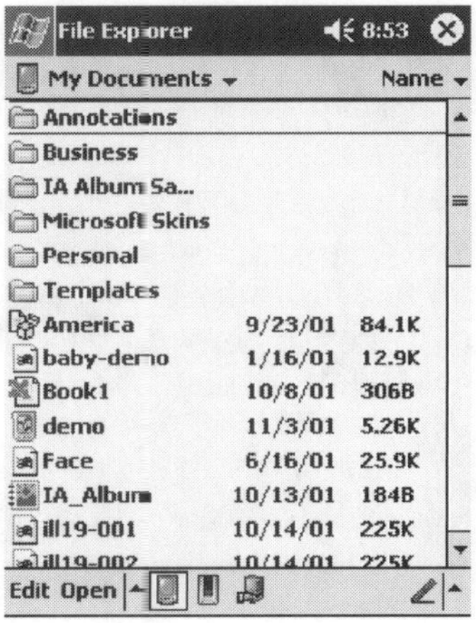

This folder contains everything
on the storage card.

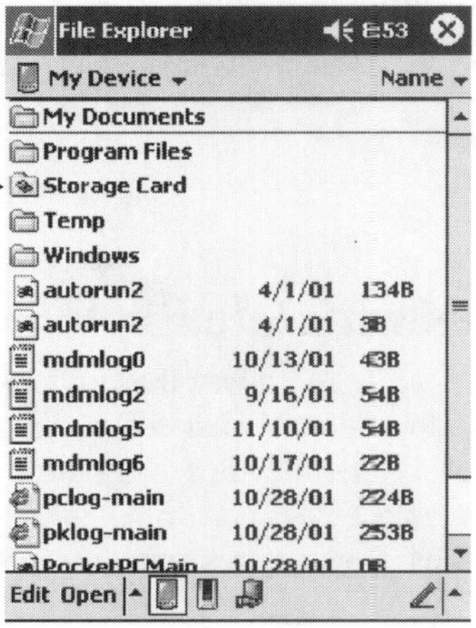

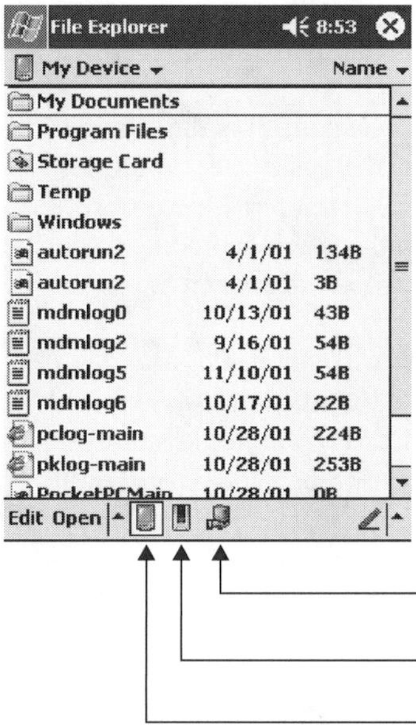

On the Command bar, there are three buttons, as shown
in the image on the left, to switch between. These include*/
internal storage, storage cards, and network shares.

Network shares

Storage cards

Internal storage

Network shares are storage locations on file servers or workstations that share files among users on a network. When you tap network shares, or the Open command, the Open dialog box shown on the right appears:

Enter the full path to the network share using the Universal Naming Convention (UNC), which has the form \\[*server name*]\[*share name*]. For example, to open a share with the name Music on a computer named Fred, enter \\Fred\Music.

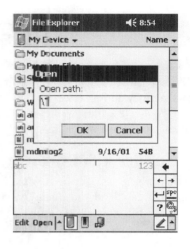

You cannot directly open a file on a network share. Instead, you must first copy the file to the Pocket PC, and then open it. However, you can create a shortcut to a file on a network share and paste it on a Pocket PC, which does not copy the entire file to the Pocket PC. Because shortcuts only point to files, when you open the shortcut, you actually open the file across the network. To create a shortcut, tap-and-hold on a file and then tap Copy. Switch to the destination location on the Pocket PC and tap Edit | Paste Shortcut. The only way to open a shortcut is by using File Explorer. You will not see shortcuts in the various program List views, such as Pocket Word.

The process is the same for opening a file or folder in Folder view; all you do is tap the item. When you tap a file, it will open in its associated program on the Pocket PC. File Explorer does not display file extensions, but an icon appears with each filename to indicate the file type.

Organize Files with Folders

Typically, you will not use File Explorer to open a file; instead, you will start a program, such as Pocket Word, and then open a file from its List view. You will, however use File Explorer to move files between folders and to create new folders.

A folder can be created in two ways: you can tap-and-hold the stylus on an open space in Folder view and tap New Folder on the pop-up list, or tap Edit | New Folder. When you do, a new folder appears with its name selected so that you can enter a new name, as shown here on the right.

To move or copy a file into a folder, you use Cut, Copy, and Paste. File Explorer does not support drag-and-drop, but tap-and-hold makes the process much easier. To move a file to another folder, tap-and-hold the stylus on the filename, tap Cut on the pop-up list, open the destination folder, tap-and-hold the stylus on the folder, and then tap Paste on the pop-up list.

TIP   *To paste a file into a folder, tap Edit | Paste.*

Copy a file by using the same process, except tap Copy on the pop-up list instead of Cut. If you paste a copy of a file into the same folder, File Explorer will automatically change the filename by adding *Copy of* to the beginning of the filename.

To delete a file, tap-and-hold on the filename and then tap Delete on the pop-up list. To change the name of a file, tap Rename on the pop-up list, and then enter the new filename.

Send Files with E-Mail

You can send any file as an e-mail attachment from File Explorer. Tap-and-hold on a filename, and then tap Send Via E-mail on the pop-up list. Inbox starts and creates a new e-mail message with the file attached, as shown in the following image:

This is the file attachment ——————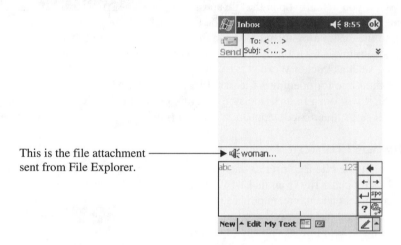
sent from File Explorer.

Complete and send the e-mail message as instructed in Chapter 20.

Beam Files with Infrared

Files can be transferred to another Pocket PC from File Explorer by using infrared. Line up the infrared ports of the two devices and set up the receiving device. To send a file from File Explorer on a Pocket PC, tap-and-hold on a filename and then tap Beam File on the pop-up list. A message box appears on the screen of both devices to indicate that the file was transmitted.

How to ... Receive Files via Infrared with Pocket PC 2000

Before a Pocket PC 2000 device can receive files with infrared, the infrared port must be turned on and set to receive files. Tap Start | Programs | Infrared Receive, and then line up the infrared port with the device that is sending the file. A message will appear on the screen indicating that communication has been established and that a file is being transferred. After the file is received, it is stored in the My Documents folder.

The infrared protocol that Pocket PC 2002 uses is different than the one used by Pocket PC 2000. If you want to use infrared to transfer a file on a Pocket PC 2000 device to a Pocket PC 2002 device, you have to use the legacy infrared support on the Pocket PC 2002 device. To receive the file on the Pocket PC 2002 device, tap Start | Programs Infrared Receive, and then line up the infrared port with the device that is sending the file.

Wrapping Up

Pocket PCs have features that are similar to Windows running on desktop computers. You use the Start menu to start programs and to switch between running programs. Files are stored in folders in a hierarchical manner in the same way as on desktop computers, and you use File Explorer to browse and manage files and folders. The Today screen is the closest thing to the Windows desktop on Pocket PCs, but the purpose of the Today screen is to provide an overview for your information rather than display program shortcuts. The Today screen also provides a way for you to personalize your Pocket PC by selecting different themes, which display pictures on the screen and change the colors of the Navigation and Command bars. In the next chapter, you'll learn how to personalize your Pocket PC for your preferences and tastes.

Chapter 3

Personalize Your Pocket PC

How To...

■ Change the Pocket PC personal settings

■ Use the Pocket PC input methods to enter information

■ Manage running programs using a program task manager

■ Change the Pocket PC appearance

It is easy to overlook the second *P* in Pocket PC, the one that stands for *personal*. Yet of all the computers made, Pocket PCs may be the most personal of all. The information they store—appointments, addresses, and tasks—is very personal for most people, and rarely will more than one person share a Pocket PC. So it makes sense for you to want to configure your Pocket PC to conform to your needs and tastes.

The Pocket PC software provides several ways to personalize your device. There are settings for entering owner information, setting passwords, programming hardware buttons, and configuring input methods. In fact, there are four different input methods for you to chose from, enabling you to pick the one that works best for you. If the input methods included with your Pocket PC do not work well for you, there are others provided by third-party companies.

Many people find the Start menu and the methods for starting and closing down programs cumbersome. There are several programs available that help manage the programs running on a Pocket PC. If you prefer a simple menu of icons to launch programs, you can use one of the many Today screen plug-ins that provide such a menu. In fact, the Today screen is one of the most customizable parts of the Pocket PC, and a variety of plug-ins exist that change the appearance of the screen, as well as add functionality.

As you can see, there are several ways for personalizing your Pocket PC—making it reflect you, its owner. In this chapter, we'll go over the personal settings in detail and show you how to enter data into your Pocket PC. We'll also take a look at the different program task managers and Today screen plug-ins available for the Pocket PC.

Change the Personal Settings

The Personal tab is where you personalize the Pocket PC by changing settings tailored to the way you work. In this section, we'll go over how to use each of the icons on the Personal tab. Table 3-1 contains a summary of what you do with each icon.

Program Hardware Buttons

In Chapter 2, you learned that part of the specification for Pocket PCs are hardware buttons. The hardware buttons may be located in different areas on the device. The purpose of these buttons is to make it easier for you to navigate within the device and start applications; you can program

3

Icon	Name	Description
Buttons	Buttons	Specifies which application a button will start.
Input	Input	Configures options for character recognition and the onscreen keyboard. Also configures word completion and voice record formats.
Menus	Menus	Specifies the program shortcuts that appear on the Start menu. Also turns on the New button, and specifies the items that appear on the New Button menu.
Owner Information	Owner Information	Enter personal information, such as address and phone number, here. Includes a Notes field that can be used to enter additional information not included with the owner information. Both sets of information can be configured to display when you turn on your device.
Password	Password	Creates or changes the password on your device and specifies whether you want to enable password protection for the device.
Sounds & Notifications	Sounds & Notifications	Changes the volume of your device, as well as the type of sound that is made for particular events.
Today	Today	Changes the appearance of the Today screen with themes and plug-ins.

TABLE 3-1   Icons on the Personal tab of the Pocket PC Settings

most of these buttons to start any application that you like. The following are some specifics of hardware buttons:

- To open the Button Properties dialog box, as shown in the following image, tap the Buttons icon on the Personal tab.

Select the button to program here.

Select what program a button will start.

■ To change the program associated with a button, first select a button in the list. Then click the triangle to the right of the Button Assignment field and select the program you want from the drop-down menu. You will see the assigned program change in the Buttons list. When finished, tap OK. If at any time you want to restore the default settings for your device, tap the Restore Defaults button.

■ The Up/Down Control tab is used to configure the Action button. The Action button is a wheel, a rocker, or a cursor pad that is used to move the cursor up or down. It is particularly useful when reading documents because you can scroll through a document while holding the device in one hand.

■ Within the Up/Down Control tab, shown on the right, you change how quickly the cursor starts scrolling and how fast it scrolls.

■ Within the Delay Before First Repeat section, move the slider left or right to control how soon scrolling starts. To control the scrolling speed, move the slider left or right within the Repeat Rate section.

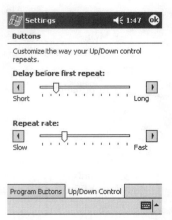

Configure the Input Methods

Pocket PC 2002 has four methods of input. The Block and Letter recognizers recognize characters that you write in the Input Panel on the screen. Microsoft Transcriber is a natural handwriting recognizer that translates what you write on the Pocket PC screen to text. Finally, you can use the onscreen keyboard to tap characters. Settings for each method are configured in the Input Settings dialog box.

The Input Properties dialog box has three tabs: Input Method, Word Completion, and Options. Use the Input Method tab to configure settings for each method. To make a change to an input method, first select it from the drop-down list, and then tap Options. There are no Block Recognizer options. When you select the Keyboard, the Input Settings dialog box changes to look like that shown at left.

Change the size of the keys on the keyboard by selecting either the Large Keys or Small Keys radic button. When you select Large Keys, you then have the option to use gestures for SPACE, BACKSPACE, SHIFT-key, and ENTER, which are made on the keyboard.

You will notice that at the bottom of the Input Settings dialog box is a sentence that contains a link, similar to the hyperlinks found on web pages. The Pocket PC settings include links to related settings; in this case, if you tap the Align link in this dialog box, the Align Screen Settings dialog box is displayed.

TIP

When you select the Letter Recognizer input method and tap Options, the screen shown at right is displayed.

When you select the Quick Stroke option, you must write all letters in one stroke. A single stroke enables you to write faster, but requires you to learn new ways to write certain letters. The Right to Left Crossbar option specifies whether you write crossbars for *t, f,* and the plus symbol (+) from right to left. If you need to write accented characters, be sure to select the Allow Accented Characters option.

TIP *Pocket PC Online Help contains demonstrations of how to write characters. To see the demonstration while the Letter Recognizer Options dialog box is displayed, go to Start | Help and then choose Demo. You can also display this help by tapping the Information button on the soft Input Panel any time that the panel is open.*

As you enter characters in the Input Panel, the Pocket PC will suggest words that you may be writing. If you tap the word that is displayed, that word will be placed wherever the cursor is located. By using this word completion feature, you can speed up data entry on your device. Use the Word Completion tab, as shown on the left, to turn word completion on or off, and to specify how many words display. It can display one to four words at a time.

You can specify how many characters you must enter before a word is suggested on this tab, as well as specify whether you want a space automatically inserted after the word or not.

Input Methods

Pocket PC 2000 has only two default input methods: Character Recognizer and Keyboard. Transcriber is included with the ActiveSync Version 3.1 CD-ROM, and is available to download from http://www.pocketpc.com.

Character Recognizer has two modes, Uppercase and Lowercase. Lowercase is the system default, and it is compatible with the Jot recognizer found on Palm-size PCs. If you have upgraded from the Palm-size PC, then you will find this mode to be consistent with what you already know. Uppercase mode works like *Graffiti*, the character recognizer found on Palm Computing devices. If you switch from Palm, then you may find this mode more familiar. On Pocket PC 2002 devices, the Block Recognizer replaces the Character Recognizer Uppercase mode.

Use the Options tab, shown on the right, to configure options wherever writing or recording is supported.

Specify the default Voice Recording Format by selecting a percentage option from the Voice Recording Format drop-down list. Selecting percentages from the drop-down list specifies the default zoom levels for writing and typing. The Pocket PC automatically capitalizes the first letter of sentences if you select that option in this dialog box. Choose Scroll upon reaching the last line, and the Pocket PC will automatically scroll the window when you reach the last line.

TIP
Each of the voice recording options affects the quality and the size of the audio file. Mobile Voice (GSM) is the recommended format because it provides good recording quality and takes far less storage than Pulse Code Modulation (PCM). PCM provides slightly better sound quality, but can take up to 50 times more storage.

Change the Start Menu

One of the first things to do with a new Pocket PC is edit the Start menu so that the programs you use most frequently are in it. By placing shortcuts to these programs in the Start menu, you decrease the number of taps necessary to start these programs. Change the contents of the Start menu by tapping the Menus icon in the Personal tab of the Settings dialog box. When you tap the Menus icon, the Menus dialog box is displayed, as shown in the illustration at left.

This list box contains all of the programs installed on the Pocket PC. Items that are selected appear on the Start menu, while the remaining items are available by selecting Start | Programs. To add an item to the Start menu, simply select the check box next to its name; to remove an item from the Start menu, deselect the check box next to the name of the program.

A feature that is unique to the Pocket PC is the New button. This feature adds a pop-up list to the New menu option on the

Command bar. Enable this feature, and a small triangle appears next to the New menu option, as shown in the following image:

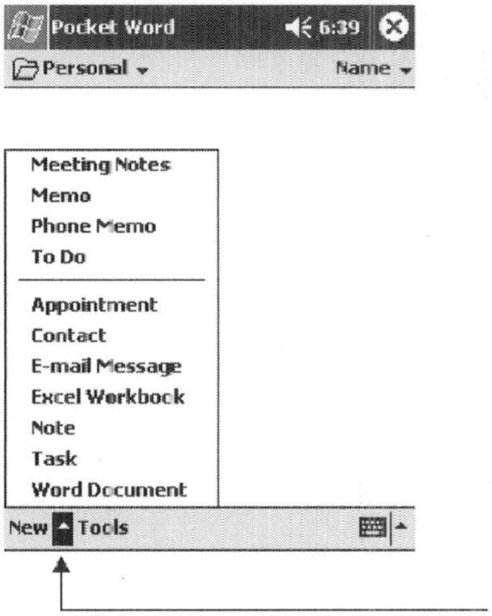

Tap here to expand the new menu list.

Tapping the triangle enables you to create a new item, such as an appointment, wherever you may be currently working on your Pocket PC. For example, suppose you are in Pocket Word editing a document when you are asked to attend a meeting. If the New button is enabled, all you need to do is tap the triangle and select Appointment. An appointment entry sheet appears for you to enter the appointment, which saves you the extra step of having to first switch to Calendar and then create the appointment.

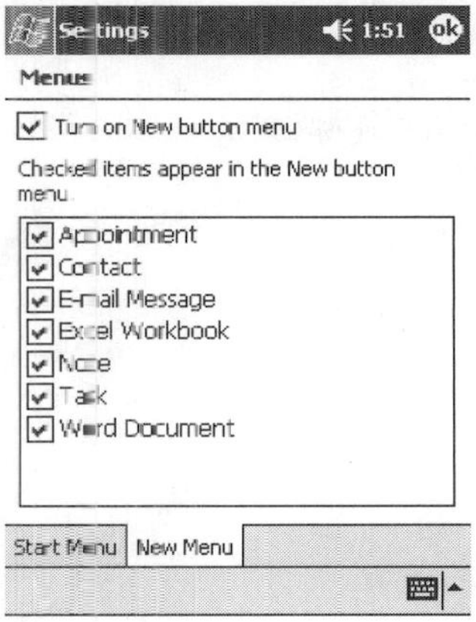

To turn the New button on or off, tap the New Menu tab to display the dialog box shown in the illustration at right.

Select the Turn On New Button Menu check box to turn the menu on, and clear the check box to turn it off. The list box in the middle of the dialog box displays the items that will appear in the list. By default, everything is selected. Remove items from the list by clearing the check boxes you do not want selected.

Edit Owner Information

With the Owner Information icon, you can enter your name and address and have them display whenever you turn on your Pocket PC. Enter this information by following these steps.

1. Tap the Owner Information icon on the Personal tab. The resulting dialog box, shown in the illustration on the right, has two tabs: Identification and Notes.

2. Enter your Name, Company, Address, Telephone number, and E-mail address in the Identification tab. To have this information display every time you turn on your Pocket PC, select the Show Information When Device Is Turned On check box. With this option selected, the information will display every time the device is turned on, and continues to display until you tap the screen.

3. Use the Notes tab to add any information you want that is not on the Identification tab. One way to use this tab is to provide a message in case your device is lost. When the device is turned on, you can have the message display along with the owner information by selecting the check box next to Show Information When Device Is Turned On.

Turn On Password Protection

You can protect the data in your device by requiring a password every time the device turns on. Tap the Password icon on the Personal tab to open the dialog box shown here.

Pocket PC 2002 supports a 4-digit password or a strong alphanumeric password, but Pocket PC 2000 devices only support 4-digit passwords. Strong alphanumeric passwords combine letters, numbers, and mixed case.

TIP *Sign-On from Communication Intelligence Corporation is a password security utility that uses your signature for authentication. Find more information about this program at http://www.cic.com.*

When you tap the Simple 4 Digit Password radio button, a numeric keypad appears for you to enter the password. A similar keypad displays for you to enter the password when you turn on the Pocket PC. Enter the password by tapping the buttons on the screen using either the stylus or your finger.

Strong alphanumeric passwords are harder to break and, therefore, provide greater security. When you tap the Strong Alphanumeric Password radio button, two fields display for you to enter a password. It is recommended to use the onscreen keyboard for entering passwords to ensure there are no translation errors. The password must be at least seven characters long, and contain a combination of upper- and lowercase letters, numbers, or punctuation.

NOTE *Strong alphanumeric passwords are case sensitive.*

You can configure how often you enter the device password by selecting a time in the Prompt If Device Unused For drop-down list. Selecting 0 minutes forces you enter the password every time you turn on your Pocket PC. Selecting 30 minutes forces you to enter the password only after the device has not been used for 30 minutes. Thus, if the device is turned off and turned right back on again, you won't have to enter the password.

TIP *It is crucial that you remember your password, because without it you will not be able to retrieve your data. If you forget your password, the only way to access your device again is to perform a full reset, which deletes all data. The process for a full reset for each device is slightly different; consult your owner's manual for details. The process usually involves removing your backup and main batteries so that your device has no power, and when you do this, all of your data will be lost.*

Change Sounds & Notifications

Using a Pocket PC is both a visual and audible experience. Sound plays a very important role in providing you with feedback. For example, when you tap a button using a stylus, you not only see the button being pressed, but you can also hear a sound. In most cases, this sound lets you know that the Pocket PC has recognized your request.

Sounds and their volumes are controlled using the Sounds & Notifications Settings dialog box. To open this dialog box, as shown in the following image, tap the Sounds & Notifications icon on the Personal tab.

Adjust volume by moving this slider.

Turn sounds on or off by selecting these check boxes.

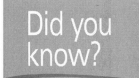

Settings for Sounds & Reminders

Pocket PC 2000 devices have a Sounds & Reminders setting that has three tabs: Volume, Sounds, and Reminders. The Notifications tab on the Pocket PC 2002 combines Sounds & Reminders settings. To change Sounds on Pocket PC 2000 devices, follow these steps:

1. Tap a name in the Event Name list, shown on the Sounds tab.

2. Tap the Sound drop-down menu at the bottom of the dialog box. Select the sound that you want from the list. If do not want a sound associated with the event, then select None from the list.

3. Once you have selected the sound that you want, preview it by tapping the Play button to the right.

4. Tap OK to save the changes.

You will notice two tabs in the Sounds & Notifications Settings dialog box. The Volume tab allows you to enable sounds for events or applications. (An event is something generated by the operating system, such as opening or closing a program.) The Notifications tab allows you to specify what you hear when you want to be reminded of appointments and tasks.

The specific sounds that you enable by selecting their check boxes on the Volume tab are the following:

- Events, such as warnings and system events
- Programs and notifications, such as alarms and reminders
- Screen taps, which you can specify as Soft or Loud by selecting the appropriate radio button
- Hardware buttons, which you can specify as Soft or Loud by selecting the appropriate radio button

There is a slider on the Volume tab that you can move to adjust the sound volume. Tap and hold the slider while dragging it to adjust the volume.

On the Notifications tab, shown in the following image, you specify what sound plays when an event occurs.

Tap here to preview the sound.

Select an event from this drop-down list.

Tap here to stop the sound preview.

First, select an event from the drop-down list, and then tap the Play Sound check box and select a sound. To preview the sound, tap the Play button.

Events can also display a message and flash the Pocket PC LED light if you select these options on the Notifications tab. When you select the Flash Light For option, you can specify how long the light flashes by selecting a number of minutes from the drop-down list.

Change the Today Screen

The Pocket PC Today screen is similar to the Windows desktop. As you see here, the Today screen can contain owner information, appointments, e-mail messages, and tasks.

Tap the Today icon on the Personal tab to configure the appearance of this screen.

TIP

You can tap each item of the Today screen to quickly start the associated application. Tap the Date icon to open the Pocket PC clock settings; tap the Owner icon to open the Owner Information settings; tap the Appointments, Unread messages, or Tasks icons to open the Calendar, Inbox, or Tasks.

Themes change the look of the Today screen, Start menu, and Navigation bar, and are new with Pocket PC 2002. Select which theme to use on the Appearance tab of the Today Settings dialog box, shown in the image at right.

To change the current theme, tap the new theme you want to use from the list box and then tap OK.

NOTE *Several programs have been developed for Pocket PCs that change the appearance of the Today screen. An overview of several of these programs is provided later in this chapter.*

To add a theme to your Pocket PC, copy the theme file, which has a .tsk extension, to either the Windows or My Documents folder on the Pocket PC. Themes can also be stored in a My Documents folder on storage cards, but they should not be in subfolders of My Documents. Chapter 7 shows you how to use ActiveSync to copy files to the Pocket PC, or you can use File Explorer to copy themes from a network share. If you want to share a theme with another Pocket PC, tap the theme, tap Beam, and align the infrared ports. To delete a theme, first tap the theme name, and then tap Delete.

If you don't want to change the appearance of the Start menu or Navigation bar, but want to change the Today screen background image, tap the Use This Picture As The Background check box, and then tap Browse to select an image. Background images can be either JPEG or GIF files and must be stored in the My Documents folder or a subfolder of My Documents.

TIP *You can combine themes and background images to further customize the Today screen appearance to your personal preferences.*

The items that can appear on the Today screen are listed on the Items tab of the Today Settings dialog box, as shown here on the right.

To add or remove items from the screen, tap the check box next to the item name. Owner Info, Calendar, Inbox, and Tasks can be moved up or down in the list by selecting the item and then tapping the Move Up or Move Down button.

Options that control what displays on the Today screen can be set for the Calendar and Tasks items. Select either, and then tap the Options button. The Today screen can display either the

3

next appointment or upcoming appointments, as well as all-day events. Task options include the number of high-priority tasks, the number of tasks due today, and the number of overdue tasks. You can also restrict the task information to a specific category.

The best time for the Today screen to be displayed is when you turn the device on for the first time each day. You might also want to have the screen display after a specified period of time has elapsed, which will happen if you tap the Display Today Screen If Device Is Not Used For [ ] Hours check box in the Today Settings dialog box. You specify the number of hours that must elapse before the screen displays from the drop-down list in the dialog box.

Enter Information on Pocket PCs

Handwriting recognition is one of the most intimate ways of interacting with computers. Writing on a computer screen with your own hand, and seeing the writing translated to text, makes the computer more personal than just a machine. It is no wonder that, from the first time handwriting recognition was introduced, it captured the imagination of computer users.

Your Pocket PC provides several ways of translating what you write to text. The Block and Letter recognizers instantly translate a letter that you write on the Pocket PC Software Input Panel to a character inserted at the cursor location. Another way is to write on the screen as you write on paper and see the results displayed on the screen in digital ink. After you finish writing, either store what was written in the digital ink form or have the Pocket PC translate the digital ink into text. Finally, you can write anywhere on the Pocket PC screen in your own handwriting, and after you finish writing, the Pocket PC translates each written word and inserts them at the cursor location.

How to ...   Install Transcriber

Transcriber is not available by default on some Pocket PC 2002 devices or any Pocket PC 2000 devices. To use it, you must install the Transcriber handwriting recognition software from the Companion (or ActiveSync) CD-ROM that comes with Pocket PCs, or download it from http://www.pocketpc.com.

Connect your Pocket PC with a desktop computer running ActiveSync. If you use the Companion CD-ROM, insert it into the CD-ROM drive, and the Getting Started screen automatically loads on the desktop computer. Click Play; click Enhance Your Pocket PC; click Tools; and, finally, click Install in the Microsoft Transcriber section of the Tools page. If you download Transcriber from the Web, browse the location where it is stored on your hard drive and run tranScriberCE_e.exe.

Follow the onscreen prompts, and install the software to the default location. After the installation finishes, a dialog box will display on the Pocket PC telling you to close documents and then reset the device. When the Pocket PC restarts, you will find that the Transcriber option has been added to the Software Input Panel options

If you prefer not to use any of the handwriting recognition methods, you can use the stylus to tap letters from an onscreen keyboard. Each letter that you tap will appear on the screen at the cursor location. In this section, you'll find instructions for using the onscreen keyboard, the Pocket PC Block and Letter recognizers, and Transcriber handwriting recognition. The process of translating digital ink is called *deferred recognition*; and because it works in many of the Pocket PC programs, instructions for using it are in the chapters covering those programs.

> NOTE *The fastest way to enter information into your Pocket PC is by using ActiveSync to synchronize data between the device and Microsoft Outlook. Chapter 6 provides instructions for using ActiveSync.*

Use the Software Input Panel

The Software Input Panel is a window on the Pocket PC screen that provides a location for writing characters or displays the onscreen keyboard. To open the window, tap the Software Input Panel button located at the bottom right-hand corner of the screen, as shown in the following image:

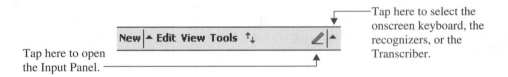

Tap here to select the onscreen keyboard, the recognizers, or the Transcriber.

Tap here to open the Input Panel.

The button image changes to indicate which of the three modes are in use. A keyboard indicates the onscreen keyboard, a blue pencil indicates the Block or Letter recognizers, and a hand and pencil indicates the Transcriber.

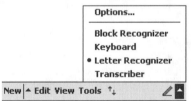

To change the input method, tap the arrow next to the Software Input Panel button to open the pop-up menu shown at left.

Tap the name of the input method that you want to use; if you select Keyboard, Block Recognizer, or Letter Recognizer, the menu closes and the panel switches to the mode that you select. When you select Transcriber, the panel closes and the button switches to the hand and pencil.

Included at the top of the pop-up menu is Options, which you can tap to open the Input Settings dialog box, as shown in the illustration on the right.

Another way to open the Input Settings dialog box is to tap Start | Settings | Input.

Enter Information Using the Onscreen Keyboard

The standard onscreen keyboard displays in the Software Input Panel, as shown in the following image:

Tap here to switch to the numeric keypad.

Tap here to switch to the special character keyboard.

To use the onscreen keyboard to enter information, do the following:

1. To enter text, tap the letters on the keyboard using the stylus. The keyboard has three different modes: standard, numeric, and special character.

2. To switch to the numeric and special character keyboards shown in Figure 3-1, tap the 123 and AU buttons, respectively, on the standard keyboard.

3. Tap SHIFT to switch the keyboard buttons to their uppercase equivalents, and the number row displays the symbols that normally display above the number row on a standard keyboard. After you enter an uppercase letter by tapping SHIFT and then tapping a letter, the keyboard switches back to lowercase, but tapping CAP locks the keyboard in CAPS LOCK.

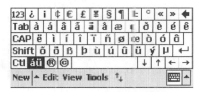

FIGURE 3-1   On the left is the numeric keyboard; on the right is the special character keyboard.

4. The standard onscreen keyboard displays small keys, but that can be switched to large keys by opening the Input Settings dialog box and selecting the Keyboard Input Method option, as shown in the following image:

These are the keyboard shortcut gestures.

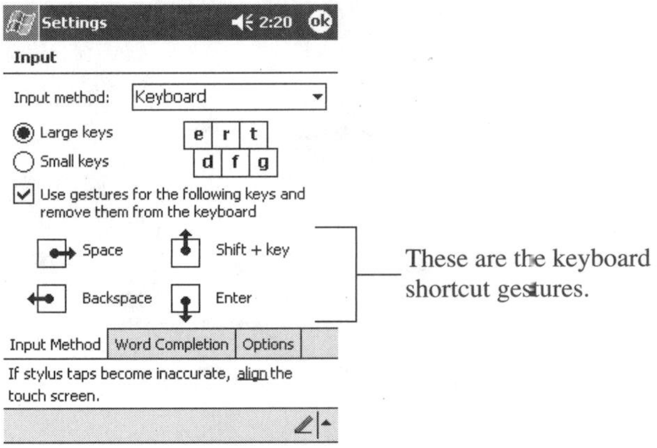

5. Tap the Large Keys or the Small Keys radio button to switch between the two different keyboard types.

The Large Keys keyboard supports gestures that you can write across the keyboard for the SPACE, BACKSPACE, ENTER, and SHIFT keys. To use the gestures shown on the Input Settings dialog box, tap the check box in the dialog box.

Enter Information Using the Letter Recognizer

To use the Letter Recognizer to enter text, tap Letter Recognizer on the Software Input Panel pop-up menu, which changes the panel, as shown in the following image:

Enter uppercase letters here.

Enter lowercase letters here.

Enter numbers here.

BACKSPACE

Move the cursor forward and back.

SPACE

Symbol keyboard

ENTER   Online Help

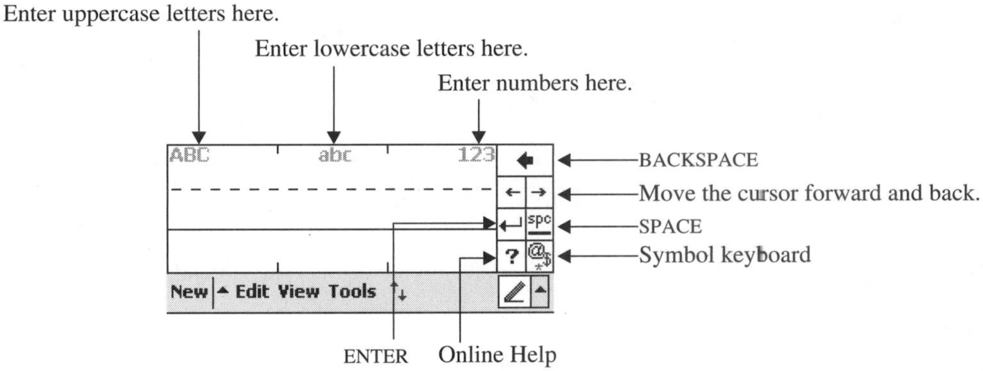

The Letter Recognizer has four areas for entering uppercase letters, lowercase letters, numbers, and keyboard commands, such as BACKSPACE and ENTER.

Drag the stylus across the panel horizontally from left to right to insert a space, and drag from right to left to delete a character or space.

The Letter Recognizer translates letters written in lowercase but you have the option of using a single stroke to enter certain letters of the alphabet. To enter characters in a single stroke, select the Quick Stroke option on the Letter Recognizer Options screen. To see demos for writing all characters, open the Letter Recognizer Online Help, and tap Demo.

The dotted middle line and the solid bottom line on the panel help the Letter Recognizer translate shorter letters and letters with descenders or ascenders. Write letters such as *o* and *c* between the midline (dotted) and baseline (solid). Write letters with descenders, such as *p,* with the top of the letter between the midline and baseline, and the descender below the baseline. Letters with ascenders, such as *b,* should be written with the ascender above the midline, and the bottom portion between the midline and baseline.

The Letter Recognizer also translates accented and special characters. Open Online Help to see demonstrations of how to enter these characters on the Input Panel.

Enter Information Using the Block Recognizer

If you switch to a Pocket PC from a Palm OS device, you may prefer using the Block Recognizer because it translates the Palm Graffiti–like character strokes to text. To use the Block Recognizer to enter text, tap Block Recognizer on the Software Input Panel pop-up menu, which changes the panel, as shown in the following image:

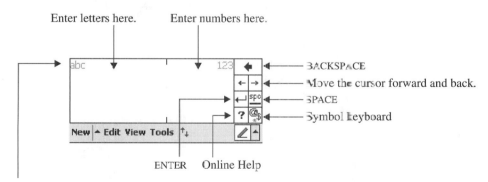

Enter letters here.   Enter numbers here.

BACKSPACE
Move the cursor forward and back.
SPACE
Symbol keyboard

ENTER   Online Help

Indicates Lowercase, Shift and Caps Lock modes.

The Block Recognizer has three areas for entering letters, numbers, and keyboard commands such as BACKSPACE and ENTER.

The first word of each sentence is automatically capitalized; otherwise, all other letters translate in lowercase. To capitalize other words, switch to Shift mode by drawing a straight line from the bottom up for at least half the length of the Input Panel. The *abc* label at the upper-left corner of the Input Panel changes to *Abc,* indicating Shift mode. To activate Caps Lock, draw two lines from the bottom up. You will know that Caps Lock is active by the *ABC* label on the Input Panel.

TIP *To see a demonstration of how to enter characters using Graffiti, tap Online Help on the Input Panel, and then tap Demo.*

You enter punctuation and symbols anywhere on the Input Panel. To enter punctuation, tap once on the panel, and then write the punctuation mark. A circle appears in the upper left-hand corner of the Input Panel, indicating punctuation mode. Enter extended characters by first drawing a slash in the Input Panel, and then writing the character. A slash appears in the upper left-hand corner of the Input Panel, indicating extended character mode.

Punctuation and symbols can also be entered by tapping the Symbol Keyboard button on the Input Panel, and then tapping an item on the keyboard, as shown in the illustration at right.

TIP *The Block Recognizer also translates accented characters, special characters, and mathematical symbols. See Online Help for demonstrations on how to enter these characters on the Input Panel.*

Word Completion

As you enter letters using the onscreen keyboard or recognizers, the Pocket PC suggests words in a pop-up window that appears above the Input Panel. Tap the word to enter it at the insertion point.

In the Input Settings dialog box, tap the Word Completion tab to configure options for word completion, as shown in the illustration at right.

When the Pocket PC suggests more words, a greater amount of space is taken up above the Input Panel, which covers up other information in the dialog box where you enter text.

Enter Information Using Transcriber

Transcriber is a natural-handwriting recognition translator for the Pocket PC. It recognizes words written in cursive, print, or mixed handwriting by using an integrated dictionary. When you select Transcriber from the Software Input Panel pop-up menu, the panel closes and you enter text by writing directly on the screen. The Input Panel button changes to the Hand and Pencil icon, as shown in the following image:

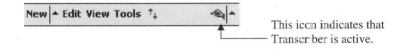

This icon indicates that Transcriber is active.

An introductory screen and icon bar will display if these items are selected in the Transcriber Options dialog box, as shown in the following image:

This dialog box opens when you select Options from the Transcriber input method in the Input Settings dialog box.

The icon bar, as shown in the following image, is a set of buttons that appear at the bottom of the screen when Transcriber is active.

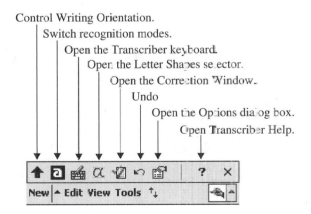

Control Writing Orientation.
Switch recognition modes.
Open the Transcriber keyboard.
Open the Letter Shapes selector.
Open the Correction Window.
Undo
Open the Options dialog box.
Open Transcriber Help.

The Control Writing Orientation arrow on the icon bar points upward relative to the selected direction of the writing. For example, if the arrow points NW, then you should write characters with an inclination of 45° from left bottom up to right top. If your writing slants letters slightly to the left, tap the arrow until it points NE.

Transcriber has three recognition modes: Unrestricted, Uppercase, and Numeric. The Unrestricted mode allows all symbols and words, and is indicated by an *a* on the icon bar. The Uppercase mode converts everything to uppercase and is indicated by an *A* on the icon bar. The Numeric mode converts numbers and some letters, and is indicated by a *12* on the icon bar.

The Transcriber keyboard provides an easy way to enter punctuation or symbols. It will remain visible until you tap OK; but if you tap the Push-Pin button, then the keyboard will close after you tap a key.

Use the Letter Shapes selector, shown at right, to configure Transcriber for your handwriting.

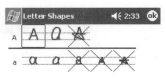

Tap each shape shown on the screen and then tap the Often, Rarely, or Never radio button to specify whether you write the letter in that shape. It's worth taking some time to go through each letter and symbol to increase translation accuracy.

The Transcriber Correction Window is new with Pocket PC 2002, and it simplifies the process of correcting translation mistakes. To open the window, first highlight a mistake, whether it's a letter, word, or phrase, and then tap the Correction icon on the toolbar. You can also use the quick-correct gesture, which is an up/down motion, over the highlight, and then tap Go To Corrector on the pop-up menu; or you can use the correction gesture, which is a check mark, to open the window, which looks like the following:

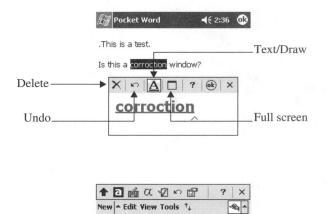

There are several gestures that you can use to direct Transcriber to perform certain actions, such as enter a RETURN or BACKSPACE. You will find these gestures in Online Help, which you can open by tapping Help on the toolbar, which looks like a question mark, or by tapping Start | Help.

There are many ways to make a correction. You can write directly over a letter or word to change it, or you can double-tap the letter or word to open the Alternates menu. From the Alternates menu, you can select an alternative letter or word from those provided, add the selection to the Transcriber dictionary, change the case of the selection, or cancel corrections.

Another method is to select the letter or word and then tap the caret underneath the text to open a menu, where you can delete the selection, replace the selection with a space, change the case of the selection, copy the selection, or replace the selection with text from the clipboard. If you double-tap the correction window in any area not over a word or the caret, a menu opens where you can erase everything in the window, cancel the previous action, copy everything in the window to the clipboard, or paste text from the clipboard into the window.

The General tab of the Transcriber Options dialog box is also used to configure the color and the width of the ink that displays when you write onscreen. The Recognizer tab of the Transcriber Options dialog box, shown in the illustration at right, provides settings for controlling handwriting recognition.

If you select the Add Space After check box, then a space is added after each translated word. If you do not connect letters when you write, select the Separate Letters Mode check box to speed up recognition. The Speed of Recognition Vs. Quality slider controls the trade-off between recognition speed and quality, with faster speed resulting in decreased quality. The Recognition Start Time slider controls the length of time after a word is written before Transcriber translates the word to text. When the slider is in the center, Transcriber will wait about a second.

How to ...   Use the Transcriber Calculator

Transcriber has a built-in calculator that can complete simple mathematical equations. Write the equation as you would text, such as **2+2=**. Transcriber recognizes this equation, performs the calculation, and translates what you wrote to **2+2=4**.

Try Alternative Recognizers

Each recognizer that comes with the Pocket PC might require you to slightly change how you write. If you have difficulty getting the recognizers to translate your handwriting, you may want to try one of several alternative recognizers available for the Pocket PC. Many of these recognizers come in trial versions so that you can try the software before purchasing it. Two alternate recognizers are PenReader and Calligrapher.

Transcriber only supports English, French, and German languages. If you write in a language other than these, you may want to consider PenReader from Paragon Software because it supports 28 different languages. It recognizes all national alphabets based on the standard Latin ABC, and there are additional recognition engines adjusted for Cyrillic and Greek alphabets. You will find more information about PenReader at http://www.penreader.com.

Calligrapher is the big brother of Transcriber. It was developed by ParaGraph, from whom Microsoft licenses code used in Transcriber. ParaGraph is also the company that developed the handwriting recognition software for the Apple Newton operating system. PhatWare Corporation recently took over distribution and support responsibilities for Calligrapher. One of the features that sets Calligrapher apart is PenCommander, which launches user-defined commands that you create using a scripting language. It also includes an integrated spell checker that you can use to check the spelling of any document that has text. There are English and International versions of this program, and you will find more information about it at http://www.phatware.com.

■ MyScript from Vision Objects adds a new Software Input Panel to Pocket PCs that enables you to write across the entire width of the panel. There are English and French versions available. Find more information about MyScript at http://www.visionobjects.com.

■ Fitaly from Textware Solution is an alternative to the onscreen keyboard. The keys are arranged for optimal input using a stylus, with 84 percent of the keystrokes clustered in a central area. People who are proficient with Fitaly have been able to enter text as fast as 50 words per minute. You will find this program at http://www.fitaly.com.

■ Resco Keyboard Pro enhances the onscreen keyboard by adding three numeric layouts, including a calculator for typing numbers or numerical expressions. Another keyboard from Resco stores phrases, which you can insert by simply tapping a button. This program can be found at http://www.resco-net.com/resco/en/default.asp.

■ AccessPanel from DeveloperOne is an additional Software Input Panel that speeds data entry by storing phrases that you can insert into documents or e-mail. It also automatically inserts information from the Pocket PC Contacts program into documents. More information about this program can be found at http://www.developerone.com.

TIP *External keyboards are also available for Pocket PCs so that you can enter information by typing. The Stowaway keyboard is very popular and can be found at www.thinkoutside.com*

Manage Running Programs

One of the most hotly debated topics between Microsoft and Pocket PC users is about exiting programs. Microsoft believes it is better to have all programs open and to jump between them, because it is much faster to switch between running programs than it is to start a program. Because of this, Microsoft does not provide a way to exit programs. Pocket PC users prefer to start, exit, and switch between programs on their devices just as they do on their personal computers.

Most Pocket PC users prefer to have more control over what programs run on their Pocket PC. Furthermore, Windows CE does not do a good enough job of managing memory, so when too many programs run, the Pocket PC slows down. Consequently, software developers have written programs that provide users with the ability to easily shut down running programs.

While there are several different program task managers for Pocket PCs, they all work in a similar way. Additional buttons are added to the Pocket PC Navigation bar at the top of the screen, and the default OK button is replaced with a button that automatically switches between Exit and OK. Tapping Exit shuts down the program.

> **TIP** *HP (Hewlett-Packard) and Compaq include their own program task managers with their Pocket PCs. The HP Task Switcher is accessible from the Today screen, and the Compaq iTask is automatically programmed to a hardware button.*

The choice of which program task manager to install is based on whether you want a number of features available from the Navigation bar, or a simple button that just shuts down programs. For example, GigaBar from ThumbsUpSoftware (http://www.gigabar.com) switches tasks, supports gestures for starting programs, browses files, shows memory and battery status, displays background images, and captures screen shots. In contrast, Go from Stellarmetrics (http://stellarm.hostme.com/Software/go.htm) adds one button to the Navigation bar for switching and exiting programs.

Did you know?

X Marks the Spot

Pocket PC 2002 adds an X button that appears to exit programs but does not. When you tap the X, the window closes and the previously opened program appears on the screen. However, tapping the X really just closes the window and does not exit the program. If you tap Start | Settings | System | Memory, and then tap the Running Programs tab, you will see the program still listed as running. Consequently, it is best to think of the X as a minimize button, and use a program task manager to shut down programs.

The support of background images, or skins, with GigaBar is popular with its users because it allows them to change the Pocket PC appearance to something they find more appealing. There are links to GigaBar skins at http://www.gigabar.com/htm/skins.html. Another program task manager that supports skins is WIS Bar, which is made by the Japanese firm Walkers Internet Service. WIS Bar displays running programs as icons on the Navigation bar, and adds icons for the Today screen, Battery, and Memory meters to the Navigation bar. You can download WIS Bar from http://www.walkers.ne.jp/ww/wisbare.html.

TaskPro Navigator from DeveloperOne does not support skins, but you can customize its colors. Taskpro Navigator adds Navigation buttons to the top of the screen, and includes memory and battery meters. You will find this program at http://www.developerone.com/pocketpc/taskpronavigator/.

Scott Seligman's PocketNav is a program task manager favored by Pocket PC users who simply want to switch between programs and shut down programs. It adds two buttons to the Navigation bar: one loads the Today screen, and the other loads the task switcher. You'll find more information about this program at http://www.scottandmichelle.net/scott/cestuff.html.

Enhance the Today Screen

The Pocket PC Today screen supports plug-ins, which provide software developers the ability to enhance the Today screen by adding more functions or changing its appearance. You can select from several programs to tailor the Today screen to your personal needs.

How to ...

Change the Overall Appearance of the Pocket PC

The skinning capabilities of Dashboard, WIS Bar, and GigaBar significantly change the appearance of a Pocket PC. However, there are parts of the Pocket PC software that these programs do not change that you can change using other software.

Stardock has brought the features of its popular WindowBlinds program to the Pocket PC. It changes the appearance of the Navigation bar and allows you to add and place as many buttons on the Navigation bar as you want. You will find this program at http://www.stardock.com/products/pocketblinds/.

You can use CETuner from Paragon Software to change the color schemes and system fonts on your Pocket PC. By decreasing the font size, more information will display on the screen, or you can make the fonts bolder so they are easier to see. This program is available from http://www.penreader.com/PocketPC/CETuner.html.

If you want to simply add something a little fun to your Pocket PC, try Pocket Mascot. This program from JGUI For Pocket PC displays a character, called a mascot, on top of any program. The mascot speaks like a comic strip, and the messages can contain help about using the Pocket PC, or they can be anything that you want displayed. This program is available at http://jguippc.tripod.com/mascot/index.htm.

Perhaps the most widely used Today screen enhancement is Dashboard from SnoopSoft. Dashboard replaces all the default parts of the Today screen with its own agenda, mail, and task viewers, and adds a program launcher. You can combine Dashboard skins with WIS Bar and GigaBar skins to change nearly the entire appearance of the Pocket PC. You will find more information about this program at http://www.snoopsoft.com/pocketpc/dashboard.html.

DeveloperOne provides several Today screen plug-ins. Normally, the Today screen only displays the number of tasks that you have, but TaskView Today lists the tasks on the Today screen. Agenda Today replaces the Calendar portion of the Today screen with all of the day's activities, including tasks. PointStart adds a list of icons that you can tap to run programs, and Phrase Today adds inspirational thoughts, quotes, and trivia to the Today screen. You will find all of these plug-ins at http://www.developerone.com/.

ScaryBear Software is another company that provides a number of Today screen plug-ins. QuickCalendar displays the current week; and if you tap the QuickCalendar window, it expands to display two months. QuickAgenda provides an overview for several days of appointments. QuickQuotes displays quotes on the Today screen, and PowerLevel displays meters for power level and memory. You will find these plug-ins at http://www.scarybearsoftware.com/.

BirthdayBoy plug-in from Gigabyte Solutions Ltd displays birthdays and anniversaries up to 31 days in advance. One version of the plug-in works with the Today screen, and another version is available for Dashboard. You can download this plug-in from http://www.gigabytesol.com/pocket.htm.

If you would like the appearance of the Today screen to change a little bit each day, check out the Today's The Day plug-in from Stellarmetrics. It displays a different image on the Today screen for each day of the week. Stellarmetrics provides instructions for how to create your own images for the plug-in, along with links to other sites that have images, at http://stellarm.hostme.com/Software/ttd.htm.

Microsoft provides a free Today screen image tool that you can download from http://www.pocketpc.com. The tool is a Today screen plug-in that displays any JPEG, GIF, or BMP image that you select. When you install the tool on your Pocket PC, an Image Entry is added to the Today screen items list. To select an image to display, tap Image and then tap Options, which opens the dialog box shown here.

Tap Browse to select an image file, which needs to be located within the My Documents folder. It's best to use images that are 240 pixels wide, but the plug-in will fit the image to the width of the screen when you tap the Fit Image To Window Width check box. You can also configure the plug-in to start programs that you enter in the Run This When Tapped field.

> **TIP**   *The Today Screen Image tool provides an easy way to add corporate logos to the Today screen.*

If you select a program that is in the Windows folder, such as the calculator, you simply need to enter the executable filename. To run programs from other folders, enter the entire path along with the executable filename. When you tap New Image Item, a second Image Entry is added to the Today screen items list, allowing you to add more than one image to the Today screen. Be careful with this feature because you cannot remove the Image Entries from the items list.

Wrapping Up

As you have seen, there are several ways for you to emphasize the personal part of the Pocket PC. Each setting and program discussed in this chapter has the purpose of tailoring the Pocket PC to your tastes and preferences. You now know how the second *P* stands for personal; in the next chapter, you'll learn how the second *C* in Pocket PC stands for computer. There are a number of system settings that control how the Pocket PC operates, and we'll take a closer look at these settings next.

Chapter 4

Change Your Pocket PC System Settings

How To...

■ Conserve battery power by adjusting the screen brightness

■ Change the date and time on your Pocket PC

■ Configure the amount of RAM used to run programs and store files

■ Monitor and manage the amount of storage space available in Pocket PCs and storage cards

■ Change regional settings

It may not look it, but your Pocket PC is a powerful computer. The Electronic Numerical Integrator And Computer (ENIAC) was the world's first electronic computer, built by the Army during World War II to compute ballistic firing tables. ENIAC weighed over 30 tons, calculated 5,000 additions per second, and stored 200 digits. A Pocket PC weighing 6.1 ounces calculates more than 300 million additions per second and can store more than 16 million digits.

One of the most powerful features of Pocket PCs is that they are designed so that you shouldn't have to change how they operate. Nowhere is this more evident than in the Pocket PC memory management features, which automatically allocate memory in the Pocket PC between storage space and program memory. However, there will be occasions when you need to make changes, and for that you use the System tab of the Pocket PC Settings screen.

Some examples of the type of system changes you may need to make include changing the Pocket PC device name if you synchronize more than one Pocket PC with a desktop computer. If taps on the screen do not properly register, fix the problem by using the Screen setting. You manage battery power by adjusting the Backlight and Power settings. In this chapter, you'll learn how to change these and other system settings on your Pocket PC.

Change the System Settings

Table 4-1 contains a summary of the icons on the System tab, which you use to change hardware settings. In this chapter, you'll learn how to use each of these icons.

Change the Device Name Using the About Icon

The Windows CE operating system runs on several different types of processors, though Pocket PC 2002 only runs on Intel StrongARM processors. Pocket PC 2000 runs on SH3, MIPS, and StrongARM processors, which means that you may need to determine what processor is in these Pocket PCs in order to install the right version of a program. The About icon on the System tab

Icon	Name	Description
About	About	Provides information about the Pocket PC version, the processor, and the amount of memory. Specifies the name of the device that is used with ActiveSync.
Screen	Screen or Align Screen	Changes the way the stylus works with the touch screen. Use this icon if you have problems getting the touch screen to recognize the exact location of the stylus.
Backlight	Backlight or Brightness	Configures the screen backlighting to conserve battery power.
Clock	Clock	Sets the current date and time on the Pocket PC. Enables the Pocket PC to act like an alarm clock.
Memory	Memory	Configures the amount of internal memory allocated for storage and program memory. Displays the amount of space available on storage cards. Shows the programs that are running and enables you to stop them.
Power	Power	Shows the amount of main and backup battery power available and configures power-saving features.
Regional Settings	Regional Settings	Enables your Pocket PC to support international settings that can be used by some programs. Also, changes the way numbers, currency, time, and dates display.
Remove Programs	Remove Programs	Uninstalls any applications that you have installed on your device.

TABLE 4-1   The Pocket PC System Settings

displays this information, and more. When you tap the About icon, the About Settings dialog box is displayed, as shown here:

As you can see, the dialog box has three tabs: Version, Device ID, and Copyrights. The Version tab displays the current version of the Pocket PC, the processor type, the amount of internal memory, whether the expansion slot is in use, and the owner's name and company. The Copyrights tab displays all the copyright information for the software that is installed on the Pocket PC.

Use the Device ID tab, shown on the left, to specify a name for the Pocket PC. This name is used to identify the device to other computers on a network. It is also used by ActiveSync to store partnership information. (See Chapter 5 for information about ActiveSync and partnerships.) Enter a name in the Device Name field. If you wish, enter information in the Description field. The Description field can contain up to 50 characters and can be used to display any information that you like.

Align the Screen

When you turned on your Pocket PC for the very first time, you aligned the Touch screen. The process involves tapping the center of a target as it moves across the screen. You will need to realign the screen if you start to have difficulty getting the Pocket PC to respond exactly as you expect when you tap on the screen.

To realign the Touch screen, tap the Align Screen icon on the System tab to open the Align Screen Settings dialog box, shown on the right.

Begin the process by tapping Align Screen. Tap the target as it moves around the screen, and the Pocket PC stores the information and returns to this dialog box. Close the dialog box by tapping OK.

Most Pocket PCs have button sequences to align the screen. For example, on a Compaq iPAQ, pressing the Navigation and Calendar buttons at the same time opens the Align Screen dialog box. Check the owner's manual of your Pocket PC to determine whether it has a similar button sequence.

Adjust the Backlight or Brightness

With this setting, you specify that backlighting be turned off when the device is on battery power and idle for a specified period of time, or on external power and idle for a specified period of time. To configure these settings, tap the Backlight icon on the System tab to open the Backlight Settings dialog box, shown at right:

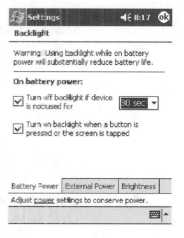

Normally, this dialog box only has tabs for Battery Power and External Power, though Compaq iPAQ Pocket PCs have an additional tab for Brightness. Both Power tabs have the same two check boxes: one to turn off the backlight if the device is not used for a specified amount of time, and the other to turn on the backlight when a button is pressed or the screen is tapped.

Select the appropriate check boxes to configure the backlight settings. If you select Turn Off Backlight, you can then select the amount of time to wait from the drop-down list. Use the Brightness tab on iPAQs to configure how bright the backlight displays. A brighter display will drain the batteries faster than a dimmer display.

Tap the Adjust Power Settings link at the bottom of the dialog box to go to the Power Settings dialog box.

Set the Clock and Alarms

When you tap the Clock icon on the System tab, the Clock Settings dialog box opens, as shown on the right: The Time tab is used to set the date and time of the Pocket PC, and the Alarms tab is used to create alarms.

The dialog box is divided in half. The top half contains the settings for the Home location, and the bottom half contains the settings for the Visiting location. Use either the Home or Visiting settings to change the date and time. Tapping the radio button next to Home or Visiting makes it available for changes. The selected location settings will be dark, while the other location settings will be grayed out.

The Home and Visiting settings are handy for travelers. With these settings, you can quickly change the date and time between two different locations. However, be aware that when you switch between the two, appointment times on the calendar will change to correspond with the new time zone.

To change the date, tap the down arrow to the right of the date to open the date picker, and then follow these steps:

1. To change the month, tap the month that is currently displayed, and then select the desired month from those that are listed. Another way to change the month is to tap the left or right arrows to move forward or back one month at a time.

2. To change the year, tap the year that is currently displayed. Use the spinner buttons to increase or decrease the number of the year.

3. To change the date, simply tap the date on the calendar.

There are two ways for you to change time.

■ Tap any part of the digital clock to select it, and then tap the up or down arrows to the right of the clock to change the value.

■ Move the arms in the analog portion of the clock by tapping-and-holding an arm on the screen. Drag the arm in the direction you want it to go. As you move the arm, the display in the digital portion of the clock will change.

When you tap OK after making any change to the clock settings, a dialog box will display asking whether you want to save the changes. Tap Yes, and the dialog box will close with the changes in effect. Tap No, and the dialog box will close without saving the changes. Tap Cancel, and you return to the Clock dialog box without saving any changes.

Set Alarms

In addition to changing the date and time of your device, you can also use the clock to set alarms. Four different alarms are available to go off at specified times throughout the day. To set an alarm, tap the Alarms tab to open the dialog box shown here:

Select this check box to → turn the alarm on or off.

Tap here to set the time of the alarm.

To set alarms, follow these steps:

1. Tap the field that contains <Description>, and enter a description of the alarm.

2. Select the day of the week for the alarm from the date abbreviations located below the description. More than one day can be selected by tapping each day of the week.

3. Tap the time to open a window that displays an analog and digital clock. Use either clock to set the alarm time, and then tap OK.

Once you have set the alarms, activate them by selecting the check boxes to the left of the alarm descriptions. The alarms you create stay in the Alarms tab, and they stay active even after they go off for the first time. Unless you clear the check boxes, the alarms that you create will go off when the designated times occur every day.

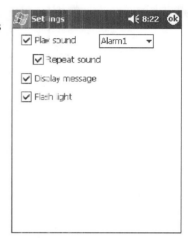

The dialog box shown on the right appears when you tap the Bell icon (located above the time setting) and controls what happens when an alarm goes off.

In this dialog box, you specify whether a sound should be made, whether that sound will repeat, whether a message will be displayed on the screen, and whether the alarm light should flash when the alarm goes off.

You can change the sound that the alarm plays by using the drop-down list next to the Play Sound option. Tap the down

Select Home and Visiting Cities in Pocket PC 2000

Pocket PC 2002 does not display city names for the Clock home or visiting sections like Pocket PC 2000 does. Instead, Pocket PC 2002 displays U.S. time zones, as well as city or country names outside the United States. If you have a Pocket PC 2000 device, you can change the home and visiting cities by following these steps:

1. Tap the Home or Visiting radio button so that the settings are available.

2. Tap the down arrow to the right of the city name and scroll through the list to find the city you want. When a city is selected, the time zone field will change.

If you cannot find a city that you want, select a city that is in the same time zone as the one you want. If the time zone displayed is not correct, change it by tapping the down arrow and selecting the correct one from the list.

arrow button to expand the list and select the sound that you want. The sound plays once it is selected.

An alarm can be any WAV file stored in the Windows folder. You can also make your own alarms using the Notes voice recording function, as described in Chapter 13.

Adjust Memory

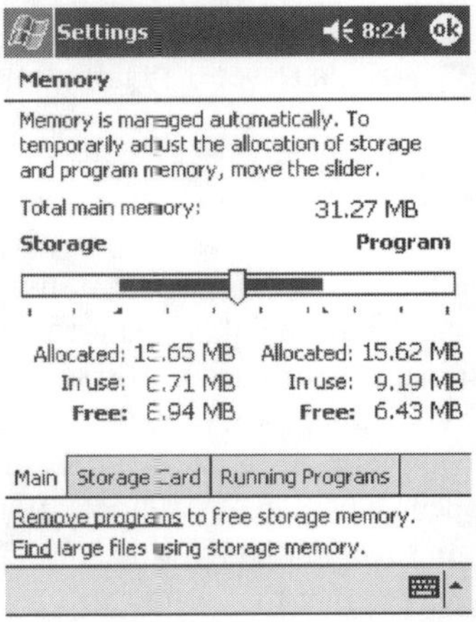

In Chapter 2, you learned how Windows CE uses RAM for both file storage and program execution. The total amount of memory in your device is divided between storage space and program execution. Use the Memory Settings dialog box, as shown on the right, to change how much memory is allocated for each.

To open the Memory Settings dialog box, tap the Memory icon on the System tab. To adjust the allocation of internal memory between Storage and Program memory, tap-and-hold the stylus on the slider, and then drag it left or right. After the slider moves, the numbers next to Allocated, In Use, and Free change to reflect the new setting.

Pocket PCs automatically adjust between storage and program memory as more programs run. In most cases, you will not need to manually change this setting.

The Storage Card tab, shown here on the right, shows you the total amount of storage card memory, how much is in use, and how much is free.

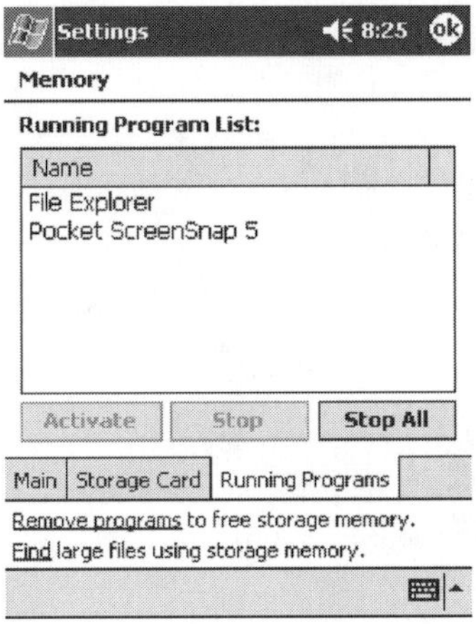

The Running Programs tab, shown on the left, shows the programs that are currently running. You can switch from one program to another, stop a particular program, or stop all the programs.

To switch to a program, select it from the Running Program List, and then tap Activate. To stop a program, select it from the Running Program List, and then tap Stop. To stop all the programs that are running, tap Stop All.

> **TIP**   *In Chapter 3, you find information about third-party programs that help you manage running programs.*

Manage Power

Most of the time your Pocket PC will run on battery power. Managing that power so that it lasts as long as possible is an important skill. Tap the Power icon on the System tab to open the Power

4

How to ... Manage Storage Space

Several programs and Today screen plug-ins are available that show you how much storage space is available without having to use Pocket PC memory settings. Other programs are available for compressing files and searching for large files so that you can free up storage space. You might consider installing one of the following programs to monitor and manage the amount of space available in your Pocket PC and on your storage cards.

- Disk'n Power Suite 2.5 from Carry-on' Crew adds storage space, program memory, and battery indicators to the Today screen. You will find this program at http://www.pocketgear.com.

- PowerLevel 2.8 from ScaryBear Software is a Today screen plug-in that displays battery power and memory information. You will find this program at http://www.scarybearsoftware.com/powerlevel.html.

- SpaceLeft, free from Tillanosoft, simply shows you the amount of storage space left in the Pocket PC and on storage cards. You can download this program from http://tillanosoft.com/ce/sleft.html.

- Compress files using the PC-compatible ZIP/UNZIP utility Resco Zipper, available at http://www.resco-net.com/resco/en/default.asp. Another compression program is HandZip from CNetX. You will find this program at http://www.cnetx.com/HandyZIP/.

- Repair and format storage cards using Flash Format from CneX, which is available at http://www.cnetx.com/format/.

- Find out which files take up the most storage space by using Where is my RAM? (WIMR?) from Rolf Olsen. You will find this free program at http://mypaq.net/mySoftware/ wimr/index.shtml.

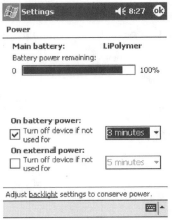

Settings dialog box, shown on the right. This dialog box provides you with information about the status of your main and backup batteries.

At the bottom of the dialog box are two check boxes for turning off the Pocket PC—one for when it runs on battery power and the other for when it runs on external power. Select the check boxes to have the Pocket PC turn off after a specified amount of time lapses. Select the amount of time from the drop-down lists.

TIP *Tap the Backlight link at the bottom of the dialog box to open the Backlight Settings dialog box.*

How to ...

Manage Battery Life

All Pocket PCs use batteries for power. After a period of time, the batteries either need to be replaced or recharged. The trick is to extend the life of the batteries because Murphy's Law dictates that the time to change the batteries is when you need your device the most. The following is some advice to help prolong battery life:

- Use the Backlight settings to adjust the brightness of the display on your device. The brighter the display, the more power is being consumed.

- Configure the battery power portion of the Backlight settings so that the backlight automatically turns off after a short period of time.

- Configure the Power settings so that the Pocket PC automatically turns off if it is not in use after a short period of time.

- Turn off sounds.

- Use peripherals that have low power ratings. Most cards that have the *Made for Windows CE* logo are designed for low power consumption.

- Remove storage cards and microdrives that are not being used. If a card is inserted in your device, it may draw power.

- Program a button in Windows Media Player to toggle the screen on and off, and program other buttons to control playback. Turn the screen off when playing music.

- Play music from CompactFlash cards rather than from microdrives. Microdrives have moving parts, thus they consume more power than CompactFlash storage cards.

- Keep your Pocket PC in its cradle and charging whenever possible. The lithium ion battery technology used in Pocket PCs does not have the same memory problems that exist with other battery technologies.

- Use a power-level monitor plug-in for the Today screen that easily shows you how much battery power is left. An example is PowerLevel from ScaryBear Software at http://www.scarybearsoftware.com/powerlevel.html. If you use a program task manager like WIS Bar or GigaBar, you can configure them to display the power level at the top of the screen.

Some Pocket PC brands drain batteries faster than others. If battery life is a concern, you may want to check message boards or newsgroups on the Internet to find out which device has the longest battery life. Some Pocket PC devices have removable batteries, which you can replace with a spare battery when necessary.

Change the Regional Settings

Although English may be used around the world, there are differences in how it is spoken, and different ways for writing numbers, currency, time, and dates. You can customize your Pocket PC so that these items display in a manner consistent with various locations. The Regional Settings dialog box, as shown in the illustration on the right, is used to make these changes. To open the Regional Settings dialog box, tap the Regional Settings icon on the System tab.

As you can see, five tabs are available in this dialog box: Region, Number, Currency, Time, and Date. The Region tab displays a drop-down list that contains preconfigured settings for different parts of the world. Selecting one of these configurations will automatically configure the appropriate settings in the other four tabs. If you wish to further customize any of these settings, tap a tab and select an item from any one of the drop-down lists.

Remove Programs

Chapter 7 shows you how to manage programs using ActiveSync. ActiveSync is used to install programs on your device, and it can also be used to remove programs. However, you might need to remove a program while you are away from your desktop. Tap the Remove Programs icon on the System tab to open the Remove Programs dialog box, as shown in the illustration on the right.

This dialog box displays all of the programs that have been installed. To remove a program, tap on it to select it and then tap Remove. A warning message dialog box will display asking whether you are sure that you want to remove the program. If you tap Yes, the program is deleted and irretrievable, so be judicious in your use of this feature!

Wrapping Up

The system settings shown in this chapter are available on all Pocket PCs, but each brand of Pocket PC may include additional settings that are unique to that device. You will find more information about these settings in the owner's manual that comes with the Pocket PC.

The Pocket PC has the same computing power as any other stand-alone computer, but it is not designed to work alone. Instead, Pocket PCs form partnerships with desktop computers to exchange data, install software, and back up everything. In the next chapter, you will learn the many ways in which you can connect Pocket PCs with desktop computers.

Chapter 5

Connect Your Pocket PC with Desktop Computers

How To...

- Prepare to install Microsoft ActiveSync on a PC
- Install Microsoft ActiveSync
- Change ActiveSync connection settings
- Connect Pocket PCs to desktop computers by using infrared
- Connect Pocket PCs to desktop computers by using Ethernet networking
- Connect Pocket PCs to desktop computers by using modems

Why did you buy your Pocket PC? One reason may be to carry information, normally stored on desktop computers, wherever you may go. You probably want to use your Pocket PC to update and add information, and then automatically copy those changes to the desktop computer at the next opportunity. Similarly, while you are away, changes may be made to the information on the desktop that you will want to automatically copy to the Pocket PC. This synchronization ensures that information is current on both the Pocket PC and desktop computer.

Your Pocket PC is designed to be a companion to your desktop computer—your PC away from your PC. Vital to this design is the desktop software called *ActiveSync,* which enables the communication between the Pocket PC and personal computer. In this chapter, you'll learn how to install ActiveSync and how to connect your Pocket PC with desktop computers. Chapter 6 shows you how to configure ActiveSync to synchronize information between Microsoft Outlook and Pocket Outlook. In Chapter 7, you learn how to use ActiveSync to manage files and folders on your Pocket PC, back up or restore data, and install or remove programs

Introducing ActiveSync

ActiveSync has undergone several significant upgrades over the years. In fact, it wasn't until recently that the software became known as ActiveSync. When Windows CE was first sold, the software was called H/PC Explorer (Handheld PC Explorer); then Windows CE Services; and finally, ActiveSync.

The changes between the versions have been significant. At first, H/PC Explorer only synchronized with Microsoft Schedule+ and did not run on Windows NT. These issues were quickly resolved with Version 1.1 of the program, which supported Microsoft Outlook and Windows NT Version 4.0.

The next major release of the program came with the introduction of the Palm-size PC. Obviously, H/PC Explorer did not appropriately identify the software that now also worked with Palm-size PCs; therefore, the name changed to Windows CE Services. This version of the program included many significant features, such as the ability to synchronize with more than one desktop computer, continuous synchronization, file synchronization, e-mail synchronization, and application manager. A later release, timed with the release of the H/PC Professional, added support for synchronization of Pocket Access databases and made installation and performance improvements.

ActiveSync Version 3.5 is the most recent release of the desktop software, and along with the name change is a dramatic difference in how Windows CE devices communicate with desktop computers. Prior versions communicated via the dial-up networking software built into Windows 9x and NT, but ActiveSync Version 3.5 uses its own network communications.

ActiveSync only works with devices that run Windows CE Version 2.0 or newer. If your device runs Version 1.0, you must use H/PC Explorer to connect it to your desktop computer. You will find H/PC Explorer at http://www.microsoft.com/windowsce/products/download/hpcexpl1.asp.

5

Because Windows CE Services uses built-in dial-up networking, it has several problems. One problem is that a PC cannot connect to a Windows CE device and the Internet at the same time unless the PC has the latest version of the dial-up networking software. Another problem is that if Internet Explorer is configured to automatically make a call to an ISP, it will start dialing the telephone number whenever the device connects. The only way to get around this problem is to configure Internet Explorer to not automatically call the ISP, or upgrade to Internet Explorer Version 5.

ActiveSync solves these problems by not using the built-in networking software on the desktop computer. With ActiveSync, your desktop computer can connect to the Internet and a Pocket PC at the same time. It will not cause Internet Explorer to dial the Internet whenever your device connects.

Another problem with prior versions of the software is the complexity of changing the connection speed. Prior versions require changes to be made on both the desktop computer and the device. ActiveSync automatically detects the connection speed of the device so that all you need to do is change the speed at one location.

ActiveSync can use the serial port of desktop computers for communication; but with prior versions, you had to manually disable serial communication if you wanted to connect another device to the same port. For example, you may want to connect a digital camera to the same serial port. ActiveSync now automatically detects when another program tries to use the port, and it offers to disable serial communications automatically. Unfortunately, you still have to re-establish serial communications in ActiveSync once you have finished using the serial port with the other software.

The first steps to use ActiveSync are installing the software on a desktop computer and establishing a connection between the Pocket PC and the desktop. These two steps are the focus for this chapter.

Prepare for Installation

Included with your Pocket PC is a copy of the ActiveSync software on a companion CD-ROM. Normally, you will use that CD-ROM to install the software on your PC. However, before you install the software, check the Microsoft website at http://www.pocketpc.com to verify that it is the current version. You may have a Pocket PC that does not have the current version of ActiveSync because a newer version was released after your version shipped from the factory.

Even if the version of ActiveSync on the CD-ROM is the same, you may still want to download the version from the Microsoft website because it may be a newer build of the same version. Microsoft often releases newer copies of ActiveSync as different builds that have the same version number. Save the program that you download to a directory on your personal computer, and remember its location because you will run that program to install ActiveSync.

Before you begin installing ActiveSync on your personal computer, verify that it meets the following minimum requirements:

- Microsoft Windows NT Workstation Version 4 with Service Pack 3, or Windows 98/2000/XP

- Microsoft Outlook 98 or later

- Microsoft Internet Explorer 4.01 SP1 or later

- 16MB of RAM for Windows 95/98, 32MB of RAM for Windows NT Workstation 4, and 64MB of RAM for Windows 2000 or Windows XP

- Hard disk with 12 to 65MB of available space, depending on the features that you select during installation

- Available 9-pin or 25-pin serial port, infrared port, or USB port

- One CD-ROM drive, if installing from CD-ROM

- VGA graphics card or a compatible graphics adapter at 256 colors or higher

NOTE   *USB support only works with Windows 98, Windows ME, Windows 2000, or Windows XP.*

Microsoft Outlook must be installed on the personal computer before installing ActiveSync. You will find a copy of Outlook 2002 on the companion CD-ROM that comes with Pocket PC 2002 devices, and Outlook 2000 is included with Pocket PC 2000 devices. If you install ActiveSync before installing Outlook, you must re-install ActiveSync after installing Outlook. Follow the instructions that come with Outlook to install it on your personal computer.

NOTE   *ActiveSync 3.1 also supports Microsoft Schedule+, but ActiveSync 3.5 does not synchronize with Schedule+.*

Pocket PCs connect to personal computers by using a cable bundled with the device. Some manufacturers include a cradle in which you place the Pocket PC to establish communication. Plug one end of the cable into the cradle and the other into a universal serial bus (USB) or serial port on the personal computer, as described in the user manual that came with the device. If the device does not have a cradle, then plug one end of the cable into the device.

NOTE   *If you connect a Pocket PC to a desktop computer with USB, do not connect the Pocket PC with the desktop until instructed to do so by the ActiveSync installation program.*

Install ActiveSync on Desktop PCs

If the CD-ROM that came with your Pocket PC has the most current version of the software, insert it in the CD-ROM drive of your personal computer. An opening screen loads with a picture of a Pocket PC and four buttons on the right. Click Start Here to open the following dialog box, which provides the three first steps for setting up your Pocket PC:

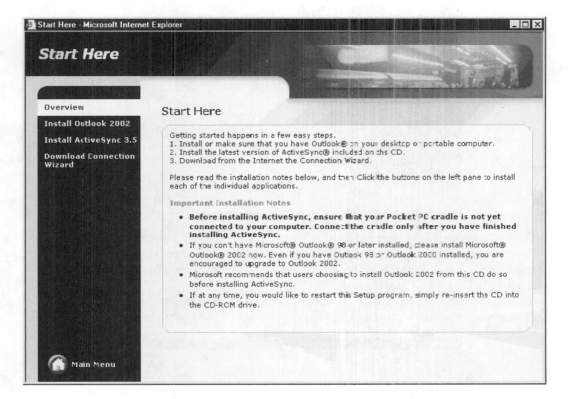

As mentioned previously, before you install ActiveSync you must first install Outlook; if Outlook is not on your Pocket PC, first click Install Outlook 2002.

NOTE   *Use the Connection Wizard to configure Internet and Local Area Network (LAN) connections on your Pocket PC. Instructions for using the Connection Wizard are provided in Chapter 19.*

Click Install ActiveSync 3.5, and then click Install on the next screen to start the ActiveSync setup program. If Autorun is disabled on your PC, you can start the setup program by using Windows Explorer to open \MS\ACTSYNC\Main on the CD-ROM and run setup.exe. The setup program starts by opening the ActiveSync Program Window dialog box, as shown in the following image:

During setup, the ActiveSync program copies files to the personal computer and the software configures the PC to connect with your device. At each step of the process, click Next to continue to the next step of the installation, click Back to go backward one screen, or click Cancel to stop installation. To display Online Help, click Help.

To begin the software installation, click Next in the Program Window. In the next program window, as shown here, select the location where you want ActiveSync to be installed:

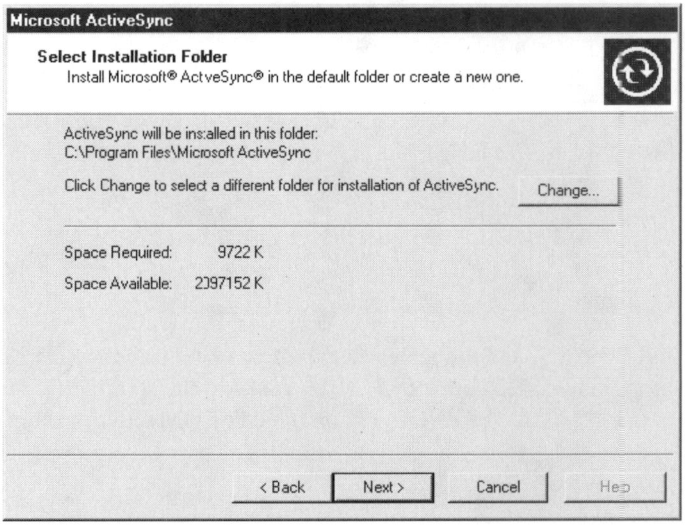

Click Change to open a window in which you browse the folders on the PC hard drive to select the installation location. Once you select the location, click Next to begin installation.

After the program files copy to your PC, the Get Connected wizard will start, as shown in the following image:

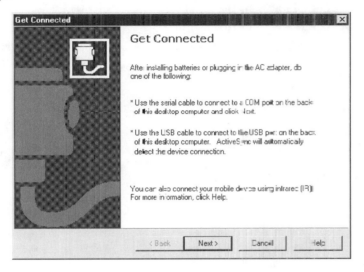

Make sure that your device is connected to the USB or serial port of the PC so that the wizard will find it.

When you click Next, the wizard begins checking each serial and USB port on the PC to find the Pocket PC. If the PC has an infrared port, it will be included among the ports the wizard checks. If you currently use the infrared port, you must start ActiveSync on the device before the Get Connected wizard starts searching ports. The process for using ActiveSync via the infrared port is described in more detail later in this chapter. Once the device is found on a port, ActiveSync is configured to use that port for future communications.

How to ...   **Troubleshoot ActiveSync Connections**

ActiveSync Online Help has a troubleshooting wizard that helps fix communication problems. You will also find an online ActiveSync troubleshooter at http://www.microsoft.com/mobile/pocketpc/howdoi/activesync.asp. The following are some troubleshooting tips that I have gathered through my experience:

■ Several people have had problems connecting Pocket PCs to desktop computers with USB cables or cradles. Many of these problems can be avoided by installing the latest version of ActiveSync because it fixes bugs that existed in prior versions.

Some USB hubs cause problems for ActiveSync, so it is best to plug the Pocket PC USB cable directly into the desktop computer.

■ If the desktop computer does not detect that the Pocket PC is connected, click File | Connection Settings on the desktop and verify that the USB or Serial connection options are selected.

■ If you connect a Pocket PC with a desktop computer before installing ActiveSync, the PC may end up using the wrong USB drivers and ActiveSync will not be able to detect the Pocket PC. Start Device Manager on the desktop computer and remove the Windows CE USB devices. Then re-install ActiveSync and connect the Pocket PC when instructed by the installation program.

■ In some instances, the Get Connected wizard may not find a device that is attached to a COM port. Typically, this happens because another program, such as a digital camera communications program, has the port locked for its use. Check to make sure that none of these programs are running.

■ Another potential cause is an interrupt conflict, which can happen if you are connecting the device to COM3 or COM4, and COM1 or COM2 are in use. COM1 shares an interrupt with COM3, while COM2 shares an interrupt with COM4. If this is a problem, try changing the interrupt of the port you are trying to use.

The next step is to create a partnership between the PC and the device. A partnership defines how information synchronizes. Every Pocket PC can only have partnerships with two different PCs, but a PC can have partnerships with more than two devices.

TIP   *Sync Manager from Kelbran Software enables you to create more than two partnerships on a Pocket PC. You can find Sync Manager at http://kelbran.com/.*

For example, a partnership can be created between your Pocket PC and a PC at home and another at the office. Once the two partnerships exist, the device cannot create a partnership with a third computer unless one of the previously created partnerships is deleted. However, if everyone in a family of four has a Pocket PC, each one can create a partnership with the same PC at home. There is one exception to the two-partner rule for Pocket PCs: if you chose to synchronize Inbox, then the maximum number of partner PCs is one.

Once ActiveSync configures the port, it will start the New Partnership wizard, as shown in the following image:

The New Partnership wizard asks whether you want to set up a partnership between the device and the PC. If you select Yes, the wizard continues; if you select No, the wizard will stop and your device will connect to the PC as a guest.

TIP   *A Pocket PC can connect to any PC as a guest, regardless of how many partnerships the device has.*

When you connect a Pocket PC to a personal computer as a guest, you cannot synchronize information between the two, but you can browse files and folders, back up and restore the device, and install programs to the device. You can also use Desktop Pass Through to access the Internet or LAN (Local Area Network).

NOTE   *Desktop Pass Through is a new feature that only works with Pocket PC 2002 and ActiveSync 3.5. Pocket PC 2000 does not support Desktop Pass Through. Instructions for using Desktop Pass Through are provided in Chapter 19.*

5

If you decide to create a partnership, the wizard displays the New Partnership program window, as shown in the image on the right. From this window you configure all of the possible synchronization settings between the device and the PC. These settings are described in more detail in Chapter 6.

When you click Next on the New Partnership program window, you see the Setup Complete program window. When you click Finish on the Setup Complete program window, ActiveSync will begin synchronization, as shown in this illustration:

The horizontal bar indicates the synchronization progress; the window also displays how many items will synchronize and estimates the amount of time synchronization will take. When synchronization is complete, the ActiveSync program window will look like the image shown here:

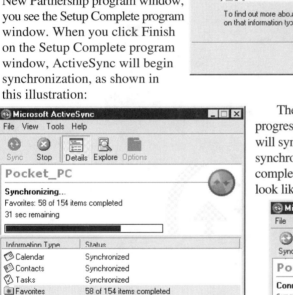

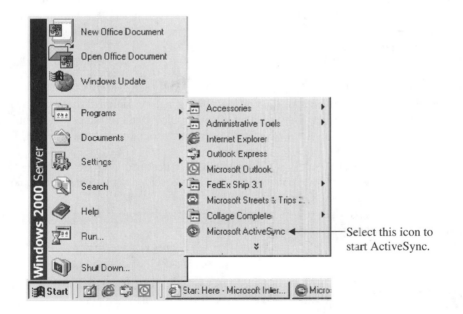

The ActiveSync installation program places the desktop shortcut icon, shown at left, on the desktop of your computer.

The ActiveSync installation program also adds an icon to the System Tray. When a device connects, the System Tray icon turns green; otherwise, it is grayed out. Double-click either icon to manually start ActiveSync.

> **TIP**   *By default, ActiveSync is configured to automatically start whenever a device connects. To stop ActiveSync from automatically starting, you need to change the synchronization mode, which is described in Chapter 6.*

Start ActiveSync on Desktop PCs

Unless you have configured ActiveSync for manual synchronization, you typically start ActiveSync by placing the Pocket PC in its cradle. If you configure ActiveSync for manual synchronization, you will need to start ActiveSync and then click the Sync toolbar button.

To start ActiveSync without a connection, double-click the System Tray icon or the desktop shortcut icon. The setup program also places a shortcut in the Start menu, as shown in the following image:

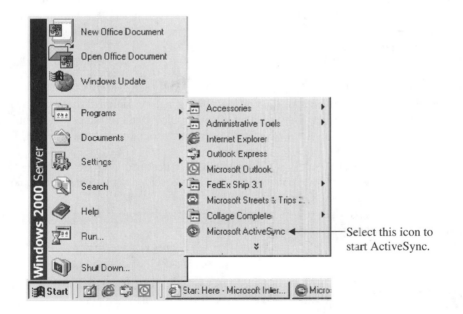

When you start ActiveSync while no device is connected, the program window looks like the screen shown on the right:

The name of the last device that synchronized with the PC is shown in the program window, along with the date and time of the synchronization. You also see details of the partnership between the device and the PC, which include all the synchronized information types. To turn the Detail Display on or off, click Details.

TIP *The partnership information is stored on the PC by the name of the device. If you synchronize more than one device with the PC, be sure to give each device a unique name. Chapter 4 provides instructions for changing the name of Pocket PCs.*

Most of what you do with ActiveSync is not available unless a device is connected, but you can configure the synchronization options by clicking the Options toolbar button. Instructions for configuring the synchronization options are provided later in this chapter. You can also delete partnerships and configure the connection settings.

Change Desktop ActiveSync Connection Settings

Assuming that ActiveSync is not configured for manual synchronization, it loads when you connect a device to the PC. It first determines whether a partnership exists; if it does, synchronization begins. If no partnership is found, ActiveSync starts the Partnership wizard, which is described in Chapter 6.

Normally, the connection settings configure when you connect your device to the PC for the first time, and they don't need to be changed after that. However, on some occasions, the connection settings may need to be changed or reset.

One such occasion is when you use the PC Serial Communications port to communicate with another device, such as a digital camera. If you connect a digital camera to the port, ActiveSync starts, determines that it is not a Pocket PC, and then displays the dialog box shown here:

When you click Disconnect COM Port, ActiveSync disables communication to the port, and the next time you attempt to connect a Pocket PC, ActiveSync will not start.

To restart communication via the COM port, first connect the Pocket PC, start ActiveSync, and click File | Get Connected. The Get Connected wizard starts, just as it did during installation, and searches all ports for a Pocket PC. When the Pocket PC is found, the connection settings configure and synchronization begins.

If you want to use a different serial port for ActiveSync, connect the cable to the new port, start ActiveSync, and then start the Get Connected wizard. The wizard will find the Pocket PC, change the connection settings, and start synchronization.

NOTE   *If you have problems establishing communication between the device and the PC, see the How To sidebar earlier in this chapter for troubleshooting tips.*

5

To manually change the connection settings, click File | Connection Settings to display the Connection Settings dialog box, as shown here:

The Serial Communications option has been disabled on this PC. →

Serial Communications is turned on or off by clicking the Allow Serial Cable or Infrared Connection to this COM Port check box. Specify which port to use by selecting one from the drop-down list. The dialog box displays the current status of the COM port. ActiveSync will also communicate via a network or Remote Access Service (RAS) connection if the box for network connections is selected. If you do not want the ActiveSync icon to be displayed in the System Tray, clear the Show Status Icon in Taskbar check box.

Change Serial Connection Speed

Increasing the serial connection speed decreases how long it takes to synchronize the Pocket PC with a PC. ActiveSync automatically detects the speed of the Pocket PC, so all you need to do is change the speed on the device.

TIP
The default connection setting for Pocket PC 2000 is Serial Port @ 19200, which is the slowest connection speed. The fastest setting is Serial Port @ 115k, with other settings in between. If you have difficulty establishing a connection using the 115k setting, try the Serial Port @ 57600 setting. Pocket PC 2002 defaults to USB connections.

To change the serial port speed on a Pocket PC 2002 device, start ActiveSync on the Pocket PC and tap Tools | Options. Select the serial port speed from the Enable Synchronization When Cradled Using drop-down list.

To change the speed on Pocket PC 2000, follow these steps:

1. Tap Start | Settings.
2. Tap the Connections tab.
3. Tap the PC icon.
4. Select the serial port speed from the drop-down list.
5. Tap OK.

NOTE
If you intend to automatically synchronize when you connect Pocket PC 2000 devices, make sure the check box next to Automatically Synchronize When Using Serial Cable is Connected is selected.

Connect with Desktop PCs by Using Infrared

Infrared is light beyond the color red in the spectrum that is not visible to the human eye. Data is sent between transmitters and receivers that are within a line of sight, such as with television and stereo remote controls. Every Pocket PC includes an infrared port that can be used for wireless synchronization with desktop computers.

TIP
If you synchronize different brands of Pocket PCs with a PC, you will find yourself constantly unplugging and switching cables because each device manufacturer uses a different cable. Infrared is wireless, making it easier to synchronize multiple devices with a PC by eliminating the need to switch cables.

To synchronize using infrared, you need software and an infrared port for your PC, but you do not need to install software on your device because each is already configured for infrared communication. For PCs running Windows 95, you need to install the Windows 95 Infrared Support Software, which you can find on the Microsoft web site at http://www.microsoft.com/windows95/downloads/. Windows 98, Windows 2000, and Windows XP have built-in infrared support, but Windows NT Version 4 requires third-party software, such as QuickBeam from Extended Systems.

Many notebook computers have built-in infrared ports. but most desktop computers do not. To add an infrared port to desktop computers, you must install an infrared serial or USB adapter, such as JetEye PC from Extended Systems.

After you install an adapter on a PC, the next step is to configure ActiveSync to use the infrared port. Start ActiveSync and click File | Connection Settings. Make sure the Allow Serial Cable Or Infrared Connection To This COM Port is selected, select Infrared Port from the drop-down list, and then click OK.

TIP

If Infrared Port is not listed in the drop-down list, run the Get Connected wizard so that ActiveSync recognizes it as an available port.

To start synchronization, first line up the infrared port of the Pocket PC with the PC adapter, and then start ActiveSync on the Pocket PC. Tap Tools | Connect Via IR to open the dialog box shown on the right.

Line up the infrared port of the Pocket PC with the PC port and the ActiveSync icon in the System Tray will turn green, indicating that the connection is established. To close the connection, tap Stop on the Pocket PC.

Connect with Desktop PCs by Using Ethernet Networking

While infrared is convenient, it is bound by the maximum serial port speed of 115,000 bits per second; much faster connections are possible with an Ethernet network. Pocket PCs are capable of synchronizing with a PC using a network, as well as connecting to mail servers and the Internet. This section focuses on using a network connection to synchronize with a PC, and Chapter 19 covers how to connect to the Internet.

NOTE

You may want to connect your Pocket PC to a network ct work. The instructions in this section will work in your office, but you will need information about your network at work, which a LAN Administrator can provide. For this section, assume that you will create the network connection at home. Chapter 16 addresses issues specific to using Pocket PCs at the office.

Ethernet synchronization can only happen between a Pocket PC and PC that are already in a partnership. Therefore, the first step is to create the partnership using either a serial, USB, or infrared port. Next, you must set up both the PC and Pocket PC for network communication.

NOTE

Many good books have been written about building an Ethernet network, details of which are beyond the scope of this book. Included here are the instructions for setting up network connections to work with Pocket PCs. If you do not know how to configure networking on your PC, a good place to start is at http://www.helmig.com/j_helmig/basics.htm.

Configure a PC for Network Synchronization

The following must be set up on the PC in order to configure a PC for network synchronization:

■ An Ethernet network interface card must be installed. You can find these cards at computer stores, and they usually come with the instructions and drivers that you need to install the card. Most of the cards that you will find are designed for unshielded twisted-pair (UTP) cable. UTP cables have RJ-45 jacks that look like phone jacks but are wider. You may also find cards that support coaxial cable, but UTP is more popular and easier to work with; so for the rest of these instructions, I assume that is what you are using

> **TIP**
> *Sometimes UTP cables are referred to as 10baseT, though 10baseT is really a specification for an Ethernet standard. You will also see the term Category 5, which refers to the EIA/TIA 568 Commercial Building Wiring Standard. Category 5 UTP cable is certified for transmission speeds up to 100Mbps, and I recommend that you only use Category 5 UTP cable.*

■ You will need a UTP cable to connect the PC to a hub. A hub is required for networking more than two computers with UTP cable, but a connection can be made directly between the PC and the Pocket PC with a crossover cable. I recommend that you use a hub, and you can find inexpensive ones at any computer store. Plug one end of the cable into the hub and the other into the card in your PC. Most hubs and cards have lights that indicate when a connection is established.

■ Install the Client for Microsoft Networks and the TCP/IP protocol. If you do not use Dynamic Host Configuration Protocol (DHCP) you must assign a TCP/IP address and subnet mask to your PC. Network devices use DHCP to automatically obtain TCP/IP addresses from a server on a network. Many home broadband gateways and routers, like the Linksys Etherfast router, act as a DHCP server. Pocket PCs and Windows computers use DHCP by default, so that all you need to do to connect to the network is plug the network cable into the network card.

> **NOTE**
> *In a private network at your home, you may use TCP/IP addresses that are part of a group of addresses set aside for private networks, defined in RFC 1918. These addresses cannot be used on the Internet. The available private address space blocks defined by RFC 1918 are listed here (Class A, B, and C blocks):*
>
> *10.0.0.0 ....10.255.255.255*
> *172.16.0.0.........172.31.255.255*
> *192.168.0.0.......192.168.255.255*

Finally, configure ActiveSync on the PC for network connections. Click File | Connection Settings, and make sure Allow Network (Ethernet) And Remote Access Service (RAS) Server Connections With This Desktop Computer is selected.

Configure a Pocket PC for Network Synchronization

In order for your Pocket PC to connect to an Ethernet network, it needs three things: a network interface card, a cable, and Ethernet drivers. The network interface cards for Pocket PCs are available as either PC cards or CompactFlash cards. If you have an NE2000-compatible card, it may work with your Pocket PC. Check Chris De Herrera's Ethernet Connectivity FAQ at http://www.cewindows.net/wce/20/ethernet.htm to find a complete list of the cards that work with Pocket PCs.

Many of the Ethernet cards include a cable, but if yours does not, then you will need a cable to connect the card to the hub. If you choose to use a crossover cable, you will plug one end into the Ethernet card on the PC and the other end into the adapter connected to the device.

Pocket PCs include some Ethernet drivers in Read Only Memory (ROM), which you can verify by tapping Start | Settings | Connections | Network Adapters. One driver found on all Pocket PCs is the NE2000-compatible Ethernet driver, which is a generic driver that works with many different Ethernet cards. Other Ethernet cards designed to work for Pocket PCs will include drivers that you will need to install on your Pocket PC.

If you use the generic NE2000 driver with an Ethernet card, the Pocket PC will display a message box asking which driver to use when you insert the card. Enter **ne2000** in the message box and tap OK. Some cards will require you to enter the driver name every time it is inserted into the Pocket PC. To avoid having to enter the driver repeatedly, download and install a shareware NE2000 driver from http://www.sbm.nu/englisch/windowsce/sbm-ne2000/index.htm.

After the Ethernet and network adapter drivers are installed, you must configure the adapter for your network. Tap Start | Settings | Connections | Network Adapters, tap the name of the adapter you are using, and then tap Properties. The Driver Settings dialog box, as shown in the following, will be displayed:

The Driver Settings dialog box looks the same for every Ethernet driver listed in the Network Adapters dialog box, but the window title displays a different driver name.

The Driver Settings dialog box is used to configure the TCP/IP protocol information. To configure these settings for your Pocket PC, follow these steps:

1. If you use a DHCP server, verify that the Use Server-Assigned IP Address radio button is selected and skip to step 5.

2. If you do not use a DHCP server, tap the Use Specific IP Address radio button and enter an address in the IP Address field.

3. Enter an address in the Subnet Mask field.

4. Enter an address in the Default Gateway field.

5. Tap the Name Servers tab.

6. In the Primary WINS field, enter the TCP/IP address of the PC that the device is synchronizing with. This will be the same address that you entered for the earlier "Configure a PC for Network Synchronization" section of this chapter.

7. Tap OK to save the changes, and a dialog box is displayed telling you that the settings will take effect the next time the adapter is inserted in the device.

CAUTION *Step 6 is critical for using a network connection for synchronization with Pocket PC 2000. The Connection Manager of the Pocket PC 2002 automatically handles the WINS (Windows Internet Name Service) configuration so that you don't need to configure this setting. Before using a network connection, you must establish a partnership between the device and the PC.*

TIP *In large networks, WINS normally runs on a dedicated server. The instructions here are for home networks; but if you connect a device to a network that has a WINS server, its address can be put in the Primary WINS field. The partner PC must be registered with the WINS server so that it can provide its TCP/IP address to the device.*

The final step in configuring Pocket PC 2002 devices for network synchronization is to tell Connection Manager which settings to use with the network card. Connection Manager is a new feature with Pocket PC 2002 that centralizes all connection settings in one place. Use it to configure dial-up connections to the Internet or a LAN. Instructions for using Connection Manager are provided in Chapters 16 and 19.

To synchronize a Pocket PC 2002 with a desktop computer over a network, start Connection Manager by tapping Start | Settings | Connections | Connections, to open the Connections Settings dialog box, as shown here on the right:

From the My Network Card Connects To drop-down list, select Work and tap OK.

Synchronize with a PC using an Ethernet Network

Now that everything is configured, you are ready to synchronize across the network. Insert the Ethernet card into the PC card or CompactFlash slot of the device, and plug the UTP cable into the card and the hub. Start ActiveSync on Pocket PC 2002 devices by tapping Start | ActiveSync or Start | Programs | ActiveSync to open the image shown at right:

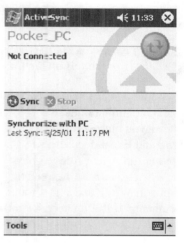

Tap Sync to start synchronization, and tap Stop to close the connection.

5

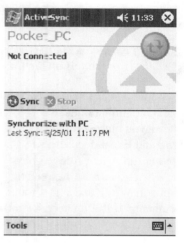

NOTE   *To start ActiveSync on Pocket PC 2000 devices, tap Start | Programs | Connections | ActiveSync.*

TIP   *If you have a Socket Communications Ethernet card, you can configure its driver to automatically start ActiveSync whenever the card is inserted. See the documentation that came with the card to use this setting.*

You can configure the Pocket PC to automatically synchronize at scheduled time intervals, as well as automatically disconnect by tapping Tools | Options in ActiveSync.

Access Shared Folders

One of the primary reasons why LANs are built is to allow network users to share files with each other. Windows 95/98/2000 and Windows XP all have the capability to share folders for access by other computers on a network. Pocket PC 2002 devices can access these shared folders by using File Explorer. To access a shared folder, connect the device to the network, start File Explorer, and tap Open or the Network Share icon, as shown here:

Tap here to open a network share.

Tap here to switch back to the device.

Enter the UNC path for the share in the Open Path field and tap OK. The UNC path is the combination of the PC name and the share name in the format \\[PC Name]\[Share Name]. For example, to access the Documents share on a computer named Fred, enter \\Fred\Documents.

> **TIP** *If a network share is already open on the Pocket PC, tapping the device and Network Share buttons on the Command bar switches between folders opened at either location.*

While you can open network shares using File Explorer, there are limitations on what can be done. One limitation is that you cannot directly open a Word or Excel document from a share; instead, you must copy the documents to the Pocket PC and then open them. You can copy Pocket Word and Excel documents to a network share, but the files are not converted as they are when copying files using ActiveSync.

When you install ActiveSync on a desktop computer, the installation program looks for Microsoft Word; and if it is found, the program adds a file type so that it can open Pocket Word documents. Unfortunately, a similar file type is not added to Excel. If you need to copy a Pocket Excel document directly to a network share, you can save the workbook in the Excel 97/2000 format and then copy the file to the network. Chapter 11 provides the instructions for saving files in the Excel 97/2000 format from Pocket PC. Chapter 10 has similar instructions for saving Pocket Word documents in the Word 97/2000 format.

Connect with Desktop PCs Using a Modem

With remote networking, Pocket PCs can synchronize data using a modem, allowing you to synchronize wherever a telephone line is available. Once the connection is established, it is used to synchronize data between a PC and the device.

> **TIP** *Plan to only synchronize data when using a modem. You cannot manually start a backup or install software by using ActiveSync on a Pocket PC. ActiveSync can be configured to automatically back up a Pocket PC whenever a connection is made, but backups over a dial-up connection are very slow. Software can be installed from the PC once a connection is made, but require assistance from someone at the computer. See Chapter 17 for tips on backing up data while away from your PC.*

In order to synchronize using a modem, the Pocket PC and desktop computer must already be in a partnership. You must also configure ActiveSync on the desktop for dial-up connections. Click File | Connection Settings and make sure Allow Network (Ethernet) And Remote Access Service (RAS) Server Connections With This Desktop Computer is selected.

To use a modem to synchronize data, you will need a dial-up server to receive the call and Connection Manager configured to dial that server. The connection may be with a RAS that provides access to an entire network, or with a PC that only provides local access. If the connection is with a RAS, then the PC in the partnership must be on and logged into the network.

Install Dial-Up Server on Windows 98/ME

In order to establish a dial-up connection between a Pocket PC and a PC running Windows 98/ME, you will need to install the Windows Dial-Up Server. The Dial-Up Server is not automatically installed with Windows 98/ME. To install it, follow these steps:

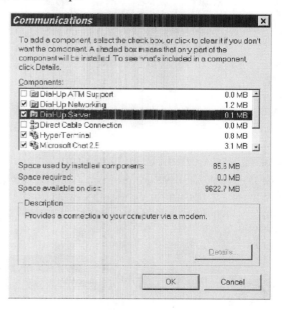

1. Open the Windows 98/ME Control Panel and double-click Add/Remove Programs.

2. Click the Windows Setup tab.

3. In Add/Remove Programs Properties, double-click Communications.

4. Select the Dial-Up Server check box, as shown on the right, and then click OK:

5. Click OK again.

The Dial-Up Server software adds a menu option to Dial-Up Networking. To find it, select Start | Programs | Accessories | Communications | Dial-Up Networking, and then select the Connections menu. The menu has an additional item for Dial-Up Server, as shown here:

When you select this item, the Dial-Up Server dialog box is displayed, as shown in this illustration:

Turn on the Dial-Up Server by selecting the Allow Caller Access radio button. Click Change Password to assign a password that must be entered when a modem connects. Clicking Server Type enables you to select either a PPP server or a Windows for Workgroups server. You can leave this setting at the default, which is PPP, because that is the type of client connection used by Pocket PCs.

When you click OK, the Dial-Up Server software starts and adds an icon to the System Tray, as shown in the following image, indicating that it is ready to receive a call

The Dial-Up Server icon

To turn off the Dial-Up Server, double-click the System Tray icon, select No Caller Access, and click OK.

Configure Connection Manager

The Pocket PC ActiveSync program automatically uses the Connection Manager Work Settings if it detects a modem. To configure Connection Manager, tap Start | Settings, tap the Connections tab, and then tap Connections. The Connections Settings dialog box opens, as shown in this illustration:

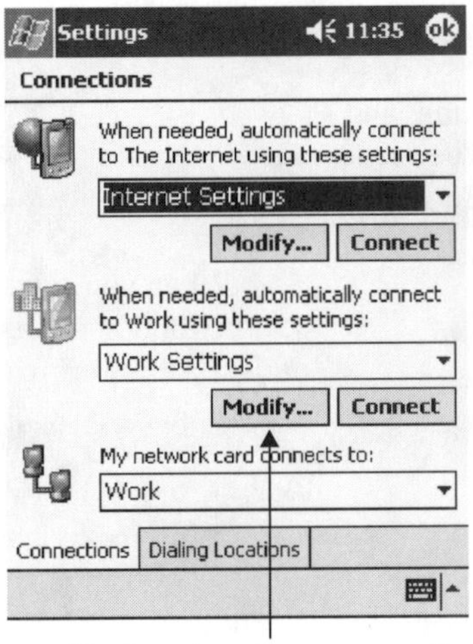

Tap here to set up a connection
to your desktop computer.

Tap Modify for the Work Settings, and then tap New on the Modem tab of the Work Settings screen. There are three screens for entering information about the connection. On the first screen, enter a name for the connection, select the modem and baud rate, and then tap Next. On the second screen, enter the phone number and then tap Next. Leave the default settings as they are on the third screen and tap Finish, which returns you to the Work Settings screen.

You do not need to configure the VPN and Proxy Settings tabs of the Work Settings screen if the Pocket PC dials a desktop computer. If the modem connection is for a corporate network, then you may need to configure these two tabs. The instructions for that are in Chapter 16.

Synchronize with a Desktop PC Using a Modem

Now that you have a dial-up server set up and running, and Connection Manager configured on your Pocket PC, you are ready to connect to the server and synchronize information. Connect a telephone line to the modem in your device, and then start ActiveSync by tapping Start | ActiveSync or Start | Programs | ActiveSync if the ActiveSync icon is not in the start menu. Tap Sync to start synchronization and the Network Log On screen, shown on the right is displayed:

If the connection is for a Windows 98/ME Dial-Up Server, and you assigned a password, you must enter it in the Password field. Connections for remote access servers require a username; password; and, possibly, a domain name if you are connecting to a Windows NT network.

> TIP   *If you use dialing locations, you must select the location to use on the Dialing Locations tab of Connection Manager before starting synchronization. Chapter 19 provides more information about dialing locations.*

Once the connection is made, ActiveSync will determine whether a partnership exists with the computer and then will begin synchronization. During synchronization, the green icon on the ActiveSync screen spins and the progress displays at the bottom. When synchronization is

complete, the icon stops spinning and the status changes from Synchronizing to Connected. To end the session and disconnect the call, tap Stop.

If you want ActiveSync to automatically disconnect the call once synchronization is complete, tap Tools | Options, and then tap the Schedule tab to open the screen on the right.q

Tap the When Manually Synchronizing Disconnect When Complete check box. You can also schedule your Pocket PC to automatically synchronize at scheduled intervals by tapping the Automatically After check box and selecting a time from the drop-down list.

Wrapping Up

Microsoft ActiveSync supports four ways to connect Pocket PCs to desktop computers: serial/USB cable or cradle, infrared, Ethernet network, and modem. The majority of the time you will use a serial or USB connection because the hardware needed for that connection is provided with the Pocket PC. Infrared, Ethernet, and modem connections provide flexibility by either supporting multiple brands of Pocket PCs or enabling you to synchronize while not being physically near the desktop computer.

The purpose for all of these connection types is to synchronize data between Pocket PCs and desktop computers. As you might guess, there are a variety of different settings in ActiveSync that control what information is synchronized. In the next chapter, you'll learn how to change these synchronization settings.

Chapter 6

Synchronize Data with Desktop Computers

How To...

- ■ Use the Partnership wizard to create partnerships between Pocket PCs and desktop computers
- ■ Configure synchronization settings
- ■ Resolve synchronization conflicts

Synchronization is the process of keeping information consistent on a Pocket PC and a desktop computer. What and how information is synchronized is stored in a *partnership,* which is created between Pocket PCs and desktop computers by using the ActiveSync Partnership wizard.

Whenever information changes on one side of the partnership, synchronization changes the information on the other side so that it matches. For example, if you create a new task on your PC, that task is copied to your Pocket PC at the next synchronization. If you then mark the task complete on the Pocket PC, it will be marked complete on the PC after another synchronization.

If the same piece of information is changed on both the PC and the device, ActiveSync will identify the conflict and provide you with the opportunity to designate which change you want to keep. How ActiveSync resolves conflicts depends on how you configure conflict resolution.

ActiveSync matches each of the main sections in Outlook with corresponding programs on the Pocket PC using the same names: Calendar, Contacts, Inbox, Notes, and Tasks. Favorites and AvantGo correspond with parts of Internet Explorer.

> **TIP**
> *ActiveSync does not synchronize with Outlook Journal. Chapter 12 provides instructions for using Crown Logic Corporation's CLC Journal to synchronize with Outlook Journal. You will find CLC Journal at http://www.crownlogic.com/.*

In this chapter you'll learn how to use the Partnership wizard to create and delete partnerships between Pocket PCs and desktop computers. You'll also learn how to configure synchronization settings for all the information types that ActiveSync supports, change how synchronization starts, resolve synchronization conflicts, and change file conversion settings.

> **TIP**
> *ActiveSync only supports the synchronization of the Outlook primary Calendar, Contacts, and Tasks folders. You cannot synchronize with any Calendar, Contacts, or Tasks subfolders unless you use a third-party synchronization program, such as Intellisync from Puma Technology. However, ActiveSync 3.5 does support synchronization of Inbox subfolders with Pocket PC 2002 devices.*

How to ... Synchronize with Programs other than Microsoft Outlook

ActiveSync only synchronizes with Outlook. If you want to synchronize your device with other desktop Personal Information Manager programs, you must use a third-party synchronization program. Third-party synchronization programs include these

- Intellisync from Puma Technology, http://www.pumatech.com
- XTNDConnect PC from Extended Systems, http://www.extendedsystems.com/products/pcsync/
- PDASync from Laplink, http://www.pdasync.com
- CompanionLink, http://www.companionlink.com/

Create a Partnership

Partnerships exist between Pocket PCs and desktop computers and contain all of the information that ActiveSync uses to synchronize data between the two. Normally, you create a partnership by using the Partnership wizard the first time you connect the device to the PC.

> **TIP** *Partnerships can only be created by using either a serial, USB, or infrared connection between the device and PC. Partnerships cannot be created with a network connection.*

When you connect a Pocket PC to a desktop computer for the first time, ActiveSync first determines whether a partnership exists. If the partnership does not exist, the Partnership wizard starts by displaying the following dialog box.

Select Yes to create a new partnership or No to connect the device to the PC as a guest. Guest connections cannot synchronize data but can perform all the other functions provided by ActiveSync.

The only way to start the Partnership wizard is to connect a device to a PC running ActiveSync to which the device does not have an existing partnership. You cannot manually start the Partnership wizard.

Select Yes to create a partnership, and then click Next to select the synchronization settings, as shown in the dialog box to the right.

In this dialog box, select which information you want to synchronize between the Pocket PC and desktop computer by checking the boxes next to each information type. Select the type and click Settings to configure synchronization of each information type. The details for changing synchronization settings are provided later in this chapter. For now, select the information types and then click Next.

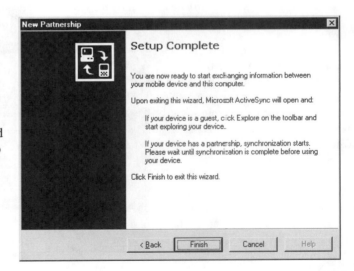

If a partnership already exists between the Pocket PC and a desktop computer, the Partnership wizard will ask you to select the number of partnerships prior to the synchronization settings. The next part of this section explains how to create two partnerships.

The final dialog box of the Partnership wizard, as shown here, tells you that it has all the information it needs to create the partnership.

Click Back to return to the previous dialog boxes and make changes; Click Cancel to stop and not synchronize or click Finish to close the Partnership wizard and start synchronization.

How to ... Synchronize with Macintoshes

Microsoft ActiveSync only runs on Windows desktop computers; there is not a version for Macintoshes. You can synchronize a Pocket PC with a Macintosh running Virtual PC, but that does not provide synchronization with native Macintosh applications. Information Appliance Associates is developing a native Macintosh synchronization program called PocketMac. You can find more information about this program at http://www.doctorce.com.

Create Two Partnerships

A Pocket PC can be in a partnership with two PCs that have different names. This is commonly done to synchronize a Pocket PC with a PC at home and another at work. Before you decide to create a second partnership, you need to consider a number of issues:

- You will not be able to synchronize Inbox information between the Pocket PC and either PC. Inbox synchronization only works for Pocket PCs in one partnership.

- If possible, both computers should use the same version of Microsoft Outlook. You can synchronize a Pocket PC between two different versions of Outlook, but doing so may introduce synchronization problems.

- Both computers should synchronize the same information and have the same synchronization settings.

- All of the information in the Pocket PC will synchronize to both PCs.

- Synchronizing a Pocket PC with two PCs can be more complicated because it adds another place where information can change. Keep in mind that changes that you make at work and then synchronize to your Pocket PC will then appear on your home PC when you synchronize the device with it.

The process of creating a second partnership is much the same as creating the first partnership. You will need a copy of ActiveSync installed on the second PC, along with Microsoft Outlook. Follow the steps for installing ActiveSync and using the Get Connected wizard, described in Chapter 5.

When you connect the device to the second PC for the first time, the Partnership wizard will start. After you tell the wizard that you want to set up a partnership and click Next, the dialog box to the right is displayed.

This dialog box only displays if the device is already part of another partnership. If you select Yes, the wizard will delete the previous partnership information on the device so that a partnership is created only with the second computer. Select No to create a second partnership with the computer without deleting any existing partnerships.

New Partnership

Select Number of Partnerships
Select whether you want to synchronize with just this computer.

Your device can have up to two partnerships or a partnership with only this computer. Do you want your device to have a partnership and synchronize with only this computer?

○ Yes, I want to synchronize with only this computer

Remove any existing partnerships on my device and set up a new partnership with just this computer.

○ No, I want to synchronize with two computers

Set up a partnership with this computer, but do not remove any existing partnerships on my device.

[< Back] [Next >] [Cancel] [Help]

NOTE *If you select Yes in this dialog box, the previous partnership will be deleted from the Pocket PC. The next time you connect the device with the previous PC, the Partnership wizard will start.*

After you select the number of partnerships, the wizard will continue through the same steps as when the first partnership was created and then start synchronization. If ActiveSync finds information on both the PC and the Pocket PC during synchronization, the Combine or Replace dialog box displays. With this dialog box you indicate whether you want to combine the information found on both the PC and Pocket PC, replace the information on the Pocket PC with what is on the PC, or not synchronize any of the information. Select the option that you want and then click OK.

Combine or Replace

⚠ The following information type on your mobile device has items that have not been synchronized with this computer before.

Information Type: Calendar, Contacts, Tasks, Favorites, Notes

○ Combine the items on my device with the items on this computer.

○ Replace the items on my device with the items on this computer.

○ Do not synchronize this information type at this time.

[OK] [Cancel]

When information is combined from the PC and Pocket PC, it is possible for ActiveSync to find duplicate information. If this happens, the Remove Duplicate Items dialog box displays, as shown in the following image:

Select the duplicate items that you want deleted and click Remove Selected or click Remove All to delete all of the duplicate items. If you want to keep the duplicates, click Keep All.

Remove Duplicate Items

ActiveSync has found duplicate items in your Outlook data file. Choose Remove All (recommended) to remove all duplicate items. The original copy of each item will be kept; only the duplicate copies will be removed.

Type	Description
Contact	John Doe

[Remove All] [Remove Selected] [Keep All]

6

TIP *ActiveSync does not do a good job of detecting all duplicate entries. In just about every instance, combining information leads to duplicate entries that then have to be manually deleted. Because of this, it is a good idea to make a backup copy of the Outlook data file prior to creating a second partnership.*

If your device is already in two partnerships and you attempt to create another partnership, the Partnership wizard will display the following dialog box.

In order to create the new partnership, you must delete one of the two existing partnerships listed in the dialog box, or click Cancel to stop the Partnership wizard.

TIP *Sync Manager from Kelbran provides a way to create partnerships with more than two desktop computers. You will find Sync Manager at http://kelbran.com/.*

Delete Partnerships

You can delete partnerships with either the Partnership wizard or manually within ActiveSync. The Partnership wizard will delete existing partnerships when you select Yes, I Want To Synchronize With Only One Computer in the Select Number of Partnerships dialog box.

To manually delete a partnership, first start ActiveSync on the PC. Only the open partnership in ActiveSync, indicated by the name of the device in the program window, can be deleted. If the PC has partnerships with more than one device and the one you want to delete is not displayed, open the partnership to be deleted by selecting File | Mobile Device and then the name of the device.

To delete the partnership, select File | Delete Partnership, and click Yes on the Confirm Partnership Deletion dialog box, as shown in this image.

When you delete a partnership, all of the synchronization information is removed from the PC, but any backup files of the device will not be deleted.

If file synchronization is included in the partnership, you will be asked whether you want to delete the Synchronized Files folder. Check the contents of the folder on the PC to determine whether the files should be deleted. Click Yes to delete the files from the PC, or click No if you do not want to delete the files.

How to ... Prevent Accidentally Deleting All Information

Once a partnership is created between a Pocket PC and a desktop computer, all changes, including deletions, will be synchronized. For example, if you delete a contact on the Pocket PC it will be deleted from the PC during the next synchronization. If all of the information is deleted from the PC, then during the next synchronization, all of the information will be deleted from the Pocket PC.

It is always a good idea, despite the fact that a copy of the data exists on both the device and desktop, to back up your device. You can prevent ActiveSync from deleting all information by manually deleting the partnership. The PC will restore the information when you re-create the partnership and synchronize the device.

Configure Synchronization Settings

Not only can you specify which information types to synchronize, but you can also control how much of the information to synchronize by changing the settings for each information type. In order to conserve storage space, some of the default settings limit the amount of information that synchronizes. To change these settings, either click the Options button on the ActiveSync toolbar or select Tools | Options to open the Options dialog box, as shown in the illustration to the right.

The information types known to ActiveSync are listed in the middle of the dialog box. In the left column are the information types, as the Pocket PC knows them, such as Calendar and Contacts. The right column displays the Windows application for each information type, such as Microsoft Outlook.

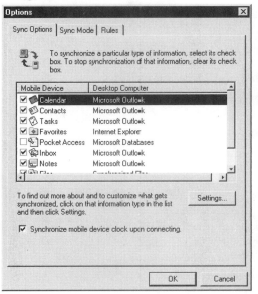

TIP   *Click either column head to sort the list of information types.*

Each checked information type synchronizes with the Pocket PC currently displayed in the program window. For example, the following dialog box shows the ActiveSync program window where Pocket_PC is the current Mobile Device:

Click here to toggle the information type display on or off.

Click here to open the Options dialog box.

The Pocket PC device name

The name of the device displayed is the last one to synchronize with the PC.

Use the Options dialog box to configure the synchronization settings for the Pocket PC named in the ActiveSync program window. To select a different device, select File | Mobile Device and then the device name. The name of the device, along with the date and time of its last synchronization, will appear in the program window. When you open the Options dialog box, it will show the information types that synchronize with that device.

> **TIP** *A quick way to change synchronization settings is to double-click the information type in the ActiveSync details or click Details to display the ActiveSync details.*

To change the synchronization settings for an information type, first select it in the list and then click Settings. The following sections describe settings for the basic information types.

> **NOTE** *The ActiveSync synchronization settings only control the information on desktop computers being sent to Pocket PCs. Once data is on a Pocket PC, it will appear on all partner desktop computers.*

Change Calendar Synchronization Settings

From the Calendar Synchronization Settings dialog box, as shown in this illustration, synchronize all appointments by selecting Synchronize All Appointments. If you only want to synchronize a select number of past and future appointments, select the Synchronize Only The radio button and then select the number of past and future appointments from the drop-down lists. To only synchronize appointments in specific categories, select Synchronize Only Those Appointments In The Following Selected Categories and then select the categories from the ones that are listed.

Click OK to save the changes and close the dialog box.

TIP *The categories will not be listed unless the device is connected with the PC.*

Change Contact Synchronization Settings

From the Contact Synchronization Settings dialog box, as shown here, synchronize all contacts by selecting the top radio button. To synchronize only specific contacts, select the middle radio button and then select the contacts that you want to synchronize with from the list. If you only want to synchronize contacts in specific categories, select the bottom radio button and then select the categories from the ones that are listed.

Click OK to save the changes and close the dialog box.

Change Inbox Synchronization Settings

Inbox synchronization occurs between the Pocket PC Inbox application and the Outlook Inbox. With these synchronization settings, you control the size and number of messages that synchronize and you select the Outlook Inbox subfolders that you want to synchronize with your Pocket PC 2002 device.

NOTE *Pocket PC 2000 does not support the synchronization of Outlook Inbox subfolders.*

ActiveSync does not synchronize the Deleted Items, Drafts, Outbox, or Sent Items folders. When you delete an e-mail, it is moved to Deleted Items, but ActiveSync removes that e-mail from the Deleted Items folder and deletes the e-mail from the Outlook Inbox. ActiveSync moves new e-mail from the Outbox folder on the Pocket PC to the Outlook Outbox folder. New e-mail messages written on your Pocket PC and synchronized to Outlook are sent using the default e-mail service in Outlook.

The inbox synchronization settings are different between Pocket PC 2000 and Pocket PC 2002. When you open the ActiveSync Inbox information type for Pocket PC 2000 devices, the Inbox Synchronization Settings dialog box displays, as shown in the image to the right.

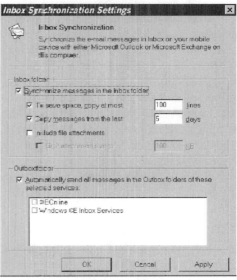

To specify the maximum size of inbox messages, check To Save Space Copy At Most and enter a number in the Lines field, or clear the check box to synchronize entire messages. Check Copy Messages From The Last box and enter a number in the Days field to specify how many days worth of messages to synchronize. To include attachments, check the Include File Attachments box, and if you want to limit the attachment file size, check Limit Attachment Size To and then enter a number in the KB field. These settings work the same for Pocket PC 2000 and 2002 devices.

To turn on outbound mail synchronization, check Automatically Send All Messages In The Outbox Folders Of These Selected Services, and then check the services. This setting tells ActiveSync which Windows CE Inbox e-mail services to use for retrieving outbox items.

When you open the ActiveSync Inbox information type for Pocket PC 2002 devices, the Mail Synchronization Settings dialog box displays, as shown in the image to the left.

The Outlook Inbox mail folders display in the middle of window, with subfolders indented beneath Inbox. Select the check box next to the subfolders that you want to synchronize with the Pocket PC.

The Mail Synchronization Settings window for Pocket PC 2002 devices does not have an option for selecting Inbox e-mail services for sending mail. Only those items in the Outbox folder of the Inbox ActiveSync service will be transferred to the desktop computer.

Click OK to save the changes and close the dialog box.

Change Task Synchronization Settings

The Task Synchronization Settings dialog box, shown here, controls how tasks are synchronized between Outlook and Pocket Outlook.

To synchronize complete and incomplete tasks, select Synchronize All Tasks. If you only want to synchronize incomplete tasks, select Synchronize Only Incomplete Tasks. You can control how active tasks synchronize by selecting the Synchronize Only The [ ] Past Weeks of Active Tasks and [ ] Future Weeks Of Active Tasks radio button. Select the number of past and future weeks from the drop-down lists. To only synchronize tasks in specific categories, select Synchronize Only Those Tasks In The Following Selected Categories radio button and then select the categories in the list.

Click OK to save the changes and close the dialog box.

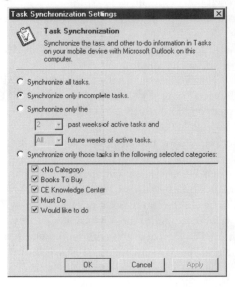

Change File Synchronization Settings

Pocket PCs synchronize files between specific folders on the PC and the device. The PC files that synchronize with the device are stored in subfolders of My Documents. For example, a Pocket PC named *Sammy* synchronizes files stored in the \My Documents\Sammy My Documents folder. Everything stored in the Pocket PC \My Documents folder synchronizes with desktop computers.

NOTE   *Only files located in internal storage on Pocket PCs synchronize with a PC.*

The File Synchronization Settings dialog box, shown here, displays the PC location of synchronized files for the Pocket PC.

You cannot change this location from this dialog box, but you can add or remove files that are in the list of synchronized files.

Click Add to browse a file and copy it to the synchronized files folder, or select a file in the list and then click Remove to delete a file from the synchronized files folder. If the device is connected and continuous ActiveSync is enabled, the changes that you make will update immediately on the device. Otherwise, the changes will occur at the next synchronization.

How to ... Change the Synchronized Files Folder on the PC

When file synchronization is enabled, ActiveSync creates a folder for the synchronized files in the My Documents folder on the PC. The folder name is the combination of the Pocket PC name and My Documents.

Editing the registry on the PC can change the location of the synchronized files on the PC. Do not make this change unless you are familiar with editing the registry. Because any error in the registry can have disastrous effects, it is wise to back up the PC before making any changes. It is also a good idea to back up the device before making this change in case the contents of the synchronized files folder is deleted.

Change the location for synchronized files by performing the following steps:

1. Run regedit on Windows 95/98/ME; run regedt32 on Windows NT/XP/2000.

2. Select HKEY_CURRENT_USER | Software | Microsoft | Windows CE Services | Partners | [Partner ID] | Services | Synchronization. The name of the [Partner ID] key is different for each device in a partnership with the PC. You'll find the device name in the DisplayName value of this key.

3. Double-click the Briefcase Path value of the Synchronization key and enter the drive letter and full directory path for the new location. It is a good idea to write down the contents of this value before changing it.

4. Close the registry editor.

During the next synchronization, the files will be written to the new location on the PC.

Change Notes Synchronization Settings

There are no setting changes for Notes synchronization, but there are two ways that Notes synchronizes with desktop computers. If you select the Notes information type in ActiveSync, then notes on your Pocket PC will synchronize with the main Notes folder in Outlook. If you do not select the Notes information type, but File Synchronization is selected, notes on your Pocket PC will synchronize with the synchronized files folder on the PC.

NOTE *Notes synchronization does not support Outlook Notes subfolders or categories.*

Change Favorites Synchronization Settings

The Favorites information type synchronizes your favorite website addresses and pages to your Pocket PC. Chapter 22 provides instructions for selecting website addresses and pages for synchronization. Synchronizing a large number of web pages may be slow, and can use up a lot of storage space. To save space, you can configure the ActiveSync Favorite Synchronization Settings so that images or sounds do not synchronize to your Pocket PC, or so that it only synchronizes certain web pages.

To stop the synchronization of a page, clear the check box next to the corresponding page listed on the General tab of the Favorites Synchronization Options dialog box, as shown on the left.

To stop synchronizing all pages, click Clear All.

To stop images or sounds from synchronizing to your Pocket PC, clear the Synchronize Images or Synchronize Sound check boxes on the Customize tab of the Favorites Synchronization Options dialog box, as shown in the image below:

To limit the number of linked web pages that synchronize to your Pocket PC, right-click the Favorites link in the Mobile Favorites folder on the desktop computer, and then click Properties. Select the number of linked pages to download on the Download tab. For example, if you set the number of linked pages to zero, only the page that you select will download to the computer. If you set the linked pages to one, then the current page, and every linked page, will download.

TIP

Web pages first synchronize from the Internet to your desktop computer, and then synchronize to your Pocket PC. If the web page doesn't appear on your Pocket PC, click Tools | Synchronize in Internet Explorer on the PC, and synchronize the web page.

Change AvantGo Synchronization Settings

AvantGo provides a way to synchronize web content to a Pocket PC. In order to use AvantGo you must first create an account at http://avantgo.com. Chapter 22 provides additional instructions for using AvantGo.

When you select the AvantGo information type and then connect your Pocket PC, the Internet settings, such as port and proxy settings, are automatically configured. If you need to change the AvantGo synchronization settings, double-click the AvantGo information type to open the AvantGo Connect dialog box, as shown on the left.

Use the Servers tab to configure the AvantGo server. If you need to change your AvantGo password, select AvantGo.com and click Properties to open the Server Profile screen, as shown below:

If a problem occurs during synchronization and there is no AvantGo content on your Pocket PC, select the Refresh All Content At Next Sync check box on the Server Profile screen.

The Connection tab of the AvantGo Connect setting screen, shown on the left, displays information about the proxy servers used by AvantGo. If you need to change these settings, you can either click Autodetect Now, in which case AvantGo will check the settings on your PC and make any necessary changes, or click Change and manually enter the settings.

Change the Synchronization Mode

By default, ActiveSync continuously synchronizes while the Pocket PC is connected to the PC. The synchronization mode can be changed to only synchronize when the Pocket PC is first connected or only when you initiate synchronization.

To change the synchronization mode, either click Options or select Tools | Options and then click the Sync Mode tab, as shown on the right.

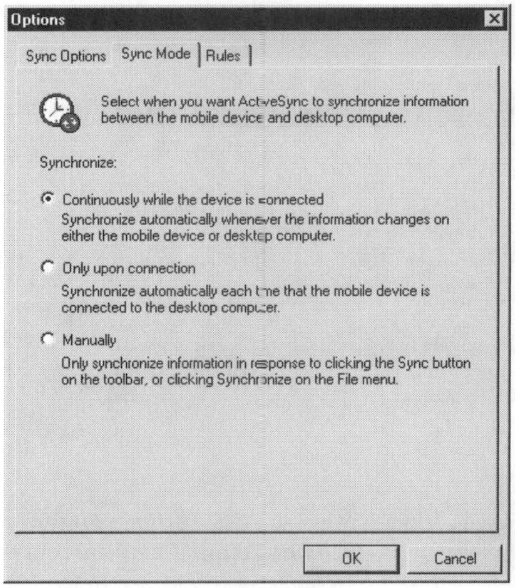

Select the radio button of the desired mode setting and then click OK.

Resolve Synchronization Conflicts

When a conflict occurs during synchronization, the item is marked as unresolved in ActiveSync and on the Pocket PC, unless you tell ActiveSync how to handle conflicts. To change the conflict resolution settings, open the Options dialog box and select the Rules tab, as shown below.

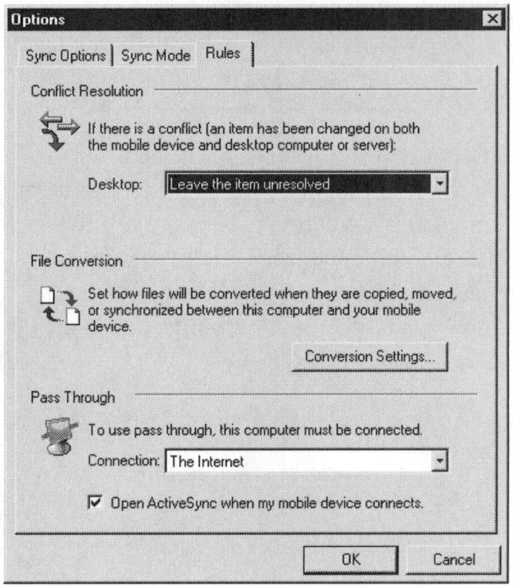

Three settings are available: Leave The Item Unresolved, Always Replace The Item On The Device, or Always Replace The Item On The Computer. Select the setting you want and click OK.

Conflicts usually occur when an item is changed on the Pocket PC and PC before synchronization. If ActiveSync is configured to leave items unresolved, the number of unresolved items for each information type displays and a Resolve Items link appears, as shown here:

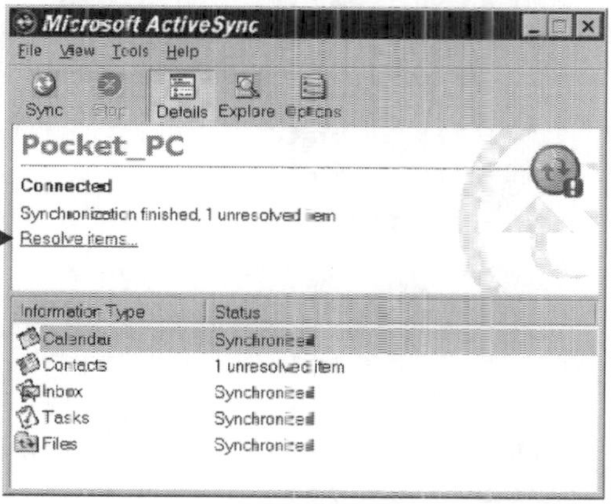

Click here to
resolve items.

When you click Resolve Items, the Resolve Conflict dialog box shown to the right displays.

Tell ActiveSync how to resolve each conflict by clicking the Action drop-down list and selecting an item. The options include replacing the desktop item with the mobile device item, replacing the mobile device item with the desktop item, or skipping the item. If you skip the item, ActiveSync will continue to indicate that at least one unresolved item exists.

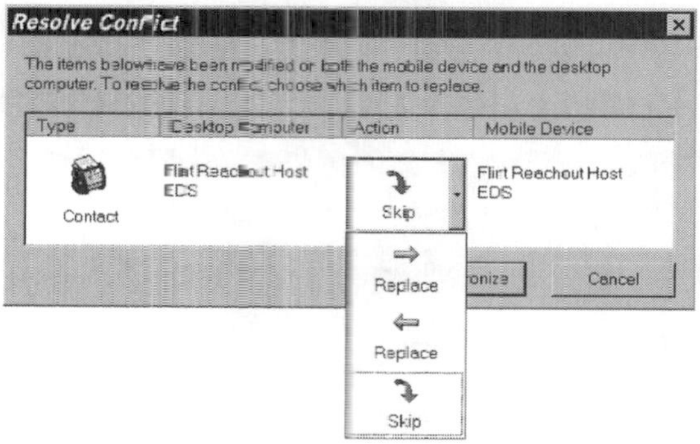

How to ...   Fix Persistent Conflicts

One of the problems that can occur with synchronization is that one or more ActiveSync information types report conflicts that are not resolved, no matter how conflict resolution is configured. This problem, along with many other synchronization problems, is often caused by problems with the Outlook data file on the desktop computer.

The Inbox Repair Tool, scanpst.exe, is installed on all PCs running Microsoft Outlook. If you have problems synchronizing data, you should use this tool to scan the Outlook data file, outlook.pst. To use the repair tool, follow these steps:

1. Disconnect the Pocket PC from the desktop computer and exit Outlook.

2. Search your desktop computer for the filename *outlook.pst,* and make note of the file location.

3. Search your desktop computer for the filename *scanpst.exe.*

4. Start the repair tool by double-clicking *scanpst.exe* in the Search Results window.

5. Click Browse and select *outlook.pst* using the information provided in step 1.

6. Click Start.

The Inbox Repair Tool will scan through the *outlook.pst* file and fix any problems that+ it finds. You may want to run the repair a second time if the first scan identified several problems.

Configure File Conversion Settings

ActiveSync converts files when they are copied, moved, or synchronized between the Pocket PC and desktop computer. To specify whether or not conversion is to take place and how files are converted, click Conversion Settings in the Rules tab of the Options dialog box. The File Conversion Properties dialog box opens, as shown in the image on the left.

Turn file conversion on or off by selecting the check box on the General tab. Select the Device To Desktop tab of the File Conversion Properties dialog box, as shown in the illustration on the top of the following page, to change conversion settings for files moved from the device to the PC. To make a

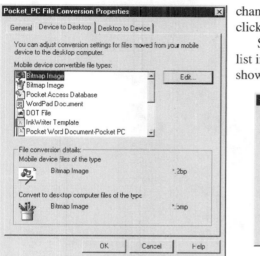

change, select a file type from the list and then click Edit.

Select the desktop file type from the drop-down list in the Edit Conversion Settings dialog box, as shown in the image below, and click OK.

Click OK on the File Conversion Properties dialog box to save the change.

The process for changing the file conversion settings of files moved from the desktop to the device is the same. Select the Desktop to Device tab, select a file type, click Edit, select a new file type, and then click OK.

Wrapping Up

The primary reason to connect Pocket PCs to desktop computers is to synchronize data with Microsoft Outlook. ActiveSync synchronizes data between the Pocket PC Calendar, Contacts, Tasks, Notes, and Inbox programs with their counterparts in Microsoft Outlook. It also provides synchronization for Internet Explorer Favorites and web pages, as well as AvantGo. Software developers may also use ActiveSync to synchronize data between other Pocket PC applications and desktop counterparts.

Synchronization is not the only reason for connecting a Pocket PC to a desktop computer. As you will see in the next chapter, you can also use ActiveSync to manage files and folders on the Pocket PC, to back up and restore data, and to install programs.

Chapter 7

Manage Your Pocket PC from Your Desktop

How To…

■ Explore Files and Folders

■ Copy, Delete, and Rename Files and Folders

■ Back Up and Restore a Pocket PC

■ Install and Remove Programs on a Pocket PC

■ Use Desktop Pass Through

As you have seen in the previous two chapters, there are a variety of different ways to connect Pocket PCs with desktop computers and to synchronize data. Synchronization is not the only reason for connecting Pocket PCs with desktop computers. ActiveSync also provides ways for managing Pocket PCs, such as exploring files and folders, copying, deleting and renaming files and folders, backing up and restoring Pocket PCs, installing and removing programs, and connecting to networks. In this chapter, you will learn how to use ActiveSync to perform all of these functions.

Explore Files and Folders

All versions of ActiveSync enable the user to browse files and folders from a PC on a connected Pocket PC. In fact, it is the only way to browse older Palm-size PCs unless third-party software is installed on the device. Browsing with H/PC Explorer was done in a separate program window, but since Windows CE Services, device files and folders may be browsed from within Windows Explorer.

How to … Protect Your Pocket PC Against Viruses

There are currently no known viruses that affect Pocket PCs, and so far there has been greater concern about Pocket PCs spreading viruses to desktop computers than virus attacks on Pocket PCs. The purpose of VirusScan for Pocket PCs from McAffee for Pocket PC is to scan files on Pocket PCs from desktop computers to prevent the desktop from infection. After you install the McAfee software, Pocket PCs are scanned for viruses every time they connect to the desktop computer. You will find more information about McAfee VirusScan for Pocket PCs at http://www.mcafee.com/myapps/vsw/handscan/ov_pocketpc.asp.

Currently, Trend Micro's PC-cillion for Wireless from Trend Micro is the only virus scan program that runs on Pocket PCs. You will find this program at http://www.antivirus .com/free_tools/wireless/. The number of virus scan programs should increase for Pocket PC 2002 because Microsoft has added virus scan APIs application program interfaces to Pocket PC 2002.

Browse Files and Folders

You can browse files and folders on a connected Pocket PC are browsed either within Windows Explorer or by using ActiveSync. As you can see in Figure 7-1, when ActiveSync is installed on the PC, a Mobile Device item is added to Windows Explorer.

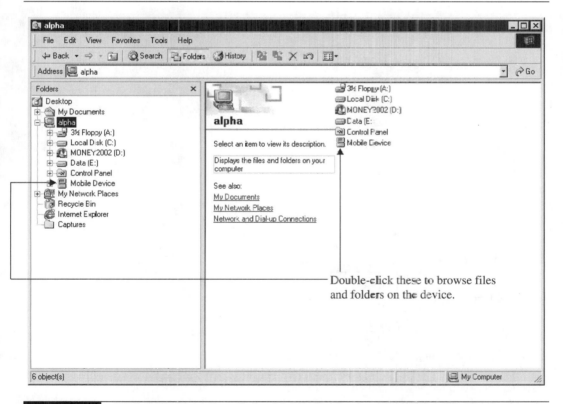

Double-click these to browse files and folders on the device.

FIGURE 7-1   With ActiveSync installed, a Mobile Device item is added to My Computer, shown here as *alpha*.

If a Pocket PC is connected, double-clicking the Mobile Device icon in Explorer will display the device's files and folders of the device. The process of browsing files and folders on a Pocket PC is similar to browsing the hard drive of a PC. You open folders by double-clicking their icons, but double-clicking a file filename opens a Properties dialog box, rather than opening the file.

To use ActiveSync to browse a connected Pocket PC, click the Explorer button icon on the ActiveSync toolbar or select File | Explore. An Explorer window will open, as shown here:

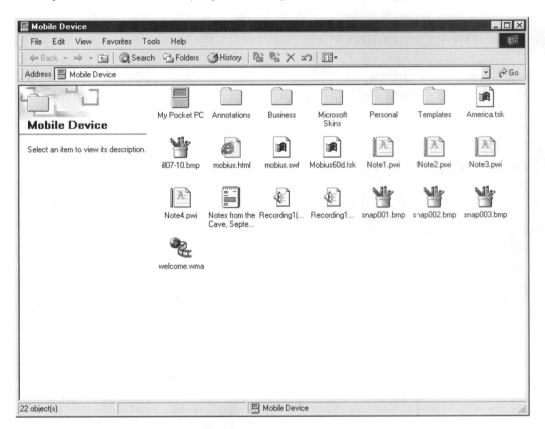

To open a folder, double-click its icon and double-click a filename to open a Properties dialog box.

Copy, Delete, and Rename Files and Folders

The processes for copying, deleting, and renaming files and folders on a Pocket PC using ActiveSync are the same as on a PC. You can copy files and folders within locations on a Pocket PC, such as between the My Documents folder and the Storage Card folder, and between the Pocket PC and desktop computer.

To copy files or folders, use either the drag-and-drop method or copy and paste. ActiveSync will automatically convert files if file conversion is enabled. See Chapter 6 for instructions on configuring file conversion.

> **TIP** *Use File Synchronization to copy a file to a Pocket PC or desktop PC while the two are not connected. Move or copy the file to the Synchronized Files folder of either, and the file will be copied at the next synchronization.*

Delete a selected file or folder by simply pressing the DELETE key or select File | Delete. Items deleted using ActiveSync are not backed up to a Recycle Bin prior to deletion. Rename a selected file or folder by selecting File | Rename, or by right-clicking the item and then selecting Rrename.

Back Up and Restore Files

While synchronization keeps copies of your personal information on both the Pocket PC and desktop computer, it does not back up program settings or files not stored in the Synchronized Files folder. The best way to ensure that you can restore a Pocket PC to its current state is with regular backups using ActiveSync.

> **NOTE** *ActiveSync does not back up files or folders that are on storage cards. If you want to back up data on storage cards, you need to use a third-party program, such as CF2Desktop from Information Appliance Associates at http:// www.doctorce.com/cf2desktop.htm.*

Automatic backups execute if you configure ActiveSync to automatically back up whenever the device connects. To make this configuration, connect the Pocket PC to the desktop computer and then select Tools | Backup/Restore to open the following dialog box.

Check the Automatically Back Up Each Time The Device Connects check box and then click OK. The next time the device connects, a backup will run immediately after synchronization.

TIP *The only way to use ActiveSync to back up a device with a modem connection is by configuring ActiveSync to automatically perform backups. Keep in mind, however, that a backup with a modem connection may take a long time. It is faster to back up Pocket PCs to storage cards, and you will find instructions for running such backups in Chapter 17.*

Automatic backups occur every time you connect a Pocket PC, extending the time of synchronization. If you do not want backups to automatically occur, you can manually back up a Pocket PC by connecting the device to the desktop PC and then selecting Tools | Backup/Restore. Click the Back Up Now button on the Backup tab and the backup will start, as shown in the following dialog box:

Backup In Progress   ☒

Now backing up to 'Backup.stg'
Please do not use the device until backup is finished.

■■

Copying: \Program Files\AOL Instant Messenger\AIM.exe

Cancel

NOTE *Do not use the device until the backup is finished.*

Define the Backup Type

ActiveSync will run either a full or incremental backup. An incremental backup only backs up changes since the last backup, while a full backup backs up all information every time. Incremental backups are quicker than full backups and, therefore, work well with modem connections.

To define the backup types, select Tools | Backup/Restore, select either the Full Backup or Incremental Backup radio button, and then click OK.

Define Where to Store the Backup

ActiveSync backups are written to the PC hard drive. By default, the backup filename is Backup.stg and is stored in a folder with the name of the device in the \Program Files\ Microsoft ActiveSync\Profiles folder. For example, if the device has the name Pocket_PC, the Backup.stg file is stored in \Program Files\Microsoft ActiveSync\Profiles\Pocket_PC. On Windows 2000 and Windows XP desktops, the files may be stored in a subfolder of Documents and Settings. For example, for a user named Frank, the backup files may be in \Documents and Settings\Frank\Application Data\Microsoft\ActiveSync\Profiles\Pocket_PC.

TIP *Two files that contain partnership information are also in this the backup folder. These files have the names outstore.dat and repl.dat. If you want to back up the partnership information stored on the PC, back up these two files.*

You may want to change the location of the backup file to a hard drive that has more storage space, or to make it easier to back up on the PC. To change the location where the backup file is written, do the following:

1. Select Tools | Backup/Restore.

2. Click Change.

3. Select a new location in the Select Backup Set dialog box.

4. Click Save to close the Select Backup Set dialog box.

5. Click OK to close the Backup/Restore dialog box.

Restore from a Backup

ActiveSync restores data from the backup file on the PC to the Pocket PC. During the process, all of the contents in the Pocket PC are replaced by the items in the backup, and the Recycle Bin is emptied. Restore does not overwrite a Pocket PC password.

Before you do perform a restore, there are a few things to be aware of. First, if you change the country settings on the Pocket PC prior to the backup, then you must make sure the Pocket PC is set to the same country settings before the restore; otherwise, the restore will not work. Second, the restore will replace everything within internal storage on the Pocket PC. If files have been written on the Pocket PC since the backup, you should copy them to a storage card or a PC before running Restore; otherwise, the files will be lost. Finally, while you can back up a Pocket PC using a network connection, you must restore a Pocket PC using either a serial, USB, or infrared connection.

To restore from a backup file, follow these steps:

1. Connect the Pocket PC to the desktop computer. If the Partnership Wwizard starts, follow the instructions to create the partnership.

2. Close any programs that may be running on the Pocket PC.

3. Select Tools | Backup/Restore and then select the Restore tab.

4. Click Restore Now. Do not do anything with the Pocket PC while the restore runs.

5. After the restore completes, soft-reset the Pocket PC.

7

How to ...

Control Pocket PCs from Desktop Computers

Some people find it awkward to work with Pocket PCs while they are docked in cradles and connected to PCs. Virtual CE from BitBank Software fixes this problem by enabling you to manipulate Pocket PCs from desktop computers while they are attached by cradles or over Ethernet networks. In addition to remotely controlling Pocket PCs, Virtual CE enables you to display Pocket PC screens on projectors and to capture difficult screen shots. You can download Virtual CE from http://www .bitbanksoftware .com/ce/index.htm.

Install and Remove Programs

Most Pocket PC software includes a setup program that you run on a PC to install software to the device. Setup programs usually store copies of the Pocket PC installation files on the PC and then run ActiveSync Add/Remove Programs to install the program on the device. With this process, ActiveSync tracks the Pocket PC software that has been installed, and it can be used to reinstall software without having to rerun the installation program.

To remove a program from a device, use either the Remove Programs setting on the Pocket PC or the ActiveSync Add/Remove Programs. Chapter 4 provides the instructions for using the Control Panel setting.

Use ActiveSync to Install Programs

To use ActiveSync to install software, you must first connect the Pocket PC to the desktop computer. The connection can either be as a partner or as a guest. After the connection is made, select Tools | Add/ Remove Programs. ActiveSync determines what programs are installed on the device and then displays the Add/Remove Programs dialog box, as shown here:

> NOTE
>
> *If the check box next a program is grayed out, that it means the program was installed on the Pocket PC using a desktop computer other than the one you are currently using.*

The checked programs listed in the dialog box are installed on the Pocket PC, and those not checked are available for installation. To install one of these programs, select its check box and then click OK. If a storage card is inserted in the device, the following dialog box will display, asking whether to install the program in main memory or on the storage card.

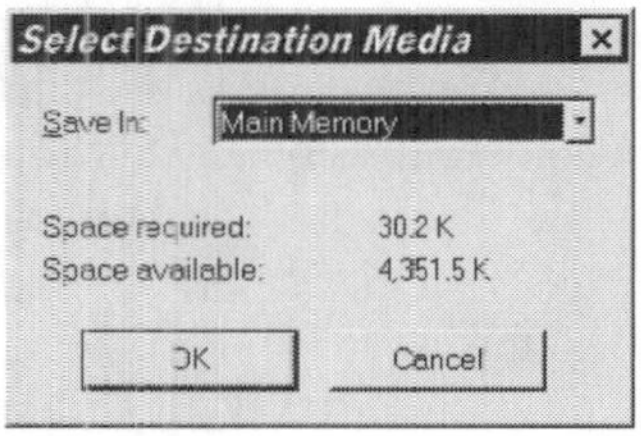

Select the location from the Save In drop-down list and then click OK.

TIP *If the option Install Program Into The Default Installation Folder option on the Add/Remove Programs dialog box is checked, then the Select Media dialog box will not display.*

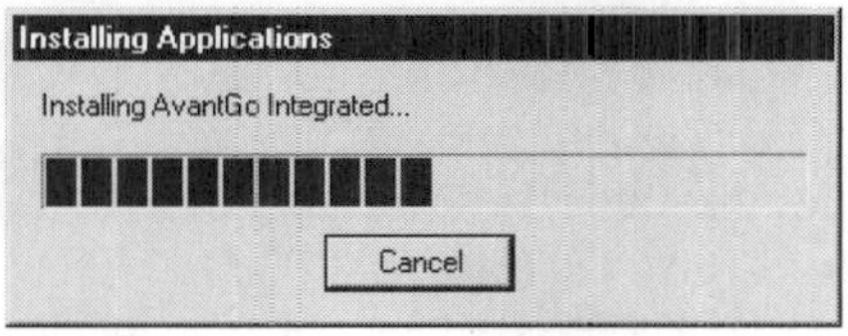

As the software is installed, the box shown at left indicates its progress.

Click Cancel to stop the installation. Once installation is complete, the following dialog box displays:

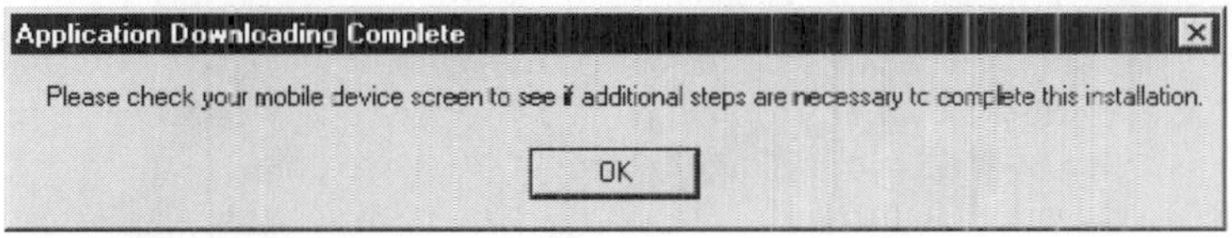

Click OK to clear the dialog box, and then check the device to see if there are any instructions displayed on the screen.

How to ... **Install Programs Directly Using a Desktop Computer**

ActiveSync provides the easiest, but not the only way, to install programs on a Pocket PC. You can install programs onto Pocket PCs without using ActiveSync by manually copying a CAB file to the Pocket PC and then running it. Pocket PC CAB files contain compressed copies ofies program files and execute directly on Pocket PCs.

The challenges with installing programs in this way are first, finding the CAB file to copy to the Pocket PC and second, insuring that you copy the right version of the CAB file. The second challenge is only an issue for Pocket PC 2000 devices, due to the fact that different brands use different processors. All Pocket PC 2002 devices use the same processor, so this issue is nonexistent.

If a Pocket PC program has already been installed from a desktop computer, you will probably find the CAB files for that program in the \Program Files\Microsoft ActiveSync folder on the Pocket PC desktop computer. The standard Pocket PC software installation process that most programs follow creates a subfolder in the Microsoft ActiveSync folder on the PC and copies the Pocket PC installation files to that folder. ActiveSync then copies those files to the Pocket PC and installs the program to the Pocket PC. If the installation files are not found in such a subfolder, you may find them elsewhere on the PC's hard drive, or they may be stored in a compressed file that you downloaded from the Internet.

Unfortunately, there are no standards for naming CAB files. Most software developers include the processor type in the CAB file name to help determine which CAB file goes with each processor. If you have a Compaq iPAQ or UR There @migo Pocket PC Pocket PC 2000 device, or any Pocket PC 2002 device, look for files that indicate ARM processors. Hewlett-Packard 520 and 540 series Jornadas have SH3 processors, and Casio E-115, E-125, EM-500 and EG-800 Pocket PCs have MIPS processors.

Use Windows Explorer or ActiveSync Explorer to copy the CAB file to the Pocket PC. Then use File Explorer on the Pocket PC to browse to the file location and tap the CAB file to install the program. Usually, after installation is complete, the CAB file is deleted. If you don't want the CAB file deleted, use Windows or ActiveSync Explorer to make the file read-only.

Information Appliance Associates has developed a Windows ActiveX control called CEWebInstallX that installs programs to Pocket PCs directly from web pages. You will find more information about this control at http://www.doctorce.com.

Use ActiveSync to Remove Programs

To use ActiveSync to remove a program from a Pocket PC, connect it to the PC and then select Tools | Add/Remove Programs. The Add/Remove Programs dialog box will display, with the programs installed on the Pocket PC checked, as shown next:

Add/Remove Programs

Select a program's check box if you want to install it on your
mobile device, or clear the check box if you want to remove the
program from your device.

Note: If a program that you installed is not listed, the program was
not designed to be used on your mobile device.

☑ Macromedia Flash Player 4 for the Po...		
☑ Microsoft Internet Explorer Tools for ...	18.4 K	
☑ Microsoft Money for the Pocket PC	374.8 K	
☑ Microsoft Power Contacts	18.2 K	
☑ Microsoft Reader		

Program description

Space required for selected programs: 0.0 K
Space available on device   7,384.5 K
☐ Install program into the default installation folder

Remove from both locations
To remove the selected program from both
your device and this computer, click Remove.   [Remove...]

[OK]   [Cancel]   [Help]

These programs are
installed on the Pocket PC.

To remove a program from the Pocket PC, clear the check box and then click OK. A message box will display indicating that the program is being removed. When finished, the Add/Remove Programs dialog box closes.

If you reopen the Add/Remove Programs dialog box, you will see that the removed program is still listed. It remains in the list because the installation files are still on the PC. If you want to remove the program from both the Pocket PC and the desktop PC, clear the program's check box and then click Remove.

Use Desktop Pass Through

New with Pocket PC 2002 is Desktop Pass Through, which is a feature that enables the Pocket PC to access the Internet while it is connected with desktop computers. The feature only works with ActiveSync 3.5 and is not available for Pocket PC 2000.

> **TIP**   *Any Pocket PC application that works with the Internet will work using Desktop Pass Through.*

Pass Through uses the same Internet connection used by the desktop computer. If you access the Internet on the desktop by using a modem, then you will need to establish a connection to the Internet before using Pass Through.

> **TIP**   *Desktop Pass Through works with ActiveSync Guest connections, so you can access the Internet via Pass Through from any desktop computer with ActiveSync installed on it.*

Desktop Pass Through is always available, though you can change the configuration to specify whether to connect to the Internet or a LAN (Local Area Network) To make this change, click Tools | Options | Rules in ActiveSync on the desktop computer to open this the following dialog box:

Options   ☒

Sync Options | Sync Mode | Rules

Conflict Resolution

If there is a conflict (an item has been changed on both the mobile device and desktop computer or server):

Desktop: Leave the item unresolved   ▾

File Conversion

Set how files will be converted when they are copied, moved, or synchronized between this computer and your mobile device.

Conversion Settings...

Pass Through

To use pass through, this computer must be connected.

Connection: The Internet   ▾

☑ Open ActiveSync when my mobile device connects.

OK   Cancel

Settings   ◀€ 9:02   **ok**

Connections

When needed, automatically connect to The Internet using these settings:

Internet Settings   ▾

Modify...   Connect

When needed, automatically connect to Work using these settings:

Work Settings   ▾

Modify...   Connect

My network card connects to:

The Internet   ▾

Connections | Dialing Locations

These drop-down list selections should be the same.

The selection in the drop-down list of the Desktop field (left image) should be the same as the selection in the drop-down list of the My Network Card Connects To field (right image) in the Connection Manager on the Pocket PC. If there is a proxy server on the network for accessing the Internet, you will need to set the drop-down lists to Work.

Wrapping Up

Pocket PCs are designed to work as an extension of your desktop computer. ActiveSync enables the partnership between Pocket PCs and desktop computers by providing for data synchronization and device management. Now that you know the basic functions of your Pocket PC and connecting how to connect it with desktop computers, it is time to learn how to use software to make the most of your Pocket PC. Perhaps the most important of these programs is Pocket Outlook, with its Calendar, Contacts, and Tasks components, which you will learn how to use in the next chapter.

7

Part II

Make the Most of Your Pocket PC

Chapter 8

Manage Appointments, Tasks, and Contacts

How To...

- ■ Schedule appointments
- ■ Store addresses
- ■ Track tasks
- ■ Search for appointments, addresses, and tasks
- ■ Use the New Button menu on the Pocket PC to create appointments, contacts, and tasks

Today's fast pace and hectic schedules have made time management an important skill. The fundamental tools for managing time include a calendar for appointments, an address book for contact information, and a task list to keep track of what needs to be done. Despite all of the capabilities that Pocket PCs provide, you probably bought your device to help manage these three things.

In this chapter, you'll learn how to use the Calendar, Contacts, and Task programs on the Pocket PC. You will use each of these programs frequently throughout the day to enter and look up information. The programs provide a search capability that helps you quickly find information based on a word or phrase. With the Calendar recurrence scheduling capability, creating an appointment that occurs on the same day and time every month is as easy as completing one screen, which eliminates the need to write the appointment on multiple entries in a day planner.

Calendar and Contacts are integrated with Inbox, the e-mail program on your device that is covered in Chapter 20. From Calendar, you can schedule a meeting with people by retrieving their e-mail addresses from Contacts and e-mailing a meeting request. From Contacts, you can send an e-mail by simply selecting an entry in the contacts list and tapping a button.

Appointments, addresses, and tasks can be sent to other Pocket PCs by using the infrared port, making it easy to share information with other people. Perhaps even more important, as you read in Chapter 6, the information in these three programs can be synchronized with your desktop computer, enabling you to work with the same information whether you are sitting at your desk or in a taxi cab.

Use Pocket Outlook on Your Pocket PC

Calendar, Contacts, and Tasks may be the most frequently used programs on your Pocket PC. Each program contains information that you use constantly throughout the day. Need to schedule an appointment? Start Calendar. Need to look up an address? Start Contacts. Been given another assignment? Start Tasks.

You will want to quickly retrieve the information stored in these three programs; the Pocket PC is designed to help you achieve this goal. By default, shortcuts for Calendar, Contacts, and Tasks are placed in the Start menu. If the shortcuts are not in the Start menu, you will find them in Programs, which you open by tapping Start | Programs.

Each program is also assigned to a hardware button. An exception is the Casio Pocket PC, which only assigns Calendar and Contacts to hardware buttons, assigning the third button to the Casio menu. You can use the button settings program on Casio Pocket PCs to change the assignments of all the hardware buttons, including the third button, which you can assign to Tasks.

> TIP
>
> *If you assign Calendar, Contacts, and Tasks to hardware buttons, consider moving their shortcuts from the Start menu to the Programs menu. By doing so, you will make space for other programs that you can place in the Start menu for quicker access. To make this change, tap Start | Settings | Menu and clear the check box next to the menu item.*

The instructions for starting Calendar, Contacts, and Tasks in this section use the Start menu. However, keep in mind the hardware buttons that you can use to quickly start each of these programs.

8

How to ... Quickly Create Appointments, Contacts, or Tasks Using the New Button Menu

The Today Screen has a New button, which you can tap to open a pop-up list with options for creating appointments, contacts, tasks, e-mail messages, and more. Using this menu from the Today Screen saves the step of first opening the program and then tapping New, but Calendar, Contacts, and Tasks do not have this feature.

The New Button menu fixes this problem by adding a pop-up list everywhere that the New button appears, but it is not turned on by default. To enable this feature, tap Start | Settings | Menus, and then tap the New Menu tab to open the Menus dialog box, as shown in the following image.

Tap the first check box to turn on the
New Button menu, select the items that you
want to appear on the menu and tap OK.
After you turn on the menu, you will see a
triangle to the right of New. When you tap
the triangle, the New Button menu pop-ups
up with Appointment, Contact, and Task
options, which you can tap to create the
desired item.

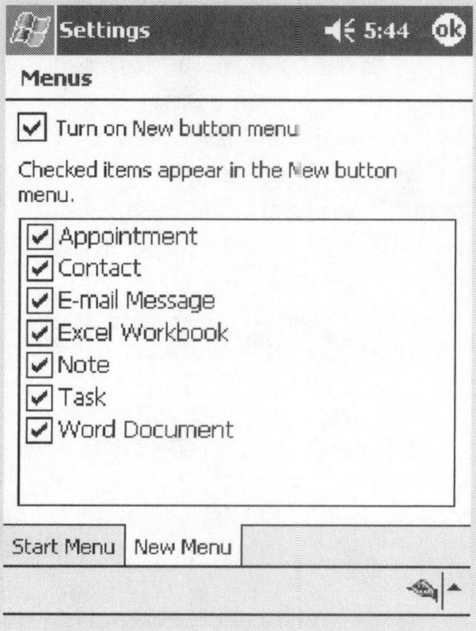

Schedule Appointments Using Calendar

The Calendar program is the Pocket PC companion to the Calendar folder in Microsoft Outlook.
ActiveSync synchronizes appointments that you enter in Calendar on the Pocket PC with the
Calendar folder in Outlook, as explained in Chapter 6. To enter an appointment, first start
Calendar by tapping Start | Calendar, which opens the program window shown in Figure 8-1.

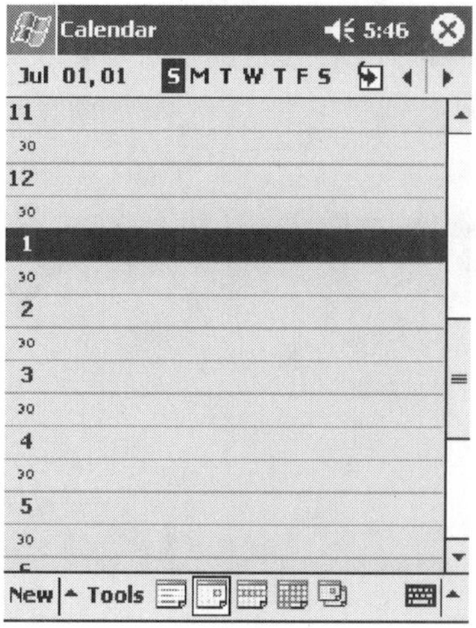

FIGURE 8-1   The Calendar menu and toolbars are at the bottom of the screen.

View Your Schedule in Calendar

You can view your schedule by day, week, month, and year. Calendar also provides an Agenda view that summarizes your appointments for each day. Unlike the Handheld and Palm-size PCs, the Agenda view on Pocket PCs does not list active tasks.

Did you know?

Switching Views

The method for switching between Calendar views is different in the two releases of Windows for Pocket PCs. In both releases, pressing the calendar Hardware button cycles through views, but Pocket PC 2002 replaces the View menu with the following five buttons on the Command bar:

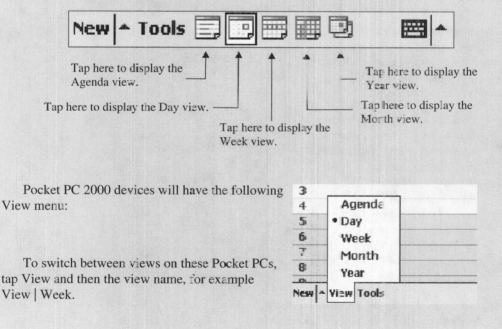

Tap here to display the Agenda view.

Tap here to display the Day view.

Tap here to display the Week view.

Tap here to display the Year view.

Tap here to display the Month view.

Pocket PC 2000 devices will have the following View menu:

To switch between views on these Pocket PCs, tap View and then the view name, for example View | Week.

8

Each view has buttons, as shown in this image, for moving forward and backward, and for returning to the current date:

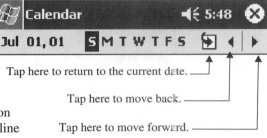

Tap here to return to the current date. ──────
Tap here to move back. ──────
Tap here to move forward. ──────

You can use the hardware navigation button to move forward and backward through the calendar in the Week view. In the Month and Year views, the navigation button scrolls the screen up and down one line at a time; in the Agenda and Day views, the navigation button moves the scroll bar up and down.

View One Day of Appointments   To display your schedule in the Day view, tap the Day View button and the program displays, as shown in the following image:

All-day events are displayed here.

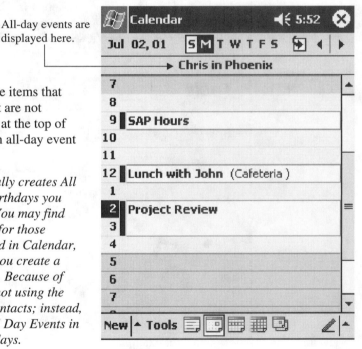

All-day events, which are items that you associate with a day, but are not scheduled for a time, appear at the top of the screen. An example of an all-day event is an anniversary or holiday.

TIP   *Outlook automatically creates All Day Events from birthdays you enter in Contacts. You may find the All Day Events for those birthdays duplicated in Calendar, particularly when you create a second partnership. Because of this, I recommend not using the birthday field in Contacts; instead, manually create All Day Events in Calendar for birthdays.*

Appointments display in the middle of the screen and, by default, list in one-hour slots. To change the slot sizes to 30-minute increments, tap Tools | Options, and then tap the Show Half Hour Slots check box. More space is taken up on the screen when you use half-hour slots.

The left edge of the appointment screen has a bar indicating its status. Any slot shown as free time (indicated with a white bar) means that another appointment could be scheduled in that time slot. Appointments can be free, tentative (light blue), busy (dark blue), or out-of-office (purple), each shown as a different color.

Icons are used to provide information about an appointment, such as whether a reminder is set, or the whether the appointment recurs. By default, the icons are turned off, yet they can be turned on by tapping Tools | Options to display the Options dialog box, as shown in the image on the left:

These icons will not be displayed on appointments.

These icons will be displayed on appointments.

Tap on each of the icons that you want to be displayed so that the icon turns dark (meaning it is selected), and then tap OK. The icons appear on the appointment in the Day view, as shown in the image on the right:

This icon indicates a recurring appointment.

This icon indicates that the appointment has a note.

Each appointment can have more information than is displayed in the Day view. To see the details, tap on the appointment to open it in a Summary view, as shown in image on the right:

The Summary view provides all of the information about the appointment on one easy-to-read screen.

Tap the date at the top of the calendar screen to display a date picker, which you can use to select a different date to be displayed. Remember that you can use the buttons on the main Calendar screen for returning to the current date or for moving backward and forward through the dates.

Tap OK to close the Summary view.

View a Week of Appointments   The Week view displays appointments for the workweek, with each day in a column, as shown in the image to the right:

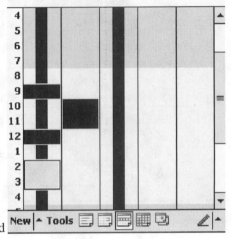

To switch to this view, tap Week view. Appointments appear as blocks with different colors, indicating statuses of free, busy, tentative, and out-of-office. All-day events are indicated by a bar running down the column. To display the appointment information, tap a block to show the information at the top of the screen.

To change the number of days that display in the Week view, tap Tools | Options and then select 5-day week, 6-day week, or 7-day week in the Week View drop-down list. Tap OK to save the change and close the Options dialog box.

To move to a different week in the year, tap the month at the top of the screen to display a date picker, which you use to select a different date to be displayed. To switch years, tap the year at the top of the screen and select a year from the drop-down list that displays. Tap the column head of a day in the Week view to switch to the Day view for that day.

View a Month of Appointments   To display the calendar one month at a time, tap the Month View button to switch to the Month view, as shown in the following image:

Indicates a morning appointment

Indicates an all-day event

Indicates an afternoon appointment

Indicates morning and afternoon appointments

Appointments display as filled blocks, with a solid block indicating morning and afternoon appointments. If a day has only a morning appointment, the upper-left corner of the filled block displays. A filled-in lower-right corner of a block indicates afternoon appointments. An all-day event is indicated by an empty block with a blue border.

A black box over a day indicates the current date. Tap the month at the top of the screen to display a drop-down list that you can use to select a different month to be displayed. To change the year, tap the year at the top of the screen and select a different year from the drop-down list. To switch the display to the Day view for a specific date in a month, tap the date on the calendar.

View a Year of Appointments The Year view displays every month of a year. To switch to the Year view, tap the Year View button to display the screen on the right:

The current date is indicated by a black square. Each month in the Year view is limited to five lines, so a sixth line of dates is indicated by a slash (/).

To display a different year, tap the year at the top of the screen and select another year in the drop-down list. To switch the display to the Month view, tap the name of the month you want displayed. To switch to the Day view, tap a date in the Year view.

Indicates multiple dates. ———

How to ... Display Week Numbers In Month View

Pocket PC 2000 devices only display week numbers in the Week view, but Pocket PC 2002 adds the ability to display week numbers in the Month view. To turn week numbers on, tap Tools | Options, tap Show Week Numbers, and tap OK. In Week view, the number displays at the upper right of the screen; in Month view, the week numbers display along the left edge of the screen. Week numbers on Pocket PC 2000 devices do not correspond to European or actual week numbers. For example, the week that begins on Sunday, December 30, 2001 is called Week 53. This problem is fixed on Pocket PC 2002 devices.

View a Daily Agenda The Agenda view, as shown in the image to the right, summarizes appointments and all-day events on one screen:

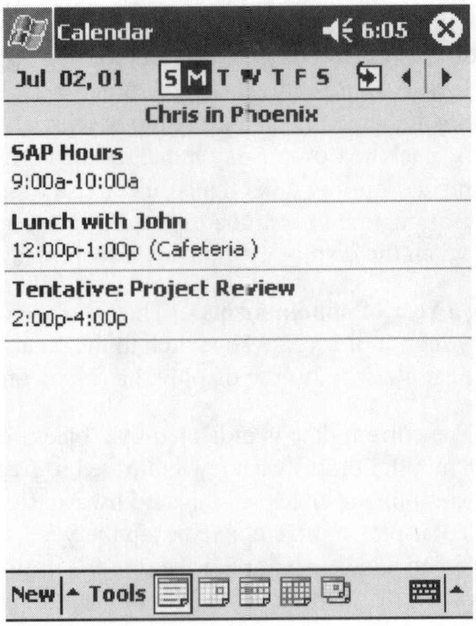

All-day events display at the top of the screen, and appointments list in rows by time. Current appointments display in a darker font on the screen, and past appointments are grayed out.

Tap the date at the top of the agenda to display the date picker, which you use to go to a specific date. Tap the date on the calendar to go to that date in the Agenda view. You can also use the buttons along the top of the screen to move through the days of the week or to return to the current date.

Tap an event or appointment in the Agenda view to open the appointment in the Summary view.

Create an Appointment in Calendar

To create an appointment in Calendar, tap New to open the dialog box shown in Figure 8-2.

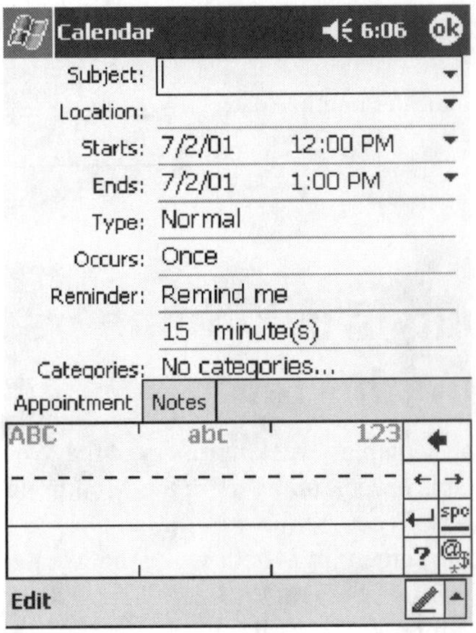

FIGURE 8-2   The New Appointment dialog box.

When this dialog box opens, the Subject field is selected, and the Software Input panel at the bottom of the screen is open and ready for you to enter a description for the appointment. Enter a description of the appointment in the Subject field and enter a location for the appointment in the Location field. The Location field is a drop-down list containing locations from previous appointments. If the new appointment is at a location that you already entered, you can select it from this list.

TIP   *The Subject field is also a drop-down list that contains words commonly used in appointments. Unfortunately, this list doesn't change, and there is no way to add words to the drop-down list.*

Enter dates in the Starts and Ends fields by tapping the date that is displayed to open the date picker, as shown in the image on the right:

Tap a date on the calendar to select it for either field. You can use the arrows at the top of the calendar to move backward and forward a month at a time or tap the month to jump to another month that appears in a pop-menu. The date that you select for the Starts field automatically appears in the Ends field.

Starting and ending times are displayed in drop-down lists, which contain times in half-hour increments. Tap the values in the drop-down lists to set the starting and ending times for the appointment. If you opened the dialog box from within the Day view, the Starts and Ends fields will contain the date and time selected in the Day view.

8

TIP   *A quick way to enter starting and ending times from the Day view is to select a group of slots and then tap New. The dialog box opens with the Starts and Ends fields populated with the starting and ending time that you selected in the Day view.*

By default, Calendar creates appointments that have starting and ending times, which is indicated by the Type field with the value of Normal. To create an all-day event, tap the Type field and select All Day from the drop-down list that appears. When All Day is selected, the times in the Starts and Ends fields are removed.

Appointments can be scheduled multiple times by selecting a *recurrence pattern*. The default setting for each appointment is to occur once, as indicated by the value of the Occurs field.

To schedule the appointment for multiple dates, tap the Occurs field to display the items shown in the image on the right:

The items will be different, depending on the day of the week, day of the month, and date that you select.

The appointment shown in Figure 8-2 is being scheduled on Monday, July 2, 2001. Select Every Monday from the Occurs drop-down list to schedule the appointment at the same time on every Monday. Select Day 2 Of Every Month to schedule the appointment for the second day of each month. If you want to schedule the appointment for that specific date—in this case, July 2—every year, select Every July 2.

If none of the items in the drop-down list meet your requirements, tap <Edit pattern...> to start the Recurrence wizard. The Recurrence wizard has three dialog boxes with questions that help you create a customized recurrence pattern. The dialog box is shown in the image on the left:

In the first dialog box, you set the starting and ending times for the appointment. Typically, the times that you originally set are the ones you want to use. If the starting time is correct, you can change the ending time by expanding the Duration drop-down list and tapping a value in the list. Tap Remove Recurrence to close the Edit Pattern dialog box and delete the recurrence.

You can also change the times in the dialog box by tapping them to open the following dialog box (shown to the right):

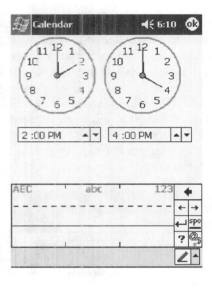

The clock and time field on the left side of the dialog box show the starting time, and on the right is the ending time. Change the times by either tapping the clock faces to move the hands of the clock or tapping the up and down arrows on the digital display. Tap OK to save the times that you select.

Tap Next to open the second dialog box of the Recurrence wizard, and tap the buttons along the top of the dialog box to define a recurrence time. When you tap Daily, two radio buttons appear, as shown in the image below:

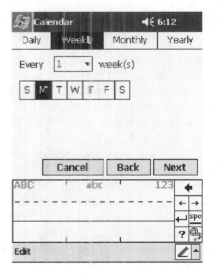

To schedule the appointment for multiple days, select a number from the Every [   ] Day(s) drop-down list. Tap Every Weekday to schedule the appointment on every weekday.

Tap the Weekly tab to change the dialog box, as shown in the image below:

Tap the days in the week that you want to schedule the appointment; more than one day can be selected. Select a value from the Every [   ] Week(s) drop-down list to schedule the appointment for several weeks on the days that you select.

8

Tap Monthly to define a monthly recurrence pattern, as shown in the image on the right:

The pattern can be defined for a specific date in a month (such as the second), for a select number of months, or for a day in a week (such as the third Monday) for a select number of months. Tap the radio button of the option you want, and select the values from the drop-down lists.

Tap Yearly to define a yearly recurrence pattern, as shown in the image below:

The yearly pattern is similar to the monthly pattern. Your options are to schedule the appointment for the same date and month each year, or for the day in a week of the month that you select. Tap the radio button of the option that you want, and select the values from the drop-down lists.

Tap Next to define the starting and ending dates of the recurrence pattern, as shown in the image below:

Select the start date by using The Pattern Starts drop-down list. Select the end date by choosing one of the three options available for defining the end date: the recurrence pattern does not end, it ends on a date that you select, or it ends after a select number of occurrences. Tap the radio button of the option that you want and select the appropriate values from the drop-down lists.

After you select the starting and ending dates of the recurring appointment, tap Finish to return to the Appointment dialog box. The Occurs field will contain <Edit pattern...> to indicate that a customized recurrence pattern has been created for the appointment.

The Reminder field on Figure 8-2 sets the time when you will be notified about the upcoming appointment. Turn the reminder notification on or off by tapping the field and selecting either None or Remind Me from the drop-down list. The second line of the Reminder field defines the amount of time prior to the appointment that notification occurs. For example, a reminder can be set for one day before the appointment. Tap the number in the field to set the amount of time, and tap the minutes portion to select either minutes, hours, days, or weeks.

Appointments assigned to categories can be filtered in any of the Calendar views by tapping View | Categories. In order to filter appointments, you must first assign them to a category, which you do by setting a value for the Categories field. Tap the field to display a list of categories, and then tap the check box next to the categories listed to assign them to the appointment.

The Attendees field is used to create a meeting, and is explained in the "Schedule a Meeting Using Calendar" section. The Status field is a drop-down list containing Free, Tentative, Busy, or Out-Of-Office. The item that you select from the list changes the color of the bar on the left side of the appointment in the Day view and is used to indicate how the time should be treated when scheduling other appointments.

Tap the Sensitivity field to display a drop-down list that contains Normal and Private. If you select Private, the appointment will be private in Outlook and Exchange after it is synchronized with a desktop computer. Other Outlook and Exchange users may view Normal appointments.

8

Did you know?

Time Zones Affect Appointments

If you change the time on your Pocket PC by tapping Start | Settings | System | Clock and the time zone of the time you choose is different, then you will also change the times for your appointments. This is because every appointment time includes the current time zone. For example, if you are in the Eastern time zone and create an appointment for 10:00 A.M., changing the clock to the Central time zone will cause the appointment time to change to 9:00 A.M.

Unfortunately, the way your Pocket PC treats time zones means that you have to keep in mind where you will be on the day of the appointment. If you are going to be in Chicago tomorrow, which is in the Central time zone, for a 10:00 A.M. appointment, you can either not change the Pocket PC clock when you are in Chicago, or you can create the appointment for 11:00 A.M. EST (Eastern Standard Time).

As you can tell, appointment times can become very difficult for those who travel. Information Appliance Associates provides CorrectTime, which will reset appointments to their original times after you change the Pocket PC clock. CorrectTime can be downloaded from http://www.doctorce.com/correcttime.htm.

Enter Notes for Appointments

Appointment notes can contain text, drawings, recordings, or writing in digital ink. To enter a note, tap the Notes tab to display the portion of the Appointment dialog box that functions in a manner similar to the Notes program explained in Chapter 13.

To make a recording, press-and-hold the hardware record button. Your device will beep and begin recording. Stop the recording by releasing the button. Once the recording is finished, an icon is inserted into the note, which you tap to play back the recording.

Schedule a Meeting Using Calendar

In Calendar, meetings are appointments with attendees. When you create a meeting in Calendar, an e-mail containing the meeting request is sent to the people that you select in the Appointment dialog box. To send the e-mail, Inbox must be configured with an e-mail service, as outlined in Chapter 20.

The process of creating a meeting is the same as creating an appointment, but with one additional step—you select participants in the Attendees field. Create a new appointment and complete the fields in the dialog box as needed. Tap the Attendees field to display the dialog box shown on the right, which lists names and e-mail addresses:

The names listed in the dialog box are entries in Contacts that each contain an e-mail address. A name may appear in the list more than once if it has more than one e-mail address (for example, a home and a work e-mail address). Tap the check box next to a person's name to select that person as a meeting participant.

Complete the fields on the Appointment dialog box and tap OK to create the meeting. The meeting will display in the Calendar Day view just like an appointment, but it contains a graphic to indicate that it is a meeting, as shown in the following image:

This icon indicates a meeting.

An e-mail message of the meeting request is placed in the Outbox of the e-mail service that you select in Calendar. To select the e-mail service in Calendar, tap Tools | Options and select the service in the Send Meeting Requests Via field, as shown in this image:

The e-mail message will be sent the next time you use Inbox to send and receive e-mail, unless you select ActiveSync for the e-mail service. If ActiveSync is used, the request will move to Outlook during the next synchronization.

This shows which e-mail service is used for meeting requests. →

Edit the Appointment Category List

Appointments can be filtered on categories so that only appointments belonging to a certain category display. You assign categories in the Appointment dialog box while creating the appointment. The category list contains several default items and is shared by Calendar, Contacts, and Tasks.

Did you know?

Meeting Attendees Are Visible With Pocket PC 2002

You cannot see the attendees for meetings in Calendar that have been sent to you in Outlook on Pocket PC 2000 devices. On Pocket PC 2002 devices, you will see the first six lines of meeting attendees.

You add items to the category list when you create an appointment or edit an existing appointment. Tap the Categories field on the Appointment dialog box to open the image on the right:

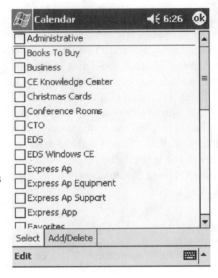

Tap the Add/Delete tab, enter the new item in the box, and tap Add. You also use this dialog box to delete items from the category list. To delete an item, select it in the list and then tap Delete.

Filter Appointments by Categories

Filters help you focus on specific groups of appointments by only displaying entries belonging to a category that you select. In order for filters to be useful, you must assign appointments to categories.

> **NOTE** *Categories do not appear in the Tools menu if there are no appointments assigned to a category.*

To filter appointments on a category, tap Tools | Categories, tap the check box next to the categories that you want to display, and then tap OK. To clear the filter and display all appointments, tap Tools | Categories, tap the check boxes of the categories selected and tap OK.

> **NOTE** *To filter appointments on Pocket PC 2000 devices, tap View | Categories.*

Edit and Delete Appointments

Tap appointments listed in the Day and Agenda views to display the Appointment Summary screen. You can also open the Appointment Summary screen from the Week view by tapping the appointment block and then tapping the summary that appears at the top of the screen.

To edit the appointment, tap the Edit command at the bottom of the screen. The Appointment dialog box opens for you to make any changes by either tapping the fields or tapping the Notes tab. Tap OK to save the changes.

Did you know?

The Edit Command Is New

The Edit command has been added to the Summary view of all the Pocket Outlook programs in Pocket PC 2002. In the prior version, you simply tapped the top part of the summary screen to edit the appointment, task, or contact information, or tapped the bottom part of the screen to edit notes. Microsoft added the Edit command for two reasons: The first reason is that many users found it too easy to accidentally edit an item. The second reason is to support hyperlinks, which are now available in Contacts and can be tapped to open a web page in Internet Explorer.

Appointments listed in Day, Week, or Agenda view can be copied, moved, or deleted by tapping-and-holding the stylus on the appointment that you want to edit and then tapping either Cut, Copy, or Delete from the pop-up list that appears. When you tap Delete, a confirmation dialog box displays, asking whether or not you want to delete the appointment.

To paste an appointment that you either cut or copied, tap-and-hold the stylus on an open time slot in either Day, Week, or Agenda view, and then tap Paste in the pop-up list that appears.

Find Appointments in Calendar

To search for appointments in Calendar, tap Start | Find to open the dialog box on the right:

Enter the word or phrase that you want to search for in the Find field, expand the Type field drop-down list, tap Calendar, and then tap Go.

Find will search through all appointments and list the entries containing the word or phrase in the Results portion of the dialog box. Tap an entry in the list to open the Summary view of the appointment; when you tap OK on the Summary View dialog box, you return to the Find dialog box.

You can search for entries in other Pocket Outlook programs by tapping their entry in the Type drop-down list, or by tapping the Pocket Outlook entry to search across all of the programs. The procedure for searching and viewing each type is the same.

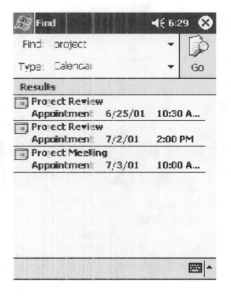

8

Send and Receive Appointments via Infrared

Any appointment in Calendar can be sent to another Pocket PC using the infrared port on the device. To send and receive appointments with infrared, follow these steps:

1. On the receiving Pocket PC, tap Start | Programs | Infrared Receive.

2. Start Calendar on the Pocket PC sending the appointment, tap-and-hold on the appointment that you want to send, and then tap Beam Appointment.

3. Line up the infrared ports of the two devices.

Once the connection is established, the appointment will be transferred and the sending Pocket PC will display the dialog box shown on the right:

The receiving Pocket PC will display a similar dialog box indicating that the appointment was received.

Did you know?

Send and Receive Via Infrared with Pocket PC 2000

The process for receiving appointments, tasks and contacts via infrared is different with Pocket PC 2000. To receive these items on Pocket PC 2000 devices, start Calendar, Tasks, or Contacts and tap Tools | Receive Via Infrared. When you send appointments, tasks, and contacts from Pocket PC 2000 devices, the menu option is different. To send, tap-and-hold the item, and then tap Send Via Infrared.

Configure Calendar Options

Several Calendar options can be set by tapping
Tools | Options to open the Options dialog box
on the right:

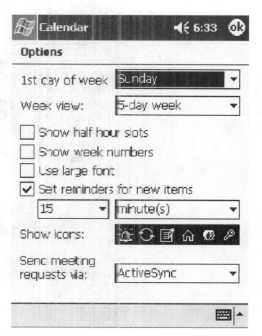

By default, the first day of the week is Sunday,
but you can change it by selecting a day from the
1st Day Of Week drop-down list. To set the
default number of weeks in the Week view,
expand the drop-down list and tap 5-day week,
6-day week, or 7-day week.

To have Calendar show half-hour slots, week
numbers, or use large fonts, tap the check boxes
for each in the dialog box. To have Calendar
automatically set reminders for appointments, tap
the Set Reminders For New Items check box.
Select the default time for the reminder notification
by tapping the appropriate drop-down lists.

Tap the information icons that you want to be
displayed on appointments in the Day view. The
dark icons will be displayed on the appointment.
Meeting announcements are sent using the Inbox
e-mail service that you select in the Send Meeting
Requests Via drop-down list.

Store and Retrieve Addresses Using Contacts

The Contacts program is the Pocket PC companion to the Contacts folder in Microsoft Outlook.
ActiveSync synchronizes addresses that you enter in Contacts on the Pocket PC with the Contacts
folder in Outlook, as explained in Chapter 6. To enter an address, first start Contacts by tapping
Start | Contacts, which opens the program window shown in Figure 8-3.

As you can see in Figure 8-3, the Contacts program on the Pocket PC does not have a toolbar
along the top of the screen. The Command bar at the bottom of the screen replaces the menu
and toolbars.

View Addresses in Contacts

Your contacts are listed in alphabetical order by last name in the program window. At the top of
the program window, as shown in Figure 8-3, are the alphabetical tabs, which you tap to move
through the list. Tapping a tab multiple times moves through contacts by jumping to entries that
start with each letter on that tab.

TIP   *Press-and-hold the hardware navigation button or rocker, and after a brief pause the
alphabet will scroll in large letters. Release the button to scroll to the first contact
matching the letter displayed on the screen.*

Categories drop-down list

Quick Find box

Alphabetical index tabs

```
      Contacts            ◀€ 6:44  ⊗
 All Contacts ▾   [                    ]
 #ab| cde| fgh |  ijk | lmn|opq| rst |uvw| xyz
 Anderson, Ray     (906) 555-1212    h
 Brown, Derek      (425) 555-1212    w
 Bush, Steve       (425) 555-1212    w
 Dunn, Jason       (425) 555-1212    w
 Hersey, Chris     (425) 555-1212    w
 Kumpula, Jim      (425) 555-1212    h
 Moraska, Sue      susie@nomail.com e
 Palmer, Steve     (906) 487-1234    h




 New | ▲ View Tools            ▦ ▲
```

FIGURE 8-3   The Contacts List view on a Pocket PC

The Quick Find box is above the alphabetical tabs and is used to find names in the list. Tap the box and start entering a name. As the letters are entered, the display will scroll and eventually show the name that is being entered.

Each contact in the list is displayed with the last name first and the first name last, unless it is a business, in which case the business name is displayed. Also included with each contact is a phone number or e-mail address, indicated by a blue letter to the right of the contact (*w* is work telephone number; *h* is home telephone number; *m* is for mobile number, *p* is pager number, *f* is fax number, *e* is e-mail).

If a contact has multiple telephone numbers and e-mail addresses, the work telephone number will be displayed by default. To change what is included with the contact in the list, tap the blue letter and select the desired item from the pop-up list that displays.

To view the address information for a contact, tap its entry in the Contacts list to display the Contact Summary view, as shown in the image on the right:

Tap OK to close the Contacts Summary view and return to the Contacts list. The Contacts Summary view is a new feature available only on the Pocket PC, and it only displays information that has been entered for a contact.

Contact Summary View Changes

Did you know?

The order of the fields that display in the Contacts Summary view is different between the two releases of Windows for Pocket PCs. Pocket PC 2000 lists all of the contact's phone numbers and e-mail addresses before displaying street addresses. Pocket 2002 groups the work and home fields together so that work phone numbers, street address, and e-mail addresses display first, then home numbers and addresses. The Pocket PC 2002 Contacts Summary view provides hyperlinks for e-mail addresses and web pages, which launch Inbox and Internet Explorer. Pocket PC 2002 devices that have integrated mobile phones provide hyperlinks to phone numbers. To dial a number all you need to do is tap the hyperlink.

8

Change the Contact List View

To view your contacts by company, tap View |
By Company to change the List view, as
shown in the image to the right:

Each company name is listed alphabetically
with a number to the right indicating the number
of contacts in that company. Tap the company
name to display the contacts indented beneath
the company name. Tap the company name a
second time to collapse the view and only
display the company name.

NOTE *View By Company is not available with Pocket PC 2000.*

Tapping View | By Name switches the List view back to the default listing. The Outlook File
As setting defines the default listing. Unfortunately, to change the default view you have to edit
each of your contacts in Outlook. If you wish to make this change in Outlook, follow these steps:

1. Start Outlook.

2. Open the contact that you want to change.

3. Click the File As drop-down field, as shown in the following image:

4. Select the option that you want and click OK.

The next time you synchronize your Pocket PC, the contact will be listed using the option you select.

How to ... Have More Power Over Contacts

One of the most frustrating aspects of the Pocket PC 2000 software is that the Contacts program does not allow you to change how contacts display in the List view. Microsoft partially addresses this issue with Pocket PC 2002 by adding the View By Company command.

While some will find this addition to Contacts useful, others will find it still does not provide the power they want over how contacts are listed. Fortunately, Web Information Solutions has written a program that addresses this shortcoming.

Pocket Informant by Web Information Solutions is a very popular alternative to all the Pocket Outlook programs. It can display contacts by first name, last name, and company name. This program also provides an Agenda view that lists appointments and tasks for each day, as well as more informative Week and Month views. You can also link appointments, contacts, and tasks to each other and to files on your Pocket PC. For more information and a trial version of the program, go to http://www.pocketinformant.com.

8

Create New Contacts

Tap New to open the Contacts dialog box:

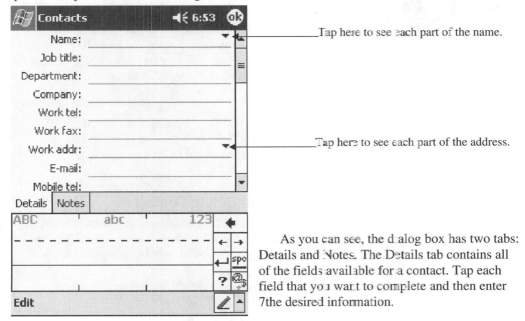

Tap here to see each part of the name.

Tap here to see each part of the address.

As you can see, the dialog box has two tabs: Details and Notes. The Details tab contains all of the fields available for a contact. Tap each field that you want to complete and then enter the desired information.

The Name and Work Address fields include detail indicators (downward pointing triangles) that you can tap to display the different parts of the field. You can enter the information directly in the field or tap the details indicator and enter the different parts of the field separately, as shown in the image to the right:

Telephone numbers on the dialog box automatically include the area code that you define in the Contact Options. To change the area code, tap Tools | Options, enter the number in the Area Code field and tap OK.

Tap the Categories field on the Contacts screen to display the category list. Assign the contact to one or more categories by tapping the check box next to the items in the list. If the category that you want to use is not available in the list, tap the Add/Delete tab, enter a category in the empty box, and tap Add. When you tap the Select tab, you will notice that the check box next to the category you entered is automatically assigned to the contact.

Contact notes can contain text, drawings, recordings, or writing in digital ink. To enter a note, tap the Notes tab to display the portion of the Contacts dialog box that functions in a manner similar to the Notes program explained in Chapter 13.

Tap here to play the recording.

To make a recording, press-and-hold the hardware record button. Your device will beep and begin recording. To stop the recording, release the button. Once the recording is finished, an icon is inserted into the note, as shown in the image on the left.

When you have finished entering all the information for the contact, tap OK, and the contact will be added to the Contacts list.

Edit and Delete Contacts

To edit a contact, first tap its entry in the Contacts list to open the Contacts Summary view; then tap Edit. Tap the Notes tab to edit the contact notes.

NOTE   *On Pocket PC 2000 devices, tap any item displayed in the Contacts Summary view to open the contact's Detail view, where you can edit any of the fields for the contact.*

To copy or delete entries in the Contacts list, tap-and-hold the stylus on the contact that you want to edit; then tap Create Copy or Delete Contact from the pop-up list that appears. When you tap Delete Contact, a confirmation dialog box displays, asking whether or not you want to delete the contact.

When you tap Create Copy, a copy of the contact that you selected inserts into the Contacts list. You can then edit the entry that was added to the Contacts list.

How to ... Create a Contact Template

You might find yourself creating many contacts with the same information, such as for people who work for the same company. One trick you can use to help speed up entering these types of contacts is to create a template that contains all of the duplicate information. By using the template, you save yourself the time spent entering the same information repeatedly. Follow these steps to create a template:

1. Tap New to create a new contact.

2. Enter the company name as the first name of the contact, and enter **_Template** for the last name. By using an underscore for the first character of the last name, you ensure that the template appears at the top of the Contacts list.

3. Complete the remaining details, such as the work address and category, that are shared by all the contacts.

4. Tap OK to add the template to the Contacts list.

The template contact will appear at the top of the list. To create a new contact using the template, tap-and-hold the template and then tap Create Copy. Tap the copy of the template that was added to the list and edit the fields as needed for the new contact you are creating.

Edit the Contact Category List

Contacts can be filtered on categories so that only contacts belonging to a category display. You assign categories in the Contacts dialog box while creating the contact. The Category list contains several default items and is shared with Calendar and Tasks.

To add an item to the Category list, expand the Categories drop-down list, as shown in the image on the right, and tap More:

The title of the drop-down list changes to Show when the list is expanded.

Tap the Add/Delete tab, enter the new item in the box, and tap Add. You also use this tab to delete items in the Category list. To delete an item, select it on the Add/Delete tab and then tap Delete.

The Category list can also be edited from the Contacts dialog box. Tap the Categories field on the Contacts dialog box to open the Contacts List and then tap the Add/Delete tab.

Filter Contacts by Categories

Filters help you focus on specific groups of contacts by only displaying entries belonging to a category that you select. In order for filters to be useful, you must assign contacts to categories. Use the Categories drop-down list to quickly filter items by the category that you select.

The title of the Categories drop-down list changes to show the currently displayed category. To filter tasks on a category, tap the Categories drop-down list and tap the category that you want to display. If the category is not in the drop-down list, tap More, tap the check box next to the categories that you want to display, and then tap OK.

Clear the filter and display all contacts by expanding the Categories drop-down list and tapping All Categories.

> TIP   *Use the Recent entry in the Categories drop-down list to display the contacts you have recently added, edited, or viewed.*

How to ...   Display Contacts Not Assigned to a Category

A problem on Pocket PC 2000 devices is that you cannot display contacts not assigned to a category, which means if you use categories you might not find a contact, since it won't display. A No Categories option has been added to the Categories drop-down list in Pocket PC 2002. When you select this option, only the contacts that have not been assigned to a category will display.

Find Contacts

To search for entries in Contacts, tap Start | Find to open the Find dialog box. Enter the word or phrase that you are searching for in the Find field, expand the Type field drop-down list, tap Contacts, and then tap Go.

Find will search through all contacts and list the entries containing the word or phrase in the Results portion of the dialog box. Tap an entry in the list to open the contact, and tap OK in the Contacts dialog box to return to the Find dialog box.

You can search for an entry in other Pocket Outlook programs by tapping it in the Type drop-down list; the procedure for searching and viewing each type is the same.

Send E-Mail to a Contact

To send e-mail to a person from Contacts, tap-and-hold on the person's entry in the Contacts list, and then tap Send E-mail To Contact on the Context menu. Inbox will start and create a new e-mail message using the contact's e-mail address. If the contact does not have an e-mail address, Inbox will still create a new message, but the e-mail Address field will be blank.

Complete the message, tap Send, and you will return to Inbox. Return to Contacts by pressing Hardware or tapping Start | Contacts.

TIP   *On Pocket PC 2002 devices, you can also send e-mail from a contact's Summary view by tapping the e-mail address. You can also open the contact's web page by tapping the URL entered in the web page field on the Summary view.*

8

Send and Receive Contacts via Infrared

Any entry in Contacts can be sent to another Pocket PC using the infrared port on the device. To send and receive contacts with infrared, follow these steps:

1. On the receiving Pocket PC, tap Start | Programs | Infrared Receive.

2. Start Contacts on the Pocket PC sending the contact, tap-and-hold on the contact that you want to send, and then tap Beam Contact.

3. Line up the infrared ports of the two devices.

Once the connection is established, the contact will transfer and the sending Pocket PC will indicate that the contact has been received.

Configure Contact Options

Set several options in the Options dialog box, as shown in the image on the right, by tapping Tools | Options:

Tap the check boxes next to Show ABC Tabs, Show Contact Names Only, or Use Large Fonts to change how the contact list displays. Enter the Area Code and select the Country/Region to be used for new contacts. Tap OK to save the changes and close the dialog box.

Manage Your Tasks

The Tasks program is the Pocket PC companion to the Tasks folder in Microsoft Outlook. ActiveSync synchronizes tasks that you enter in Tasks on the Pocket PC with the Tasks folder in Outlook, as explained in Chapter 6. To enter a task, tap Start | Tasks, which opens the program window shown in Figure 8-4.

Tasks	◀€ 8:44 ⊗
All Tasks ▾	Priority ▾

- ☐ ! Complete checklist
- ☐ A Passion For Books
- ☐ Add more code for database com
- ☐ **Complete Report**
- ☐ Constantine's Sword
- ☐ Create debug handling routine
- ☐ Document test system config
- ☐ Explain differences between cf sl
- ☐ Read travel books
- ☐ Sign contract
- ☐ UPS batteries in Southfield
- ☐ ↓ Doco fileservers

New ▲ Tools   ▦ ▲

8

As you can see in the figure, the Tasks program on the Pocket PC does not have a toolbar along the top of the screen. The Command bar at the bottom of the screen replaces the menu and toolbars, and overall the screen looks less busy.

View Your Tasks

Tasks display in the main program window in one complete list. To the left of each task is a check box that you tap to mark a task as complete. Immediately to the right of the check box is the Priority column, which displays exclamation marks for high-priority tasks, an arrow pointing down for low-priority tasks, and nothing for normal tasks. The description of the task takes up the remaining space for each item.

Above and to the left of the Tasks list is the Categories drop-down list. The "Filter Tasks by Categories" section explains how to use the Categories drop-down list to change what displays in the Tasks list.

To the right of the Categories drop-down list (and above the Tasks list) is the Sort drop-down list. The title of the Sort drop-down list displays the name of the item used to sort the list. In Figure 8-4, the Tasks list is sorted by Priority. Tap the title to expand the drop-down list, as shown in the image to the right:

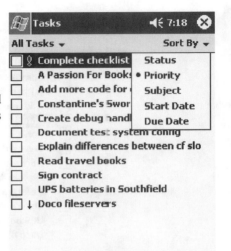

You can sort the tasks list by Status, Priority, Subject, Start Date, and Due Date. A task has either an active or a complete status, and when the list is sorted by status, active tasks appear before complete tasks. To change the sort order of the Tasks list, expand the Sort drop-down list and then tap an item in the list.

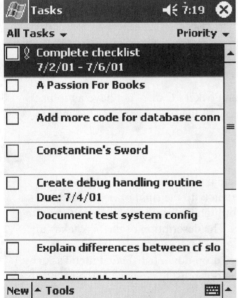

Task start and due dates do not appear in the Tasks list unless you enable them. To display start and due dates, tap Tools | Options and then tap the Show Start And Due Date check box. When the dates are enabled, each task will occupy two lines in the Tasks list, as shown in the image on the left:

Past due tasks are displayed in red in the Tasks list. To increase the font size, tap Tools | Options, and then tap the Use Large Font check box.

Each task can have more information than is displayed in the Tasks list. To see the details, tap on the task to open it in a Summary view, as shown in the image on the right:

The Summary view is a new feature found only on Pocket PCs. It provides all of the information about the appointment on one easy-to-read screen. The top part of the screen displays the task details and can be expanded by tapping the down arrows of the task's start and due dates and category assignments. The bottom part of the screen displays notes.

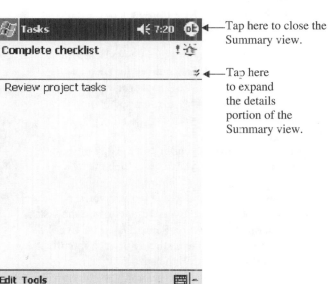

Tap here to close the Summary view.

Tap here to expand the details portion of the Summary view.

Create New Tasks

Tap New to open the Tasks dialog box and create a new task. The dialog box has two tabs: Task and Notes. On the Task tab you enter the all of the details about the task. The Subject field is a drop-down list, which you can use to select words commonly used in task subjects. By using the drop-down list you can speed up data entry, but unfortunately the list does not change, and you cannot add words.

Dates are entered in the Starts and Due fields by tapping the field to open the date picker shown on the right:

Tap a date on the calendar to select it for either field. You can use the arrows at the top of the calendar to move backward and forward one month at a time, or tap the month to jump to another month that appears in a pop-up list. The date that you select will automatically appear in the field.

NOTE   *A task cannot be assigned a start date without a due date. However, a due date can be assigned without a start date.*

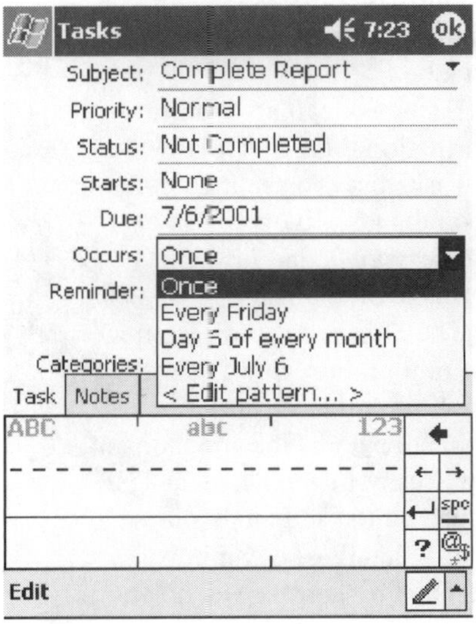

Tasks can be created multiple times by selecting a recurrence pattern. The default setting for each task is to occur once. To make the task appear multiple times, tap the Occurs field to display the items shown in the image on the right:

The items will vary depending on the day of the week, day of the month, and date on which the task is created.

The task shown in the image is being created on Friday, July 6, 2001. Select Every Friday to add the task to the task list on every Friday. Select Day 6 Of Every Month to add the task on the sixth day of each month. If you want to add the task on the specific date every year—in this case, July 6—then select Every July 6.

If none of the items in the drop-down list meet your requirements, tap <Edit pattern...> to start the Recurrence wizard. The Recurrence wizard has three dialog boxes, the first of which is shown below:

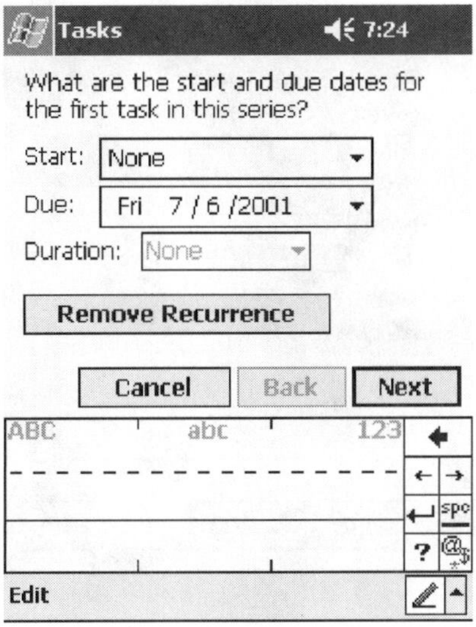

In the first dialog box you set the Start and Due dates for the task. Typically, these will have been already entered prior to creating the recurrence pattern. If the start date is correct, you can change the due date by expanding the Duration drop-down list and tapping a value in the list. Tap Remove Recurrence to delete the recurrence and close the dialog box.

Tap Next to open the second dialog box of the Recurrence wizard. Tap the buttons along the top of the dialog box to define a recurrence time. When you tap Daily, two radio buttons appear, as shown in the image at right:

To create the task on multiple days, tap the first radio button and select a number from the Every [   ] Day(s) drop-down list. Tap the Every Weekday radio button to create the task on every weekday.

Tap Weekly to define a weekly recurrence pattern, as shown in the image below:

Tap the days in the week for which you want to create the task; you can select more than one day. Select a value from the Every [   ] Week(s) drop-down list to create the task for several weeks on the days that you select.

Tap Monthly to define a monthly recurrence pattern, as shown in the image below:

The pattern can be defined for a specific date in a month (such as the sixth), for a select number of months, or for a day in a week (such as the first Friday) for a select number of months. Tap the radio button of the option you want, and select the values from the drop-down lists.

Tap Yearly to define a yearly recurrence pattern, as shown to the right:

The yearly pattern is similar to the monthly pattern. Your options are to create the task on the same date and month each year, or for the day in a week of the month that you select. Tap the radio button of the option you want, and select the values from the drop-down lists.

Tap Next to define the starting and ending dates of the recurrence pattern, as shown in the image below:

Select the starting date by using The Pattern Starts drop-down list. Three options are available for defining the end date: the recurrence pattern does not end, it ends on a date that you select, or it ends after a select number of occurrences. Tap the radio button of the option that you want and select the appropriate values from the drop-down lists.

After you select the start and end dates of the recurring task, tap Finish to return to the Tasks dialog box. The Occurs field will contain <Edit pattern...> to indicate that a customized recurrence pattern has been created for the task.

> **TIP** *You may have problems synchronizing recurring tasks between your Pocket PC and Outlook. If you create a recurring task, only edit it on the Pocket PC; otherwise, the task may not be re-created for each occurrence.*

The Reminder field on the dialog box sets the date when you will be notified about the upcoming task. Turn the reminder notification on or off by tapping the field and selecting either None or Remind Me from the drop-down list. The second line of the Reminder field defines the date for the notification. Tap the date on the second line to display the date picker, and tap a date on the calendar for when you want the reminder notification to occur.

Tasks assigned to categories can be filtered in the Tasks list by using the Categories drop-down list. In order to filter tasks, you must first assign them to a category, which you do by setting a value for the Categories field. Tap the field to display a list of categories, and then tap the check box next to the categories listed to assign them to the task.

Enter Notes for Tasks

Task notes can contain text, drawings, recordings, or writing in digital ink. To enter a note, tap the Notes tab to display the portion of the Tasks dialog box that functions in a manner similar to the Notes program explained in Chapter 6.

To make a recording, press-and-hold Hardware Record. Your device will beep and begin recording. Stop the recording by releasing the button. Once the recording is finished, an icon is inserted into the note, which you tap to play back the record.

Use the Task Entry Bar

The Task Entry Bar provides a quick way to enter tasks, but it is disabled by default. To display the Task Entry Bar, tap Tools | Entry Bar. When the Task Entry Bar is enabled, an extra row is added beneath the Categories and Sort drop-down lists, as shown here:

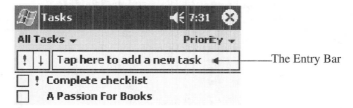

The Task Entry Bar includes two priority buttons and the task subject. Set the task priority to either high or low by tapping the exclamation mark or arrow. To create the subject, tap Tap Here To Add A New Task on the bar and enter the task subject.

When you have finished entering values on the Task Entry Bar, tap ENTER on the Software Input panel to add the new task to the Tasks list.

Edit and Delete Tasks

Tap an item in the Tasks list to display the Task Summary screen; then tap Edit to open the task information. To edit the task notes, tap the Notes tab, make any necessary changes to the fields in the dialog box, and then tap OK to save the changes.

NOTE
On Pocket PC 2000 devices, tap the top part of the Task Summary screen to edit the task information and tap the bottom part of the screen to edit notes.

To copy or delete a task, tap-and-hold the stylus on the task that you want to edit and then tap either Create Copy or Delete Task on the Context menu that appears. When you tap Delete, a confirmation dialog box displays, asking whether or not you want to delete the appointment.

Edit the Task Category List

Tasks can be filtered on categories so that only tasks belonging to a given category display. You assign categories in the Tasks dialog box while creating the task. The Category list contains several default items and is shared with Calendar and Contacts.

To add an item to the Category list, expand the Categories drop-down list and tap More. Tap the Add/Delete tab, enter the new item in the box, and tap Add. You also use this dialog box to delete items in the Category list. To delete an item, select it in the list and then tap Delete.

The Category list can also be edited from the Contacts dialog box. Tap the Categories field to open the dialog box and then tap the Add/Delete tab.

Filter Tasks by Categories

Filters help you focus on specific groups of tasks by only displaying entries belonging to a category that you select. In order for filters to be useful, you must assign tasks to categories. Use the Categories drop-down list to quickly filter items by the category that you select.

The title of the Categories drop-down list changes to indicate the category currently being displayed. To filter tasks on a category, tap the Categories drop-down list and tap the category that you want to display. If the category is not in the drop-down list, tap More, tap the check box next to the categories that you want to display, and then tap OK.

To clear the filter and display all contacts, expand the Categories drop-down list and tap All Categories.

TIP   *Use the Recent entry in the Categories drop-down list to display the tasks that you have recently added, edited, or viewed.*

The Categories drop-down list has two items useful for looking at tasks. Select Active Tasks to list all tasks with a start date before and on the current date. Tasks not assigned a start date are always active. Select Completed Tasks to list all tasks marked complete.

TIP   *You can select a category and Active Tasks or Completed Tasks to display the active or completed tasks for a category.*

How to ... Display Tasks Not Assigned to a Category

A problem on Pocket PC 2000 devices is that you cannot display tasks not assigned to a category, which means if you use categories, you might miss a task, since it won't display. A No Categories option has been added to the Categories drop-down list in Pocket PC 2002. When you select this option, only the tasks that have not been assigned to a category will display.

Find Tasks

To search for entries in Tasks, tap Start | Find to open the Find dialog box. Enter the word or phrase that you want to find in the Find field, expand the Type field drop-down list, tap Tasks, and then tap Go.

Find will search through all tasks and list the entries containing the word or phrase in the Results portion of the dialog box. Tap an entry in the list to open the task, and tap OK in the Tasks dialog box to return to the Find dialog box.

You can search for entries in other Pocket Outlook programs by tapping their entries in the Type drop-down list. The procedure for searching and viewing each type is the same.

Send and Receive Tasks via Infrared

Any entry in Tasks can be sent to another Pocket PC using the infrared port on the device. To send and receive tasks with infrared, follow these steps:

1. On the Pocket PC receiving the task, tap Start | Programs | Infrared Receive.

2. Start Tasks on the Pocket PC sending the task, tap-and-hold on the task that you want to send and then tap Beam Task.

3. Line up the infrared ports of the two devices.

Once the connection is established, the task will transfer, and the sending Pocket PC will indicate that the task has been received.

Configure Task Options

To set three task options, tap Tools | Options to open the dialog box on the right:

Tap Set Reminders For New Items to have reminders automatically created for new tasks. To add the start and due dates to the Tasks list, tap Show Start And Due Date. Tap Use Large Font to increase the size of the font used for the Tasks list. Tap OK to save the changes that you make and close the Options dialog box.

Wrapping Up

Pocket Outlook provides the tools that help you manage your time. Recurring appointments are easy to schedule in Calendar because you only have to enter the appointment information once, and your Pocket PC automatically enters that appointment on all the other days you select. The Tasks program provides the same functionality, reminding you of tasks that you must complete at regular intervals. All of your addresses are stored in Contacts, which make it easy to retrieve a phone number or an e-mail address. In Chapter 9, you'll see how Pocket PC 2002 provides more power to Contacts by integrating all of the phone numbers with a dialer program. The combination of Contacts, the dialer program, and integrated mobile phone hardware enables you to make phone calls using your Pocket PC.

Chapter 9

Call a Friend from Your Pocket PC

How To...

- ■ Purchase an Pocket PC with mobile phone capabilities
- ■ Make and receive phone calls using Pocket PCs
- ■ Manage phone call information
- ■ Change phone, service, and network settings

Chances are you own a mobile phone, and have had one long before you even considered buying a Pocket PC. Today, mobile phones are one of a growing number of gadgets we consider essential and must be carried with us at all times. Pocket PCs are in that list of essential gadgets, but for many lugging a phone and a Pocket PC around all day is one gadget too many. The answer, according to analysts and hardware manufacturers, are devices that integrate mobile phone and personal digital assistant (PDA) features.

Over the last several years there has been considerable talk about integrated devices, which are often called *smart phones*. In fact, Microsoft competitors have taken a lead in developing such devices. Palm Computing works with several mobile-phone manufactures, such as Kyocera, in developing integrated devices, and the Kyocera Smartphone has been on the market for many months. The VisorPhone is a Springboard module that turns a Handspring Visor handheld, which runs the Palm OS, into a mobile phone.

Mitsubishi, Sagem, Siemens, Zess, and Cesscomm sell integrated devices that run Pocket PC 2000 in Europe. These devices run the standard Pocket PC software, with the mobile-phone functions added by the hardware company. Consequently, the mobile-phone software functions differently on each of these devices and adds a software development burden to companies that usually focus on designing and producing hardware.

Pocket PC 2002 directly supports mobile-phone hardware to provide a standard user interface for phone functions across all devices. Very little has been said about the phone capabilities of the Pocket PC 2002 because the integrated devices will not be available in the United States until the spring of 2002, at the earliest. In this chapter, you'll receive an introduction to the phone features in Pocket PC 2002, though some of the information may change by the time the devices become available.

NOTE   *You will not see the phone features on standard Pocket PCs discussed in this chapter.*

Buy a Pocket PC Phone

Several companies sell integrated devices, but the total numbers sold have not been nearly as high as the number of mobile phones or even handheld computers sold. The challenge is designing a device that is large enough to be useful as a handheld computer, while being small enough to be carried around and used as a phone. With the trend of mobile phones becoming smaller, integrated devices feel and look like bricks in comparison.

The Microsoft solution to this dilemma recognizes that no one hardware design will be right for everyone. One part of the Microsoft solution is Pocket PC 2002 and its mobile-phone capabilities, which is designed to be the best handheld computer capable of making phone calls. The second part of the Microsoft solution is a smart-phone platform code named Stinger. Stinger is designed to be the best mobile phone that also has some handheld computing capabilities.

The two Microsoft solutions are targeted at two different types of users. People who frequently use cell phones, or want to carry one small device, will prefer Stinger phones because they are small and optimized for use in one hand. Those who do not frequently use cell phones, yet use handheld computers, will prefer a Pocket PC integrated with a phone so that they don't have to carry multiple devices.

Trying to decide which Microsoft solution is right for you? First determine how frequently you make phone calls, and then determine whether you can live with the trade-offs of one solution over another. A Stinger phone will be smaller than a Pocket PC, but it will not have all of the features available on handheld computers. An integrated Pocket PC is larger than most mobile phones, and can be awkward when holding it up to your ear. You will most likely want to use a hands-free microphone with any integrated Pocket PC.

We do not have enough information about the Microsoft smart phones to provide adequate coverage of them in this book. In this chapter, the focus is on the mobile-phone extensions of Pocket PC 2002, with the intention of providing enough information to provide you with an idea of how these integrated devices may work.

The Pocket PC 2002 launch event provided some information about what these integrated devices might be like. At the event, mmO2 announced the O2 xda, which will be the first integrated device running Pocket PC 2002. The O2 xda only supports the communication protocols used by European phone systems, and will start selling there in early 2002. It uses the same 206Mhz StrongARM processor, 32MB of ROM, 32MB of RAM, and built-in secure digital slot as other Pocket PCs. It is expected to have 3.5 hours of talk time and 150 hours of standby time.

While the O2 xda will only be available in Europe, similar integrated devices will also be available in the United States. Compaq plans to start selling the Wireless Expansion Pack for the GSM/GPRS networks by the end of 2001. The expansion pack will add mobile phone features to the iPAQ Pocket PCs. As more announcements of new products are made, you will find information about them at http://www.pocketpc.com.

Make and Receive Phone Calls

The mobile-phone features in Pocket PC 2002 are only available with integrated devices and add-on products. You will not be able obtain the Phone application unless you buy one of these products. When you turn on a Pocket PC that is integrated with a mobile phone, you will see a Phone Notifications icon as shown in the image to the right: The phone searches for a connection, and when one is found it shows signal strength in the form of bars to the right of the icon.

Phone Notifications icon

Turn the phone on or off by tapping the Phone Notifications icon. By default the phone is always on, even when you have the Pocket PC turned off.

Make Phone Calls

There are several ways for you to make a phone call, depending on the number that you want to dial. One way to make a call is to simply dial a number using the Phone application, which you start by tapping Start | Programs | Phone. Tap the numbers on the keypad and then tap Talk. The image to the right shows a call in progress:

Tap End to complete the call and hang up.

NOTE   *Some Pocket PCs with integrated mobile phones will have dedicated hardware buttons for Talk and End, which are similar to the buttons on mobile phones.*

The Phone application supports speed dialing, which uses phone numbers that you program into storage locations. To speed dial a number, tap-and-hold on the speed dial location on the keypad and Phone application will dial the associated number. If the speed dial location is a two-digit number, tap the first digit and then tap-and-hold the second digit. You can also tap Speed Dial on the keypad and then tap a number in the following list:

Did you know?

Pocket PC Phones Use GSM

There are several different mobile-phone technologies, but Global System for Mobile Communications (GSM) is the preferred technology for Pocket PC phones because it is available around the world. GSM is widely used throughout Europe, but there is much less use of it in the United States. VoiceStream Wireless provides the majority of GSM service in the United States, but AT&T Wireless is in the process of converting their network to GSM, and Cingular Wireless also provides some GSM service.

Most of the GSM service providers are upgrading their networks to support General Packet Radio Service (GPRS), which adds data communications to their networks. Most Pocket PC phones will be designed to use GSM for voice communications and GPRS for data communications.

GSM phones use Subscriber Identification Module (SIM) cards, which are smart cards that store mobile-phone service settings and user preferences. In some cases SIM cards contain contact information, which you can access as speed dial numbers on Pocket PC phones. You can also import contacts from SIM cards to the Pocket PC.

If you already subscribe to a GSM service, you should be able to use a Pocket PC phone with that service by simply transferring the SIM card from your phone to your Pocket PC.

While speed dialing can be handy when making calls from the Phone application, you will most likely store all phone numbers in Contacts. The Contacts program on integrated Pocket PCs is enhanced to support dialing phone numbers. To dial a number from the Contacts list view, tap-and-hold the contact. On the pop-up menu, tap Call and the type of phone number displayed. For example, if the contact's work number is displayed in the list view, Call Work Tel will display in the pop-up menu, as shown in the image to the right:

| Create Copy |
| Delete Contact |
| Send E-mail to Contact... |
| Beam Contact... |
| Call Work Tel |
| Add Speed Dial Work Tel |

TIP *To change the number for a contact that displays in the list view, tap the letter to the right of the number in the Contacts list view and then select a number from the pop-up menu.*

Another enhancement to Contacts is that phone numbers display as hyperlinks in the Contacts summary view, as shown in the image to the right:

To make a call, simply tap any one of the phone numbers in the summary view.

Contacts	☰ ◀ 2:08 ok
Frank McPherson	
Freelance Writer	
(425) 555-1212	Work tel
(425) 555-1212	Work fax
frank@fmcpherson.com	E-mail
(425) 555-1212	Home tel

NOTE *When you make a call from Contacts, the Phone application does not display. Instead, a notification displays showing that a call is connected. Tap the Phone Notification icon at the top of the screen to end the call.*

All the calls that you make or receive are tracked in the Call Log. You can review the Call Log and make calls from

| Summary | Notes | |
| Edit Tools | | ⌨ ▲ |

9

that log by tapping Call Log on the keypad and then tapping a number in the list, as shown in the image on the right:

You can filter the Call Log to show missed calls, outgoing calls, incoming calls, or calls sorted by caller name. In the following image, tap the Show drop-down list at the upper left of the Call Log screen and select an option from the list:

How to ... Take Notes During Calls

If you want to take notes during a call, tap the icon shown in the following image:

Edit Tools

Tap here to create a note.

The Pocket PC Notes application starts for you to write notes. Notes taken during a call are associated with the phone number so that you can open the note from within the Call Log. In order to take notes during a call, you will need to use a hands-free microphone or the speakerphone functionality that may be available with integrated Pocket PCs.

Receive Phone Calls

When the Pocket PC receives a call, a notification bubble appears on the screen with options for Answer and Ignore. Tap Ignore to silence the phone and transfer the call to voice mail if it is included by the mobile-phone service, or tap Answer to receive the call. If the Phone application is running, you can also tap Talk to answer a call. Finally, if you use an integrated device that includes a Talk hardware button, press the button to receive the call just as you do with mobile phones.

Manage Calls

Every call that is made, received, or missed is entered in the Call Log. To view the contents of the log, tap Call Log on the keypad to open the following screen:

Tap here to filter items in the Call Log.

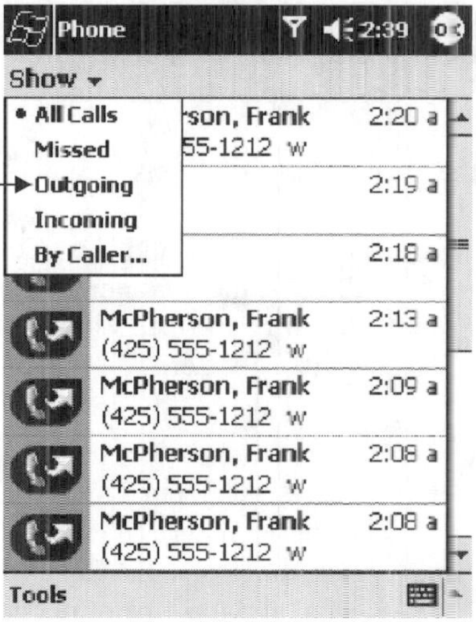

9

How to ... Use the Wireless Radio for Data Communications

Integrated Pocket PC phones may be sold by mobile-phone service providers who will provide voice and data service for the phones. The Pocket PC 2002 Communication Manager is designed to use the wireless radio built into the device or added to the device. To use the phone to connect to the Internet, you will need to create a new connection in the Connection Manager Internet settings and select the wireless radio as the modem. Chapter 19 provides instructions for configuring Connection Manager.

You can filter the items in the Call Log by selecting one of the following items from the drop-down list.

- ■ **All Calls**   Shows all the calls made, received, or missed in chronological order
- ■ **Missed**   Shows only those calls that were not answered
- ■ **Outgoing**   Shows only those calls made from the phone
- ■ **Incoming**   Shows only those calls made to the phone
- ■ **By Caller**   Shows only those calls associated with a single caller

If a note was created for a call, an icon will appear next to the call entry in the log; tap the icon to open the note. Tapping within the white space of an entry in the log displays a tooltip showing the date, time, and duration of the call.

To delete all the items in the Call Log, tap Tools | Delete All Calls. You can also delete a select number of entries from the log by tapping Tools | Options to display the Call Log Options screen:

Select an item from the Delete Call Log Items Older Than drop-down list and tap OK.

The Call Log Options screen displays call statistics. You can view the total time spent on all calls, the total number of calls, and the total time since the last time the Call Log was reset. Tap Reset to reset the call statistics to zero.

Program Speed Dial

There are two ways to add a speed-dial number. To create a speed dial from a contact, tap-and-hold the item in the Contacts list view and then tap Add Speed Dial and the type of phone number displayed. For example, if the work phone number is displayed, tap Add Speed Dial Work Tel, as shown in the image to the right:

The other way to create a speed dial is to tap Speed Dial on the keypad of the Phone application and then tap New, which opens the screen shown in the image to the right:

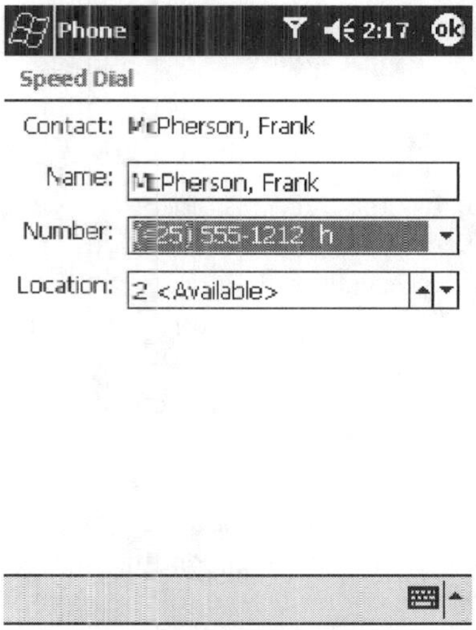

Select the name of the contact for the speed dial, the phone number for the speed dial, and the speed-dial location. There are 99 speed-dial locations for you to use. Tap OK to save the speed dial.

Configure the Pocket PC Phone

To change the phone settings, tap Tools | Options in the Phone application. Alternatively, you can choose Start | Settings | Phone. The settings screen has three tabs: Phone, Services, and Network.

Change the Phone Settings

The Phone tab, as shown in the image to the right, displays the phone number, which is read from the SIM card:

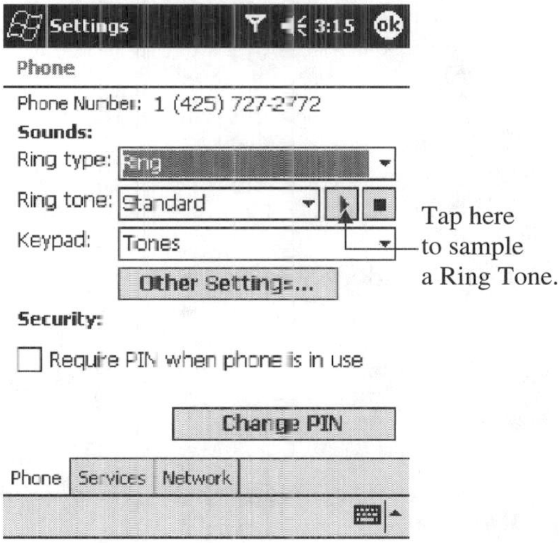

The Ring Type and Ring Tone settings configure how the Pocket PC reacts to an incoming call. Ring Type specifies the type of notification you receive for an incoming call. If you select a Ring Type option, you can sample and select a Ring Tone. You cannot select a Ring Tone if you select the Vibrate Only ring type.

The Keypad field specifies what you hear when using the dialer. You can set the keypad to Beep or Off to not be disruptive in public places. Other Settings opens the Pocket PC Sounds and Notifications settings, where you can set phone, volume, and system sounds.

Select the Require PIN When Phone Is In Use check box to prevent unauthorized use of the Pocket PC phone by requiring that a PIN be entered to use the phone. Tap Change PIN to change the PIN. Emergency 911 calls can be made at any time without first entering a PIN.

NOTE *Instructions for changing the Pocket PC Sounds and Notification Settings are provided in Chapter 4.*

Change the Services Settings

You use the Services tab, as shown in the following image, to access and configure services provided by your mobile-phone service provider:

To configure a setting, select the service and then tap Get Settings.

The Caller ID setting controls whether or not your phone number displays to the person you call. You can prevent your number from being displayed by tapping Disable Caller ID.

Call Forwarding configures the service to forward calls made to the phone depending on the status of the phone. You can configure the following forwarding options:

- **Unavailable** Forwards calls if the phone is turned off or unreachable

- **Busy** Forwards calls when the line is busy

- **No answer** Forwards calls if you do not answer the phone

Call Waiting allows you to receive a second call during a call. To turn call waiting off, tap Do Not Notify Me.

Voice Mail and SMS configures the voice mail and Short Message Service (SMS) access numbers.

NOTE *Short Message Service provides text messaging between mobile phones.*

TIP *Speed dial location 1 is automatically configured for accessing voice mail.*

Change the Network Settings

The network settings allow you to select which mobile-phone network the Pocket PC phone will use. The selection remains active until you change it, lose the network signal, or change the SIM card. The currently registered network displays on the Network tab, as shown in the image to the right:

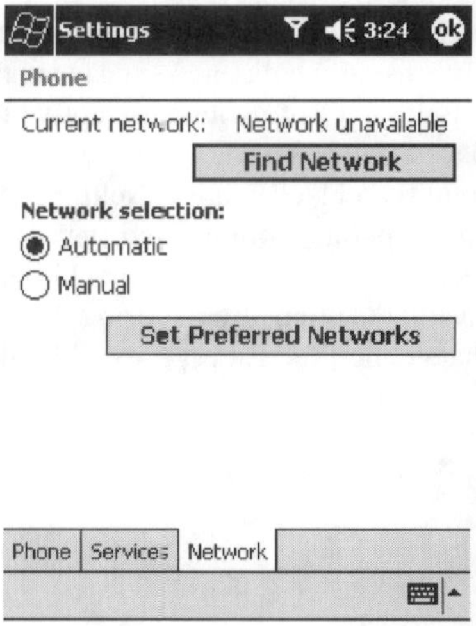

In this image, the phone was not able to find a network. To change this, tap Find Network to start the network selection process.

The phone will search for a network using the criteria specified in the Network Selection portion of the screen. If you select Automatic, the phone will select a network from those you specify as preferred networks. If you select Manual, the phone will search for all available networks and list them. You can then select the network that you want to use from the list.

Tap Set Preferred Networks to specify the networks the phone should use and the order in which they should be accessed.

Wrapping Up

Pocket PC 2002 is designed to be a great handheld computer that is also capable of making phone calls. Whether or not you want to use your Pocket PC as a phone will depend on your mobile phone needs. In this chapter, you have seen how the phone software might work on Pocket PCs. Keep in mind that phone software is still being developed, so information in this chapter may change by the time integrated Pocket PC phones are sold.

In the future you might be able to call a friend using your Pocket PC, but right now you can use your Pocket PC to write a letter to that friend. In the next chapter, you'll learn how to use Pocket Word to create and edit documents.

9

Chapter 10

Create Documents with Pocket Word

How To...

■ Create and save documents

■ Edit and format documents

■ Add handwriting, drawings, and recordings to documents

■ Send documents via e-mail

■ Beam documents using infrared

Pocket Word enables you to use your device for more than just storing personal information and retrieving e-mail. With Pocket Word, you can create letters, memos, or notes wherever the need arises. Pocket Word is similar to Microsoft Word, but its purpose is to complement the desktop software, rather than replace it. Because of this, Pocket Word does not have many of the formatting features—such as tables and footnotes—that you find in Microsoft Word. With Pocket Word, though, you can instantly write documents wherever you are and then transfer the document to a desktop computer for further editing.

NOTE   *When a Word document that contains a significant amount of formatting is transferred to a Pocket PC, most of the formatting will be lost when you edit the document on a Pocket PC. This also applies to e-mail attachments that you receive and return to the sender.*

Use Pocket Word on Your Pocket PC

Unlike the desktop version, Pocket Word cannot do any of the following:

■ Create outlines

■ Password-protect documents

■ Print documents

■ Create tables

■ Create numbered lists

Figure 10-1 shows the differences between the Pocket Word program window on the Pocket PC and Word on a desktop computer. At the bottom of the Pocket Word screen is the Command bar, which contains menu items similar to the menu bar on the desktop version of Word. Each item of the Command bar is summarized in Table 10-1. By default, the toolbar is not displayed, but tap the blue arrows button to the right of Tools, and the toolbar will show or hide.

The Command bar   Tap here to open the toolbar.

FIGURE 10-1 The Pocket Word program window on the Pocket PC (left) and the Microsoft Word program window (right)

NOTE Command bar *is a new term created by Microsoft to refer to the bar at the bottom of the screen on the Pocket PC.*

Menu Item	Function
Edit	Copy, move, or delete text in documents using Cut, Copy, and Paste. Search for and replace words in documents. Change how text in the document looks by selecting fonts and changing paragraph alignment.
View	Control how the document displays by wrapping text to window and enlarging text using Zoom. Change between Writing, Drawing, Typing, and Recording modes.
Tools	Check spelling, count words, and convert digital ink to text. Send the document via infrared or e-mail. Delete the document, and save it using a different filename.

TABLE 10-1 Pocket Word Command Bar Items on a Pocket PC

Spell Check and Word Count With Pocket PC 2002

Spell check and word count are the two features added to Pocket Word in Pocket PC 2002. If you have one of the original Pocket PCs that has not been upgraded, you will not be able to run spell check or word count.

Create, Open, and Save Documents

To start Pocket Word, tap Start | Pocket Word, and the File List View window, shown in Figure 10-2, displays. Tap New to create a blank document in the program window.

In order to create documents using a template, the New Button menu must be enabled on your Pocket PC. To enable the New button, follow these steps:

1. Tap Start | Settings.

2. In the Personal tab, tap Menus.

3. Tap the New Menu tab.

4. Check the box next to Turn On New Button Menu.

5. Tap OK.

Tap here to change folders.

Tap here to change how filenames are sorted.

Pocket Word	◀ 6:27 ❌	
All Folders ▾		Name ▾
A Numbered List	6/3/01	1k
Another copy	6/3/01	5k
Doc1	6/3/01	1k
MEETING PLANNER	6/3/01	1020b
This is a list	6/3/01	760b
WOW	6/2/01	728b

New | ▴ Tools

Tap here to create a new document.

FIGURE 10-2   The Pocket Word File List window on the Pocket PC

When you start Pocket Word, you will notice that to the right of New is a vertical line and up arrow, as shown in the following image:

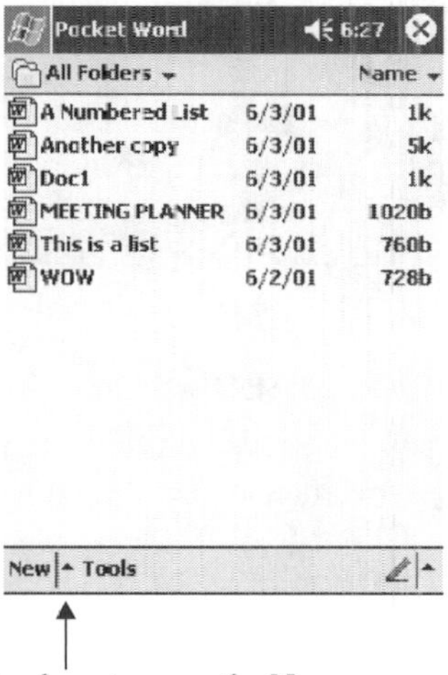

Tap here to open the New pop-up menu.

Tap the up arrow to open a pop-up menu and select a template listed at the top. Four templates come pre-installed: Meeting Notes, Memo, Phone Memo, and To Do.

> **TIP**
>
> *The pop-up menu also contains options for creating the following: Appointment, Contact, E-mail, Excel Workbook, Note, Task, and Word Document. These options are available wherever you see New, enabling you to create these items quickly, regardless of what application is currently running.*

Use the File List View window shown in Figure 10-2 to create new documents or to open, copy, delete, or move existing documents. By default, all documents in the My Documents folder, and any subfolders, will display. If there is a folder on a storage card named My Documents, then its contents, and the contents of its subfolders, will be merged into the list. Tap the down arrow next to All Folders to display the Folders drop-down list, as shown here:

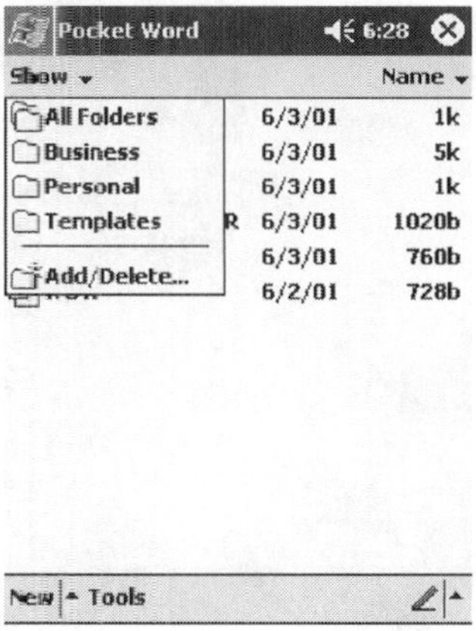

Select a folder name from this list to display its contents. If you tap the Add/Delete item of the drop-down list, you can create, rename, and delete subfolders.

> **TIP**
>
> *Pocket PCs will only look for documents stored in the My Documents folder. If you want your documents on a storage card, it is best to create a My Documents folder on the card and then store the documents in it.*

As you see in Figure 10-2, the files are sorted by name. To sort them by Name, Date, Size, or Type, tap the arrow to the right of Name. Notice that the sort that you select displays on the top line.

To open a document, tap the filename in the list. Tap-and-hold on a filename to display the pop-up menu shown here:

| Create Copy |
| Delete |
| Select All |
| Send via E-mail... |
| Beam File... |
| Rename/Move... |

Tap Create Copy and another copy of the file using the same filename appears with a copy number added to the filename. For example, if you select Create Copy for the file named Foo, then the filename Foo(1) will be added to the list. Tap Delete to delete the file that you selected and tap Rename/Move to bring up a dialog box in which you can specify a new filename, folder, and storage location.

Edit Your Pocket Word Documents

The Pocket Word Edit menu provides the tools for editing text in a document. With the commands in the Edit menu, you copy text, delete text, search for text, and replace text.

TIP   *To count the number of words in a document Tap Tools | Word Count.*

How to ... Create Document Templates

Document templates save time by creating documents that already contain text. Your Pocket PC comes with four templates that are listed in the New pop-up menu. To create your own template and add it to the menu, follow these steps:

1. Start Pocket Word, create a new document, and enter the text that you want in the document every time you use the template.

2. Tap Tools | Save Document As.

3. Enter a name for the template. Tap the Folder drop-down list, select Templates, and then tap OK. You will want to keep the Type as Pocket Word Document and the Location at Main memory. The template can be placed on a storage card, but it will not be available if the card is not inserted in the Pocket PC.

4. Tap OK to close out of the document.

To use your template, tap the up arrow next to New and then tap the name of your template in the pop-up menu. You can also create document templates using Microsoft Word on your desktop computer. Just create a document in Word and save it in the Templates folder, which is in the Pocket PC My Documents folder on the desktop. During the next synchronization, the template will be copied to your Pocket PC. See Chapter 6 for instructions on setting up file synchronization between your Pocket PC and desktop computer.

Copy Text in a Pocket Word Document

To copy or move text within a document, follow these steps:

1. Select the text by tapping-and-holding the beginning of the text to be selected, drag to the end, and release.

2. Tap Edit | Copy to copy text or Edit | Cut to move text.

3. Tap at the location where you want the text to be inserted.

4. Tap Edit | Paste.

TIP *A shortcut on the Pocket PC is to tap-and-hold on the selected text and then choose Copy, Cut, or Paste from the pop-up menu.*

Delete Text in a Pocket Word Document

To delete text from a document, select the text and then tap Edit Clear. To select all of the text in a document, tap Edit | Select All.

If you make an edit that you do not like, you can remove it by selecting Edit | Undo. If you performed multiple edits, continue to select Edit | Undo to remove each edit that was performed. The opposite is Edit | Redo, which restores each edit that was removed using Edit | Undo.

Search for a Text String in a Pocket Word Document

To search for a word or phrase in a document, tap Edit | Find/Replace to open the Find dialog box, as shown on the left:

Enter the search text in the Find What field. If you want to search only for a word, select Match Whole Words Only; if you want to search only for words using a specific case, select Match Case. Once you have entered the text, tap Find. The first instance of the text in the document will be

How to ... Revert to the Previously Saved Document

The Undo command recovers mistakes that you make one at a time. For example, if you enter a line of text in a document and then decide to remove it, tapping Edit | Undo Typing removes the text one character at a time. If you make a number of edits to a document, you might want to cancel them all, but unlike Word 2000, there is no Close menu command or button. To cancel all the changes you made since you opened the document, tap Tools | Revert to Saved and then tap Yes when Pocket Word asks whether you want to undo all document changes.

highlighted, and a bar will appear above the Command bar that contains four buttons, as shown on the right:

Tap Next to move to the next occurrence of the text in the document. Tap the Close button, which looks like an *X,* to stop searching for text.

Replacing text is a similar process. Tap Edit | Find/Replace and then tap the Replace button. Enter the text to be replaced in the Find What field and the new text in the Replace With field. If you want to match whole words, or case, be sure to select the appropriate check boxes and then tap Find. A bar appears with buttons for Next, Replace, Replace All, and Close; the first instance of the text to be replaced is highlighted. To skip the instance and move to the next, tap Next; to replace the text, tap Replace. The text is replaced and the search continues to the next occurrence of the text. If there are no more occurrences, a dialog box displays saying that Pocket Word has finished searching the document. Tap Replace All to replace all occurrences of the text being replaced without a prompt for direction from you.

Check the Spelling in Your Pocket Word Documents

To check the spelling in a document, tap Tools | Spell Check. Questionable words highlight and a pop-up menu appears near the word, as shown on the left:

Tap one of the recommended words at the top of the pop-up menu to replace the highlighted word. If the word is correct, tap Ignore, and the next questionable word will highlight. Tap Ignore All to skip the remaining instances of that word in the document. When you tap Add, the highlighted word is put in the Spell Check Dictionary so that the word will not be highlighted as questionable in the future.

How to ... Edit the Spell Check Dictionary

Words that you add to the Spell Check Dictionary are stored in a file named Custom. The file does not have an extension and it is in the Windows folder on your Pocket PC. It is a text file that you can edit using Notepad on your desktop computer. To edit the file, copy it to your desktop using ActiveSync Explorer, open the file, and add or remove words. Save the file and then copy it back to the Windows folder on your Pocket PC with ActiveSync Explorer. Chapter 7 provides instructions for using ActiveSync Explorer to copy files between a Pocket PC and desktop computer.

Format Your Pocket Word Documents

Text displayed in a document can use different fonts and be aligned left, center, or right. Paragraphs can also be indented in a couple of different ways. To make these changes, use the Format and Paragraph options from the Edit menu.

Apply formatting to existing text by first selecting the text and then choose the desired option. If you specify the formatting that you want before typing text, then anything that you entered will display as specified. Most formats can be specified using the toolbar buttons, as well as through menu selections. The Pocket PC pop-up menu that appears when you tap-and-hold on selected text includes the same Format and Paragraph menu options that are in the Edit menu.

On the right is the Format dialog box on the Pocket PC:

Select fonts and font sizes from the appropriate drop-down list. Select font color from the Line/Font drop-down list. In addition to the standard font styles, you can also select Highlight, which emulates yellow highlighting over the text, and Strikethrough, which runs a line through text.

To specify paragraph formatting, select Edit | Paragraph and the Paragraph dialog box shown on the left appears:

Align text Left, Center, or Right by selecting from the Alignment drop-down list. To indent the margins, use the arrows in the Left and Right fields to change the indent value. If you want the first line to be indented, or a hanging indent, select it from the Special field; the size of the indent is specified in the field directly beneath the Special field. Select the Bulleted check box to create a bulleted list. Numbered lists cannot be created on the Pocket PC.

> **TIP** *You can work around the lack of support for numbered lists in Pocket Word by creating a document template that contains the numbers 1 through 10 down the left side. Save it with the filename Numbered List and store it in the Templates folder. Then, to create a new document with numbered lists, start Pocket Word and select the Numbered List template in the New pop-up menu.*

Use the Four Pocket Word Modes

The View menu is primarily for switching between the four modes of Pocket Word: Writing, Drawing, Typing, and Recording. Each of the modes can be used separately or combined to create documents that contain handwriting, drawings, text, and recordings. By default, Pocket Word starts in Typing mode. In Typing mode, you enter text into the document using the soft input panel, and text appears in the body of the document above the panel.

Express Yourself with the Pocket Word Writing Mode

Switching to Writing mode enables you to write directly on the screen with the writing displayed in digital ink, as shown in Figure 10-3. The screen background changes from blank to ruled, and the toolbar changes to include additional buttons. As you write toward the bottom of the screen, Pocket Word automatically scrolls to the next page so that you can continue writing. Most of the Edit menu functions work in Writing mode, and the toolbar provides shortcuts to the formatting options. To select handwriting, tap-and-hold the stylus on the screen, wait until the cursor appears, and then drag the stylus across the writing that you want to select. Once the text is selected, you can then edit it, such as cutting and pasting, or apply formatting. For example, if you want to change the ink color, select Edit | Format, tap the Line/Font drop-down list, and select a color.

The Pocket Word Tools | Recognize command converts handwriting to text. Use the command to convert the entire document, or select a portion of the document and then use the command. To correct words not properly recognized, tap-and-hold the word and select Alternates; a list of possible words will display. Tap the correct word in the list to replace the incorrect word.

Pocket Word Drawing Mode

In Drawing mode, you use the stylus to draw on the screen. Gridlines appear to help you draw. Once you lift the stylus off the screen, a drawing box appears, indicating the boundaries of the

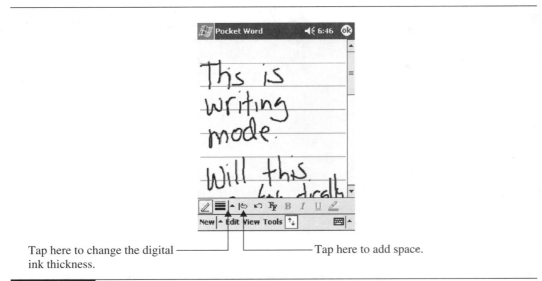

Tap here to change the digital ink thickness.

Tap here to add space.

FIGURE 10-3   Writing Mode in Pocket Word

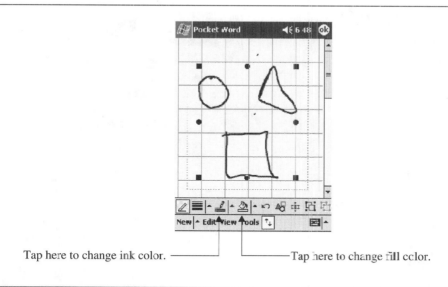

Tap here to change ink color. ─────────────────────┘   └─────────────Tap here to change fill color.

FIGURE 10-4   Drawing Mode in Pocket Word

drawing. Additional lines that touch the drawing box become part of the drawing. The toolbar, shown in Figure 10-4, provides shortcuts to formatting options. Tap the Ink Color button to change the color of what is drawn on the screen. To select an object, tap-and-hold it until the cross appears, then lift the stylus; or follow these steps:

1. Tap-and-hold the stylus on the screen.

2. Drag the stylus across the object that you want to select.

3. Lift the stylus.

Little squares and circles surround a selected object, as shown here:

Once an object is selected, a variety of changes can be made, as described in Table 10-2.

The options in Table 10-2 are also possible for multiple objects. To select multiple objects, press-and-hold Action while tapping each object. Three additional changes are available for multiple objects, as described in Table 10-3.

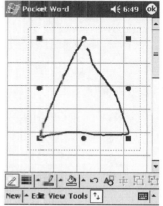

To	Do
Switch from Drawing to Edit mode	Tap the Pen button on the toolbar.
Resize the object	Tap-and-hold one of the square boxes around the object and then drag the stylus to change the size.
Rotate the object	Tap-and-hold one of the circles around the object and then drag the stylus in the direction to rotate.
Change the line color	Tap Edit | Format and select the color from the Line/Font drop-down list, or tap the up arrow next to the Line button on the toolbar and select a color.
Change the fill color	Tap Edit | Format and select the color from the Fill color drop-down list, or tap the up arrow next to the Fill button on the toolbar and select a color.
Change the line thickness	Tap Edit | Format and select an option from the Pen Weight drop-down list, or tap the up arrow next to the Line button on the toolbar and select an option.
Undo an edit	Tap Edit | Undo Style, or the Undo button on the toolbar.
Create a copy of the object	Tap-and-hold the object and select Create Copy from the pop-up menu.
Make the shape a perfect rectangle, circle, triangle, or line	Tap-and-hold the object, select Shape, and then select the desired shape.

TABLE 10-2 Pocket Word Drawing Mode Formats

Be Heard with the Pocket Word Recording Mode

Use the Pocket Word Recording mode to embed voice recordings into a document. Recordings are made by either using the Recording Mode toolbar or with the Record Hardware button of the Pocket PC. To use the Recording mode, follow these steps:

1. Tap Edit \| Recording.
2. Tap Record on the toolbar.
3. Begin speaking into the microphone after the beep.
4. Stop recording by tapping Stop.

To	Do
Align objects left, right, top or bottom, and center vertically or horizontally	Tap the Alignment button on the toolbar and select the option.
Group objects	Tap the Group Objects button on the toolbar.
Ungroup objects	Tap the Ungroup Objects button on the toolbar.

TABLE 10-3 Drawing Mode Formats for Multiple Objects

Using the Record Hardware button is easier, just follow these steps:

1. Press-and-hold Record Hardware until you hear a beep.

2. Continue to hold the button and speak into the Pocket PC microphone.

3. Release the button to stop recording.

Two beeps will sound, and the new recording appears in the document as an Embedded icon, as shown here:

Recording Mode toolbar ⟶

Tap the Embedded icon to play the recording and use the toolbar buttons to control the playback.

Text can be added to the document while in Recording mode, enabling you to annotate the recordings. Recordings may be played in either the Typing or Writing modes, but not in the Drawing mode. If the document is uploaded to a desktop computer, the recordings can be played in Microsoft Word by double-clicking the Embedded icon.

Use the View Menu to Change the Screen Display

The View menu is also used to control the screen display. To hide or show the toolbar, tap View | Toolbar. Turn Wrap to Window on or off by tapping View | Wrap to Window. Use View | Zoom to change the display size by selecting from one of the five settings in the menu.

Share Documents Easily with Other Users

Pocket Word makes it easy to share documents with other people by including the capability to send documents via infrared or e-mail. Use infrared to send a document to another Windows Powered device by following these steps:

1. If the receiving device is a Handheld PC, open Windows Explorer and tap File | Receive. The Handheld PC will not recognize the document as a Pocket Word file, but rather as an Inkwriter file.

2. If the receiving device is another Pocket PC, tap Start | Programs | Infrared Receive.

3. On the sending device, which has a document open in Pocket Word, tap Tools | Beam Document and line up the infrared ports.

NOTE *If your device is running the first release of Windows for Pocket PCs, tap Tools | Send Via Infrared.*

Once the two devices recognize each other, the file will transfer to the receiving device. When the transfer is complete, the sending device will indicate that one file has been sent, and a Close button will appear, which you tap to return to Pocket Word.

To send a document via e-mail, tap Tools | Send Via E-mail, and a new e-mail message will open with the document as an attachment. Enter an e-mail address, subject, and message, and then tap Send. Inbox will send the message the next time you connect to the Internet and retrieve e-mail.

Copy and Delete Pocket Word Documents

To create another copy of the document currently open in Pocket Word, tap Tools | Save Document As, and the Save As dialog box will display. Enter a new filename, select the location where you want the file stored and tap OK. Tap Cancel to close the dialog box and not save the document.

Tap Tools | Delete Document and then tap Yes on the Confirmation dialog box to delete the currently open document. The document deletes and you will return to the Pocket Word List View window.

Wrapping Up

Because Pocket Word does not have all the features of Microsoft Word, I use it primarily for creating text, and then transfer documents to a PC for formatting. As you have seen in this chapter, Pocket Word has all the features needed for creating new documents, including spell check and word count.

Spreadsheets are important documents for people who analyze financial data. In the next chapter you will learn how to use Pocket Excel to create and edit spreadsheets on your Pocket PC.

How to ... **Add Fonts to Your Pocket PC**

Like Windows 2000, Windows CE uses True Type fonts, and each Windows CE device comes with six different fonts. You can add fonts to your Pocket PC by simply copying the font file from your desktop computer to the device. On your desktop computer, the default location for your computer fonts is the \Windows\Fonts folder. If you want to transfer a font from your desktop computer to your Pocket PC, use Windows Explorer and ActiveSync to copy a font file to the \Windows\Fonts folder on your Pocket PC. Once the font is copied, do a soft reset and then start Pocket Word. Check the Fonts drop-down list to verify that the font is now available. See Chapter 7 for directions on how to copy files from your desktop computer to the Pocket PC using ActiveSync.

Chapter 11 Crunch Numbers

How to...

- Create Pocket Excel workbooks
- Add data and formulas to workbooks
- Edit and format workbooks
- Password-protect workbooks
- Make calculations using the Pocket PC calculator

Of all the types of software that have been written for personal computers, spreadsheets may have had the most impact. Indeed, it wasn't until VisiCalc and Lotus 1-2-3 that businesses began to use personal computers, perhaps launching the entire personal computer industry. The appeal of the spreadsheet is its tremendous versatility, such as tracking hours, managing budgets, or creating *what if* scenarios.

Pocket Excel provides similar versatility for your Pocket PC. In this chapter, you'll learn how to use Pocket Excel to create workbooks that crunch numbers. You'll learn how these workbooks can be transferred to a desktop computer, beamed via infrared to other Windows-powered devices, or e-mailed to your friends via the Internet. Because workbooks may contain sensitive information, you'll also learn how to protect your data by assigning a password to workbooks. Finally, for those times when all you need to do is add some numbers, you'll learn how to use the Pocket PC Calculator application.

Pocket Excel on the Pocket PC

Pocket Excel is similar to the version of Excel that you run on your desktop computer, except that you cannot create graphs and charts, and you cannot print spreadsheets. Nor does it support macros or the Visual Basic for Applications programming language. Yet, like Excel, Pocket Excel spreadsheets can have 256 columns, but only 16,384 rows—versus the 65,536 in Excel. Nonetheless, Pocket Excel features do allow you to create spreadsheets that will meet the majority of your needs. In this section, you'll learn about Pocket Excel for the Pocket PC and how to use it to create and save workbooks, work with data, password-protect workbooks, and send workbooks via e-mail or infrared.

Figure 11-1 shows the differences between the Pocket Excel program window on the Pocket PC (left) and Excel on a desktop computer (right). At the bottom of the screen on the left is the Command bar, which contains menu items similar to the Menu bar on the desktop version of Excel. Each item of the Command bar is summarized in Table 11-1. By default, the toolbar is not displayed, but tapping the blue arrow button to the right of Tools will display or hide the toolbar.

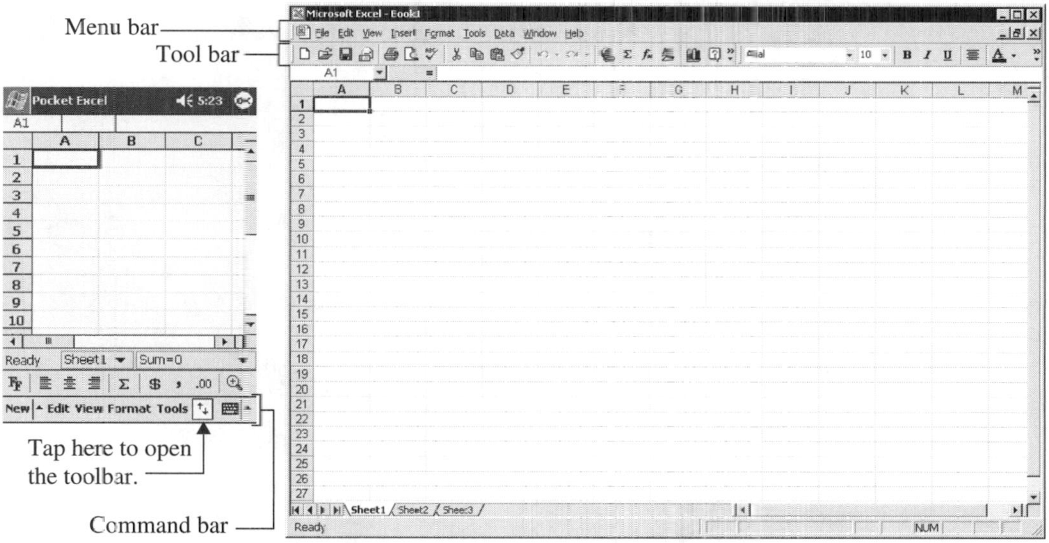

Menu bar
Tool bar
Tap here to open the toolbar.
Command bar
Pocket Excel
Microsoft Excel - Book1

FIGURE 11-1 The Pocket Excel program window on a Pocket PC and the Excel program window on a desktop computer

Menu Item	Function
Edit	Copies, moves, or deletes data in spreadsheets using Cut, Copy, and Paste. Searches for and replaces data in spreadsheets. Assigns passwords to workbooks.
View	Controls how the spreadsheet displays by turning scroll bars, the Status bar, and row and column headings on or off. Also includes the commands to split spreadsheets, freeze panes, display the spreadsheet as a full screen, and zoom the display.
Format	Changes the appearance of data in cells, along with the appearance of rows and columns. Also includes commands for adding, renaming, and modifying sheets, as well as inserting and deleting cells.
Tools	Sorts and filters data. Inserts functions and symbols, and defines cell names. Sends workbooks via infrared and e-mail, and names and deletes workbooks.

TABLE 11-1 Pocket Excel Command Bar Options

Start Pocket Excel

To start Pocket Excel, tap Start | Programs | Pocket Excel, and the List View window, as shown in the following image:

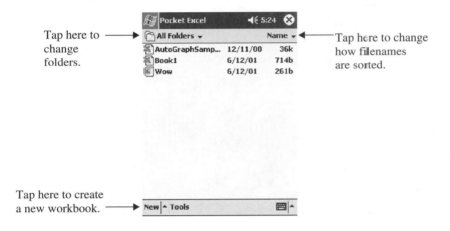

Tap here to change folders.

Tap here to change how filenames are sorted.

Tap here to create a new workbook.

How to ... Graph Your Pocket Excel Data

While Pocket Excel does not create graphs, you can generate graphs on your Pocket PC from Pocket Excel data by using AutoGraph from DeveloperOne. To create a graph with AutoGraph, first select and copy data in Pocket Excel, and then paste it into AutoGraph. You can then create bar, column, descriptive bar, pie, XY scatter/line, line, and stock-trend graphs. After you create a graph, it can be saved to a bitmap file, or copied to the clipboard and pasted in Pocket Word or a graphics editor. More information and a trial version of AutoGraph are available at http://www.developerone.com.

SpreadCE from Bye Design Ltd. is a spreadsheet program that you can use instead of Pocket Excel. It provides the same functionality described in this chapter, plus it adds macros and graphs. Unlike AutoGraph, the charts you create in SpreadCE stay within the spreadsheet, and they change as you update the data for the chart. You can open and save Pocket Excel files in SpreadCE, but charts will only be saved in Excel 97 format—which is the default file format for the program. More information and a trial version of this program are available at http://www.byedesign.freeserve.co.uk.

> **NOTE**   *If you start Pocket Excel with no workbooks stored in the My Documents folder, the program automatically creates a blank workbook and skips the List view.*

Use the List View window to create new workbooks or to open, copy, delete, or move existing workbooks. By default, all workbooks in the My Documents folder, and any subfolders, will display. If there is a folder on a storage card named My Documents, then its contents, and the contents of its subfolders, will be merged into the list. Tap the down arrow next to All Folders to display the folders drop-down list, as shown here on the right.

Select a folder name from this list to display its contents. If you tap the Add/Delete option of the drop-down list, you can create, rename, and delete subfolders.

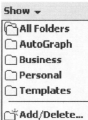

> **TIP**   *Pocket PCs will only look for documents stored in the My Documents folder. If you want your documents on a storage card, it is best to create a My Documents folder on the card, and then store the documents in it.*

To open a workbook, tap the filename in the list. Tap-and-hold a filename to display the pop-up menu shown at left.

| Create Copy |
| Delete |
| Select All |
| Send via E-mail... |
| Beam File... |
| Rename/Move... |

Tap Create Copy to place another copy of the file, using the same filename with a copy number added to the filename. For example, if you select Create Copy for a file named Foo, the filename Foo(1) will be added to the list. Tap Delete to delete the file that you selected, and tap Rename/Move to open a dialog box in which you can specify a new filename, folder, and storage location.

Create a New Workbook

Tap New on the Command bar in Pocket Excel to create a blank workbook, as shown in the following image:

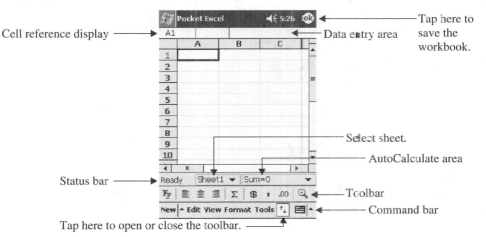

In order to create workbooks using a template, the New Button menu must be enabled on your Pocket PC. To enable the New Button menu, follow these steps:

1. Tap Start | Settings.
2. On the Personal tab, tap Menus.
3. Tap the New Menu tab.
4. Select the check box next to Turn On New Button Menu.
5. Tap OK.

When you start Pocket Excel, you will notice that to the right of New is a vertical line and an up arrow. Tap the up arrow to open a pop-up menu, and select a template listed at the top. One template, Vehicle Mileage Log, comes pre-installed on your Pocket PC.

Save Workbooks

When you tap OK in Pocket Excel, the current workbook writes to the My Documents folder and is given a default filename, unless you are editing a previously saved workbook. To assign a filename to a workbook, tap Tools | Save Workbook As to open the Save As dialog box. Enter a filename, select a file type and storage location, and then tap OK.

TIP *To add your own templates to the New Button menu, create a workbook, tap Tools | Save Workbook As, select the Templates folder, select the Pocket Excel Template type, and then tap OK.*

Normally, you should leave the file type as Pocket Excel Workbook. If the file is synchronized with a desktop computer, it will be converted to the Excel file format. However, if you write the file to a storage card that will be read on a PC that does not have a copy of ActiveSync installed, then you will need to specify an Excel file type corresponding to the version of Excel on that PC.

TIP *When you tap OK in Pocket Excel, the List view will replace the application program window. To rename a workbook in the List view, tap-and-hold on a workbook name, select Rename/Move from the pop-up menu, and then enter a filename.*

Move Around in Workbooks

Spreadsheets tend to grow in size, making it difficult to quickly move through cells. The Define Name command and the Go To command help with this problem. By using the Define Name command, you can give a cell a name, and then use the Go To command to move the cursor to that cell.

To assign a name to a cell, follow these steps:

1. Tap on a cell to select it.

2. Tap Tools | Define Name to open the Define Name dialog box, as shown on the right.

3. Enter a name in the Names In Workbook field.

4. Tap Add.

5. Tap OK to close the dialog box.

After the name is assigned, it will appear in the cell name display area. If you want to assign a name to a range of cells, select the range in step 1, and then enter the name in the Names In Workbook field.

To use the name with the Go To command, first tap Tools | Go To to open the Go To dialog box, as shown in the following image.

Select the Cell Reference Or Name radio button, enter the name in the field, and then tap OK. The cursor will move to the cell, or range of cells, assigned to that name. The Current Region radio button selects the region of cells around the current cell. Cell references also work with the Go To command. For example, entering **F18** in the dialog box moves the cursor to cell F18 in the spreadsheet.

> **TIP** *The cell reference display area can also be used to move to cells within a sheet. Tap the display, enter the name or reference, and then tap ENTER on the soft input panel.*

The Go To command works across all spreadsheets in a workbook. To use the Go To command to move to a cell reference in another sheet, enter the sheet name, an exclamation mark, and the cell reference in the Go To dialog box. For example, to move to cell A1 in Sheet1, enter **Sheet1!A1**.

> **TIP** *The Go To dialog box retains the last entered cell reference or name, and can be used to quickly switch between cells. For example, if the cursor is currently in cell F18, and you enter **A1** to move to that cell, the next time the Go To dialog box opens, it will contain F18. To quickly switch back to it, just tap OK.*

A workbook may contain more than one sheet, and the sheet selector in the Status bar is available to move between them. Tap the down arrow in the sheet selector to display a pop-up list of the sheet names, and then tap the name of the destination sheet.

Add Data and Formulas to Workbooks

Entering data into Pocket Excel is a simple process. First, select the cell in which you want to enter data, open the soft input panel, write the data, and then tap ENTER or move to another cell. If the cell is not visible on the screen, use the Go To command by selecting Tools | Go To, as described in the preceding section.

TIP *Entering data on a Pocket PC is easier when using the keyboard buttons on the soft input panel. Chapter 3 contains information on how to use these buttons.*

What is written appears in the data entry area, and as the following image shows, three buttons appear to the left of that area for canceling the entry, entering the value in the cell, and opening the Insert Function dialog box:

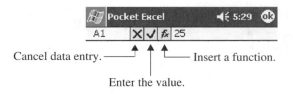

Cancel data entry. ——— ┗━ Insert a function.

Enter the value.

Use Fill to Quickly Enter Data

To quickly enter a series of data in a range of cells, enter the first value in a cell, select the range, and tap Edit | Fill to open the Fill dialog box, as shown on the right:

To copy the value entered in all cells in the range, tap the Copy radio button, select the fill direction from the Fill drop-down list, and then tap OK. The value will be copied into all the cells in the range.

TIP *The fill direction is based on the range. If a column of cells is selected, then the direction is up or down; but if a row of cells is selected, the direction is left or right.*

If you want the range to contain a series of data, such as the numbers one through ten, follow these steps:

1. Select a cell and enter the starting value.

2. Select the range of cells starting with the cell selected in step 1.

3. Tap Edit | Fill.

4. Tap the Series radio button.

5. Select the direction from the Fill drop-down list.

6. Select the series type:

   ■ **AutoFill**   Select AutoFill to create a series based on the contents of the first cell. The first value must be a day of the week or month, or, text followed by a number. For example, a range starting with Value1 will be filled with Value2, Value3, and so on.

- **Date**   Select Date to create a series of dates. Specify which part of the date to increment by selecting Day, Month, or Year from the drop-down list. The series will increment by the amount entered in the Step Value field.

- **Number**   Select Number to create a series of numbers that is incremented by the value entered in the Step Value field. For example, to create a series of even numbers, the first value must be even, with a step value of two.

7.   Tap OK to create the series.

The starting value of a date series must contain at least a month and a date. Other values will generate unexpected results.

Enter Formulas

Every formula begins with the equal sign plus one or more of the following: values, cell references, name references, operators, and functions. The result of the formula displays in the cell in which it was entered. For example, if cell A1 contains the value 10, cell B1 the value 5, and C1 the formula =A1−B1, then the number 5 will display in cell C1.

To enter a formula, first select the cell that you want to contain the result, enter the equal sign, enter a combination of one of the following, and then tap ENTER:

- **Values**   These are otherwise known as constants. They can be numbers, characters, text, or dates.

- **Cell references**   The two-character identifier made by the intersection of the column and row headers. For example, G6 is the cell at the intersection of column G and row 6. An example of cell references in a formula is =A1+B1. To use cell references of multiple sheets in a formula, add the sheet name and an exclamation mark before the reference. For example, the formula =Sheet1!A1+Sheet2!A1 adds the values in the A1 cell of both sheets and places the result in the selected cell.

- **Name references**   Names that you assign to a cell using Tools | Define, as described earlier in this chapter. An example of a name reference in a formula is =Assets−Liability. Name references of multiple sheets can also be used in formulas, such as, =Sheet1!Total+ Sheet2!Total.

- **Operators**   Operators are arithmetic, comparison, or reference. Arithmetic operators perform basic mathematical operations such as addition, subtraction, multiplication, and division. Comparison operators compare two values, and the result is either true or false. Reference operators combine a range of cells for calculations.

- **Functions**   Functions are predefined formulas that return a result, based on constants or references passed to it as arguments. For example, the formula =POWER(2,3) displays the value 8. If 2 were entered in cell A1, and 3 in cell B1, the formula =POWER(A1,B1) would also display the value 8.

11

Pocket Excel supports many functions, and you can find a list of the functions in Online Help. If you have Excel on your desktop computer, you can find more information about the functions in its Online Help.

NOTE   *Pocket Excel does not support all of the functions available in the desktop version of Excel.*

Fortunately, the Insert Function dialog box is available to assist in adding functions to formulas. Tap Tools | Insert Function to open the Insert Function dialog box, as shown on the right.

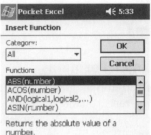

TIP   *Another way to open the Insert Function dialog box is to tap Function in the data entry area.*

The functions are listed in the middle of the dialog box; to narrow the list of options, select an item from the Category drop-down list. Tap a function to add it to the formula in the data entry area. When you add a function to a formula, it will include a template between the parentheses for its arguments, e.g., POWER(*number,power*). The template items must be replaced with either a value or a reference, e.g., POWER(2,3).

TIP   *A description of each function displays in the Insert Function dialog box when you tap a function name in the list.*

Some functions return a result based on a range of values. Use the reference operators, such as A1:A10 and A1, B1, C1, to identify a range. You could type all the references, but it is quicker to select the range using the pointing device, as described in the following steps:

1. Begin entering the formula.

2. Select a function that takes a range of numbers as an argument. The template of these functions contains three periods, such as, COUNT(*value1,value2,...*).

3. Delete the template items of the function in the data entry area.

4. Select the range of values in the spreadsheet. As you do, the cell references will appear in the data entry area.

5. Tap ENTER.

TIP   *If a name is assigned to a range of cells using the Tools | Define Name command, then that name can be used with functions that require a range of values.*

The most common function that you will use is Sum, and the AutoSum button on the toolbar provides a quick way to insert the sum of a range of cells into a spreadsheet. To use AutoSum, follow these steps:

1. Select the cell in which you want to insert the sum.

2. Tap AutoSum.

3. Select the range of cells to be summed.

4. Tap ENTER.

> **TIP**   *AutoSum automatically selects a range of cells adjacent to the selected cell. The selection starts with the first cell above the selected cell, and continues until finding a blank cell. If the cell immediately above is blank, then a range of adjacent cells to the right will be selected.*

Change the View in Workbooks

Pocket Excel provides multiple ways to change the view of a workbook. These commands are particularly useful with the small displays of the Pocket PC. The horizontal scroll bar, the vertical scrollbar, the Status bar, and row and column heads are turned on and off by selecting the appropriate command from the View menu. Turning off these elements allows more of the spreadsheet to display in the program window.

Split the Screen

By splitting the screen display horizontally or vertically, you can see different parts of the spreadsheet at the same time. To split the screen, tap View | Split, and the screen will split above and to the left of the selected cell, as shown here on the right.

If you want to split the screen horizontally, select a cell in column A, and then tap View | Split. To split the screen vertically, select a cell in row 1, and then tap View | Split. To remove the split, tap View | Remove Split.

Adjust the screen split by moving the horizontal and vertical bars. To make the adjustment, tap-and-hold the stylus on the bar, and then drag it in the direction you want it to move.

Freeze Panes

Freezing panes locks a column or row in place while you scroll through the rest of the spreadsheet. This is typically done to display column and row heads of data beyond the screen. To freeze panes on a spreadsheet, first select the cell where you want to freeze panes, and then tap View | Freeze Panes. All rows above the current cell, and all columns to the left of the current cell, are frozen. Lines will appear above and to the left of the cell, indicating the location of the panes. To unfreeze panes, tap View | Unfreeze Panes.

Change the Screen Display

The Zoom command changes the display size of items in the spreadsheet, allowing more rows and columns to display. To zoom the display, tap View | Zoom, and then select the magnification.

Create a custom zoom setting by tapping View | Zoom | Custom, and then enter a value in the Custom dialog box, as shown on the right.

> Pocket Excel   ◀€ 5:35 ⓞⓚ
> **Custom Zoom**
> Zoom: 100% ◀ ▶

Zoom settings apply to the entire workbook, and they are saved when you save the workbook.

To display even more columns and rows, tap View | Full Screen. All that appears are the cell reference and data entry areas, along with the spreadsheet rows and columns. To exit the Full Screen view, tap Restore.

Adjust Column Width and Row Height

Changing the size of columns and rows will display more or less of the data that they contain. To change the size of a column, tap-and-hold the stylus on the right edge of the column head, and then drag the stylus left or right. To adjust the row height, with a stylus, tap-and-hold the bottom edge of the row head, and then drag the stylus up or down. Another way to change row height and column width is to tap Format | Cells, enter values in the Row Height and Column Width fields, and then tap OK.

Automatically adjust the size of a column to the width of its longest value by double-tapping the right edge of the column head, or tap Format | Column | AutoFit. To size a row automatically, double-tap the bottom edge of the row head, or tap Format | Row | AutoFit.

Hide Rows or Columns

Hiding a row or column removes it from the display, but does not delete the contents from the workbook. To hide a row or column, follow these steps:

1. Select a cell in the row or column to be hidden.
2. To hide a row, tap Format | Row | Hide.
3. To hide a column, tap Format | Column | Hide.

To display a hidden row or column, follow these steps:

1. Tap Tools | Go To.
2. Type a reference for a cell, such as E4, in the hidden row or column.
3. Tap OK.
4. To display the hidden row, tap Format | Row | Unhide.
5. To display the hidden column, tap Format | Column | Unhide.

Insert, Rename, Move, and Delete Sheets

By default, each new workbook contains three sheets. To insert another sheet into a workbook, tap Format | Modify Sheets. Tap Insert, enter a name for the sheet, and then tap OK. The Modify Sheets dialog box is also used to rename, delete, and move sheets.

How to ...   View Your Spreadsheet in Landscape

By now you have probably thought to yourself, "Wouldn't it be great to view a spreadsheet in landscape?" Indeed, by default, the Pocket PC portrait display only shows three columns in Pocket Excel, though spreadsheets tend to have many more columns. If you own one of the original HP Jornada 540, 545, 547, or 548 Pocket PCs, you can take advantage of a hidden feature that rotates the screen in landscape. First, if your Jornada Pocket PC has password-protection turned on, turn it off and then follow these steps:

1. Hold down Action.

2. Tap-and-hold the time display in the upper right-hand corner of the screen.

3. Tap Run on the pop-up menu.

4. Type **rotate r** in the Run dialog box, and then tap OK.

5. Reset your Pocket PC.

6. Realign the touch screen by holding the power button down until the Align Screen window displays.

Repeat these steps to switch the display back to portrait mode. Newer HP Jornada Pocket PCs may not have this hidden feature.

Two software developers have created programs that enable you to switch the display to landscape on other Pocket PCs. Both programs also increase the screen resolution by changing the way pixels display on the screen. Higher resolutions display text smaller, and therefore show more information; but you might find text harder to read, so the programs provide Zoom and Pan functions. JS Landscape from Jimmy Software runs on the Casio and the color Compaq iPAQ Pocket PCs, but does not run on HP Jornada Pocket PCs. You will find information about JS Landscape at http://www.jimmysoftware.com. The Nyditot Virtual Display provides higher resolutions than JS Landscape and runs on HP Jornada Pocket PCs. You will find information about Nyditot Virtual Display at http://www.nyditot.com.

To rename a sheet, select it in the sheets list, tap Rename, enter a new name, and then tap OK. To delete a sheet, select it in the sheets list and then tap Delete. To move a sheet, select it in the sheets list, and then tap Move Up or Move Down to move the sheet in the list.

Edit Data in Workbooks

As each cell is selected, its contents display in the data entry area. To edit the contents, place the cursor in the area by tapping the area, and then use the soft input panel to edit the data. If you

Tap-and-Hold is New With Pocket PC 2002

Pocket PC 2002 adds tap-and-hold to Pocket Excel. When you tap-and-hold anywhere in a spreadsheet, a pop-up menu appears for Cut, Copy, Paste, Insert, Delete, Clear, and Format Cells. This pop-up menu is not available in Pocket PC 2000.

intend to replace the contents of a cell, just select it and begin writing, and the contents are replaced.

 If you decide that you do not want the edit after it is made, restore the previous contents by using the Edit | Undo command.

Move Cell Contents

Use the following steps to move the contents of a cell or range:

1. Select the cell or range.
2. Tap Edit | Cut.
3. Select the cell in which you want to paste the data.
4. Tap Edit | Paste.

Copy Cell Contents

The processes for copying the contents of a cell or range are similar; just follow these steps:

1. Select the cell or range.
2. Tap Edit | Copy.
3. Select the cell in which you want to paste the data. For a range, select the upper-left cell.
4. Tap Edit | Paste.

If you only want to paste formulas, values, formats, or everything except borders, select Edit | Paste Special in step 4 of the preceding list to display the Paste Special dialog box, as shown in the illustration on the right.

Tap the radio button of an option and then tap OK.

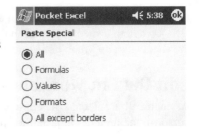

> TIP   *The cell or range selected during a copy operation remains selected until you perform another copy. With this feature, you can paste multiple copies of a selection in the workbook.*

If you want to copy the contents of a cell or range to adjacent cells, use the Edit | Fill command by carrying out the following steps:

1. Select the cell or range containing the data and the adjacent destination cells.
2. Tap Edit | Fill.
3. Tap the Copy radio button to select the fill type.
4. Select the direction of the destination cells from the Fill Direction drop-down list.
5. Tap OK.

Find or Replace Cell Contents

To find a number or text in a cell value or formula, tap Edit | Find/Replace to open the Find dialog box, as shown in the image on the right, and then follow these steps:

1. Enter a value in the Find What field.
2. Select the Match Case or Match Entire Cells check boxes as needed.
3. Specify whether to look in the cell values or formulas from the Look In drop-down list.
4. Tap OK.

To replace a number or text in a cell value or formula, tap Edit | Find/Replace to open the Find dialog box, and then tap Replace to open the Replace dialog box, as shown in the following image.

Enter values in the Find What and Replace With fields, select the Match Case or Match Entire Cells check boxes as needed, and then tap Find. The first instance of the value being searched for is highlighted, and a toolbar appears with buttons for Next, Replace, Replace All, and Close. Tap the appropriate button on the toolbar, or tap Close to stop the search.

Clear Cell Contents

To clear the contents of a selected cell or range, tap Edit | Clear and select one of the following options:

- **Contents**   Removes the data in the cell, but not the format of the cell.

- ■ **Formats**　Removes the format of the cell, but not the data.
- ■ **All**　Removes the data in the cell and the format of the cell.

If you want to clear the entire contents of a column or row, first select a cell in the row or column, and then tap Format | Delete Cells to open the following Delete Cells dialog box.

Tap either Entire Row or Entire Column, and then tap OK. When a column is deleted, its contents are replaced with the contents of the column to the right. The contents of a deleted row are replaced with the contents of the row immediately below it.

The Shift Cells Left and Shift Cells Up options specify how the contents of a selected cell or range are replaced. For example, if you select cells G3, H3, and I3, and then select Shift Cells Up, the contents in cells G4, H4, and I4 will replace the contents of the selected cells.

Insert Cells

The Format | Insert Cells command inserts a row or column in the location of the current cell. When you select the command, the Insert Cells dialog box displays, as shown in the following image:

When you insert a column, the contents of the column shift to the right and rows shift down. Selecting Shift Cells Right or Shift Cells Down specifies the direction that the selected cell or range will move when the cells are inserted.

Format Data in Workbooks

Pocket Excel provides a variety of ways to format the display of data in a workbook. Select a cell, or a range of cells, and then tap Format | Cells to open the Format Cells dialog box, shown next:

With this dialog box, you can change the cell size, format the display of numbers, alignment, font, and borders (and fills) by making changes in the tabs and then tapping OK.

> **TIP** *Tap a row or column head to select the entire row or column, and then change the formatting for the entire selection.*

Change the Cell Size

The Size tab has fields for the row height and column width in pixels. Changing the values of these fields changes the entire row or column of the current cell. The default row height is 12.75 pixels and the default column width is 9.00 pixels.

> **TIP** *You can also change the row height or column width right on the spreadsheet. To change row eight, tap-and-hold the line underneath the row number and drag up or down. To change the column width, tap-and-hold the line to the right of the column letter and drag left or right.*

Format Numbers

Ten predefined formats exist for numbers: Number, Currency, Accounting, Date, Time, Percentage, Fraction, Scientific, Text, and General. You can also customize the format of numbers. By default, every number in a spreadsheet has a general format. To apply a format, first select a cell or range, select a format from the Category list, configure the format, and then tap OK. As you change the settings, a sample of the format will display in the dialog box. The following list summarizes each number format:

- **Number** Changes the display to show the number of decimal places specified. Negative numbers display based on the format selected from the Negative Numbers drop-down list. To include a 1,000 separator, check the Use 1000 Separator box.

- **Currency** Adds the currency symbol to the display when Use Currency Symbol is checked. The symbol is based on the settings that you define using the Regional Settings icon in Pocket PC Settings. This format also defines the number of decimal places and negative numbers.

- **Accounting** Adds the currency symbol and decimal places to the display. Negative numbers are formatted using parentheses and cannot change.

- **Date** Enables you to change the date in 11 different ways by selecting the format from the list. When you enter a value into a cell that contains a number, followed by a forward slash and then another number, Pocket Excel will automatically assume you are entering a date. By default, the date will appear as specified in the Pocket PC Regional settings.

- ■ **Time**   Has six different formats, which you select from the list. When you enter a value into a cell that contains a number, followed by a colon and then another number, Pocket Excel will automatically assume you are entering a time. The default format is specified in the Pocket PC Regional settings.

- ■ **Percentage**   Adds the percent symbol at the end of a number, and you select the number of decimal places in the Decimal Places field.

- ■ **Fraction**   Changes the display of a calculated value, such as =1/4 from a decimal of 0.25 to a fraction. To specify the number of digits in the fraction, select from the Type field. To enter a fraction in a cell, the fraction must be preceded by an equal sign; otherwise, the value will be treated as a date.

- ■ **Scientific**   Displays the value in scientific notation, using the number of decimal places that you specify.

- ■ **Text**   Forces the contents of a cell to be formatted as text, even when a number is in the cell.

Create a Custom Format   If none of the pre-existing formats meet your needs, you can create a custom format by creating a template using format codes. Pocket Excel includes several predefined templates that you can select and customize. The templates contain four sections of format codes, which are separated by semicolons. The sections define positive numbers, negative numbers, zero values, and text, in that order. If only two sections are specified, the first is used for positive numbers and zeros, and the second for negative numbers and text. When only one section is specified, it is applied to all numbers. To skip a section, include the ending semicolon for that section. Pocket Excel uses the same format codes as Excel, and you can find the codes in the Excel Online Help.

Change Alignment

To align cell contents, first select the cells to be changed, open the Format Cells dialog box, and tap the Align tab, as shown in the illustration on the right.

Options in the Horizontal group change the position of values left to right within the cell, and options in the Vertical group change the position of values top to bottom within the cell.

NOTE   *Unless you change the row height, you will not notice much change when selecting vertical alignment options.*

If you enter text that is longer than the cell width, it will not display completely within the cell. To see the complete text in the cell, select Wrap Text in the Align tab.

Change Font Settings

The Font tab of the Format Cells dialog box, as shown in the illustration on the right, provides settings to change the display of text or numbers.

To change the font, first select the cells, tap Format | Cells, tap the Font tab, select the changes, and then tap OK.

Change the font by selecting a font from the Font drop-down list. Selecting a value from the Size drop-down list changes the font size, and selecting the appropriate check boxes sets the font styles to Bold, Italic, and Underline. To change font colors, select a color from the Color drop-down list.

Change Borders and Fills

To change the cell color, use the Borders tab of the Format Cells dialog box, as shown here on the right.

Select the border color from the Borders drop-down list, and select the options in the Border group to indicate which sides of the border to change. To change cell colors, select a color from the Fills drop-down list.

Work with Data in Workbooks

As your spreadsheets grow with data, you may want to hide some data so that you only see a subset, or you may want to change the order in which the data is entered so that similar values are grouped together. The Pocket Excel Sort and AutoFilter tools enable you to change the order of data and decrease the amount of data in the display.

Filter Data

A filter uses values in columns to decrease the number of rows that display below the point where the filter is created. Where the filter starts depends on how it is created. If only one cell is selected, the filter will begin in row 1, but if a range of cells is selected, the filter will begin in the row that contains the range. Figure 11-2 shows a filter that starts in row 5.

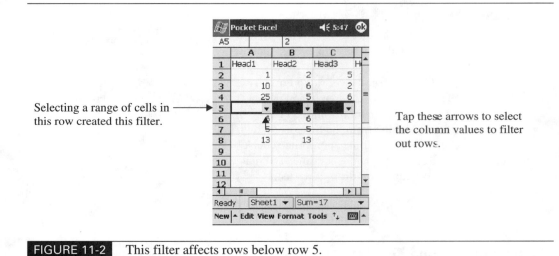

Selecting a range of cells in
this row created this filter.

Tap these arrows to select
the column values to filter
out rows.

FIGURE 11-2   This filter affects rows below row 5.

This filter will not change rows above row 5, but the rows below it will change.

To filter data, follow these steps:

1. Select a cell, or a range of cells, in a row.

2. Tap Tools | AutoFilter.

3. Tap the arrow in one of the columns to open a drop-down list.

4. Select a value from the drop-down list.

Only the rows containing the value that you selected will display below the location of the filter. For example, if the number 5 is selected in Figure 11-2, only row 7 will display; rows 6 and 8 will be hidden, and rows 1 through 5 will continue to display. To remove the filter, tap Tools | AutoFilter.

Custom filters provide more control over what rows display. To create a custom filter, select Custom from the Filter drop-down list, and the Custom AutoFilter dialog box, as shown in the following image, displays:

Select the filter criteria
from these drop-down
lists.

Select the filter value
from these drop-down
lists.

The two drop-down lists at the top of the dialog box contain the filter criteria, such as Is Greater Than and Is Not Equal To. The two drop-down lists at the bottom of the dialog box contain the filter values that are in the column below the filter.

You can have your filters define two sets of criteria by selecting values in the second drop-down lists and selecting one of the middle radio buttons. For example, you could create a filter that showed rows in which the column value is greater than 3 and less than 9.

In addition to the column values and the custom filter selection, you will also see All and Top 10 in the AutoFilter list. Selecting All clears the filter and displays all of the rows; selecting Top 10 displays rows that contain the top ten values in the column.

Sort Data

The Pocket Excel Sort command enables you to change the order of rows in a selected range of cells based on values in columns. To sort data, first select a range of cells, and then tap Tools | Sort to open the following Sort dialog box:

Up to three columns can be included in a sort, which you select from the drop-down lists, and they are used in order from top to bottom. By default, the sort is in ascending order unless the check box for the column is cleared, in which case the sort is in descending order. If the range of cells includes a header row, and Exclude Header Row From The Sort box is selected, then the header titles appear in the drop-down lists rather than the column references, and the row is not included in the sort.

> **TIP** *If a range of cells is not selected, the Sort command will automatically select all adjacent rows and columns of the selected cell for the sort.*

Password-Protect Workbooks

A password can be assigned to workbooks so they will be secure. Without entering the password, the workbook cannot be opened. To create passwords, follow these steps:

1. Tap Edit | Password.

2. Enter the password in the Password field.

3. Enter the same password in the Verify Password field.

4. Tap OK.

5. Save the workbook.

When you open the workbook, the Password prompt will display and the password will have to be entered. Don't forget the password; without it, you will not be able to open the workbook, nor will you be able to synchronize the workbook with your desktop computer!

> **TIP** *To remove passwords, select Edit | Password, delete the contents of the Password field, tap OK, and then save the workbook.*

If you synchronize a Pocket Excel workbook that has a password, ActiveSync will prompt you for the password during synchronization. After entering the correct password, a copy of the file will be written to the synchronized files folder of your desktop computer, but the password will no longer be assigned to the workbook. Excel workbooks that contain passwords will not synchronize with your Pocket PC; and during synchronization, a message box will display telling you that the file cannot be converted.

Share Workbooks

Pocket Excel makes it easy to share workbooks with other people by including the capability to send workbooks via infrared or e-mail. To use infrared to send a workbook to another Windows-powered device, follow these steps:

1. If the receiving device is a Handheld PC, open Windows Explorer and tap File | Receive.

2. If the receiving device is another Pocket PC, tap Start | Programs | Infrared Receive.

3. On the sending Pocket PC, which has a workbook open in Pocket Excel, tap Tools | Beam Workbook, and line up the infrared ports.

> **NOTE** *If your device is running Pocket PC 2000, tap Tools | Send Via Infrared.*

Once the two devices recognize each other, the file will transfer to the receiving device. When the transfer is complete, the sending device will indicate that one file has been sent, and a Close button will appear that you tap to return to Pocket Excel.

To send a workbook via e-mail, tap Tools | Send Via E-mail and a new e-mail message will open with the workbook as an attachment. Enter an e-mail address, subject, and message, and then tap Send. Inbox will send the message the next time you connect to the Internet and retrieve e-mail.

The Pocket PC Calculator

Pocket Excel is useful for *what if* scenarios, but it can be overkill if all you want to do is add a bunch of numbers. For these simple mathematical tasks, your Pocket PC includes a standard calculator application.

> **TIP**   *Some Pocket PCs include alternative calculators stored in ROM. For example, HP Jornadas include OmniSolve. Several alternative calculators are available for download from the Internet.*

Use Calculator

To start Calculator, tap Start | Programs | Calculator, and the following program window will display:

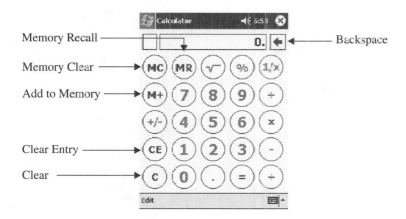

Tap the buttons on the screen to use the calculator. If you want to copy a value in the display into a document, tap Edit | Copy, and then paste it into the document.

Wrapping Up

Pocket Excel enables you to analyze numbers and track information, and the Calculator is ideal for quick arithmetic. You can also use Pocket Excel to manage money, but you may prefer to use Pocket Money because it synchronizes with the desktop version of Microsoft Money. In the next chapter, you learn how to keep track of your finances using Pocket Money.

11

Chapter 12

Manage Your Money

How to...

- Install Microsoft Money
- Synchronize Microsoft Money
- Set up accounts in Microsoft Money
- Use Microsoft Money to track how you spend and save money
- Use Microsoft Money to track your investments

As you have seen, Pocket PCs can be used to manage most of your personal information, from contacts, appointments, and tasks to Pocket Word documents and Pocket Excel spreadsheets. You may also want to manage your money on your Pocket PC. You can use Pocket Excel, but an even better solution may be Microsoft Money.

Microsoft Money is a financial information management program that runs on Pocket PCs. With this program, you can track financial information such as checking accounts, savings accounts, credit cards, and investments. If you run Money 2002 (the most current version) on a desktop computer, all of your data can be synchronized between it and your device. Transactions that you enter on your Pocket PC will automatically synchronize to your desktop and update account balances.

In this chapter, you learn how to install Microsoft Money on your device and how to configure ActiveSync to synchronize data between Microsoft Money and Money 2002. You also learn how to work with transactions, categories, and payees. Finally, you learn how to track your investments by downloading stock quotes from the Internet.

> NOTE *Microsoft Money came pre-installed in ROM of Pocket PC 2000 devices, but it is a separate program that you must install on Pocket PC 2002 devices.*

Install Microsoft Money

If you plan to synchronize with Money 2002 on a PC, and it is not already installed, you should install it first. Microsoft provides Money Microsoft as a free download that you will find at http://www.microsoft.com/mobile/pocketpc/downloads/money.asp.

To install Microsoft Money for Pocket PCs, your desktop PC must be running Windows 95, 98, NT4 (SP4 or greater), Windows 2000, or Windows XP. The PC must have 70MB of available hard disk space, 16MB of RAM, and at least a 90MHz Pentium processor. Microsoft Money requires 500K of storage space available on the Pocket PC for installation.

To install Microsoft Money on a Pocket PC, first connect the device with a desktop computer. Use Windows Explorer to browse to the location where you downloaded Microsoft Money, and then run mppc2002.exe. The software installs like any other Pocket PC program, using ActiveSync's Add/Remove Programs function. The installation program may ask to replace files on your device, which you should do by tapping Yes in the dialog box that appears.

Synchronize with Microsoft Money 2002

Microsoft Money Version 2 for Pocket PCs will only synchronize with Microsoft Money 2002 on a desktop PC. If you do not have Money 2002, you will need to upgrade the program before you can synchronize with a Pocket PC.

CAUTION   *There are some reports on the Internet newsgroups that you can synchronize Microsoft Money Version 2 with Money 2001 if you install the Microsoft Money Synchronization Update for Pocket PC for Money 2001. You will find the synchronization update at www.microsoft.com/mobile/pocketpc/downloads/money.asp. This work-around is not supported by Microsoft.*

Synchronization of Microsoft Money data can only occur between one Pocket PC and one desktop computer. This rule applies for multiple Pocket PCs synchronizing with the same PC, as well as for synchronizing a Pocket PC with multiple PCs

If you intend to synchronize your Pocket PC with Money 2002, you should not enter information on the Pocket PC before synchronizing. During the first synchronization, ActiveSync will detect data on the Pocket PC and give you the chance to combine the data with Money 2002. However, there is always a chance that a problem can occur and data will be lost. To prevent that from happening, it is best not to enter any data on the Pocket PC before synchronizing with Money 2002.

TIP   *Do not disconnect or turn off your Pocket PC while synchronizing with Money 2002, or you may experience problems with the program. If this occurs, start ActiveSync on your desktop computer, double-click the Microsoft Money information type, click the Tools tab, and then click Sync All to force a full resynchronization of your Money data.*

12

How to ... Synchronize Money Data After Installing Money 2002 on a PC

We recommend that you do not add data to Microsoft Money on your Pocket PC until you install Money 2002 on your desktop computer. However, if you do input Money data on your Pocket PC, here is how you can safely synchronize that data to a new Money file on a PC. Before you follow these steps, you should back up your Pocket PC following the instructions in Chapter 7.

1. Install Microsoft Money on your desktop computer.
2. Run Microsoft Money on your desktop. On the initial Money Setup Assistant screen, click Start Here. This will create a blank Money file.
3. Exit Microsoft Money on your desktop.

4. Connect your Pocket PC with the desktop and reinstall Microsoft Money for the Pocket PC.

5. When prompted on the Pocket PC, tap OK to reinstall.

6. This step is very important, otherwise you will lose the Microsoft Money data on your Pocket PC. When prompted on the Pocket PC, tap No to deleting any existing Money databases on your Pocket PC.

7. When prompted on the Pocket PC, tap Yes To All, when asked to replace existing files.

8. The install will end on the Pocket PC at the Items tab for the Today screen settings. Leave this screen open and connect your Pocket PC to the desktop computer.

9. Check ActiveSync to verify that the Money data synchronizes.

10. Once synchronization completes, you can close the Today Screen settings on the Pocket PC

Configure Synchronization Settings

ActiveSync can be configured to limit the amount of data that synchronizes to a Pocket PC, which can speed up synchronization. To configure synchronization, connect your Pocket PC to your desktop PC and then perform the following steps on the PC:

NOTE *By default, Microsoft Money synchronizes the last four weeks of data. Data older than four weeks is removed from the Pocket PC as it ages, but it will remain on the PC. You can choose to synchronize all data, but this will require more storage space if you have a lot of transactions.*

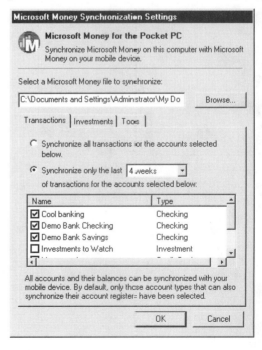

1. Double-click the Microsoft Money entry in the Details section to open the Microsoft Money Synchronization Settings dialog box shown here.

2. By default, ActiveSync selects the current Money 2002 file for synchronization. You can change the file by clicking the Browse button.

3. ActiveSync can be configured to synchronize all transactions for selected accounts, or only a defined

amount of transactions. Select the radio button for the setting that you desire; and to limit the transactions to a defined period of time, select a value from the drop-down list.

4. All of the accounts in the Money 2002 file are listed in the dialog box, which you can select for synchronization by clicking the check box next to each entry. If you clear the check box, the account will not synchronize to the Pocket PC—though if the account was previously synchronized, it will not be deleted from the Pocket PC.

5. The Investments tab is used select the investments to synchronize between the Pocket PC and desktop PC. Select a radio button to synchronize all investments, or only the investments that you select in the dialog box, as shown on the right:

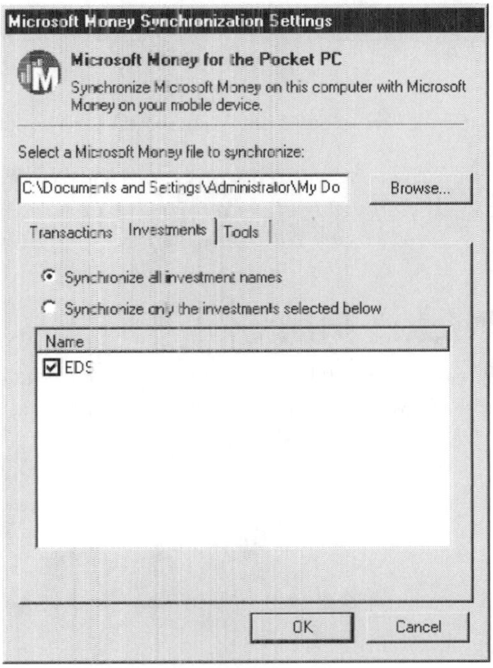

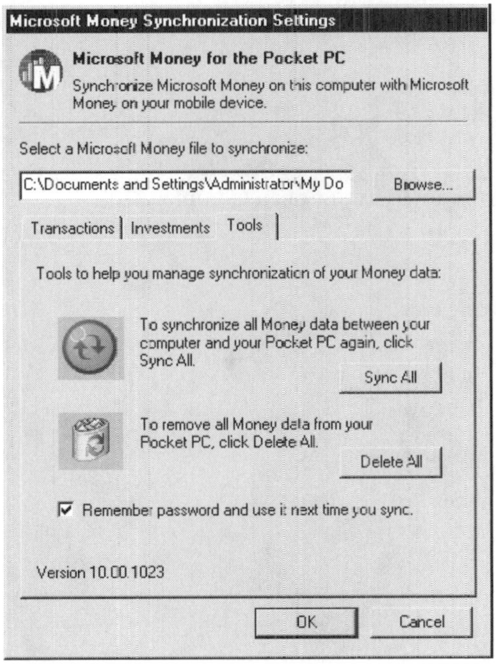

6. The Tools tab, shown at left, provides options for fixing problems that may occur during synchronization. Click Sync All to initiate a full resynchronization of your Money data. The Sync All button is grayed out if the Pocket PC is not connected to the desktop computer. Click Delete All to delete all of the Money Data on your Pocket PC. If you protect your desktop Money data with a password, you will be prompted to enter that password each time Money synchronizes. You can select the Remember Password And Use It The Next Time You Sync check box if you prefer not to enter the desktop password during synchronization.

12

If the Microsoft Money data on your Pocket PC becomes out of sync with your desktop computer, click Delete All to remove the data from your Pocket PC, and then click Sync All to restore the data on the desktop to the Pocket PC.

Click OK to save the Microsoft Money synchronization settings and close the dialog box.

 You can assign a password to the Microsoft Money data file on your Pocket PC by tapping Tools | Password. This password is different than the password that you assign to Money 2002 on your PC.

Use Pocket Money

Microsoft Money has five views: Account Manager, Account Register, Categories, Investments, and Payees. The current view is always displayed at the top of the screen, as shown here:

Tap here to open the
View drop-down list.

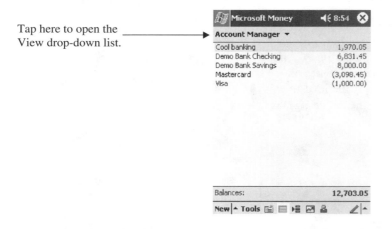

To switch between views, select one from the View drop-down list, or tap a Command bar button, as shown here:

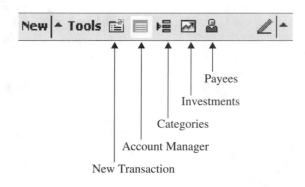

Create, Edit, and Delete Accounts

Microsoft Money can store as many accounts as you want, depending on the amount of storage memory available. All of the data is written to the Pocket PC data store, which is the same place where the Pocket Outlook data is written. This data cannot be written to a storage card, and the Pocket PC data store is limited to 16MB.

In addition to possibly affecting how much Pocket Outlook data your device can hold, the speed of Microsoft Money will be impacted if you choose to store a great deal of data on your device.

To create a new account in Microsoft Money, you will need to provide a name for the account and select an account type. Microsoft Money on Pocket PCs does not support all Money 2002 account types, but the account types it does support are Cash, Checking, Credit Card, Line of Credit, and Savings. Any new account that you create on your device will be added to Money 2002 during the next synchronization.

To create a new account, tap New on a Pocket PC, and the dialog box shown on the right appears:

Enter a name in the Account Name field, and select the type of account that you want to create in the Account Type drop-down list. All of the other fields in the dialog box are optional, though you will probably enter an amount in the Opening Balance field. Tap the Display Account On Today Screen check box if you want to see the account balance on the Today screen. The Optional tab provides fields for storing an Account Number, Institution Name, Contact Name, and Phone Number.

Once an account exists, you can edit its details at any time. You can also edit some of the details for accounts that have been created in Money 2002. When you make changes, they will be uploaded to Money 2002 during the next synchronization.

12

How to ... Display Money Information on the Today Screen

Microsoft Money Version 2 account balances and investment information can be displayed on the Pocket PC's Today screen. During installation, a Money entry is added to the Today screen items, which you view by tapping Start | Settings | Today, and then tapping the Items tab. Clear the Money check box to remove the Money information from the Today screen. Select the Money item, and then tap Options to select the accounts and investments you want to see on the Today screen.

NOTE *Information for accounts enabled for online banking cannot be edited on Pocket PCs.*

To edit an account, tap-and-hold on the account name in the Account Manager view and select Edit Details on the pop-up menu. You can edit most of the details for an account except the account type. If you want to change the account type, you must delete the account and create another with the new type.

When you delete an account, you also delete all of the transactions it contains. You cannot, however, delete an account that has been synchronized with Money 2002 from a Pocket PC. You must use Money 2002 to delete synchronized accounts. To delete an account, tap and hold on the account name in the Account Manager view and select Delete Account from the pop-up menu.

Use Accounts and the Account Register

When you start Microsoft Money, the Account Manager view displays, which is the main view of the program. This view displays the name and balance for each account, as well as the total balance for all accounts. To see the transactions for an account, tap the account name in the Account Manager view. You can also switch to the Account Register by expanding the View drop-down list and tapping Account Register, which opens the program window on a Pocket PC, as shown next:

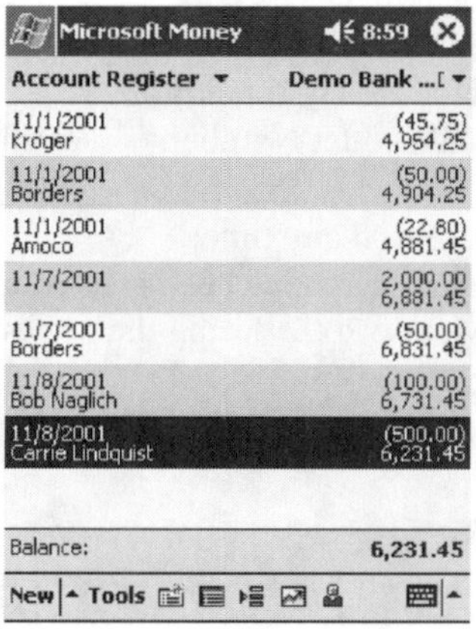

Tap here to select a different account.

You will notice that the current account displays in the upper right-hand corner. If you want to switch to another account, tap the drop-down list triangle next to the account name and tap an account name in the list, as shown here:

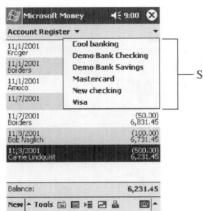

Select an account from this list.

Enter Transactions

Microsoft Money for the Pocket PC is designed so that entering transactions is fast and easy. Many of the fields that you complete while entering a transaction contain default values; for instance, the default type for all new transactions is Withdrawal. AutoFill automatically enters the most recently used amount, category, and subcategory for the last transaction for a payee.

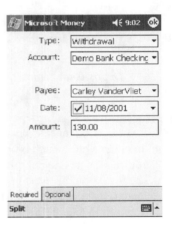

NOTE *AutoFill is an option that must be turned on. The process for setting options in Microsoft Money is explained later in this chapter.*

Microsoft Money supports three transaction types: Withdrawal, Deposit, and Transfer. A withdrawal is a transaction that removes money from an account; deposits add money to accounts. A transfer moves money from one account to another. You can enter new transactions from any view by tapping the New Transaction button on the Command bar or, if you are in the Account Registry view, tapingp New. When you create a new transaction, the screen shown on the right appears.

To enter a new transaction, do the following:

1. Select Withdrawal, Deposit, or Transfer from the Type drop-down list.

2. Select an account from the Accounts drop-down list.

3. Enter a payee in the Payee field, or select an entry from the drop-down list. AutoFill will attempt to determine which payee you are entering, and will automatically display one previously entered into the field based on the letters you enter.

4. Select a date from the Date pop-up menu.

5. Enter a value in the Amount field.

At this point, you have completed all of the fields required for the transaction; and if you tap OK, the transaction will appear in the Account Registry. However, you can complete optional fields by tapping the Optional tab, as shown here:

Tap the Optional tab to display this dialog box.

The most frequently used field on the Optional tab may be Check Num. in which you enter a check number for withdrawal transactions. If AutoFill is enabled, and the last transaction for the payee was a check, the next available check number for the account will be automatically entered in this field.

NOTE   *Deposits and transfers do not include the Check Num field on the Optional tab.*

Categories and subcategories are downloaded from Money 2002 during synchronization. Select values from each drop-down list to complete these two fields. You can also enter a new item in either field, which is automatically entered in the category list and uploaded to Money 2002 during the next synchronization.

The Status field is used to set the transaction status to C for cleared, R for reconciled, or V for void; and you can use the Memo field to enter a short note for the transaction. When you have finished entering all of the information for the transaction, tap OK.

Transfer Money Between Accounts   Transfers move money from one account to another; and to accommodate this, the dialog box changes when you select the transfer transaction type. As shown on the right, two fields appear in the dialog box, From and To.

Transfer out   Transfer in

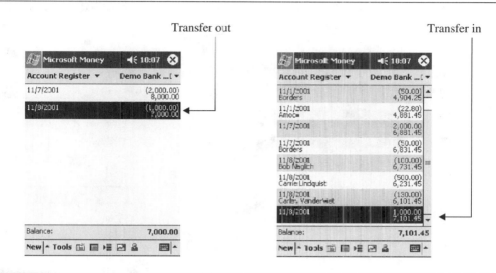

FIGURE 12-1   On the left is the Account Registry view for a source account after a transfer;
on the right is the Account Registry view for the destination account.

To transfer money from one account to another, select the source account in the From
drop-down list, and the destination account in the To drop-down list. Complete the rest of the
fields in the dialog box like any other transaction. Figure 12-1 shows the Account Registry for
the source and destination accounts after a transfer is complete.

Split Transactions   Categories and subcategories are used to track how money is spent. It is often
the case that financial transactions should be split into multiple categories. For example, one purchase
at a computer store may include hardware and software, and you might want to track the amount of
money that you spend on each category. Microsoft Money's split
transaction functionality enables you to track your finances at this
level of detail.

While you can split any withdrawal or deposit, you cannot
split a transfer. To enter split transactions, do the following:

1. Create a new transaction.

2. Complete the Payee and Amount fields.

3. Tap Split to open the Split Transaction dialog box,
   shown on the right.

12

4. Tap New to open the dialog box shown at right:

5. Enter the amount, category, subcategory, and description for a part of the transaction, and tap OK.

6. As each part of the transaction is entered, the Unassigned amount will change, as shown next.

7. Repeat steps 3 and 4 for each part of the transaction.

8. Tap OK.

Another way to enter a split transaction is to skip entering the amount in step 2. Enter each part of the transaction, and then tap Adjust Total. The dialog box shown at right appears.
Tap Yes, and the total for the transaction will equal the sum of the split items. Tap OK to return to the Split Transaction dialog box.

If you tap the Optional tab, you will see that the Category field contains the word "Split," and the Subcategory field is grayed out, as shown on the left.

Edit and Delete Transactions

Editing a transaction in an Account Register is simple. Tap the transaction that you want to edit, make the changes, and tap OK. To delete a transaction on a Pocket PC, tap-and-hold on the transaction, and on the pop-up menu, tap Delete Transaction. You will be asked to confirm that you want to permanently delete the transaction. Tap Yes to permanently delete the transaction. During the next synchronization, the transaction will also be deleted from Money 2002.

Create, Edit, and Delete Categories

One of the reasons you might want to use Microsoft Money is to see where you are spending your money. With that information, you can create a budget that reflects your spending habits. Microsoft Money's method for tracking money is to assign transactions to categories and subcategories.

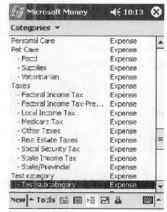

Categories stored in Microsoft Money are listed in the Categories view. To open the view, tap Categories in the View drop-down list or tap the Categories command bar button, as shown on the right:

Expense categories are listed first and are in alphabetical order. Subcategories are indented underneath categories, and provide more specific detail about the transaction. For example, a Computers category may have hardware and software subcategories to identify how money is spent on computers.

Prior to synchronization, the Category view is empty. The first time you synchronize Microsoft Money on a Pocket PC with Money 2002, the Category view is populated with the Money 2002 categories. When you create a new category on your Pocket PC, it will be added to Money 2002's categories during the next synchronization.

You can create as many categories and subcategories as you want—but keep in mind that this information, along with everything else in Microsoft Money, is kept in internal storage. The more information you store, the slower Microsoft Money will run.

To create a new category from within the Category view, tap New to open the New Category/Subcategory dialog box shown on the right.

> **TIP**   *Categories and subcategories can also be created while you are entering a new transaction, as described in the previous section of this chapter.*

Enter the category name in the Name field, and tap the appropriate radio button to specify whether it is an income or expense category. Tap the Subcategory Of radio button and select a subcategory name from the drop-down list if you are creating a subcategory. You can also enter a short description for the category or subcategory in the Memo field. Tap OK to add the item to the Category view.

> **NOTE**   *Because subcategories belong to categories, you can only create a subcategory for a category that already exists.*

12

The only parts of a category that can change after it is created are the Name and Memo fields. If you want to change the category type, you must delete the category and create a new one. To change these items for a category, tap the category name in the Category view, change the entries in the Name field, and tap OK.

Any category or subcategory can be deleted; and when you delete a category, all subcategories that it contains are also deleted. Transactions in Microsoft Money that are in a deleted category or subcategory remain, but are no longer part of the category. However, the same transactions in Money 2002 are not changed, and therefore the category may not be deleted in Money 2002. If that is the case, then the category will re-appear in Microsoft Money after the next synchronization.

> **NOTE** *Categories and subcategories that you delete in Microsoft Money will only be removed from Money 2002 if they are not used in any transactions.*

To delete a category or subcategory, tap-and-hold on the item and select Delete Category from the pop-up menu.

Create, Edit, and Delete Payees

Payees are people or organizations to whom you pay money or from whom you receive money. Typically, payees are created when you enter a transaction in Microsoft Money, but they may also be created in the Payee view. To see a listing of the payees entered in Microsoft Money, tap Payees in the View drop-down list, or tap the Payee Command bar button, to open the dialog box shown on the right.

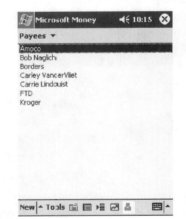

To create a new item in the Payee view, tap New and complete the fields in the dialog box. Only the Name field is required; when you have finished, tap OK to add the item to the list of payees. During the next synchronization, the item will be added to the list of payees in Money 2002.

Any payee that you enter in Microsoft Money or Money 2002 can be edited. To edit an item in the Payee view, tap the item, make the changes to the fields, and then tap OK.

Every transaction in Microsoft Money requires a payee; therefore, you can only delete payees that are not used in any transactions currently on your Pocket PC. Microsoft Money will prevent you from deleting a payee included in transactions and will display a warning box. When you delete a payee from Microsoft Money, it will also be permanently deleted from Money 2002 during the next synchronization.

To delete an item in the Payee view on a Pocket PC, tap-and-hold on the item and tap Delete Payee on the pop-up menu.

Create, Edit, and Update Investments

Of course, checking and savings accounts are not the only places in which we put our money. Investments in stocks and mutual funds are increasingly becoming an important way for us to save and make money. People who make investments like to keep current on the performance of their holdings; and today, a number of ways exist for you to obtain stock quotes. One of those ways is with software like Microsoft Money and Money 2002.

With Microsoft Money, you can keep track of the value of your investment portfolio either directly online or by synchronizing with Money 2002. The first step in tracking this information is to enter the market symbols and the amount of shares that you hold by using the Investment view, which you open by selecting Investments in the View drop-down list or tapping the Investments Command bar button.

To enter an investment, tap New; this will open the New Investment dialog box, shown on the right.

In the dialog box, enter the name of the investment, its symbol, and the number of shares you hold. If you want the investment to display on the Today screen, tap the Display Investment On Today Screen check box. Tap OK to save the investment information and close the dialog box. If you know the investment's last price, you can enter it, but it is not required.

After the investment is entered, it appears in the Investments view, as shown on the left.

You do not need to enter the number of shares that you hold, and you can simply provide a name and symbol to obtain a stock quote. Entries in the Investment view cannot be edited. To delete an entry, tap-and-hold on it, and then tap Delete Investment on the pop-up menu.

Perhaps the most important part of the Investment view is its ability to download stock quotes from the Internet. Microsoft Money retrieves quotes from the MSN MoneyCentral web site. The quotes are provided by Standard & Poor's Comstock and are delayed at least 20 minutes.

In order to download stock quotes to your Pocket PC, you must create and use an Internet connection (described in Chapter 19). Connect the Pocket PC to the Internet, and then tap Tools | Update Investments or tap the Update toolbar button. Microsoft Money will download the latest market prices for your investments and display them in Investment view. If you enter an invalid symbol for an investment, the market value will display "Invalid Symbol."

TIP *Stock quote prices may be updated by using a direct Internet connection. If you connect to the Internet using a proxy server, you must provide the address and port number in Microsoft Money's options, as described in the next section.*

Change Settings

There are some options in Microsoft Money you may not notice at first, but would find very useful. These include using AutoComplete+, assigning Money to a hardware button, and downloading stock quotes from the Internet. To change these options, tap Tools | Options to open the Options dialog box, shown here on the right.

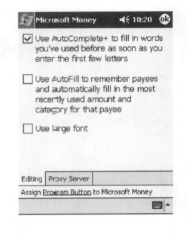

The Editing tab is used to turn AutoComplete+ on or off, to turn AutoFill on or off, and to turn large fonts on or off. AutoComplete+ fills in words you have used before as soon as you enter the first few letters. AutoFill remembers payees and automatically fills in the most recently used amount, category, and subcategory for the payee. It also automatically fills in the next check number if you are entering a check. The Use Large Font setting switches the font display in Microsoft Money between normal and bold, with Use Large Font represented as bold. To turn AutoComplete+, AutoFill, and Use Large Font on, the check boxes next to each item in the tab.

Microsoft Money can be assigned to a hardware button on your device. The Options dialog box on the Pocket PC includes a link that you can tap to open the Button Settings dialog box. Follow the instructions provided in Chapter 3 for assigning programs to hardware keys, and tap OK to return to the Microsoft Money Options dialog box.

Stock quotes can be downloaded from the Internet using a direct network connection. Many local area networks provide connection to the Internet through a proxy server. If that is the case, and you want to download stock quotes, you must configure the Proxy Server tab in the Options dialog box. When you tap the Proxy Server tab, the dialog box shown on the right will appear.

Tap the check box so that Microsoft Money uses the proxy server. Enter a URL or TCP/IP address in the HTTP field, and enter a number in the Port field. Typically, the port number will be 80, but consult your network administrator to confirm this value.

Tap here to use a proxy server.

How to ... Synchronize with Quicken

Unfortunately, there is no Pocket version of Quicken. There are some Pocket PC programs that do support Quicken's QIF file format, which you can use to export information out of Quicken and import to a Pocket PC. A few alternatives to Microsoft Money include.

- **PoQuick Money Professional** http://www.mastersoftmobilesolutions.com/
- **Cash Organizer** http://www.inesoft.com/eng/index_shtml
- **PocketMoney** http://www.catamount.com/PocketMoney.html

Set Passwords

You can assign a password to Microsoft Money that has to be entered each time you start the program. To assign a password to Microsoft Money, tap Tools | Password. Enter a password in the New Password field, enter it a second time in the Confirm Password field, and then tap OK.

Wrapping Up

Because a Pocket PC is very portable, you'll find it easy to record financial transactions as you shop. Then, when you return home, all you need to do is synchronize your Pocket PC to update the financial information on your desktop computer. The combination of Microsoft Money, a Pocket PC, and synchronization with your desktop PC provides an example of how you can use a Pocket PC as part your normal routine.

Pocket PCs are also great note-taking tools. In the next chapter, you will learn how you can make both handwritten notes and voice recordings on your Pocket PC, and then later synchronize them to your desktop computer.

12

Chapter 13 Take Notes

How To...

- Create notes in digital ink or text
- Make voice recordings
- Change the voice recording format
- Send notes and voice recordings via e-mail
- Beam notes and voice recordings to other devices
- Synchronize notes with Outlook
- Manage and search for notes on your Pocket PC
- Synchronize Outlook Journal entries using CLC Journal

If you need to write a quick note, what do you use? Before I started using my Pocket PC, I would write notes on pieces of paper and stick them somewhere easy to find. On my desk at work I would have these notes scattered everywhere, and over time my workspace would look very cluttered. Inevitably a note that had an important phone number or an appointment would be lost, causing me to either lose time hunting for the phone number or miss a meeting.

Now that I have my Pocket PC, I store phone numbers in Contacts and enter appointments in Calendar, but there are still times when I just need to jot a quick note and for that I turn to the Notes application on my Pocket PC. Of course, I could use Pocket Word, but I have found Notes to be better suited for this task.

As you will learn in this chapter, Notes can be configured to store what you write in digital ink or translated to text. Since I usually need to write these notes very quickly, I use digital ink, and use Pocket Word for creating documents in text. For those times when writing is not convenient, you can use your Pocket PC to make voice notes, which are stored and retrieved along with all your handwritten information. Finally, Notes on your Pocket PC can be synchronized with the Notes folder in Outlook or synchronized as individual files in the My Documents folder. Think of Notes, configured for digital ink, as your electronic notepad, which neatly stores all your information in one place and never runs out of paper.

Create, Open, and Save Notes

To create notes, tap Start | Notes to start the Notes application. If Notes is not listed in the Start menu, then tap Start | Programs | Notes. The application will open in List view, as shown in Figure 13-1. Simply tap on a filename in the List view to open the note. Tap New to create a blank note page that is ready for handwriting, text, or recordings. Tap OK to save the note and return to the List view.

Write Notes

Writing notes is as simple as using a paper notepad. When you create a note by tapping New, the screen displays a ruled page similar to paper. If you write directly on the screen, your handwriting

Tap a filename to open a note. ⟶

Tap here to create a new note. ⟶

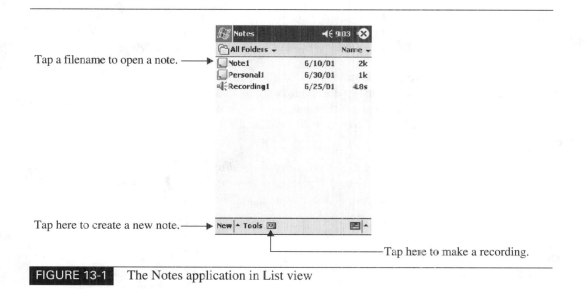

Tap here to make a recording.

FIGURE 13-1   The Notes application in List view

will appear as digital ink, as shown in Figure 13-2. Notice the Pencil button on the Command bar; the square indicates that Notes is in Writing mode. Tapping Pencil will switch to Typing mode, enabling you to put text into the note using the soft input panel.

Tap here to switch between Writing and Typing mode. The square indicates Writing mode.

FIGURE 13-2   Notes has two modes, Writing (shown here) and Typing.

> TIP
>
> *By default, Notes is configured for Writing mode, which displays all of your handwriting in digital ink. If you want your handwriting to always be translated to text, tap Tools | Options from the List view and then select Typing from the Default Mode drop-down list.*

If you tap Tools | Recognize, all handwriting in the note converts to text. You may also narrow the conversion down to only a portion of the handwriting by first selecting it and then tapping Tools | Recognize. To make corrections to the conversion, tap-and-hold the stylus on the incorrect word and select Alternates. Select the correct word from the list that appears. Undo the conversion by tapping Edit | Undo Recognize.

> TIP
>
> *Even though Notes does not have a Drawing mode, drawings can be made in Writing mode. However, if you use Tools | Recognize to convert an entire document to text, Notes will convert the drawing to text as well, generating some strange results.*

Edit Notes

The standard edit functions (Cut, Copy, and Paste) can be used to edit Notes. Select these functions from either the Edit or pop-up menus. To select writing, tap the stylus on the screen until the cursor appears, drag the stylus across the writing, and then lift the stylus. When selecting text, just drag the stylus across the words that you want to select and lift the stylus. Embedded recordings are also selected in this manner. Tap-and-hold the stylus on the selection to open the pop-up menu and select Cut, Copy, Paste, or Clear. These same functions are also available in the Edit menu.

To select the entire note, tap Edit | Select All. Any edit function can be undone by using the Edit menu. The Undo options in the Edit menu change according to the last edit performed. For example, if you just cut an item from the document, the Edit menu contains Undo Delete, which will replace the item cut from the document.

> TIP
>
> *To insert the current date and time into a note, tap-and-hold the stylus on the screen until the pop-up menu appears and then select Insert Date.*

Zoom Notes

Change the display size by selecting a zoom percentage from the Tools menu; for example, to increase the display size 200%, tap Tools | 200%. You cannot customize the zoom settings.

Make Voice Recordings

How often do you drive and use your computer at the same time? Not very often, I hope, or I would like to know what roads you travel on so that I can avoid them. Yet, while you shouldn't be using your computer while driving, there are probably times when you've had a thought that you would like to make sure you remember. For that you could use a cassette recorder or your Pocket PC.

Recording memos to yourself is little reason to buy a Pocket PC, but once a recording is completed, the Pocket PC capabilities shine. You can label the recordings, giving them a name that you can easily identify for later retrieval, as well as date and time stamp each recording. Recordings can be grouped together in folders and synchronized to a desktop computer. They can also be attached to e-mail and sent to anyone with an Internet e-mail address, and they can be beamed via infrared to any other Pocket PC.

You may wonder how many recordings you can store on your device. The total number of recordings is limited by the amount of storage space available. Recordings can be stored in either internal storage memory, or on a storage card. Your Pocket PC creates files in the Waveform (WAV) audio format, and there are different types of WAV files. Depending on which format you select, and its recording quality, a three-second recording can require 1 to 28KB of storage. Approximately one hour of recordings can take up to 1MB of space.

Storage space is not your only consideration; using the microphone and other peripherals drains batteries faster, decreasing the amount of recording time. If you plan to make long recordings, make sure the battery is fully charged and remove any unnecessary peripherals.

Create Recordings

Your Pocket PC is designed to work like a tape recorder. To make a recording, press-and-hold the Record hardware button. Your device will beep and begin recording. Stop the recording by releasing the button. The recording is stored on your device and is included in the Notes List view with a default filename. To play a recording, tap its filename, and use the buttons on the recording toolbar to control the playback.

How to ... Create a Customized Alarm

Your Pocket PC comes with several different sounds that are used for reminders in Calendar and Tasks and as a general alarm. You can record your own customized alarm using Notes. First, create the recording that you want to use, then tap-and-hold on the file and rename the file to something easy to remember. Then, start File Explorer and copy the file from the My Documents folder to the Windows folder. To use the recording for reminders, tap Start | Settings | Sounds & Reminders; then tap the Reminder tab and select your recording from the Sound drop-down list. To create an alarm, tap Start | Settings | System | Clock, then tap the Alarms tab. Tap the Alarm button and select your recording from the Play Sound drop-down list.

13

Recordings can also be created in Notes by tapping Record on the Command bar to open the Recording toolbar, as shown in the following image:

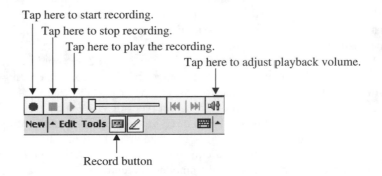

Tap here to start recording.

Tap here to stop recording.

Tap here to play the recording.

Tap here to adjust playback volume.

Record button

Tap the Record button on the toolbar to begin recording and the Stop button to end recording.

TIP *The default filename for text notes and recordings is based on the folder name in which the item is stored. For example, if you select a folder named Projects in the Notes List view, then notes and recordings will have the default name of Projects and a number, such as Projects1.*

If you make a recording while a note is open, it will be embedded in the note. Once the recording is finished, an icon is inserted into the note, as shown in the following image:

Play the recording by tapping the icon.

TIP *Speak directly into the microphone to create good recordings. Check the user manual of your Pocket PC to locate the microphone.*

How to ... Change the Format of Voice Recordings

Recordings are created using one of several formats available on your Pocket PC. Which format to use depends on your personal preferences for sound quality and how much you want to record. Higher quality recordings require more storage space.

To change the recording format, tap Start | Settings | Input and then tap the Options tab on the Input screen. Tap the Voice Recording Format drop-down list to expand the list of available formats and then select the format you want to use. The Pulse Code Modulation (PCM), Global System for Mobile (GSM) telecommunications 6.10 and Mobile Voice formats come standard with Pocket PC 2000, but Pocket PC 2002 does not include Mobile Voice. Compaq only provides the standard formats; Casio adds TrueSpeech, and HP adds HP Dynamic Voice. The Casio and HP formats are optimized for their hardware and only run on their Pocket PCs, so you cannot play a TrueSpeech recording on an iPAQ.

Of the standard formats, PCM provides the highest quality, and the drop-down list provides several different bit rates of this format in either mono or stereo, which you can select to balance between quality and storage space. GSM 6.10 provides medium quality recordings and Mobile Voice provides the lowest quality recordings. PCM and GSM 6.10 can be played on Windows desktop computers, but Mobile Voice cannot be played on anything but Windows Powered devices. For this reason, make sure you select either PCM or GSM 6.10 as the format to use if you plan to e-mail recordings to people who can only receive them on Windows desktops.

Send Notes and Recordings via E-mail or Infrared

Notes and recordings may be sent to someone via e-mail, which the receiver opens using Microsoft Word or the default WAV file player. To e-mail a note, follow these steps:

1. If the note is already open, tap Tools | Send Via E-mail.
2. If the note or recording is displayed in the Notes List view, tap-and-hold the filename and select Send Via E-mail from the pop-up menu.
3. Inbox starts with a new message and the note attached. Enter an e-mail address. (See Chapter 20 for instructions on how to use Inbox.)
4. Enter a subject.
5. Tap Send.

Depending on how you use Inbox, the e-mail will be sent the next time you connect with your Internet Service Provider (ISP) or the next time you synchronize with your desktop computer.

13

TIP *If you e-mail a voice recording and the person who receives the recording cannot play it, make sure the recording is in either the PCM or GSM 6.10 format.*

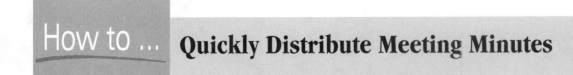

Quickly Distribute Meeting Minutes

With a large enough storage card, entire meetings can be recorded using a Pocket PC. Start Notes, create a new note, start the recording, and then place the device in the middle of the table. Make sure that everyone speaks loud enough to be recorded. Once the meeting is over, send the recording as an e-mail attachment to all of the participants. If the meeting is long, create multiple recordings of different meeting topics.

Notes and recordings can be transferred between devices using the infrared port. To perform infrared transfers, follow these steps:

1. If the note is already open, tap Tools | Beam Note.
2. If the note or recording is displayed in the Notes List view, tap-and-hold the filename and select Beam File from the pop-up menu.
3. Make sure the device receiving the transfer is set to Receive.
4. Line up the infrared ports of both devices. A sound will indicate that a connection is made, and the note will transfer.

The receiving device will indicate that one file was received and the sending device will indicate that one file was sent.

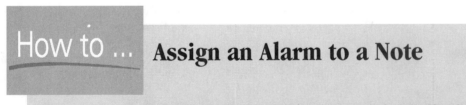

Assign an Alarm to a Note

There are many reasons to take notes; one of them is to remind yourself to do something in a couple of hours. You could create an appointment or task and set a reminder, but sometimes that is overkill when you just want to jot a quick note to yourself. Fortunately, three software developers have created solutions that provide this functionality. All of them will sound an alarm and display a written note at a set time or automatically play a voice recording at a set time.

RemindMe from Applian is available in English, German, French, and Spanish. RemindMe can display notes or play voice recordings either within a certain amount of time, say 15 minutes from now, or at a set time. You can find a trial version of this program along with more information at http://www.applian.com/pocketpc/remindme/index.htm.

BugMe from Electric Pocket is an award-winning Palm OS application that has also been written for the Pocket PC. It provides the same functions as RemindMe, plus adds the ability to change note and ink colors, as well as lock notes so they can't be accidentally deleted. A trial version if BugMe is available at http://bugme.net/bugme-pocketpc/index.html.

If you already use Pocket Informant as an alternative to Pocket Outlook, you don't need to install RemindMe or BugMe because their features are available as a Pocket Informant Alarm Note. By default, Pocket Informant assigns the Alarm Note feature to the Voice Record button on your Pocket PC, but if that is not the case on your Pocket PC, you can create an Alarm Note by selecting PI Alarm Note in the New button menu. Pocket Informant provides many more features than described here, and more information and a trial version of the program is available at http://www.pocketinformant.com.

> **NOTE**   *Items containing embedded recordings can only be opened with Pocket PCs. To send a note with an embedded recording to other devices, first remove the recording and then send it again.*

Synchronize Notes and Recordings

There are two ways to synchronize notes with a desktop computer. If you prefer to store notes in Outlook, you can configure ActiveSync to synchronize them with the Notes folder in Outlook. When Notes synchronization is disabled and File synchronization is enabled, notes are synchronized along with other files in the Pocket PC My Documents folder.

To enable the Notes ActiveSync information type on your PC, click Tools | Options and then select the Notes check box. When you synchronize the device with your desktop computer, any note on the device will appear in Outlook Notes, and notes already in Outlook will appear on the device. All note types are synchronized, including those containing digital ink and voice recordings.

> **TIP**   *Notes located on storage cards will not synchronize with Outlook.*

13

Manage Your Notes and Recordings

The best way to manage notes is by using the Notes List view. Notes are sorted by Name, Date, Size, or Type. Select one of the four sort options as shown here:

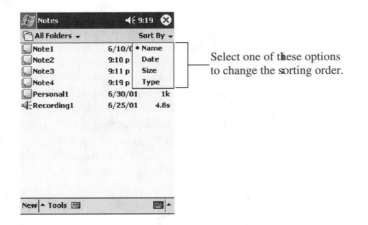

Select one of these options to change the sorting order.

Notes are copied, deleted, renamed, or moved by using the pop-up menu that appears when you tap-and-hold the stylus on a note. Table 13-1 summarizes what the pop-up menu options do.

An open note can be renamed or moved by tapping Tools | Rename/Move. To delete a note while it is open, tap Tools | Delete Note.

Menu Option	Action
Create Copy	Places a copy of the selected note in the List view. The note will have the same name with the addition of a number in parentheses, such as Note(1).
Delete	Opens a warning dialog box telling you that the selected item(s) will be permanently deleted. Tap Yes to delete or No to cancel.
Rename/Move	Opens the Rename/Move dialog box. Enter a name in the Name field to rename the note. Move the note to a different folder by selecting it from the Folder drop-down list or to a different storage location by selecting it from the Location drop-down list.

TABLE 13-1 Notes List View Pop-Up Menu Options

How to ...   Store Notes in Multiple Outlook Folders

The Notes application has a couple of limitations that affect how you can manage your notes in Outlook. One limitation is that Notes does not support categories. You can store notes in different folders on your Pocket PC, but those folders correspond with the subfolders in My Documents, not folders in Outlook. However, the folder names are inserted at the beginning of a note's subject, so that if you sort the notes by subject in Outlook, those stored in the same folder will be grouped together. Another limitation is that Notes, like Calendar, Contacts, and Tasks, does not synchronize with Outlook subfolders or public folders.

To date, no third-party developer provides an alternative to Notes that supports Outlook categories. However, HPC Notes from the Phatware Corporation does support synchronization of notes with multiple Outlook folders. For example, you can create one HPC Notes database on your Pocket PC that synchronizes with a Work folder in Outlook, and another database that synchronizes with a Home folder, therefore separating notes you take at work and at home. More information and trial versions of HPC Notes is available at http://www.phatware.com.

Search for Notes and Recordings

Pocket PCs provide the ability to search through all data stored on the device. You can search for filenames or words within documents. To search for a note, follow these steps:

1. Tap Start | Find.
2. Enter a word in the Find field.
3. Select Notes from the Type drop-down list.
4. Tap Go.

Search results display in the bottom half of the screen. Open a listed note by tapping its name.

Configure Notes

Unlike all other Pocket PC applications, you can only configure Notes from its List view. You can set several options in the Options dialog box, which you open by tapping Tools | Options. Table 13-2 lists these options, what they do, and their possible values.

13

Option	What It Does	Possible Values
Default mode	Specifies which mode Notes will be in when the application starts	Writing Typing
Default template	Specifies the template used to create new notes	Blank Note Meeting Notes Memo Phone Memo To Do
Save To	Specifies the default storage location for new notes	Main memory Storage card 1 (if available)
Record button action	Specifies what happens when you press the Hardware Record button	Switch to Notes Stay in current program

TABLE 13-2 Notes Configuration Settings

NOTE *Notes written to a storage card will not synchronize with your desktop computer.*

Synchronize the Outlook Journal using CLC Journal

If you are proficient with Outlook, you may have noticed that ActiveSync does not support synchronization with the Outlook Journal. Apparently, Microsoft felt that Journal created too much data to be synchronized with a Pocket PC, since it can be configured to automatically track every document that you open on your desktop. However, many people turn off the Journal tracking feature and manually enter information because it automatically assigns a date and time stamp to all entries.

Fortunately, Crown Logic has created Crown Logic (CLC) Journal, which synchronizes with the Outlook Journal. With this program you can create all of the different types of Outlook Journal entries on your Pocket PC, such as notes or phone calls, and then synchronize them to a desktop. The program can be downloaded from http://www.crownlogic.com.

The CLC Journal installation program adds a Journal information type to ActiveSync. With the information type enabled and CLC Journal installed on a Pocket PC, journal entries will synchronize between the desktop and Pocket PC along with all other information during synchronization. As you can see in the following image, Journal synchronization can be configured for a period of time for selected contacts or for selected categories:

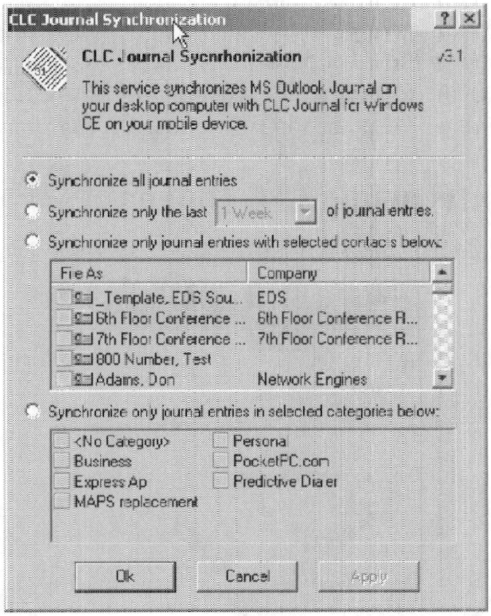

The installation program adds the Journal shortcut to the Pocket PC Start menu. When the program starts, it first displays all the journal entries in a List view, as shown below:

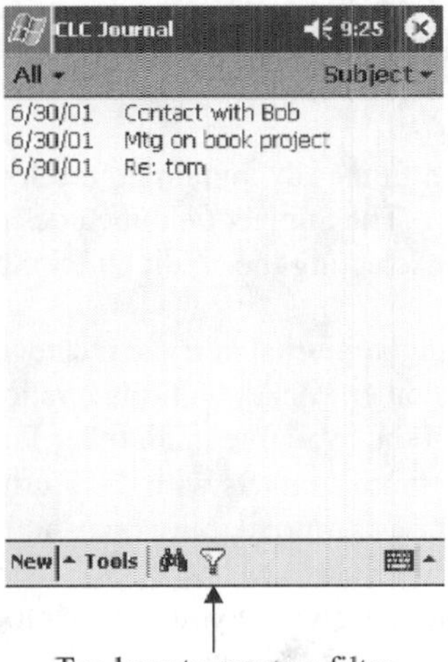

Tap here to create a filter.

13

You can filter the List view display by selecting an item from the All drop-down list at the top-left of the screen, or by tapping the Filter button. Like Notes, you can filter journal entries by category, but if you tap More in the drop-down list, you can also define filters for date ranges and months. Tap the Subject drop-down list at the top-right of the screen to sort the entries in the list.

Create a Journal Entry using CLC Journal

To create a journal entry, tap New to open the following entry screen:

Tap here to turn the timer on or off.

The screen has two tabs, with the Entry tab containing the Journal fields and the Note tab containing the text of the journal entry. The Subject field includes a drop-down list of commonly used subjects, which you can edit by selecting the <Edit Quick Subjects> entry from the drop-down list.

Tap the Categories field to assign the journal entry to a category, which may be one of the categories you already created in other Pocket Outlook applications. You can also create categories in CLC Journal, which will be available in all other Pocket Outlook applications. Tap the Contacts field to link one or more contacts with the journal entry. You will not be able to open the contact from within CLC Journal, but you can click on the contact in Outlook to open its information.

Notice the clock on the Command bar? When you tap the clock, CLC Journal will keep track of the amount of time that elapses and update the Duration field on the Entry tab. Time is rounded to the nearest minute. Tap the clock a second time to turn the timer off.

Tap the Note tab to enter the text of the journal entry. The Edit menu provides the standard edit functions Cut, Copy, and Paste, along with Undo and Redo, and the View menu provides options for zooming the display. Tap the two Command bar buttons, as shown in the following image, to insert the current date and time into the text:

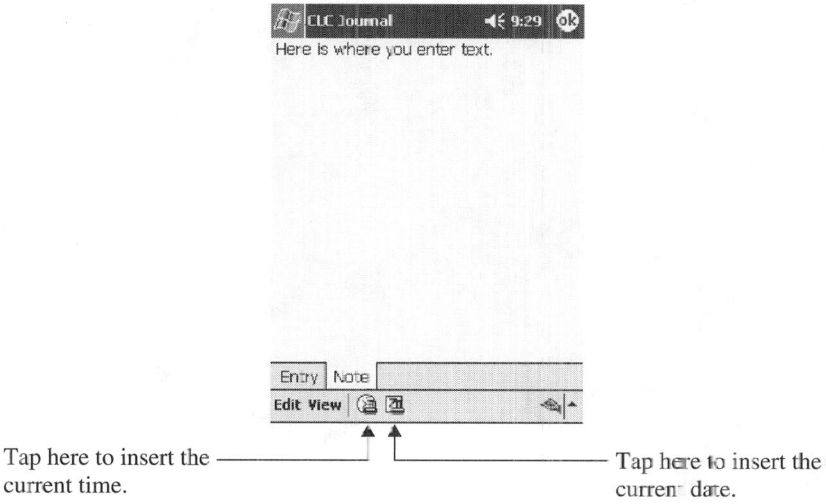

Tap here to insert the current time.

Tap here to insert the current date.

Wrapping Up

Now, whenever you need to write a quick note, reach for your Pocket PC rather than a scrap piece of paper. Anything that you need to write and throw away quickly is written with digital ink in Notes, and a backup copy of your notes is stored in Outlook by ActiveSync. Use CLC Journal to take notes during phone calls and meetings and use the time tracking option to know just how much time you spent. Up to this point all of the information that we have worked with has been words and numbers, but there are also times when we need to work with graphics. In the next chapter, you'll learn how you can create colorful drawings on your Pocket PC, as well as view pictures and Microsoft PowerPoint presentations.

13

Chapter 14

View Pictures and Presentations

How To...

■ View digital pictures

■ Edit digital pictures

■ Create drawings

■ View PowerPoint presentations

■ Create presentations

A feature that sets Pocket PCs apart from other handheld computers is their beautiful color displays. All of the new Pocket PC 2002 devices can display 64,000 colors on 3.5" or 3.8" screens. In fact, you would think that Microsoft would exploit these beautiful displays by providing a graphics program like Microsoft Paint, or a Pocket PowerPoint.

Surprisingly, Microsoft does not provide a version of Paint or PowerPoint for Pocket PCs. This omission provides an opportunity for other people to write programs to fill the void. The picture viewing, drawing, and presentation programs that we present in this chapter will not disappoint Pocket PC owners. If you enjoy drawing or taking digital pictures, or need to give presentations, you will find the Pocket PC to be very capable at these tasks.

View Pictures

Twenty years ago, the only way you could see a photo right after it was taken was by using a Polaroid Instant Camera. After you shot the picture, the photo would pop out of the camera, and the image would slowly appear on the paper after a couple of minutes. By today's standards, the old Polaroid Instant Camera is quaint compared to digital cameras that enable you to see pictures at nearly the instant they are shot.

Digital photography not only enables us to see pictures instantly, but also it has changed the way we store and transport pictures. While our parents and grandparents stored photos in albums, which lost color over time, you and I and our children are more likely to store our pictures on CD-ROMs, and the pictures will be as vibrant in the future as they were on the day they were taken.

While you might still carry pictures of loved ones in a wallet or purse, it is also likely that you will simply carry them on CD-ROM to display on a personal computer. You can even buy devices that are designed to display photos from CDs on TV screens. If you carry a Pocket PC, you can also view pictures anywhere you may be by using one of the many picture-viewing programs.

To view pictures on a Pocket PC, you will need to load them on the device, which is normally done by using a storage card. If you use a camera that stores pictures on CompactFlash, you can simply remove the card from the camera and insert it into the Pocket PC to view the pictures. All of the picture-viewing programs display pictures from a folder as thumbnails, and you can select individual pictures to display or sort the pictures to display in a slide show.

SmartMedia is another popular storage format used by digital cameras. You can view pictures with SmartMedia cards by using Pretec's CompactSSFDC SmartMedia to CompactFlash adapter. More information about this adapter is available at http://www.pretec.com.

Turn a Pocket PC into a Digital Camera

Several Pocket PC manufacturers sell digital cameras for their Pocket PCs. The cameras use the CompactFlash slot to attach to Pocket PCs, and include software for taking pictures and managing photos. Most of these cameras can use the Pocket PC's screen as a viewfinder. Hewlett-Packard's Jornada Pocket Camera works with HP Jornada 520, 540, and 560 series Pocket PCs. Casio's JK-710DC Digital Camera Card works with the Casio E-115, E-125, EG-800, and E-200 Pocket PCs. UR There sells a CompactFlash digital camera for the @migo Pocket PC. Compaq does not currently sell a camera for the iPAQ Pocket PCs, but there have been announcements from third-party developers that intend to sell cameras for the iPAQ.

All the picture-viewing programs provide a way to rotate and zoom pictures. Most provide ways to annotate pictures with text and attach voice recordings to pictures. These extra features can be really useful for recording information about the pictures when they are taken.

As stated earlier, Microsoft does not include a picture-viewing program with the Pocket PC software. However, several manufacturers bundle these programs with their Pocket PCs. In some cases, they simply include third-party programs, but others provide their own picture-viewing programs. Table 14-1 provides an overview of the picture-viewing programs available for the Pocket PC. In this chapter we will show you two of the most popular picture-viewing programs: Applian's PicturePerfect and IA Style's IA Album.

14

Program	URL
Applian PicturePerfect	www.applian.com
IA Style IA Album	www.iastyle.com
Realviz CoolViz	www.realviz.com/products/coolviz
Aidem System PhotoExplorer	www.aidem.com.tw/English.htm

TABLE 14-1   Picture-Viewing Programs for the Pocket PC

Program	URL
Resco Picture Viewer	www.resco-net.com/resco/en/default.asp
ScaryBear Software PocketPics	www.scarybearsoftware.com
TangCode Image Explorer	www.tang.btinternet.co.uk
CD Software Solutions Pocket Image	www.members.aol.com/doanc/products.html
PQView	www.bitbanksoftware.com/ce/pocketview.htm

TABLE 14-1 Picture-Viewing Programs for the Pocket PC *(continued)*

View Pictures Using PicturePerfect

Pocket PC Magazine has awarded a Readers Choice Award to Applian's PicturePerfect for Best Photo Software. You can download a trial version of Picture Perfect from http://www.applian.com/ pocketpc/pictureperfect/index.htm. When you start PicturePerfect, you will see this program window:

PicturePerfect stores pictures in albums, so to view pictures, you first create an album by tapping Album | New. You can create an empty album and add individual pictures to the album, or you can have PicturePerfect automatically create an album using all the pictures it finds on a storage card or in a folder. Albums contain information about pictures, such as where they are located, but the picture files are separate. You can open albums that you have created by tapping Album | Open, which opens a dialog box that displays all of the albums found on the Pocket PC and storage cards.

NOTE   *PicturePerfect displays pictures in the BMP, GIF, or JPEG formats.*

Pictures display in landscape, such as shown here:

The command bar has buttons to display pictures full screen, to zoom pictures, and to display thumbnails. Thumbnails provide an overview of all the pictures in an album, and also provide a quick way to move between pictures

As you can see in the illustration below, you can configure the thumbnail view to display two, three, or four pictures across the screen.

Tap the Enlarge check box to have the thumbnails occupy the entire display area, and to display a picture, tap its thumbnail.

Display Full Screen   Display Thumbnails
Display Previous Picture   Zoom
          Display Next Picture

When you tap the Zoom button, a Zoom Decrease button (as shown right) replaces the thumbnail button.

The Thumbnail button reappears when you move to another picture, or you can display thumbnails by tapping Picture | View Thumbnails. The Picture menu also contains View Full Screen, Zoom In, and Zoom Out commands.

Zoom In   Zoom Out

14

To add a picture to an album, tap Picture | Insert Picture. You can also add an entire folder's worth of pictures to an album by tapping Picture | Insert Folder. After you add a picture to an album, you can move it to another location in the album by tapping Album | Manage | Sort Album | Manually.

To view a slide show of all the pictures in an album, tap Album | Play Slide Show. The slide show displays the pictures full screen and automatically moves between pictures. You can change the speed at which pictures change in the slide show by tapping Album | Settings | Global Defaults, to open this screen:

Here, you can change the length of time a picture displays during the slide show, as well as select different transition effects and scaling.

You can jazz up slide shows by using a music file as a soundtrack. When PicturePerfect plays a slide show, it looks for an MP3 or WMA file with the same name as the album, and plays the file if it is found.

For example, if you use the default name of Album.alb and Album.mp3 is in the same folder, the music file will automatically play with the slide show.

You can also associate voice recordings to pictures in an album. To create a recording, tap Picture | Properties | Play/Record Sound; and if there is no prior recording, you will see a dialog box asking whether you would like to create a recording. Tap Yes, and you will see a recording toolbar as shown here:

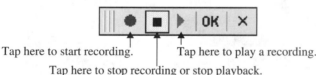

Tap here to start recording.   Tap here to play a recording.
Tap here to stop recording or stop playback.

When a picture that has a recording appears on the screen, you will see a recording button on the Command bar, as shown next:

Tap this button to play the recording.

PicturePerfect provides an easy way to share albums with other PicturePerfect users. You share an album by creating packages, which are files that contain the album and all the associated picture and sound files. To create a package, tap Album | Manage | Make Package; and to open a package, tap Album | Manage | Open Package. When you open a package, the album and all associated files are extracted into the folder where the package file is stored.

> TIP
>
> *Pocket PC Skins has a number of PicturePerfect packages that you can download to view on your Pocket PC. You will find the packages at http://www.pocketpcskins. com/album.html.*

View Pictures Using IA Album

IA Style's IA Album has won a *Pocket PC Magazine* Best Product Award for image management. A trial version of this program is available at http://www.iastyle.com/ iaalbum/index.asp. When you start IA Album, you see this program window:

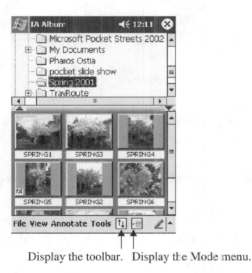

Display the toolbar.   Display the Mode menu.

The main program window has two halves: the top half displays the Pocket PC folder structure, and the bottom half displays the folder contents.

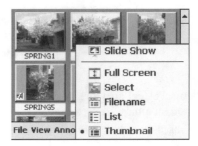

Tap the Mode menu command bar button to switch the viewing mode between filenames, list, thumbnails, individual files, or full screen as shown right:

To display one picture, double-tap either a filename or a thumbnail, or tap Select in the file list menu.

IA Album's toolbar provides quick access to many of the program's functions. The toolbar changes depending on the viewing mode; when in Select mode, the toolbar looks like the following:

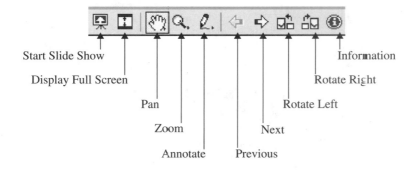

The Select mode toolbar also has three different modes, Pan, Zoom, and Annotate. The Pan mode is the default mode, and it provides buttons for moving through pictures and rotating pictures left and right.

> TIP
> *All of the toolbar functions are also available in the View and Annotate menus.*

The Select Zoom Mode toolbar, shown here, has buttons for zooming in and out of pictures, displaying a picture in its actual size, quick view, and zoom control.

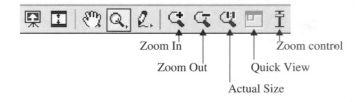

Quick View displays a thumbnail of the picture and provides a way to select a specific portion of the picture to display. The Zoom Control is a slider that you use to zoom the display in or out.

The Select Annotate Mode toolbar, shown next, has buttons for adding voice recordings, inserting text, selecting digital ink color, and selecting digital ink width.

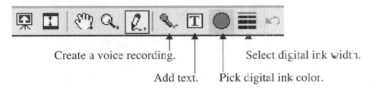

Create a voice recording.   Select digital ink width.

Add text.   Pick digital ink color.

When you tap the Voice Recording button, a toolbar appears with buttons for Record, Play, Stop, and Close. Text annotations appear in a separate window that includes a thumbnail view of the picture along with a text field.

You can also associate recordings that have already been made by tapping Annotate | Select Audio.

You can annotate a picture using digital ink when it displays full screen, or when it is in Select mode. If you draw something and want to erase it, tap Annotate | Undo Last Stroke. You can continually tap Annotate | Undo Last Stroke to erase all digital ink from a picture. A fast way to remove all annotations is to tap Annotate | Remove | All.

By default, digital ink annotations are stored in a separate file, but you can also merge digital ink with a picture, which creates a new picture file. To merge digital ink and create a new picture, tap Annotate | Merge Ink.

Be careful with merging digital ink. The original picture will be altered, and there is no way to return to the original picture without overwriting the file.

14

The toolbar for the Filename, List, and Thumbnail modes is the same, and looks like the following:

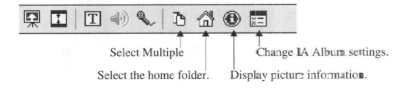

Select Multiple   Change IA Album settings.

Select the home folder.   Display picture information.

To select multiple pictures, tap the Select Multiple toolbar button and then tap the pictures you want to select.

IA Album provides tap-and-hold menus throughout the program. To perform operations on a picture file, such as Cut, Copy, or Paste, tap and hold on the picture in the Filename, List, or Thumbnail mode. You can tap and hold on a picture while it displays full screen to rotate or flip the picture, and exit the full screen view.

To display pictures in a slide show, tap the Slide Show button on the Select Mode toolbar, or tap View | Mode | Slide Show. The slide show toolbar appears on the screen, as shown here:

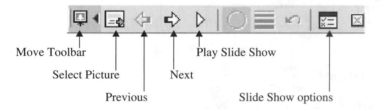

To start a slide show, tap the Play button on the toolbar. The toolbar disappears when the slide show starts playing. Tap the screen to stop a slide show.

Tap the Options button on the toolbar to change one of the many slide show options, as shown here:

You can select different slide show transitions on this option screen.

Edit Pictures

PicturePerfect and IA Album provide easy ways to view digital pictures on a Pocket PC, but they are not designed for editing pictures. For example, while IA Album has the ability to crop and resize pictures, it doesn't have a way to adjust the brightness of a picture. To make changes to a picture on a Pocket PC, you need a graphics editor such as Conduit's Pocket Artist or Idruna Software's Photogenics.

Edit Pictures with Pocket Artist

Pocket Artist is a 24-bit graphics editor for Pocket PCs. You edit pictures and create drawings at the pixel level. Pocket Artist has many of the features available with desktop graphics programs, but works within the constraints of the Pocket PC's screen size. An evaluation version of Pocket Artist can be downloaded from http://www.conduits.com/products/artist/index.htm.

When you start Pocket Artist, you see the following program window

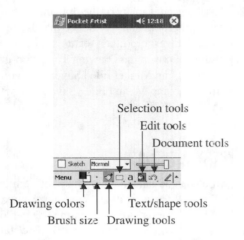

The white space on the screen is the main image document. You can think of this as your canvas for drawing, or where pictures display. The Command bar provides the program menus and the toolbar provides fast access to most of the program functions.

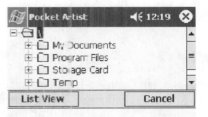

Pocket Artist can edit BMP, GIF, JPG, and 2BP image files. To open a picture, tap Menu | File | Open, which opens this dialog box:

Select the folder that contains the picture file at the top of the screen. When you select a folder, any pictures that it contains are displayed as thumbnails at the bottom of the screen. Tap the picture that you want to edit.

To zoom a picture, tap Menu | Edit and then select Zoom In, Zoom Out, or Zoom 100%. To crop a picture, first tap the Selection tool on the Command bar, and then use the stylus to draw a box around the portion of the picture you want to keep. After you make the selection, tap Menu | Tools | Crop Image.

14

To adjust a picture's brightness or contrast, tap Menu | Tools | Bright/Contrast, which opens this dialog box:

You can drag the dialog box to any location on the screen. Move the sliders left or right to adjust the brightness or contrast. As you move the sliders, you will see the changes made to the picture.

Pocket Artist provides many of the drawing features that are available in a desktop graphics program. You will notice that as you select different drawing tools, the toolbar changes to provide features specific to a tool. The image on the left shows the options in the Drawing Tools pop-up menu.

To save pictures, tap Menu | File | Save; or if you want to save the picture using a new filename, tap Menu | File | Save As. Pocket Artist can only save files in the BMP or JPG formats.

Edit Pictures with Photogenics

Photogenics from Idruna Software is an advanced paint and photo-editing program, and there are versions of the program for Pocket PCs, as well as Windows, Linux, and Amiga desktop computers. There are two Pocket PC versions of the program. The personal version provides the basic features for editing pictures and creating original artwork. The standard version includes all of the advanced features that you expect of graphics software. Both programs are available at http://www.idruna.com/.

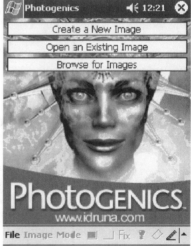

When you first start Photogenics on a Pocket PC, you see this screen:

If you are editing a picture, and know its specific location, tap Open An Existing Image. To browse through the Pocket PC folders to find an image file, tap Browse For Image. Like other Pocket PC graphics programs, Photogenics displays pictures in a folder as thumbnails.

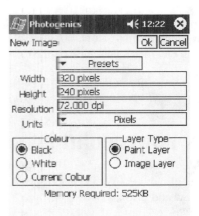

When you create a new image, you first see this dialog box, in which you specify the image's size and resolution:

The Presets drop-down list provides a number a predefined image sizes; and to create an image that fits on the Pocket PC's screen, select 320 × 240. Select the background color by tapping the Colour radio buttons.

Tap OK to create the new image file using the settings on the screen, and then the main program window appears as shown next:

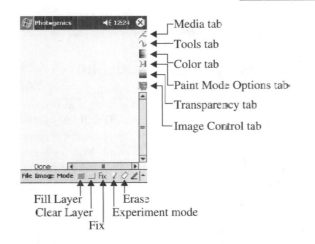

Photogenics provides a toolbar along the top right of the screen in addition to the Command bar buttons and commands at the bottom of the screen.

One of the important concepts of Photogenics is the paint layer. Imagine painting on a glass sheet that is over an existing image. You could paint on the glass without changing the image that is underneath. You could also wipe the paint off the glass if you made a mistake, or remove the glass and get rid of your painting—but leaving the original image untouched. Photogenic's paint layers act like that glass sheet, with the drawings not becoming part of an image until you decide to make the change.

The Fill Layer button causes the paint layer to be filled with a selected color or effect. You can tab the Clear Layer button to clear the paint layer and undo changes that you are not happy with, or tap the Erase button and use the stylus to "rub out" parts of the paint layer you want removed. Tap the Fix button to combine the paint layer to an image. After you tap Fix, you can no longer erase changes.

14

The Experiment mode provides a way to quickly see how a picture will look if you decide to change paint colors. For example, if you draw a red circle while Experiment mode is enabled, you can then select blue on the Color tab and the circle will instantly change to blue.

TIP *Idruna has video tutorials for Photogenics that you can download from http://www.idruna.com/resources.html.*

Show PowerPoint Presentations

Many business people rely on Microsoft PowerPoint every day as part of their job. For those people, if a Pocket PC is to replace notebook computers, they must include software that can view and display PowerPoint presentations. While Microsoft does not include a pocket version of PowerPoint with Pocket PCs, several companies provide programs that can display PowerPoint presentations on a Pocket PC. Table 14-2 lists the programs that are available; and in this section, we will present two of the most popular: CNetX's Pocket SlideShow and Conduit's Pocket Slides.

NOTE *Many of the image-viewing programs presented earlier in this chapter can be used to view PowerPoint presentations, if you export the presentation to JPEG formatted files.*

Show Presentations Using Pocket SlideShow

CNetX's Pocket SlideShow is one of many PowerPoint viewing programs for the Pocket PC. It has received *Pocket PC Magazine*'s Best Pocket PC Software and People's Choice Awards, and you can download a trial version at http://www.cnetx.com/slideshow/.

When you install Pocket SlideShow, a PowerPoint file converter is added to ActiveSync on the desktop computer. In order for file conversion to work, Microsoft PowerPoint 97 or PowerPoint 2000 must be installed on the PC. To view a PowerPoint file, use ActiveSync Explorer to copy the file to a folder on the Pocket PC.

Program	URL
CNetX Pocket SlideShow	www.cnetx.com
Conduits Pocket Slides	www.conduits.com
IA Style IA Presenter	www.iastyle.com
Presenter Inc, iPresentation Mobile Converter	www.presenter.com
Albatros Slides	www.albatros-development.com
Westtek ClearVue Presentation	www.westtek.com

TABLE 14-2 PowerPoint File-Viewing Programs for the Pocket PC

How to ...   **Project Presentations**

Colorgraphic sells a Type I CompactFlash VGA card that works with all Pocket PCs. With this card, you can project anything on the Pocket PC's screen to a computer monitor or television set. The card is capable of displaying VGA, SVGA, Wide VGA, and XGA output, as well as NTSC/Pal TV output. The card includes a standard VGA adapter for making connections to projectors, and an RCA adapter to connect to televisions. The software driver enables the display to appear in portrait or landscape, as well as centering and enlarging the display. The card can be ordered from http://www.colorgraphic.net.

Margi Systems Inc.'s Presenter-to-Go is a Type II CompactFlash card that comes with an infrared remote control, which works with the Pocket PC's infrared port. You can order this card from http://www.margi.com.

If you own a Compaq iPAQ Pocket PC, you can use the LifeView FlyJacket i3800, which is an expansion pack that includes a CompactFlash slot. The FlyJacket accepts video input from VCRs and DVD players, and supports standard VGA output as well as Composite and S-Video. You will find more information about the FlyJacket at http://www.lifeview.com.tw/web_english/ fly_jacket.html.

ActiveSync will detect that you are copying a PowerPoint file, and the following dialog box will appear.

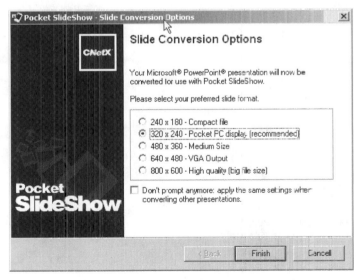

Select the screen format for the presentation on the Pocket PC. If don't plan on projecting the presentation, you should select the 320 × 240 Pocket PC display, which is the default setting. Click Finish and the file will be converted to the Pocket SlideShow format and then copied to the Pocket PC.

After the file is copied to the Pocket PC, you can open it with Pocket SlideShow. When you first start Pocket SlideShow, you see a list of the presentations on the Pocket PC that you can tap to open. An open presentation looks like the following:

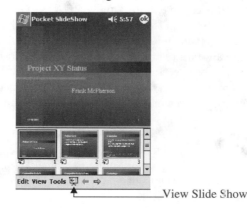

View Slide Show

All of the slides appear as thumbnails along the bottom of the screen, with the current slide shown at the top. If you prefer to see the slide at the bottom of the screen, tap View | Swap Panes and the thumbnails will move to the top of the screen.

> **TIP** *You can change the size of the slide on the screen and make more thumbnails visible by dragging the separator bar up or down.*

To view the presentation as a slide show, tap the Slide Show command bar button, or tap View | Slide Show. The slides will display on the Pocket PC's screen in landscape. You can manually move through the slide show by tapping the screen or by using the Pocket PC's Navigation button. To stop a slide show, press the Action or Navigation button or tap and hold on the screen.

If you prefer to have the slide show automatically advance, tap Tools | Options and then tap the Show tab to display the screen shown on the right.

You can manually advance slides, use the presentation times as entered in the original PowerPoint file, or specify a number of seconds between slides. If the slides automatically advance, you can specify whether the presentation should loop continuously by tapping the appropriate check box on the screen.

To view slide notes, tap View | Notes. You cannot enter notes for slides in Pocket SlideShow, so the notes you see here must be entered using PowerPoint on the desktop. Transitions that you set up in PowerPoint will appear in Pocket SlideShow, or you can set up transitions on the Pocket PC.

To specify a transition for a slide, select the slide and then tap Edit | Transition, which displays the screen shown right:

Select the transition effect from the drop-down list in the middle of the screen. A demonstration of the effect is shown using the graphic on the screen. You can specify the speed of the transition by tapping the appropriate radio button on the screen.

You can hide slides by tapping Edit | Hide Slide. When a slide is hidden, a check box appears next to the Hide Slide option in the Edit menu, and the slide number is crossed out in the thumbnail view.

Pocket SlideShow has direct support for external VGA output such as provided by the Colorgraphic Voyager VGA CompactFlash card. To configure settings for using the card, tap Tools | Options and then tap the Output tab.

How to ... Control PowerPoint Presentations Using a Pocket PC

The programs in this chapter are used to view PowerPoint presentations on a Pocket PC. SlideShow Commander enables you to view and control a PowerPoint presentation that is running on a desktop computer. When combined with wireless networking, you can use SlideShow Commander to remotely control a presentation from anywhere in a room. To use the program, you must be able to establish a network connection between the Pocket PC and desktop computer. You will be able to view the PowerPoint presentation on the Pocket PC's screen, and tap the screen or use hardware buttons to advance slides in the presentation. To obtain more information about SlideShow Commander and buy a copy of the program, go to http://www.synsolutions.com/software/ slideshowcommander/.

Create Presentations Using Pocket Slides

Pocket SlideShow does not provide a way to create new slides or edit existing slides. If you need more editing capabilities to create presentations, Conduit's Pocket Slides may be the program for you. It has all the same features as Pocket SlideShow, plus it can create and edit slides and presentation notes. An evaluation copy of Pocket Slides can be downloaded from http://www. conduits.com/products/slides/default.asp.

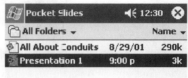

When you start Pocket Slides, you see the list view that shows the presentations that are on the Pocket PC (at right).

Tap the presentation that you want to open, or tap New to create a new presentation.

> TIP *If the New button menu is enabled, you can create a new presentation based on one of several Pocket Slides templates.*

A new presentation file is created with one slide, as shown next.

Tap here to expand the slide notes.

Tap and hold the slide title or subtitle, and tap
Edit Text on the pop-up menu to enter text on the slide.
As you can see in the illustration on the right, there are
several options available to you when entering text:

To add a new slide to the presentation, tap Edit | New Slide. The toolbar, shown next,
provides many of the functions that you need for adding items to a blank slide:

You use the slide sorter to move slides within a presentation. To switch to the slide sorter view,
tap View | Slide Sorter. The slide sorter, shown next, has command buttons for changing the slide
sorter view, hiding slides, previewing animations, setting up animations, and selecting transitions.

Change View

Hide slide

Preview Animation

Select Transitions

Set Up Animation

14

How to ... View PowerPoint Attachments

Both Pocket SlideShow and Pocket Slides require ActiveSync to convert Microsoft PowerPoint presentations for viewing on Pocket PCs. If you receive a PowerPoint file as an e-mail attachment, you will not be able to view the presentation on your Pocket PC using either of these programs. To directly view a PowerPoint file on your Pocket PC, you can use Westtek's ClearVue Viewers, which are available at http://www.westtek.com/clearvue.htm. ClearVue Viewers are available for Microsoft Word, Excel, and PowerPoint files.

The toolbar contains drop-down lists for selecting transitions between slides. To specify a transition to a slide, first select the slide and then select a transition from the drop-down list.

To view a slide show, tap View | Slide Show. Use the Navigation button to move between slides, or tap the screen. You can also use the stylus to draw on the screen during the slide show. To draw, tap and hold on the screen, then tap Stylus Mode | Pen. Clear the drawings by tapping Presentation | Erase Pen on the tap-and-hold menu. Tap Speaker Notes on the tap-and-hold menu to view speaker notes. Exit the slide show by tapping End Show on the tap-and-hold menu.

When you install Pocket Slides, a PowerPoint file converter is added to ActiveSync on the desktop computer. In order for file conversion to work, Microsoft PowerPoint 97, 2000, or 2002 must be installed on the PC. To view a PowerPoint file, use ActiveSync Explorer to copy the file to a folder on the Pocket PC.

Wrapping Up

Pocket PCs have beautiful color screens that can display pictures and presentations, and they can be much easier to carry than notebook computers when traveling. For many business people, the programs presented in this chapter make it possible for Pocket PCs to replace notebook computers. However, presentation software is not the only business tool Pocket PCs are lacking. Pocket PCs do not come with a database program, but as you will see in the next chapter, like graphics software, there are several database programs available from third-party developers to meet any database requirement.

Chapter 15

Store and Query Data

How To...

- Create databases using HanDBase
- Synchronize HanDBase data with a desktop computer
- Synchronize Microsoft Access databases to a Pocket PC
- View and Edit Pocket Access databases using Data On The Run

So far, you have learned how Pocket Outlook, Pocket Word, and Pocket Excel can be used to manage time, write documents, and calculate numbers. But there may be occasions when the information you have just doesn't fit any of these applications. If that is the case, a database may be just the program you need.

Unlike Handheld PCs, Pocket PCs do not come with Pocket Access, and Microsoft does not provide a version of it for you to install. Fortunately, several software developers have written database programs that you can download from the Internet to install on your Pocket PC. In this chapter you'll learn how to use some of these programs to create databases to store and query information.

Even though Pocket Access is not on your Pocket PC, you can still synchronize Access databases using ActiveSync, creating a Pocket Access version of the database on your Pocket PC. You can then use some of the programs covered in this chapter to view, query, and update that data on the Pocket PC. During the next synchronization the changes will be made to the desktop database.

Select a Pocket PC Database

Pocket PC database software ranges from very simple programs, designed for creating databases on your Pocket PC, to more complex programs, designed to synchronize data with enterprise databases from Oracle and Sybase. Many of the programs work with Pocket Access databases and take advantage of the synchronization capabilities that ActiveSync provides. Some of these Pocket PC programs are clients for databases stored on a desktop computer, which they access across a network.

Software vendors continually create new database programs that you can download from the Internet. Table 15-1 provides a list of the programs available at the time this book is written:

HanDBase	http://www.ddhsoftware.com
Pocket Database	http://www.pocket-innovations.com
Data On The Run	http://www.biohazardsoftware.com/dataon.htm
Wireless Database	http://kelbran.com/
HandyDB	http://www.soft4ce.com/prod03.htm
DBF View	http://www.soft-expert.ro/dbfview.htm

TABLE 15-1   Pocket PC Database Software

abcDB	http://www.pocketsoft.ca/Features.asp
Data Anywhere	http://www.smartidz.com/DataAnywhere.htm
DB Anywhere	http://www.dbanywhere.n3.net
Visual CE	http://www.syware.com
Microsoft SQL Server CE	http://www.microsoft.com/sql/evaluation/trial/CE/download.asp
Oracle 9i Lite	http://www.oracle.com/ip/deploy/database/oracle9/9ilite/index.html
Sybase SQL Anywhere Studio	http://www.sybase.com/products/databaseservers/sqlanywhere

TABLE 15-1   Pocket PC Database Software *(continued)*

Usually, you either want to create a simple database on your Pocket PC or synchronize an existing Microsoft Access database so that you can carry that data with you. In this chapter, you'll receive instructions for completing these two tasks using two of the programs in Table 15-1, HanDBase and Data On The Run.

Create Databases with HanDBase

HanDBase, from DDH Software, is one of the most downloaded programs for Palm OS devices on the Internet. DDH Software has a version of this popular program for the Pocket PC that has the following features:

- Create databases on your Pocket PC
- A wide variety of field types, such as, text, integer, float, check box, image, date, note and more
- Multiple security settings that allow one to require passwords to open databases, add records, edit records, delete records, and more
- Move or copy records between databases
- Export records to a text file
- Print records using PrintPocketCE (if installed)
- Infrared beaming of individual records and full databases between Pocket PCs and Palm OS devices
- Find, Sort, and Filter records
- Windows desktop companion program that you can use to create and edit databases for your Pocket PC
- Hundreds of databases that have already been created and are available for free from the DDH Software website

15

A 30-day evaluation version of HanDBase is available at the DDH website and the registration fee for this shareware is $24.99. Included in that fee is Pocket PC and desktop software.

In this section, you'll be introduced to this database program by going through the process of creating a database on your Pocket PC, entering data, and synchronizing the data with your desktop computer.

Install HanDBase

The process of installing HanDBase is the same as all other Pocket PC applications. First, the setup program copies files to your desktop computer, and second, ActiveSync is initiated to complete the installation to your Pocket PC. During the process you have the option of installing the software to the default location, which is internal on your Pocket PC, or on a storage card. The installation process also adds a HanDBase PPC 2.76 folder to the start menu on your desktop computer. Included in that folder is the icon for the HanDBase Desktop application.

The HanDBase program takes as much as 253K of storage space on your Pocket PC and adds this following icon to the Programs window:

Create a Database

To start HanDBase, tap Start | Programs | HanDBase. When you start the program for the very first time, the screen to the right displays.

From here you can either open an existing database that is listed on the screen or create a new database by tapping Create A New Database. In order for a database to be listed on this screen and opened from within the program, it must be stored in the My Documents folder, or a subfolder of My Documents. You can open databases stored in other locations by using File Explorer.

Let's go ahead and create a new database by tapping Create A New Database. The resulting Edit Database screen

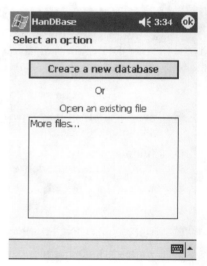

displays, as shown in the image to the right. Here you can define a database name, configure security settings, define the database fields and their order, and provide an author name and comments.

TIP *Once a database is created, you can return to this screen by tapping File | DB Properties.*

Let's create a simple database to keep track of a CD collection. The database will contain simple information such as the title of the CD, the artist, how much it cost, when it was bought, the type of music, and some comments.

To create fields, tap one of the fields listed in the scroll box on the Edit Database screen. For example, tap Field 1 to open the window shown in the next image.

Change the name of the field by selecting the contents of the Field 1 Name text box and type in the new name. To change the type of field, tap the Field Type drop-down menu and select one of the many different data types. When you select the text data type, a number of additional properties display, which you can use to configure how the field displays. One of the settings unique to HanDBase is Pixels Shown. This setting provides you with the ability to accurately control the amount of space the field occupies on the small Pocket PC screen. As a gauge, keep in mind that a letter of the alphabet is approximately 6-pixels wide, so you would enter 12 pixels to display a two-digit number. For the screens that you see in this chapter, the number of pixels is at the default setting, which is 87.

All of the fields in HanDBase can have an associated pop-up menu, which is useful for data entry. The contents of the pop-up menu can be defined when you create the field; also, you have the ability to control whether items are added to the pop-up menu when data is entered manually. To do this, tap the Popups Append check box on the field definition screen to select or deselect it.

Up to four digits can follow the decimal of Float fields, such as the Cost field for our CD database, which has been set to two places after the decimal. Date fields can be configured with default behaviors, such as automatically populating the field with the date that the record is added, the date that the record is modified, or the current date. The default is Date Record Added, but for the CD database, Ask User For Date has been selected. Pop-up fields, such as the Genre field of our database, provide a pop-up menu of items to be selected. Unlike the other fields, you only change items in this pop-up menu by editing the database properties. A default value can be assigned for this field as well.

You enter data by completing a Form view of the record. The field order on the form is defined by tapping Field Order in the Edit Database screen. To move the fields in the list, select the field name and then tap the up or down arrow.

If you wish to secure your database, tap Security Settings on the Edit Database screen. You can then configure the following options for Full Access, Password Required, or No Access: Open Database, Add Records, Edit Records, Delete Records, Edit Pop-ups, DB Properties, and Beam Data.

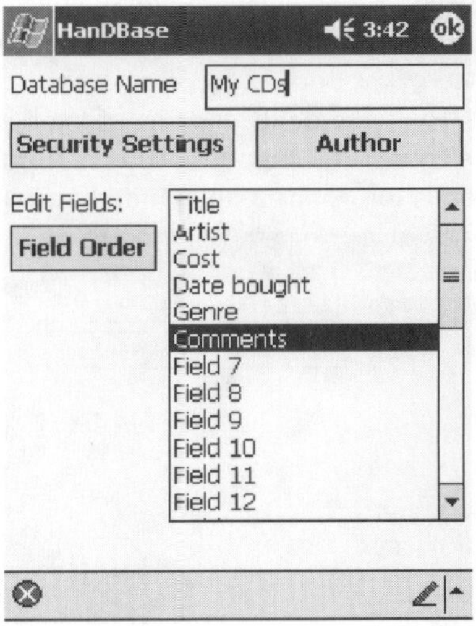

As you can see in the image to the right, there are several fields listed in the Edit Database dialog box that have not been defined.

These fields are not included in the database because their field type is set to Not-Used. Tap OK to save the database properties and to start entering data. To make changes to the database after it has been created, tap File | DB Properties.

Enter and Edit Data

Data displays in a tabular view, as shown in the following image.

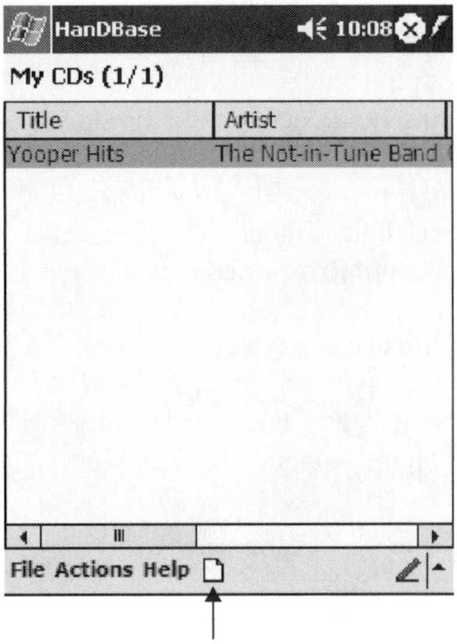

To resize the columns, tap the stylus on the right edge of the column head and drag either left or right. Slide the scroll bar left or right to view more columns in the database. (There is no way to zoom in or out like you can in Pocket Excel.)

Tap here to create a new record.

To see more database columns on your Pocket PC, use either JS Landscape or Nyditot Virtual Display, as described in Chapter 11, to change the display to landscape.

To create a record, tap New Record on the Command bar to display the Edit Record window to the right.

All of the fields are ordered from top to bottom based on the criteria you defined in the Edit Database screen. To the left of each field name is a small triangle, indicating that a pop-up menu exists for that field. Tap the name of the field to display the menu, and then tap the item you want placed in the field. To add an entry to the pop-up menu, tap the Edit Pop-up List item.

Date fields include a check box for entering the current date. Select different dates using a calendar picker, which displays when you tap the triangle to the right of the field. If you tap the field name of a date field, you'll see a pop-up menu with options including Today, Tomorrow, One Week, or No Date.

You'll recall that we defined the Genre field as a pop-up field when we created the database. Here you'll see how pop-up fields appear. The pop-up menu will display if you tap either the field or the field label. Pop-up fields can also be changed in the tabular view, but by default this is turned off. To enter data in pop-ups from the tabular view, tap File | Preferences, and then tap Allow Pop-up in List View check box.

Synchronize Data with Your Desktop

Pocket Outlook stores information in databases and provides record-level synchronization, which means that only individual records synchronize and not the entire database file. HanDBase does not provide record-level synchronization, so there is no option added to ActiveSync. The database files can be synchronized with a desktop if they are stored in the My Documents folder located internally on your Pocket PC, which is where they are written by default.

Once the file is synchronized to your desktop, it can be opened using the HanDBase Desktop program. You can then add or edit records. The next time you synchronize, the updated file will download to your Pocket PC, just like Pocket Excel or Pocket Word documents. Keep in mind, however, that if you make a change to the database file on both your Pocket PC and desktop before you synchronize, a conflict will occur. If you configure ActiveSync to automatically resolve conflicts by replacing items on either the Pocket PC or desktop, you could end up losing data.

DDH Software is developing an ActiveSync option for HanDBase that will provide record-level synchronization of databases. This option should be available by the time this book is published. You will find it at http://www.ddhsoftware.com.

15

How to ...   **Save Time by Using the HanDBase Gallery**

Because HanDBase has been available for Palm OS devices for several years, thousands of people have been using the program to create databases. Besides providing a great program, DDH Software also provides a free service of storing and cataloging databases so they can be easily found and downloaded. If you need a database, first check the HanDBase Gallery at http://www.ddhsoftware.com/gallery.html because chances are it has already been created. At the very least you'll find a database that is close to your needs, which you can then modify. If you find something useful in the gallery, the best way to pay the developer back is by contributing databases that you create to the gallery.

Synchronize Microsoft Access Databases

Even though Pocket Access is not available on the Pocket PC, you can still synchronize Pocket Access data with Microsoft Access on a desktop by using ActiveSync. Synchronization between Pocket Access and Microsoft Access is not enabled by default. It has to be turned on by selecting the Pocket Access information type in ActiveSync. As you will learn later in this chapter, the process for setting up synchronization varies depending on where synchronization is initiated.

TIP   *Pocket Access database files on your Pocket PC have an extension of .cdb, and Microsoft Access database files on your desktop have an extension of .mdb.*

Only tables, fields, and indexes are synchronized between your device and PC. You can choose to synchronize only certain fields within a table or mark information as read-only on your device.

NOTE   *Only 65,536 records can be synchronized from a host database to a Pocket PC database.*

Synchronize PC Databases

ActiveSync converts Microsoft Access files and other Open Database Connectivity (ODBC) databases to Pocket Access, but Pocket Access files will only convert to Microsoft Access. The first step for enabling database synchronization is to enable the Pocket Access information type in ActiveSync. To do that, start ActiveSync on your PC, and follow these steps:

If the device is not connected, make sure the correct device name displays in ActiveSync. If not, switch to the appropriate device by clicking File | Mobile Device and select the name of the device.

1. Click Options, or select Tools | Options to open the Options dialog box, as shown in the image to the right.

2. Select the check box next to Pocket Access.

3. Click OK.

After the Pocket Access information type is enabled for the device, the next step is to set up database synchronization. To do this, connect the device to the PC and then follow these steps:

1. If the information type details do not display, click Details on the toolbar.

2. Double-click the Pocket Access information type to open the Database Synchronization Settings dialog box, as shown in the image to the right.

3. Click Add, select a database using the Open dialog box, and then click OK. By default, Microsoft Access databases are listed, but ODBC databases can be selected from the Files Of Type drop-down list. When you select a database the Import From Database To Mobile Device dialog box displays.

4. Enter a location and filename for the Pocket Access database, and select the tables and fields

to include in the database using the Import From Database To Mobile Device dialog box, as shown in the image to the right.

TIP

Another way synchronize a database is to drag-and-drop a database file from the PC to the device. The Import From Database To Mobile Device dialog box will then open. By default, the database will be stored in the My Documents folder on the device.

5. Click OK. ActiveSync will copy the database file to the device. When that is done, the Database Synchronization Settings dialog box will display. It will have an entry for the database currently being synchronized.

NOTE

Pocket Access is one of the few ActiveSync information types that will synchronize data not stored in the internal My Documents folder. This enables you to synchronize large databases to storage cards, though if you do, it is recommended that you put the database in a My Documents folder on the storage card. Doing so ensures that database programs will be able to find and open the database.

Table synchronization is now established between the Pocket Access database on the device and the database on the PC. You can then open the database on the device and add or edit information; at the next synchronization, those changes will be copied to the PC.

Synchronization Conflicts

A synchronization conflict occurs when ActiveSync determines that a record has changed on both the device and PC. ActiveSync automatically resolves conflicts by giving the PC priority. The record from the device is written to the MSysCEC*Xxx* table in the PC Database, where *Xxx* is the original name of the table. You can check the MsysCEConflicts table to determine if a conflict occurred, and then go to the MSysCEC*Xxx* table to look at the data.

Configure Database Synchronization Options

Opening the database Properties dialog box can change the host and device file locations. To make these changes, follow these steps in ActiveSync on the PC:

1. Click Details to display the Information Types.

2. Double-click Pocket Access.

3. Select the database you want to change and then click Properties.

4. Change the contents of the Host Location or Device Location fields as desired.

5. Click OK to save changes.

Synchronize Mobile Device Databases to the Desktop

The programs Pocket Database, HandyDB, abcDB, DBAnywhere, and Visual CE listed in Table 15-1 will create Pocket Access databases on a Pocket PC, which can be synchronized with a PC running Microsoft Access. ActiveSync will not automatically synchronize a database file that is placed in the My Documents folder on the device. To synchronize a Pocket Access database to a PC, you must use the ActiveSync Explorer to copy the file.

When you drag-and-drop a Pocket Access database file to a folder on the PC, the Export From Mobile Device To Database dialog box displays, as shown in the image to the right.

With this dialog box, you specify the location on the PC where the file will be written, and you select the tables in the database to copy to the PC.

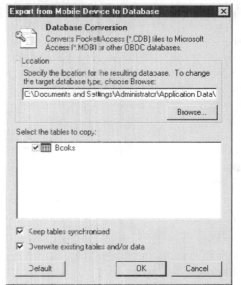

> NOTE   *By default, ActiveSync will write the database to the \Program Files\ActiveSync\Profiles\ [device name] folder on the PC.*

If you clear the Keep Tables Synchronized check box, ActiveSync will just make a copy of the database to the PC and not set up synchronization. When the Overwrite Existing Tables And/Or Data check box is selected, ActiveSync will overwrite any database files or tables that have the same filename on the PC.

After synchronization is established, you can disconnect and add data to the database on the device and the PC. At the next synchronization, ActiveSync will compare the tables in the two databases, identify the records that have been added, and then synchronize them so that both databases are current.

Stop Database Synchronization

There are two ways to stop synchronizing a database, and both involve opening the Database Synchronization Settings dialog box by double-clicking the Pocket Access information type on the ActiveSync Options screen. If you want to temporarily stop synchronization, select the check box next to the database name. To permanently remove a database, select it in the dialog box and then click Remove.

15

Work with Pocket Access Databases Using Data On The Run

ActiveSync only provides the ability to synchronize data with Microsoft Access. To view or edit the data once it is on your Pocket PC, you'll need to download and install one of the programs listed in Table 15-1. Perhaps the easiest and least expensive of those programs is Data On The Run from Biohazard Software. A trial version of this program is available at http://www.biohazardsoftware.com.

Install Data On The Run

The process of installing Data On The Run is the same as all other Pocket PC applications. First, the setup program copies files to your desktop computer, and second, ActiveSync is initiated to complete the installation to your Pocket PC. During the process you have the option of installing the software to the default location, which is internal on your Pocket PC or on a storage card.

Data On The Run requires a hefty 3,213K of storage space, with many of those programs being system files that are written to the \Windows folder on the Pocket PC. While you can install the program to a storage card, only 450K of files are written to the card, with the rest being stored internally. ActiveSync will determine whether there is enough storage space on your Pocket PC before installing the program. After the installation completes, the icon to the right is added to the Programs menu. Tap this icon to start Data On The Run.

Data On The Run

Open a Database

When Data On The Run first loads, you'll see the program window to the right.

To open a Pocket Access database that is stored in the My Documents folder, either internally or on a storage card, tap File | Open, then tap the name of the database that you want to open.

Access databases can contain several tables of records that store information. Only one table opens at a time in Data On The Run, so, immediately after selecting a database, you are prompted to select the table to open from a drop-down list of tables in the database. To open another table in the database, tap File | Open, reselect the database that you are working in, and then select the new table that you want to view.

View Data

The table that you select displays in the following Form view:

Tap these buttons to
move through records.

Tap here to create a new record.

Tap here to delete a record.

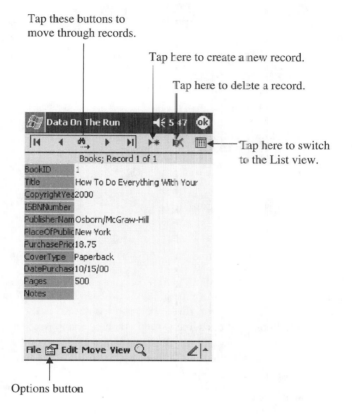

Tap here to switch
to the List view.

Options button

This Form view is automatically created by the program, and unlike other database software available for Pocket PCs, Data On The Run does not allow you to create your own forms. However, you can change the font size, the font style, and background color of the form labels by tapping Options on the Command bar.

15

Along the top of the Form view are buttons for moving through the records in the table. At the upper right of the Form view is the List View button. When you tap this button, all of the records in the table display in a tabular view, as shown in the following image:

Tap here to switch to Form view.

Tap here to move through records.

To resize the columns, tap the stylus on the right edge of the column head and drag either left or right. Slide the scroll bar left or right to view more columns in the table.

Indicators at the bottom of the screen show you how many rows are displayed, along with buttons for moving back and forth through the table for a select number of records. Tap Options on the Command bar to configure the number of records that display in the List view. Tap the Form View button to switch the display back to the default Form view.

TIP *The View menu provides commands for switching between Form and List views.*

Tap the Binoculars in either the Form or List view to jump to a specific record. If you want to go to the next record in the table that begins with an *A,* tap the last radio button, select Next from the drop-down list, select the field, and enter **A**, as shown in the image to the right.

To go to the tenth record in the table, select Record Number and enter **10** in the Record Number field. After you make a selection, tap Go!, or tap Cancel to close the dialog box.

Search for Data

While in the Form view or the tabular Form view, tap the Magnifying Glass to open the dialog box where you enter search criteria, an example of which is shown in the image to the right. Select the field to search from the Search Field drop-down list, select an operator from the Operator drop-down list, and enter the information that you want to search for in the Criteria field.

Tap Apply Filter to run the search and display the records that meet the specified search criteria in the table. To add a second field to the search, tap the Second Criteria check box, select And or Or, and then provide the search information.

The filter remains in effect until you remove it by tapping the Magnifying Glass and then tapping Remove Filter.

Edit Data

One of the reasons why you might synchronize a Microsoft Access database is so that you can edit the data when you are away from your desktop computer. Editing data using Data On The Run is very easy, but you can only edit existing data in the Form view. Simply tap the field that you want to change, make the changes, and then move to the next record to save the changes to the field.

> **TIP** *Double-tap a field in the Form view to display its contents in a separate window.*

To add or delete data from either the Form or List view, tap Edit | Add New Record or Edit | Delete Record. Add Record and Delete Record buttons are available in the Form view.

> **NOTE** *Keep in mind that if you change a record on a Pocket PC and the desktop computer before synchronizing, a synchronization conflict will occur. ActiveSync will automatically apply the change on the desktop and ignore the change on the Pocket PC.*

One of the neat features that Data On The Run provides is the ability to define a drop-down list of data that is frequently entered into a database. First, you need to select a field and then enter the items for the drop-down list by tapping Edit | Setup Drop-Down Choices. Enter an item for the drop-down list and tap Add. Tap Done when finished.

A triangle to the right of a field indicates that there is a drop-down list. When you add a record, tap the triangle to display the list, tap an item, and it will be inserted into the field.

15

Wrapping Up

Many programs written for Pocket PCs are really just databases. The programs described in this chapter provide you with the ability to create similar programs for yourself, either by creating databases on a Pocket PC using HanDBase or synchronizing Access databases and viewing them with Data On The Run. We have now completed our overview of the productivity applications available for the Pocket PC. In the next chapter, you'll learn how to best use these programs on your Pocket PC at the office.

Chapter 16

Be Productive At Work

How To…

- ■ Secure information
- ■ Send and receive e-mail from Exchange
- ■ Send and receive e-mail from Lotus Notes
- ■ Access mainframe applications
- ■ Access corporate databases
- ■ Run Windows programs

Your Pocket PC is designed to help you organize your life and to have fun along the way. While at home, you may enjoy listening to music using the Windows Media Player or reading a book using Microsoft Reader, but for many, you'll use your Pocket PC at work the most.

One of the reasons why you might have bought a Pocket PC is because a coworker has one. Personal digital assistants (PDA), whether they are Pocket PCs, Palms, or Visors, are increasing in numbers at corporations.

The extent to which you use your device at work will depend significantly on how computers at work are used and supported. Before you connect your Pocket PC to your desktop PC at work, you should find out whether your company has a policy for using PDAs. Some people will have no problem connecting their device to their desktop PC at work, while others may be restricted because of corporate policy. Unfortunately, in many cases, policies are defined out of ignorance about how Pocket PCs work.

This chapter provides information for using your Pocket PC at the office. You will find tips for connecting your Pocket PC to your desktop at work and with the corporate network. You will also learn ways to secure information, access your company's e-mail, and even run Windows programs.

Bring Your Pocket PC to Work

There are many great features built into your Pocket PC to help you be more productive at work and, it is hoped, to gain more free time to enjoy life. Obviously, you can use your device to schedule appointments, track tasks, and store contact information; yet the Pocket Office applications enable you to create documents and spreadsheets as well.

You probably already knew about all these features before you bought your device, and probably tried each as soon as you took the device out of its box. Inevitably, the time will come when you pack your Pocket PC in your briefcase and head off to work, but once you are there, how will you use your device?

Connect to Your PC at Work

You will encounter few problems using your Pocket PC at work, but you may face some hurdles connecting the device to your work computer. You will need to resolve two issues: one, the physical connection between the device and computer; and two, installing and running ActiveSync.

Make the Connection

Every Pocket PC is capable of partnering with two PCs, but most Pocket PCs only include one cable or cradle. Chances are good that you already use the cable or cradle with your home computer, so you might be faced with the prospect of carrying it back and forth between work and home. There are a few solutions to this problem.

First, check to see whether your work computer has an infrared port. For example, many notebook computers have built-in infrared ports. If the port is available, it can be used to communicate with your device. Chapter 5 provides the instructions for using infrared ports with ActiveSync.

Even if your computer does not have a built-in infrared port, you might want to add one. It can be useful for connecting with multiple devices, or connecting notebook computers to desktop computers. Attached to my home computer is JetEye PC from Extended Systems, which I find useful for connecting multiple devices. You will find more information about the JetEye PC at http://www.extendedsystems.com. The ACTiSYS Corporation has serial and USB infrared adapters that also work and can be found at http://www.actisys.com.

The second solution is to buy a second cable to use at work. All hardware manufacturers sell cables as accessories. Most of the cables sell for less than $25 and are available from the manufacturers or any online store that sells Pocket PCs. If you upgrade within a brand, you might already have two cables, so be sure to check the manufacturer's website.

Finally, you can use an Ethernet card to make the connection between your device and the desktop PC. However, before an Ethernet card can be used, you must create a partnership using a cable or an infrared port. Chapter 5 provides the instructions for synchronizing with a network connection, and later in this chapter you will learn about additional aspects of connecting your device to a corporate network.

Install ActiveSync

After you determine how you will connect the device to your computer at work, the next step is to install ActiveSync. Aside from corporate policies prohibiting the installation of software on company PCs, it is easy to install ActiveSync on PCs running Windows 98. Detailed instructions for installing ActiveSync are provided in Chapter 5.

Installing ActiveSync on PCs running Windows NT 4 and Windows 2000 is more difficult. The user ID that you use to install ActiveSync must be a local administrator on the PC. Once installed under Windows NT 4, ActiveSync will run, even if the ID is only in the local users group.

The same is not true for Windows 2000. By default, to run ActiveSync, the ID must at least be in the power users local group if ActiveSync is installed on a drive formatted with NTFS. The reason is because the Windows 2000 default security on the Program Files folder and subfolders does not provide users with write access, and ActiveSync must be able to write files in the \Program Files\Microsoft ActiveSync folder. An alternative is to modify the NTFS permissions of the ActiveSync folder so that the users group has full control over the folder.

NOTE *This problem does not occur if the Program Files folder is on a FAT partition.*

16

Work with Non-Microsoft Applications

Personal Information Managers (PIMs) have been available for many years, but they never seemed to catch on, probably because the data stored by PIMs is not as useful when anchored to a desk. Sure, when you sit at your desk you could quickly search for a telephone number or an appointment, but what happens when you are in a meeting? The solution was to print the information on paper and take it with you, but adding appointments and tasks was tedious because it required entering that information when you returned to your desk.

The synchronization capabilities of Personal Digital Assistants (PDAs) make PIMs more useful because it is easier to carry and update data. Furthermore, now that the data is in electronic form, it is much easier to share with others, and that has lead to the group scheduling capabilities that make PIMs corporate tools.

Microsoft Outlook is a popular PIM, but is certainly not the first, or only, one used by companies. Lotus Organizer has been available for much longer, and its user interface, which looks like a paper planner, is very popular. Other programs store PIM data, but specialize in contact management, such as Act!, Goldmine, and Maximizer. Collaborative software such as Microsoft Exchange Server and Lotus Notes also store PIM data.

With all of these options, there is a chance that your company uses a program other than Microsoft Outlook. If that is the case, in order for your Pocket PC to be useful at work, you will need a way to synchronize data with that program. The good news is that Pocket PCs can synchronize with programs other than Outlook. The bad news is that you may need to buy additional software because ActiveSync only communicates with Outlook.

Synchronize Data with Non-Microsoft Applications

Four programs expand the Pocket PC synchronization capabilities beyond Outlook to several different PIMs. They are Intellisync from Puma Technology, XTNDConnect PC, CompanionLink Express, or Professional from Extended Systems, and PDASync from LapLink. These programs include features not found with ActiveSync that provide more control over synchronization and address shortcomings. For example, Intellisync and XTNDConnect PC support synchronization of Outlook subfolders, which is not possible with ActiveSync.

Each of these programs synchronizes calendar, e-mail, contacts, and tasks. Both Intellisync and XTNDConnect PC give you the ability to match fields of data, providing flexibility not available with ActiveSync, which is optimized for Outlook. What may be appealing to companies is that both synchronize with Pocket PCs and Palm Computing devices, enabling them to provide a standard method of synchronization with a standard PIM.

Intellisync provides synchronization with 15 different programs, including Microsoft Exchange, Lotus Notes, and Novell GroupWise. For a current list of the programs that Intellisync supports, check the Puma Technology website at http://www.pumatech.com/intellisync.html.

In addition to synchronizing with Pocket PC and Palm Computing, XTNDConnect PC also synchronizes with Pocket Viewer from Casio. Pocket Viewer is a low-cost organizer that does not support all of the features found with the Pocket PC or Palm. XTNDConnect PC synchronizes with fewer programs than Intellisync, but does support NetManage Ecco Pro 4, unlike Intellisync. For more information about XTNDConnect PC, go to the Extended Systems website at http://www.extendedsystems.com.

CompanionLink also synchronizes with fewer programs than Intellisync, supporting versions of GoldMine, Lotus Organizer, Outlook, ACT!, and Telemagic. More information and a trial version of CompanionLink can be found at http://www.companionlink.com.

PDASync is the newest of these products and supports synchronization between a variety of Pocket PCs, Palm Computing devices, and mobile phones, with seven different desktop applications. The desktop applications it supports are Outlook, Lotus Notes, Lotus Organizer, ACT!, NetManage Ecco Pro, GoldMine, and Palm Desktop. You will find more information about PDASync at http://www.laplink.com/products/pdasync/overview.asp.

Manage Contacts

Contact managers are programs that store data in a manner similar to PIMs, but are designed for the purpose of managing relationships with people. Usually, all of the data in a contact manager relates back to a person. For example, with a contact manager you can quickly see all the appointments that you have with a particular person. Sales departments of companies commonly use these programs to help build relationships with people.

The four third-party synchronization programs described in the previous section support the synchronization of Pocket Outlook with popular desktop contact managers like ACT! and GoldMine. However, Pocket Outlook does not provide many of the features, such as linking contacts with appointments or tasks that one expects of a contact manager. If you want these features on your Pocket PC, you will have to obtain a third-party application.

One of the most popular of these applications is PocketInformant, available for download from http://www.pocketinformant.com. PocketInformant enables you to link contacts with appointments, tasks, other contacts, or files. It also provides the ability to create appointments or tasks using the contact information, which are automatically linked to the contact.

PocketInformant works with your Pocket Outlook data, so everything synchronizes with Outlook. Pocket On-Schedule Version 5 for Pocket PC from Odyssey synchronizes with On-Schedule Version 5 or Microsoft Outlook. Because of this, it is a good alternative to Pocket Outlook if you don't like Outlook.

Unlike Pocket Outlook, Pocket On-Schedule provides journaling capabilities to track contact information, and it supports multiple address books, calendars, and to-do lists. For people who find Pocket Outlook categories insufficient for separating data, Pocket On-Schedule may be a good alternative. You will find more information, and a trial version of the software, at http://www.odysseyinc.com.

16

How to ... Boost Contacts

The Power Contacts power toy from Microsoft adds three options to the Contacts pop-up menu: Create Appointment, Create Task, and Open Web Page. Create Appointment creates an appointment with the contact as the subject and attendee, Create Task creates a task with the contact as the subject, and Open Web Page starts Internet Explorer and loads the web page associated with the contact. This program is free and can be downloaded from http://www.microsoft.com/mobile/pocketpc/downloads/powertoys.asp.

Convert Files

Even though Microsoft Word and Excel are the most popular word processor and spreadsheet programs, they are not the only ones used by companies. At one time, WordPerfect and Lotus 1-2-3 were more popular, and they are still in use.

Unfortunately, there are no widely available file conversion tools for the Pocket PC that enable you to open WordPerfect or Lotus 1-2-3 files in Pocket Word or Excel. In both cases, the best way to work with these files is to save them in Microsoft formats before downloading to your device. This also means that if someone wants to e-mail a WordPerfect document as an attachment, they should first convert the file to a Microsoft format.

Chapter 6 explains how ActiveSync converts files as they move between a device and a desktop computer. Inbox also converts files so that you can easily send and receive Word and Pocket Word file attachments. But if you use any other method of transferring files, such as an FTP client or a network connection, you will have to manually convert the file to a supported format.

Pocket Word can save files in Rich Text, Plain Text, Word 97, and Word 6.0/95 formats. To save a document in these formats, tap Tools | Save Document As, expand the Type drop-down list, and select a format. Pocket Excel can save files in Excel 97, 5.0, and 95 workbook formats. To save a Pocket Excel workbook in these formats, tap Tools | Save Workbook As, expand the Type drop-down list, and select a format.

Open Adobe Acrobat Files

The Adobe Portable Document Format (PDF) has become the de facto standard for distributing documents on the Internet. This is because Adobe distributes Acrobat Reader, which is required to view PDF files, for free on the Internet. PDF files look exactly the same as printed documents and are very easy to create. For these reasons, many companies create documentation in PDF format and make it available from their websites.

Pocket PC owners have long sought a PDF viewer for their devices, and Adobe recently made this wish come true by releasing a version of Acrobat Reader for the Pocket PC. The Pocket PC version of Acrobat Reader is capable of viewing tagged and untagged Acrobat files.

Tagged files are preferable for viewing on Pocket PCs because they allow the Reader to format the text for the size of the Pocket PC screen. When you install Acrobat Reader on your Pocket PC, it adds an Acrobat file converter to ActiveSync, which attempts to convert Acrobat files to the tagged format. If the PDF file cannot be converted to the tagged format, it is copied to the Pocket PC in the untagged format. You will find more information about Acrobat Reader at http://www.adobe.com/products/acrobat/readerforppc.html.

Before Adobe Acrobat Reader, Primer PDF Viewer from Ansyr was the only Acrobat Reader for Pocket PCs. Primer supports most PDF image formats, including bookmarks, hyperlinks, and Table of Contents. It provides magnification capabilities that are important for viewing documents designed for larger PC screens. More information and a 30-day trial version of this program is available at http://www.ansyr.com/.

Access the Corporate Network

Chances are good that your computer at work is connected to a Local Area Network (LAN) so that it can access shared resources like printers and e-mail servers. The Pocket PC includes the software to enable it to connect to these networks, either by using a modem and dial-up connection or directly with an Ethernet card. You can use this connectivity to send and receive e-mail from your company mail server, or access web pages on your corporate intranet.

Gather Dial-Up Information

Today, many companies provide dial-up access to their networks to enable employees to access resources from home or on the road. The dial-up access is probably expected to work with desktop computers, while few companies provide support for Pocket PCs. This does not mean that your Pocket PC will not work with a company dial-up access, but it does mean that you may have to gather more information and probably configure the device yourself.

If you can access a corporate network using standard Windows Dial-Up Networking, you should be able to connect using a Pocket PC. You will need to gather some information in order to create a dial-up connection. If your company provides instructions for connecting using Windows, then what you need will be provided in those instructions. If the dial-up connection has already been created, you can find the information by opening the connection properties. The following is the information that you will need to create the dial-up connection on your Pocket PC:

- Do you provide a username and password in the Dial-Up Connection dialog box, or does a terminal window open after the number has been dialed (in which you enter a username and password)?

- Obtain the maximum baud rate for the connection, as well as the settings for data bits, parity, stop bits, and flow control.

- Find out whether the connection uses Point-to-Point Protocol (PPP) or Serial Line Interface Protocol (SLIP). The most common of these is PPP.

- Does the network access server or Windows NT Remote Access Server provide an IP address, or is one manually assigned? The most common configuration is server-assigned, but if it is manually assigned, then you will need the address.

16

■ Does the connection use software compression or IP header compression? The most common configuration is to use both.

■ Does the server assign addresses for name servers, or are they manually assigned? If they are manually assigned, you will need the addresses for the Primary Domain Name Server (DNS), Secondary DNS, Primary Windows Internet Name Sever (WINS), and Secondary WINS.

■ Is a proxy server used to access the Internet? If you plan on accessing the Internet from the corporate network, you will need the proxy server name, if one is used. To find the proxy server name found in Internet Explorer on desktop computers, click Tools | Internet Options; then click the Connections tab and the LAN Settings button.

■ Do you use virtual private networking (VPN) to connect to the corporate network? If you do, then obtain the host name or IP address of the VPN server.

■ Obtain the phone number for accessing the corporate network, or if you use VPN, then obtain the phone number for an Internet Service Provider (ISP).

Configure Connection Manager Work Settings

After you gather this information, you are ready to create the dial-up connection. The process for creating the connection with Pocket PC 2000 is the same as creating an Internet connection. Pocket PC 2002 introduces the Connection Manager, which simplifies the process of connecting a Pocket PC with networks.

The Connection Manager, as shown in the following image, has three sections: one for Internet connection settings, another for Work connection settings, and one more for Network cards.

Configure Internet connection settings here.

Configure Work connection settings here.

Specify what type of connection network cards use here.

Microsoft provides a Connection Manager Wizard for Pocket PC 2002 that simplifies entering the Connection Manager settings. The Wizard also configures e-mail and instant messaging settings. You can download the Wizard using a link provided on the Pocket PC companion CD-ROM. From the CD-ROM main menu, click Start Here | Download Connection Wizard. Chapter 19 discusses instructions for using the Wizard.

The Work section of Connection Manager includes a drop-down list from which you can select the settings to be used when connecting to a corporate network. In most cases, all you need to do is modify the existing Work Settings item in the list; however, if you connect to multiple corporate networks, you can create additional items in the list by selecting New.

To change the Work Settings, tap Modify, and the screen to the right displays.

The first step in configuring the work settings is to enter the dial-up information on the Modem tab located in the Work Settings dialog box. To enter the dial-up information, tap New, enter a name for the connection, select a modem, and select a baud rate. If the network provides TCP/IP addresses and name server information and you don't need to change the modem settings, just tap Next.

> **TIP** *If you want to change the name for the settings or delete the settings, tap the General tab.*

If you need to enter TCP/IP or name server information, or if you need to have a terminal window open after the modem connects so that you can log on to the network, then tap Advanced on the Make New Connection screen. The Advanced Settings screen opens, as shown on the left.

Tap the Use Terminal After Connecting check box if you need a terminal window for logging on to the network. Tap the User Terminal Before Connecting and Enter Dialing Commands Manually check boxes if you need to enter modem commands prior to the call being made. Tap the TCP/IP tab to enter the IP address that the Pocket PC should use when connecting to the network, and tap the Name Servers tab to enter IP addresses for Domain Name Servers (DNS) and Windows Internet Name Servers (WINS). Tap OK to close the Advanced Settings screen and then tap Next.

16

How to ...   Use Dial-Up Scripts

Connections that require a terminal window require the entry of information that can be automated by using dial-up scripts. Unlike Windows, you cannot create scripts in Pocket PC dial-up connections, but Peter Koch's Dialup Master supports dial-up scripts on Pocket PC 2000 devices.

Dialup Master adds a System Tray icon for quick access to dial-up connections. Dialup Master supports customized login scripts and provides an online timer in the system tray. A 15-day trial version of this program can be downloaded from http://www.moreinfo.com.au/peterepeat/.

Dialup Master does not work with Pocket PC 2002, but the program author is developing a Pocket PC 2002 version. When the new version of the program is complete, it will be posted on the web site.

NOTE   *In most cases you will not need to make changes to the Advanced settings. Your network administrator can tell you whether you need to change these settings, and can provide you with information that must be entered.*

The second screen of the Modem settings contains fields for the country code, area code, and phone number of the dial-up connection. Enter the phone number for the corporate network on this screen unless you use a VPN, in which case you enter the phone number for an ISP. After you enter the number, tap Next to open the final screen for the Modem settings.

On the last Modem settings screen, you can specify how long the modem should wait before canceling a call if it is not answered and whether the modem should wait for a dial tone before dialing. If you use a mobile phone to make the connection, you should clear the Wait For Dial Tone Before Dialing check box on this screen. A field is also available for entering extra modem commands, which the modem will execute prior to dialing the phone number. Tap Finish to save the settings and return to the Modem tab.

TIP   *To delete an item on the Modem tab, tap-and-hold the item and tap Delete on the pop-up menu.*

Virtual Private Networking Provides Access to Corporate Networks

Virtual Private Networking uses encryption to secure communication between a client and a server, and it is commonly used to enable one to use the public Internet to access servers on a private network. Typically, you first dial an ISP using dial-up networking. Then you run a VPN client, which establishes a connection with the VPN server. After a VPN connection is made, you can then run any application that requires a network connection.

Pocket PC 2002 supports Virtual Private Network (VPN) solutions that use the Point-to-Point Tunneling Protocol (PPTP). In order to configure your Pocket PC to use VPN, you will need the host name or IP address of the VPN connection. To configure your Pocket PC to use VPN, tap the VPN tab and then tap New. The screen to the left will then open.

If you need to enter TCP/IP and name server addresses for the VPN connection, tap Advanced. After you enter a name for the connection and the VPN host name or IP address, tap OK.

To delete an item on the VPN tab, tap-and-hold the item and tap Delete on the pop-up menu.

The final work setting to configure is on the Proxy Settings tab, as shown on the right.

Proxy servers are typically used by web browsers to access pages on the Internet on computers connected to a corporate network. If you need to use a proxy server, tap the two check boxes on this screen, and then enter the name for the server in the Proxy Server field. Tap Advanced if you need to change the ports for the proxy server, enter a WAP proxy server, or configure the Socks proxy server. Tap OK from any of the Work Settings tabs to save the settings and return to the Connection Manager.

16

How to ... Make VPN Connections Using the IP Security Protocol

Pocket PC 2002 does not support the IP Security Protocol (IPSec), and Pocket PC 2000 does not include PPTP. If your company requires IPSec, then movianVPN from Certicom may be the best solution. The client software runs on Pocket PC and Palm OS devices and is optimized for wireless communication. You will find more information about this product at http://www.moviansecurity.com.

V-ONE provides another VPN solution for Pocket PCs called SmartPass Pocket PC. SmartPass Pocket PC only works with the V-ONE SmartGate Server, and you will find more information about both of these products at http://www.v-one.com.

> **NOTE** *WAP proxy servers provide access to web pages that are designed for display on mobile phones. Socks proxy servers enable clients and servers of client/server applications to communicate with each other by using the Internet.*

Connect to the Corporate Network

You can connect to a corporate network directly from the Connection Manager by tapping Connect in the Work section, but you will most likely want to connect when using Inbox or Internet Explorer. Chapter 20 shows you how to configure an e-mail service in Inbox so that it uses the work settings.

Internet Explorer does not have an option for you to specify whether to use an Internet or Work connection. Instead, the Connection Manager determines which type of connection to use based on the URL you enter in the address bar or the URL you select in Favorites. If the address is a fully qualified domain name, such as www.pocketpchow2.com, Connection Manager connects to the Internet. If the address is one word, Connection Manager will connect to Work.

> **NOTE** *Internet Explorer with Pocket PC 2000 does provide a way to select a specific connection to use and to manually initiate a connection. To select a connection, tap Tools | Options | Connections and to use a connection tap Tools | Connect.*

If you access a corporate intranet that uses fully qualified domain names, you will have to either manually initiate the call using Connection Manager or configure the Internet connection to access the corporate network. You have several options for configuring the Internet connection so that it connects to a corporate network.

One option is to select Work Settings in the Internet drop-down list of Connection Manager. Another option is to configure the Internet Settings with the phone number for the corporate network, but you cannot use VPN or proxy servers with the default Internet settings. Yet another option is to create a new Internet setting, which can use proxy servers, and then select those settings for the Internet portion of Connection Manager. All of these options will require you to frequently change options for the Internet part of Connection Manager if you connect to corporate networks and ISPs.

If your corporate network uses a proxy server to connect to the Internet, you may encounter another problem connecting to intranet websites. Unlike the proxy server configuration for desktop versions of Internet Explorer, there is no way to configure Pocket PCs so that they don't use a proxy server to access intranet websites. If the proxy server on your corporate network does not support intranet websites, you may need to create two work settings in Connection Manager, one that uses a proxy server and one that does not use a proxy server.

Use Ethernet Networking

Most Pocket PCs are capable of connecting to an Ethernet network, which is used by most companies that have LANs. There are several reasons why you might want to connect your device to an Ethernet network. One is because network synchronization is much faster than using serial or infrared ports. You can also use Pocket Internet Explorer to access intranet websites, and even use a proxy server to access the public Internet. Furthermore, Inbox can also access e-mail servers that use standard Internet e-mail protocols. Before you connect your device to the network in your office, review the information in this section with your network administrator.

To connect your Pocket PC to an Ethernet network, you will need an Ethernet network card. Several companies sell CompactFlash Ethernet cards that work on Pocket PCs with Type I or Type II slots. Type II cards are larger than Type I cards and will not fit in slots only designed for Type I cards, so you need to know which type of CompactFlash slot is in your Pocket PC. The Pocket PC's user manual should tell you what type of CompactFlash slot is in your Pocket PC. Chris De Herrera maintains a list of cards that work at http://www.cewindows.net/peripherals/cfethernet.htm.

Before you can connect the Pocket PC to an Ethernet network, you must gather the following information so that you can configure the Ethernet card driver. Your network administrator can provide this information. Chapter 5 provides the instructions for using this information to configure the Ethernet card driver.

■ Does the network provide IP addresses using Dynamic Host Communication Protocol (DHCP) or are they manually assigned (static)?

■ If the addresses are static, obtain an address, the subnet mask, and the default gateway.

■ If the network provides the addresses, are the Domain Name Servers (DNS) and Windows Internet Name Servers (WINS) addresses also provided? If not, obtain the IP addresses for the Primary and Secondary DNS, and the Primary and Secondary WINS.

■ Some networks do not use WINS, so if you plan to synchronize using the network connection, you will need the IP address assigned to your desktop computer. You can determine that address by running winipcfg.exe with Windows 95/98 or running ipconfig.exe from a Windows NT command prompt. Use the IP address of the desktop computer for the Primary WINS address.

16

Connection Manager also has a role in how Pocket PC 2002 uses network cards. The third section of Connection Manager is a drop-down list that specifies whether you are using the card to connect to the Internet or Work. If you use a network card to connect to a LAN in order to synchronize with a desktop computer on that network, you must specify that the network card connects to Work.

> **NOTE** *If you specify that a network card connects to Work and the work settings are configured for a proxy server, you will not be able to access websites on the Internet unless the proxy server is available. This means that if you connect to a home network that does not have a proxy server, you will need to set the network card to the Internet to access websites.*

Use ActiveSync Desktop Pass Through

With Pocket PC 2002 and ActiveSync Version 3.5, you can access the corporate network from a Pocket PC while the device is connected to a desktop computer. The feature is enabled by default in ActiveSync, but if it is not working click Tools | Options on the desktop computer and click the Rules tab. If you need to use a proxy server to access an Internet site, be sure to select Work from the drop-down list on the Pass Through section of the Rules tab.

Secure Information

Because Pocket PCs are small, they are handy to carry around. Unfortunately, their size also makes it easy for the devices to be stolen. It is bad enough that your appointments, addresses, and tasks are at risk, but it is another thing entirely to expose confidential documents. Fortunately, you have several ways to secure the information and data in a Windows Pocket PC. This section reviews some of these methods to help you determine which way is the best for you.

Use the Power-On Password

Every Pocket PC can be assigned a password that you must enter whenever you turn on the device. The only way to access the device without the password is by performing a hard reset, which removes all information. To assign a password to your device, follow the instructions provided in Chapter 3.

> **NOTE** *Pocket PC 2002 supports strong passwords, which consist of alphabetic and numeric characters. Because strong passwords are more secure than the simple 4-digit numeric PIN used with Pocket PC 2000, they are preferred by corporations.*

Use AntiVirus Software

To date, there have been no reported instances of viruses on Pocket PCs. The focus of virus scan software vendors has been on preventing infection of desktop PCs from viruses transported on Pocket PCs. McAfee's Virus Scan for Pocket PC runs on desktop computers and scans files on the Pocket PC during synchronization. You will find more information about this product at http://www.mcafee.com.

Solutions that scan files from a desktop computer do not protect the Pocket PC from viruses that may be sent via e-mail, or downloaded off the Internet. Pocket PC 2002 includes Application Program Interfaces (APIs) that make it easier for vendors to write virus scan software for the Pocket PC. Check http://www.pocketpc.com for the latest news about what virus scan programs are available for the Pocket PC.

Store Sensitive Information in Secure Databases

It seems as though the Internet has dramatically increased the number of user IDs and passwords in our lives. Combined with account numbers and PINs, it is too much information to keep track of in anyone's head. A Pocket PC is perfect for storing and retrieving this information, but how do you protect it?

Fortunately, several programs have been written to store and protect this information. One of these programs is PassKey from AppStudio, which is an information manager that lets you store password and registration information in one encrypted database. You can use PassKey to store passwords, CD-ROM keys, and website registration information. For information and an evaluation copy, go to http://www.appstudio.com.

With *The Safe* from the German company Softwarebüro Müller, you can also store encrypted information. Unlike PassKey, this program allows you to define three fields for each record, which can contain any string. You can then determine whether or not you want to encrypt a particular record. In order to view encrypted data, you must enter a password when the program starts. For more information and an evaluation copy, go to http://www.sbm.nl/englisch/windowsce/thesafe/index.htm.

eWallet from Ilium Software has a graphical user interface that takes the form of a *wallet*. In this wallet, you can store cards that resemble credit cards, calling cards, and cards that include PINs and registration numbers. Each card can be protected with a password and encryption. Ilium Software sells versions of eWallet for all Windows CE platforms, and there is also a version available for desktop computers. For more information and an evaluation copy, go to http://www.iliumsoft.com/wallet.htm.

Assign Passwords to Documents

The Pocket Word and Excel documents that you store on your device might also contain confidential information. Unfortunately, you cannot password-protect Pocket Word documents on a Pocket PC. To password-protect an Excel spreadsheet on a Pocket PC, tap Edit | Password.

There is one problem with password-protecting documents: when you synchronize a document, the password-protection can be removed. At first, ActiveSync will not synchronize the protected file, and instead creates a synchronization conflict. If you resolve the conflict, you will be prompted for the password, and after you enter it, the password is removed from the document. Documents that are password-protected on the desktop PC cannot be synchronized to a Pocket PC.

16

Encrypt Files

Encryption is the process of converting messages and data into a form unreadable by anyone except the intended recipient. People commonly use this method to secure data transferred across the Internet. For example, the Secure Sockets Layer protocol developed by Netscape encrypts the contents of web pages before they transmit between the web server and the web browser.

Encryption can also be used to secure files, which cannot be opened unless a password is provided. While encryption is very effective for securing documents, there is a risk that if the password is lost or forgotten, the document cannot be opened. One way to protect against this risk is to store unencrypted copies of the files in a secure location. Two products, Sentry CE and PocketLock, provide encryption for Pocket PCs.

SoftWinter, Inc. sells Sentry CE, which is also available for Windows NT as Sentry 2020. Sentry CE creates an encrypted virtual volume on a Pocket PC that is compatible with their Windows NT product, which means that if the volume is on a storage card and your device fails, you still have access to the data. Encrypting a file is a simple matter of copying the file to the virtual volume and providing a password. The virtual volume can be created on a storage card, which you can then remove from the device and store for even more security. The virtual volume looks like a large file when viewed with File Explorer. You will find more information about Sentry CE at http://www.softwinter.com.

PocketLock from Applian provides simple encryption and decryption of files or folders located internally or on a storage card. It uses the Microsoft High Encryption Pack to provide eight different encryption methods. To encrypt a file or folder you simply select either using PocketLock and provide a numeric PIN. Encrypted files can by automatically decrypted from File Explorer, but they are not visible to Pocket Word or Excel. You will find more information about PocketLock at http://www.applian.com.

Connect to Corporate E-Mail Systems

You might expect Inbox to work with the Microsoft Exchange server. After all, they are both Microsoft products, why wouldn't they work together? Unfortunately, that is not the case, primarily because Exchange was not originally designed for use on the Internet. Lotus Notes and Novell GroupWise are two other popular e-mail servers used by corporations, and like Exchange, both primarily support their own clients, which do not use the Internet e-mail protocols.

Unless Internet protocol support is added to these servers, the only way to use Inbox with them is through an intermediary program. Inbox communicates with the intermediary program using Internet protocols, and the intermediary program communicates with the e-mail server using the appropriate non-Internet protocol.

The good news is that the intermediary program can run on a server and provide access to the corporate e-mail server for several clients. The bad news is that you must add a server to the corporate network, which may be beyond your capability.

You have a couple of alternatives. One is to synchronize messages between Inbox and an e-mail client running on your PC. The process for synchronization between Inbox and Outlook, explained in Chapter 20, will enable you to send and receive messages from Exchange when

Outlook is used as an Exchange client. Intellisync and XTNDConnect PC, described earlier in this chapter, are both capable of synchronizing Inbox messages with Lotus Notes clients.

Mail on the Run! from River Run Software Group is another alternative. This product includes a client that runs on a Pocket PC, and an agent program that runs on a PC running Windows 98 or NT. The agent transfers messages between the client and corporate mail servers, including Microsoft Exchange, Lotus Notes, and Novell GroupWise. You can run the agent program on your desktop computer and communicate with the device using the serial cable, dial-up, or network connection. In order to access mail remotely, you must be able to dial into the PC, which is connected to and logged on to the network, so that it can communicate with the mail server. You will find more information about Mail on the Run! at http://www.riverrun.com/motr/index.html.

Send and Receive E-Mail from Exchange

As explained in Chapter 20, Inbox is primarily an Internet e-mail client. While the latest version of Exchange includes support for Internet protocols, many implementations have this feature disabled. If the Exchange server that you use does support either the POP3 or IMAP4 protocol, then Inbox can be configured to work with the server. Follow the instructions for setting up an Internet service provided in Chapter 20.

As described earlier, companies that want to provide Pocket PC access to Exchange can install an intermediary server on their network. One product in this category is XTNDConnect Server from Extended Systems, which was formerly known as ASL-Connect. This product synchronizes Pocket PC and Palm Computing devices with Microsoft Exchange and Lotus Notes. It runs on a server on the network and can provide e-mail access to several devices at the same time. Microsoft has partnered with Extended Systems to provide a concurrent five-user, 60-day trial copy of the program. You will find more information about XTNDConnect Server at http://www.extendedsystems.com/go/mstrial/.

Send and Receive E-Mail from Lotus Notes

To say that Lotus Notes is commonly found among corporations around the world is an understatement. Recently, Lotus announced that they had reached 50 million users. The popularity of this program has created a whole new category of software called *groupware*.

Companies use groupware to provide access to free-form information stored in databases. Several copies of the same database may be kept consistent throughout a company through a process called *replication*. Replication is very similar to the synchronization process that you use to keep your Pocket PC and Outlook consistent. The difference is that the databases may be countries apart, and they use networks and messaging to pass information back and forth.

At first, Lotus Notes consisted of e-mail messages and databases. Later, PIM features and group scheduling were added to the product. The product has also been divided in two, with Notes being the client and Domino being the server, but people often refer to the two as one and call it Lotus Notes.

As you can tell, Lotus Notes has many features and can be very complicated. For a person trying to determine how to get a Pocket PC to work with Lotus Notes, things can get very confusing. First, do you want to communicate with the Notes client or the Domino server? Do you want to

16

synchronize e-mail, calendar, contacts, and tasks, or do you want access to databases? Let's see if we can sort this out.

A number of the products already described enable synchronization of e-mail, calendar, contacts, and tasks with the Lotus Notes client. Intellisync and XTNDConnect PC support Lotus Notes Versions 4.5 and 4.6, and XTNDConnect PC also supports R5. River Run sells *All in Sync! Personal,* which synchronizes with Versions 4.5, 4.6, and R5 of the Lotus Notes client.

Intermediary programs provide synchronization of PIM data between Pocket PCs and Domino servers. One these programs is XTNDConnect Server, described in the Sending and Receiving E-mail from Exchange section of this chapter. Another program is All in Sync!, which uses the same client-agent model that River Run uses in Mail on the Run! to access Exchange.

Finally, if you need access to Lotus Notes databases, you will want to look at Cadenza from CommonTime Ltd. This product is the only one designed specifically for working with Lotus Notes databases, which CommonTime specializes in developing. If you are familiar with Lotus Notes, you will find that CommonTime products provide the most support for all of its features. More information is available at http://www.commontime.com/.

Run Windows Programs

You may be painfully aware by now that the Pocket Office applications included with Pocket PCs are not the same as Microsoft Office. If you travel frequently, you may have hoped that your device could replace that notebook computer you lug around, only to have those hopes dashed when you found out that you couldn't create tables in Pocket Word. Wouldn't it be great if you could run the full copy of Microsoft Word on your Pocket PC?

Well, you can, kind of. Actually, you can work with a display of Word on your Pocket PC while the program actually runs on another computer. The process for doing this is called *network computing,* and it is similar to the mainframe programs you access with a terminal emulator.

A terminal server client runs on your Pocket PC that accesses programs running on the server. The display of those programs appears on your Pocket PC, and it seems as if you are sitting at a regular desktop computer, but all of the processing happens back at the server. This software is becoming a popular way for companies to provide remote access to its systems because it centralizes support. Programs are installed on one computer and made available to all who access it, rather than having to install programs on hundreds of notebook computers spread throughout the country.

While they work incredibly well, terminal server clients have one significant limitation: the client must be able to connect to the server in order to run applications. People who travel frequently on airplanes may find this limitation to be a problem when they want to run Microsoft Word or Excel. However, for users of Pocket PCs, these clients are the only way to run Windows programs.

Use Microsoft Mobile Terminal Server Client

The first step in using the Microsoft Mobile Terminal Server client is to obtain access to the server. The administrator will create a username and password that you will use to log on to the server. The administrator will also set you up with the programs that you will need to run.

You will also need to connect your Pocket PC to the corporate network as described in the "Access the Corporate Network" section of this chapter.

The Mobile Terminal Service client may already be installed on your Pocket PC; if not, you can download it from http://www.pocketpc.com. Install the program using the process described in Chapter 7. To start the program, tap Start | Programs | Terminal Services Client. Enter a host name or an IP address of the terminal server and tap Connect.

After a connection is established you will see the standard Windows 2000 logon screen, as shown here:

Tap these buttons to move
around on the screen.

Along the bottom of the screen are five buttons that quickly move the display around the screen. If you limit the size of the server desktop to fit the Pocket PC screen, the buttons do not display.

TIP
The Pocket PC portrait orientation limits what you can see on the Windows desktop. Use Nyditot Virtual Display or JS Landscape as described in Chapter 11 to change the screen to landscape orientation and see more of the desktop.

16

Use the stylus for mouse operations when running Windows programs, and tap-and-hold to perform a right-click. You cannot use Transcriber with terminal services, so you will need to use the keyboard, letter recognizer, or block recognizer to enter information. To end the terminal session, tap Start | Shut Down, select Logoff, and then tap OK.

NOTE
The Pocket PC Close button does not shut down the Terminal Services client. If you tap Close and then switch back to Terminal Services, you will find that your Pocket PC is still connected to the server.

How to ... Use Terminal Services with Pocket PC 2000

Microsoft has not provided a Terminal Services client for Pocket PC 2000 devices. However, there is a version of the client for handheld PCs that works on the Compaq iPAQ Pocket PC. Because the program is designed for handheld PCs it does not have the features found in the Terminal Services client for Pocket PC 2002. The Pocket PC Start button will move to the bottom of the screen, the server display is limited to 256 colors and to the size of the Pocket PC screen, and there is no support for a right-click.

> **TIP** *If you run Navigation bar replacement programs, such as WIS Bar or Gigabar, you should exit them before running the Terminal Server client; otherwise you will have problems accessing the soft-input panel.*

To install the client on an iPAQ, download the program from http://www.microsoft.com/mobile/downloads/ts-final.asp and follow these steps:

1. Connect your iPAQ to your desktop computer.

2. Run the program that you downloaded. The installation program will say that you do not have a compatible device and will leave you at the Add/Remove Programs screen. Click Cancel to close Add/Remove Programs and click Finish on the Setup screen.

3. Start Windows Explorer on your desktop computer and open C:\Program Files\ Microsoft ActiveSync\Terminal Server Client for Windows CE, Handheld PC Edition. This directory path is for a standard installation of ActiveSync and may be different if you installed to a different drive or directory.

4. Copy the file *rdp.hpc_sa1100.CAB* to a folder on your Pocket PC.

5. Start File Explorer on the iPAQ, open the folder in which you stored the file in step 4, and then tap the filename. There will be a warning that the program is designed for the H/PC, tap Yes to continue the installation.

The Terminal Server Client is installed into the \My Device\Program Files\Terminal Server Client folder, and the program name is mstsc40. You can use File Explorer to run the program or use ActiveSync to create a shortcut as described in Chapter 7.

Use Citrix Winframe

Citrix pioneered the development of server-based computing when they created and sold Winframe. The Independent Computing Architecture (ICA), also developed by Citrix, enables client devices running a variety of different operating systems to access their terminal server. Included among those devices are Pocket PCs.

Because Citrix has been selling Winframe for a number of years, a large number of corporations have it installed. If your company uses Citrix, you will be able to download and use the ICA client, which you can find at http://download.citrix.com/.

Use Other Remote-Control Applications

Remote-control software works like terminal servers because you run programs running on other computers. The difference is that the host program can only support one client session at a time. Perhaps the most popular use of these programs is to provide remote troubleshooting and helpdesk support for remote and mobile workers.

Virtual Network Computing (VNC) is a remote display system that allows you to view a desktop environment running on a machine from anywhere on the Internet. It is usually used to display an X Window environment that runs on Unix, but it will also run on Macintoshes and Windows. With a VNC Viewer running on a Pocket PC, you can access desktops running on Unix, Macintosh, and Windows computers running the VNC server. Best of all, the software is free and available for download off the Internet. To download any one of the server programs, go to http://www.uk.research.att.com/vnc/index.html. You will find a Pocket PC version of the VNC Viewer at http://www.cs.utah.edu/~midgley/wince/vnc.html.

Wrapping Up

Pocket PCs are powerful productivity tools at the office. They connect to corporate networks and synchronize with desktop computers, open Internet and intranet websites, retrieve e-mail from corporate mail servers, and run Windows programs using the Terminal Services client. A number of third-party applications are available to synchronize data with PIMs, as well as view PDF files, such as ACT! and Lotus Organizer. In Chapter 14 you learned how to use third-party programs to create and give PowerPoint presentations. You can secure the information on your Pocket PC using strong passwords and encryption software. Just as Pocket PCs are useful at the office, they are even more useful when traveling. In the next chapter you will learn how to take full advantage of your Pocket PC while you are away from your home or office.

16

Chapter 17

Travel With Your Pocket PC

How To...

■ Prepare to travel

■ Extend battery life

■ Get connected to the Internet while traveling

■ Print to different types of printers

■ Back up your device while traveling

■ Connect a GPS receiver to your device

■ Find maps to install on your device

■ Find language translators for your device

A decision to replace your notebook computer with a Pocket PC on your next business trip will depend on the amount of functionality that you need from software applications versus the convenience of less weight, longer battery life, and the "instant on" startup time provided by a Pocket PC. If you need to retrieve your e-mail, give a presentation, write documents, and create spreadsheets, then a Pocket PC will meet your needs, with much less weight and longer battery life than most notebook computers. In this chapter, you'll find many tips on traveling with a Pocket PC, along with a handy checklist that you can use while packing for your trip.

Prepare to Travel with Your Pocket PC

Murphy's Law seems to apply most often when you are on the road and away from any help. Preparation will either prevent problems or help you deal with them when they happen. Planning how you'll use your Pocket PC on your trip will reduce stress and increase productivity. There are four items that you should plan for on your trip: power, connectivity, printing, and backup.

Keep Your Pocket PC Running

Every computer ever made has at least one thing in common: they all need power in order to work. Batteries enable computers to be used in places where using a power cord is not possible. The longer the battery lasts, the more productivity you gain using the computer. Pocket PCs maximize your productivity with its design for long battery life.

Unfortunately, no matter how long a battery can last, it will either need to be replaced or recharged. Because it is so important, take the time to plan how you will power your device and recharge its batteries while traveling. Here are some tips for planning your power needs:

■ **Charge the batteries before leaving**   Batteries tend to run out at the worst possible time, like halfway through a flight while you write a report that is due the next day.

That would not be a good time to recall that the last time you charged the batteries was last week. Don't let batteries be the cause of not finishing that report; charge them the night before leaving.

■ **Pack an extra battery**   If your device uses a removable battery, then consider buying a spare battery that you can bring on long trips. Of course, make sure you charge up that extra battery before you leave on the trip.

■ **Buy an external battery pack**   Some Pocket PCs do not have replaceable batteries but do have external battery packs that connect to the power adapter port and recharge the internal battery. The next section provides more information about battery packs that you can buy.

■ **Buy an extra power adapter**   If you frequently travel to the same location, buy an extra power adapter and leave it at that location. It is also a good idea to keep adapters at your office and home. By doing this, you will lighten your luggage and avoid forgetting to pack the adapter.

■ **Pack an extension cord**   Older hotel rooms tend to have too few power outlets, which may be covered by beds and dressers, and always seem to be placed as far from the desk or table as possible. An extension cord will allow you to use your device wherever it is convenient.

■ **Pack a portable surge suppressor**   Power surges can occur anywhere, creating the possibility of destroying your device. Most computer stores carry portable surge suppressors that have two outlets and possibly two or three phone jacks, all of which protect your device from power surges.

■ **Get a power adapter for your car**   If you travel a great distance by car, consider getting an adapter that converts the car cigarette lighter into an outlet for the AC adapter of the device. With this adapter you can charge up your device while driving your car.

■ **Remove PC cards**   Modem and network cards draw extra power from the device, even if they are not being used. Only plug the cards in your device when they are being used. As an extra precaution, only use the card in your device while it is using the AC adapter. Buy a case to house extra PC and CompactFlash cards so they don't get lost.

■ **Be aware of international power differences**   Other countries have different power standards than the United States. AC adapters designed for the United States will not work in those countries. Check with the manufacturer of your device to find out if its power adapter can work in the country you plan to travel to. You many need to purchase an international power adapter for your device, or you may find it easier to buy a power conversion kit.

■ **Know the power-saving features of your device**   Most devices include features designed for extending battery life. An example of this is settings that control the backlighting of the display. Learn how to use these features, and use them while you travel.

17

How to ... Extend Battery Life with External Power Packs

The Hewlett Packard (HP) Jornada and Compaq iPAQ Pocket PCs do not have replaceable batteries, so you cannot simply replace their batteries with fresh ones when they run out. That is not a problem if you are near an outlet, but can be trouble when you are in an airplane. Fortunately, portable battery extenders exist for both brands of Pocket PCs.

The HP Jornada 520/540 series power pack is an external rechargeable battery that plugs into the Jornada A/C power port. It provides seven hours of additional battery life and can also recharge the Jornada internal battery. To recharge the power pack, all you need to do is drop it in the Jornada cradle. You can by the HP power pack at http://www.hpshopping.com.

DataNation sells the iPowerPak which recharges Compaq and Casio Pocket PCs using AA batteries. DataNation also sells the ePack Rechargable battery pack for Compaq iPAQs. Both power packs can be bought at http://www.data-nation.com.

Perhaps the most innovative external power source is Instant Power Charger from Electric Fuel. It uses a disposable cartridge that recharges the internal batteries of Casio, HP, and Compaq Pocket PCs by drawing oxygen into holes on the cartridge case. The cartridges will recharge a Pocket PC three times. The Instant Power Charger includes one cartridge, along with the cable to connect the Pocket PC. Versions are also available for most popular mobile phones. More information can be found at http://www.electric-fuel.com.

Plan How to Connect Your Pocket PC to the Internet

Next to battery life, the biggest challenge of using a Pocket PC on the road is connectivity. Most of us have become dependent on our Internet access to communicate via e-mail, and to keep abreast of news on the Web. Determining how you will access the Internet, or your office network, before you leave on a trip will help tremendously when you finally make it to the hotel room. Here are some tips to help you get connected on the road:

> NOTE *Even though these tips are for access to the Internet, they also apply to accessing corporate networks. Chapter 16 has additional information on accessing corporate networks via the Internet using virtual private networking (VPN) software.*

■ **Get the local ISP phone numbers before you leave** Most ISPs have pages on their websites that list all their phone numbers, or they will provide the numbers based on an area code and phone number that you enter. They may also have a toll-free number that you can call to obtain these numbers. Use the hotel phone number to determine what will be a local phone call. If your ISP provides a toll-free access number, find out what it is; while you may be charged more for using the number, it might be the only way to connect with the ISP at the destination.

- **Test access numbers before you leave**   If connection to the Internet is important, it may be worth the long-distance call to actually test the connection before you leave. Use remote networking to create a new dial-up connection using the access number. You will find it easier to get help while you are at home, and you can travel with the confidence that you will connect to the Internet when you reach your destination.

- **Check wireless coverage**   If your Pocket PC supports wireless connections to the Internet, check the service provider's website to verify that they provide coverage for your destination. Most providers do not charge for roaming, but coverage can be limited to metropolitan areas.

- **Know how to create and use dialing locations**   Most hotel and office phones require the entry of a number to access an outside line. The dialing locations of a Pocket PC make it easy to configure your modem to dial that number before making any call. Chapter 19 provides instructions for creating dialing locations on a Pocket PC.

- **Use a calling card**   Your ISP may not have a local-access number, or a toll-free number, that you can use at the destination. In these cases, you may want to use a phone company calling card. Unlike Windows 98, there is no special support for calling cards in Windows CE. But, you can create dial-up connections that use calling cards by putting the appropriate codes in the telephone number field of the Dial-Up Connection dialog box. Chapter 19 provides instructions for creating dial-up connections.

- **Research international requirements**   If you travel overseas and want to use your device to connect to the Internet, you will need to do some additional research. First, find out if your ISP has access numbers outside the United States; many of them do not. Next, be aware that international numbers do not include a 1 before the area code, but may require additional codes. This is best handled by using Dialing Locations and Dialing Patterns, as described in Chapter 19. The international dialing pattern is used when a dial-up connection of a country code is blank.

- **Pack a phone line tester**   Some hotels and businesses use digital phone lines that can damage the modem. The tester has an indicator light that shows whether the line is digital, which should not be used, or analog, which is safe.

- **Pack a long phone cord**   Phone jacks can be hidden behind beds and dressers, making them difficult to reach. A long phone cord can be useful for connecting your device to those phone jacks. Computer and electronics stores carry retractable phone lines that are easy to carry.

- **Pack a one-to-two phone jack adapter**   Some hotel rooms have only one phone jack and a phone without a data port. In this case, the adapter will enable you to connect your modem and the phone to the jack.

- **Pack a phone line adapter for international travel**   The phone jacks in some countries may not match the ones you use at home. Call ahead and find out if you will need a special adapter, or ask your travel agent. If you travel abroad, you may want to buy a travel kit available at most computer stores. These kits contain many different

17

adapters and tools that you may need to connect to phone systems in different countries. A good website for phone adapters is from Megellan at http://shop.gorp.com/magellans/. To find adapters on the Megellan site, do a search for *Telephone*.

- ■ **Pack a line noise filter**   Some hotels have phone systems that are not modem-friendly, and some European countries add a *tax tone* to monitor usage. The result is a reduction of signal clarity, making it difficult for modems to communicate with each other. A noise filter can reduce this problem.

- ■ **Know how to synchronize using a modem**   If it is important for you to synchronize Pocket Outlook data while traveling, you can use ActiveSync with remote networking to access your home computer. Chapter 5 provides instructions for synchronizing using a modem.

Print on the Road

The Pocket PC does not have built-in support for printing, but you can add the ability to print Pocket Word documents, plain text, or e-mail using PrintPocketCE from FieldSoftware. The program will print to HP PCL3 compatible printers, as well as variety of printers that have built-in infrared ports. A list of supported printers is available at http://www.fieldsoftware.com/PrintersSupported.htm, and you can find more information and a 30-day trial copy of PrintPocketCE at http://www.fieldsoftware.com.

Infrared provides the simplest way to connect a Pocket PC to a printer. When using PrintPocketCE, all you need to do is align the infrared ports and tap Start Printing. The FieldSoftware website lists a number of printers that have infrared ports, or you can connect an infrared printer adapter to a printer parallel port. Such adapters are available from ACTiSYS Corporation, http://www.actisys.com/actir100.html, and Extended Systems, http://www.extendedsystems.com.

TIP   *Serial printers are harder to find, but still available. You can use a serial sync cable for your Pocket PC and a null modem adapter to connect with a printer serial cable. You cannot connect a Pocket PC to a printer using a USB cable.*

If you don't plan to do a lot of printing, you might not want to purchase extra software or cables. Yet, you may find that, on occasion, you need to print a page or two. In these instances, a road warrior trick comes in handy; fax the document from your device to a fax machine.

To send faxes from your Pocket PC, you need fax software. The following two fax programs are available: WinPhone Pocket (http://www.bvrp.com/) from BVRP Software and Truefax (http://www.ksesoftware.com/) from KSE Software. Most hotels provide fax services for their customers, so call the front desk and get the fax number. Then start up either WinPhone Pocket or Truefax and send the document to that fax machine.

If you decide that you need a printer, Pentax, Hewlett Packard, Citizen, Canon, and Seiko Instruments all make portable printers. Be aware that these printers may require special paper, and they are not designed for high-volume printing. Some of these printers have built-in infrared ports, which eliminate the need for carrying and connecting extra cables.

Back Up Your Pocket PC on the Road

If you consider the information in your Pocket PC to be critical, then you ought to live by the motto "Back up early and often." The most common way to back up your device is by using ActiveSync, as described in Chapter 7. Chances are good that when traveling you will not have access to a desktop computer, yet the risk of losing data while traveling is even greater. Therefore, you need a way to back up your device without using a PC.

The best tool for backing up your device on the road is a storage card. If you already use a storage card, consider buying an extra card and only use it for backups. The extra card should be at least 32MB so it can hold all of the possible files in internal storage memory.

You could copy files to the storage card, but many devices have a better method of backup. Included is software designed to back up the entire contents of internal storage to a storage card. Backing up this way is faster than using a serial cable, so you might want use this as your main backup method. Consult the user manual of your device for instructions on using its backup software.

NOTE   *Be aware that the backup file is written in a proprietary format. If the device is lost or stolen, you will need to obtain an identical device in order to restore the files.*

For an additional level of security, use a PC storage card reader to copy the backup file from the card to a computer hard drive. You will find this to be a better method for backing up your device to a desktop computer, but it has the additional cost of the card reader. Chapter 23 has more information about card readers.

The Internet is also a useful tool for backing up files on your device. If you don't have a storage card, and you want to back up a file, attach it to an e-mail message and mail it to yourself. The e-mail and the file will stay on the mail server until it is deleted. This has the added benefit of giving you access to the file from any computer that can read e-mail from the server.

Secure Your Data

While traveling, your Pocket PC and the data it contains are at risk of being lost or stolen. Backing up your data to a CompactFlash card and then carrying that card separately from the device will help you keep a secure copy of your data with you at all times. Methods exist for securing the data even further, but come with the cost of some inconvenience and the risk of rendering data inaccessible due to lost passwords. Here are some tips for securing your data:

- Use Windows CE password protection by using the Password icon in Settings on a Pocket PC. With power-on protection enabled, a password must be entered every time the device is turned on. If you forget the password, the device will be inaccessible unless you perform a hard reset, which will remove all install applications and data from the device.

- Use password protection with Pocket Excel.

17

■ Use software that securely stores personal information such as bank account numbers and user IDs. Programs that provide this function include CodeWallet at http://www.codewallet.com/cw/home.htm, eWallet at http://www.iliumsoft.com/wallet.htm, and MediaWallet at http://www.applian.com/mediawallet/index.htm.

■ Encrypt data stored either internally or on a storage card.

> **TIP** *Chapter 16 provides more information about securing your Pocket PC.*

Turn Your Pocket PC into a Traveling Tool

Now that all of the preparations are out of the way, let's look at some additional hardware and software that turn your Pocket PC into a valuable travel tool. From time to time we all get lost while traveling and end up looking to the skies for direction. With a global positioning system (GPS) receiver, a Pocket PC can show your exact location on a map. Even if you don't have a GPS, several different mapping programs run on the Pocket PC, and with the software, you won't have to figure out how to refold the map.

> **TIP** *These GPS systems may not include maps for use outside the contiguous United States. You may want to check which systems provide maps for Alaska, Hawaii, or other countries.*

International travel presents additional challenges of overcoming language barriers. Several language translators exist that run on the Pocket PC, and using one can help you order a grilled cheese sandwich in France or Spain.

Know Where to Go and How to Get There

GPS has existed since 1973, and is operated by the United States Department of Defense. It determines a location by computing the difference between the time a signal is sent and the time it is received. The signals come from three different satellites located over the Earth. A GPS receiver uses the data to triangulate a location in latitude and longitude, which is then used to identify a spot on a map.

GPS hardware and software are very popular Pocket PC accessories. While you can buy stand-alone GPS receivers, there are several advantages to using a receiver with a Pocket PC. One is that in a car you can place the receiver wherever the signal strength is the greatest, and hold the device in your hand. Another advantage is that Pocket PCs are in color and have higher resolutions than stand-alone GPS receivers, making it easier to read the maps. Finally, Pocket PC GPS software is designed to work with storage cards, providing a significantly greater amount of space to store maps over stand-alone GPS receivers.

Several companies sell GPS receivers and software that work with Pocket PCs. Each product provides driving directions, voice prompts, route computation, and off-route warning. Maps are provided on CD-ROM and are downloaded either to internal storage on a Pocket PC or onto a storage card. Here is a summary of the GPS solutions available for the Pocket PC:

■ Pharos bundles their iGPS-180 and Pocket Navigator software along with serial cables that connect directly to Casio, Compaq, and HP Pocket PCs. The bundle is called the

GPS Navigator PocketPak, and the Pocket Navigator software can also be bought separately. You can find more information about this product at http://www.pharosgps.com/.

■ Pocket CoPilot from TravRoute is the Pocket PC version of their popular CoPilot software for PCs. Pocket CoPilot is only available in bundles that include a GPS receiver and software and include serial cables that connect directly to Casio, Compaq, and HP Pocket PCs. The software will only work with the TravRoute GPS receiver. Map data is downloaded to a Pocket PC or storage card using desktop software. This product and can be found at http://www.travroute.com.

■ The Destinator Personal Navigation System is a GPS receiver and software bundle that only works with the Compaq iPAQ. It includes the same street-level NAVTECH maps used by FedEx, OnStar, Mercedes-Benz, and Lexus. Voice prompts speak English, French, or Spanish, and detailed maps are available for the United States, Canada, and Europe. This product can be found at http://www.mecissystems.com/destinator.htm.

■ TeleType GPS sells several different receivers that work with Pocket PCs, including CompactFlash and PC Card versions that turn your Pocket PC into a very portable GPS. The CompactFlash GPS works with Casio, Compaq, and HP Pocket PCs, and the PC Card GPS only works with the Compaq iPAQ. The TeleType GPS software can be purchased separately and will work with other GPS receivers compliant with the standards of the National Marine Electronics Association (NMEA). You will find these products at http://www.teletype.com.

■ HandMap from Evolutionary Systems is a vector-based map viewer. The professional version of the software includes plug-ins to work with GPS receivers. A standard version is available as a free download from their website, but it only works with maps provided by Evolutionary Systems. More information can be found at http://www.handmap.net/.

How to ...   Connect a GPS Receiver to a Pocket PC

Most handheld GPS receivers include a serial cable designed to work with computers so that you can download maps to the GPS. If the receiver can send NMEA standard information out that serial port, you can use it with a Pocket PC. In order to use the receiver with a Pocket PC, the GPS serial cable has to be connected to a serial ActiveSync cable. Each Pocket PC hardware manufacturer sells serial ActiveSync cables for their device, which you can purchase from their website, or you can also purchase them from the Teletype website at http://www.teletype.com. To complete the connection, you will also need a null modem adapter (part number 26-264B) and a male DB9 to male DB9 gender adapter (part number 26-231), both of which you can purchase at RadioShack.

17

Plug the ActiveSync cable into your Pocket PC. Connect the null modem adapter to the serial ActiveSync cable, and then connect the gender adapter to the null modem adapter. Next, connect the GPS serial cable to the gender adapter, and then plug the GPS serial cable into the GPS receiver. This configuration will work for handheld GPS receivers or receivers designed to work with PCs, such as the DeLorme Earthmate.

Compaq sells a RS-232 cable for the iPAQ Pocket PC (part number 236251-B21) that you can connect directly to the GPS serial cable. If you purchase this Compaq cable, you do not need the null modem or gender adapter. Just plug the RS-232 cable into the iPAQ, connect the GPS receiver cable to the RS-232 cable, and then plug the GPS serial cable into the GPS receiver.

If you use a handheld GPS receiver, you might need to configure the interface for NMEA. For example, to make this change on a Garmin eMap, press Menu twice, select Setup, select the Interface tab, and then move the cursor to the Serial Data Format field. Press ENTER and then select NMEA Out. Press ESC twice to close out of the setup screen.

To use the receiver, you will need the Pharos, Teletype, or HandMap GPS programs on the Pocket PC.

View a Customized Map with Pocket Streets

Pocket Streets is a map-viewing program that displays maps created with Microsoft Streets & Trips 2002, AutoRoute 2002, or MapPoint 2002. It is only included with these programs, and is not on the ActiveSync CD-ROM that ships with Pocket PCs. Microsoft does not provide Pocket Streets 2002 for download from their website.

TIP   *Microsoft has released an update to Pocket Streets 2002 that provides support for GPS receivers and integration with Pocket Outlook. You can download the update from http://www.microsoft.com/pocketstreets/using/download.htm.*

Did you know?

Pocket Streets 2002 is Bundled with Streets & Trips 2002

Pocket Streets Version 3 is available on the ActiveSync 3.1 CD-ROM, along with several free maps. It was also available as a free download from the Microsoft website until Streets & Trips 2002 was released. You could also find a copy of Pocket Streets Version 3 with Streets & Trips 2001, AutoRoute 2001, and MapPoint 2001. Microsoft now only provides Pocket Streets 2002 with the full retail versions of the desktop software to prevent people from distributing illegal copies of maps. Pocket Streets Version 3 cannot open maps made using the 2002 versions of the desktop software, and Pocket Streets 2002 cannot open Version 3 maps.

The setup files for Pocket Streets 2002 are in the PStreets folder on the setup CD-ROM of Streets & Trips 2002, AutoRoute 2002, and MapPoint 2002. To install the program, connect your Pocket PC with a desktop running ActiveSync, and then use Windows Explorer on the desktop to open the PStreets folder on the CD-ROM and run the setup program. You can install Pocket Streets to either internal storage or a storage card following the standard software installation procedure described in Chapter 7.

Pocket Streets will run a little slower if it loads maps from a storage card.

Microsoft provides 42 maps for several metropolitan areas in the \PStreets\Maps folder on the setup CD-ROM. To use these maps, copy the file to the My Documents folder on your Pocket PC, or a My Documents folder on a storage card.

To create your own maps using Streets & Trips 2002, select a portion of the map on your desktop using the mouse, right-click within the selected area, and then click Export Map for Pocket Streets. Streets & Trips 2002 calculates the approximate amount of storage space the map will need on the Pocket PC and then prompts you for a location on your desktop to store the files.

Two files are created, a map file that has an .mps extension and a pushpin file that has a .psp extension. Copy these two files to the My Documents folder on your Pocket PC or on a Storage Card using ActiveSync Explorer as described in Chapter 7.

If you have a CompactFlash reader connected to your desktop, you can export the map file directly to a CompactFlash storage card.

When Pocket Streets starts, you first see the standard Pocket PC list view showing all the map files stored in the My Documents folder on your Pocket PC. Maps that you put in the My Documents folder on storage cards are also listed. If you do not see a map, make sure it is in the My Documents folder. Tap a map name to open the map, as shown here:

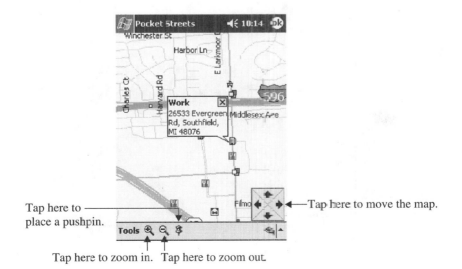

Tap here to place a pushpin.

Tap here to move the map.

Tap here to zoom in. Tap here to zoom out.

17

Tap the buttons on the Command bar to zoom the map and tap the buttons in the Navigation box to move the map.

TIP *Another way to zoom in on a map is to select an area of the map using the stylus.*

Tap the Pushpin button on the Command bar and then tap a location on the map to create a pushpin location on the map. The Pushpin Properties dialog box displays for you to enter the name of the pushpin and a note. Tap Change Symbol to change the pushpin shape on the map.

Several other mapping programs and websites exist for Pocket PCs; some are free, while others are sold as commercial software. Here is a summary of what is available and where you can get more information:

- Street Wizard from Adept Computer Solutions runs on Windows 98 and NT desktop computers, and includes Pocket PC software so you can download maps to a device. The professional version integrates with popular contact managers. You can find more information at http://www.streetwizard.com/.

- Route Planner Millennium from Palmtop Software is a sophisticated road map and route planning application that includes countries other than the United States. It runs on all Pocket PCs, and comes in English, German, French, Italian, Spanish, and Dutch versions. The software will work with GPS receivers. A complete listing of the country maps that are included is available at http://www.palmtop.nl/ce/poc_route.html.

- The Portable Internet provides maps of 135 metropolitan areas in the United States and Canada. It also provides reviews from Frommer's Travel Guides for 29 metro areas, highlighting places to stay, dine, and things to see and do. More information about this program can be found at http://www.portableinternet.com/.

- MSN Mobile at http://mobile.msn.com/pocketpc/home.asp provides a link to Expedia.com Travel, which provides access to travel itineraries, flight information, and driving directions.

Did you know?

Pushpin Bug Fixed in Pocket Streets 2002

Pushpins that you create using the desktop software are exported along with maps so that you can view them in Pocket Streets. However, you cannot open pushpins that you create in Pocket Streets with the desktop software. Pocket Streets Version 3 has a bug that causes pushpins created on the desktop to appear at the wrong locations. Fortunately, this bug has been fixed in Pocket Streets 2002.

You must first create the travel itinerary using a desktop web browser and accessing http://www.expedia.com. Expedia.com Travel also provides an AvantGo channel so that you can download information and maps to your Pocket PC.

■ AvantGo has 78 travel channels that provide information you can download to your Pocket PC and view using Internet Explorer. Amongst those channels are MapBlast! and MapQuest, which provide driving directions and maps. To obtain driving directions and maps, you enter the origin and destination addresses and then synchronize your Pocket PC. The information is then downloaded to your Pocket PC so that you have it while you travel. Instructions for using AvantGo with Internet Explorer are provided in Chapter 22. You can also access AvantGo at http://avantgo.com.

Language Translation

English is a widely used language inside and outside of the United States. Americans who do not speak foreign languages, or are learning them, rely on either interpreters or language translators. Typically, these translators will list English words and their foreign-language equivalents. Language translators are available for Pocket PCs and provide searching capabilities that make it easier to find the correct words to say. Here is an overview of some language translator software available for your Pocket PC:

■ PalmTop Software sells Windows CE versions of HarperCollins' English-French, English-German, English-Italian, and English-Spanish translators. More information is available at http://www.palmtop.nl/.

■ First Words In Hand from Burr Software provides phonetic translations of popular phrases in eight different languages. It includes audio clips of the phrases so you can hear how they are pronounced. You can also add your own phrases to this software, which you can find more information about at http://www.burroak.on.ca/fwih.html.

Hit the Road

Having read this far, you know how to plan your trip and how your Pocket PC can help you get to your destination. Now it is time to put everything together, pack it up, and head off on your trip. Before you do, here are a few final preparations.

Make Final Preparations

If you plan to work in your hotel room, ask about accommodations for business travelers when you make the reservation. Ask them if computer modems can be used in their rooms. If not, and connecting to the Internet is important, you might want to go to a different hotel.

Some hotels have business centers that have personal computers and printers available for their patrons. Find out the manufacturers of their equipment and ask them if you can use their printer with your notebook computer. (Don't bother asking about Pocket PCs; chances are good the person you talk to will know nothing about them.) This information will help you decide what printer software should be installed on your device.

17

Make sure you download all of the data files that you will need to your device or storage card. The wrong time to find out that you are missing a file is when you try to open it hundreds of miles away. The ActiveSync file synchronization capability helps with this because as long as the file stays in the synchronized files folders, you know there will be a copy on the device. Chapter 6 has all the information you need on using file synchronization.

Don't put your Pocket PC, or important components, in checked luggage. Not only do you run the risk of the luggage not showing up at your destination, but it can be stolen as well. Keep briefcases and computer bags with you at all times. Airports are popular locations for thieves.

What type of case do you use to carry your Pocket PC? If you use the case that it came with, it is probably too small to carry accessories, and may not provide enough protection. Targus (http://www.targus.com) has some nice cases, as does E&B Company (http://www.ebcases.com). Try to find a case that has enough padding to withstand normal travel abuses.

> **TIP**   *Todd Ogasawara keeps an extensive list of carrying-case vendors at http://to-tech.com/windowsce/faqs/cases.htm.*

Complete a Travel Checklist

Checklists are handy tools to help remember what to pack and what to do as you prepare for a trip. Chapter 23 has information about ListPro, a handy program designed for making and reusing lists. Unfortunately, a ListPro file cannot be attached to this book, so the next best thing is the following travel checklist, as shown in Figure 17-1.

✔ Charge all rechargeable batteries.
✔ Pack extra batteries or an external battery pack.
✔ Pack an AC power adapter.
✔ Pack a portable surge suppressor.
✔ Pack a phone line tester.
✔ Pack an extra phone line.
✔ Pack a CompactFlash or PC Card modem.
✔ Pack a backup storage card.
✔ Find ISP access numbers for your destination.
✔ Determine if you will need to print and, if so, how.
✔ Pack an extra storage card for backup.
✔ Download maps of the destination to your device.

If you are traveling outside the United States:
✔ Verify that the power adapter will work at the destination.
✔ Find out how phone calls are made at the destination.
✔ Pack an international phone line adapter.
✔ Pack a phone line noise filter.

FIGURE 17-1   Pocket PC travel checklist

Wrapping Up

Pocket PCs are made for traveling. With a little planning, you will have a happy and safe journey. When I travel, I enjoy taking along my Pocket PC and GPS so that I know where I am and how much longer I have to travel. For anyone, like me, who gets anxious when they are lost, a GPS can be a godsend. But traveling can also be boring, particularly if you fly or ride a train. Fortunately, there is a variety of entertainment software—games, music players, and eBook readers—available for the Pocket PC to help you pass the time. Chapter 18 shows you how your Pocket PC can help you unwind and relax after a long day of traveling.

17

Chapter 18

Relax with Games, Music, Books, and Movies

How to...

- Pick the best Pocket PC for playing games
- Find games to play on your Pocket PC
- Read eBooks
- Play audio books
- Play music
- Play movies and watch television shows

Having read this far, you may think that a Pocket PC is for nothing more than managing time and creating documents. Nothing could be further from the truth. When it's time to kick back and relax, a Pocket PC can be a perfect companion. With your Pocket PC you can play games, listen to music or audio books, read a novel, or even watch a movie.

If you enjoy playing computer games, you'll be happy to find Pocket PC programs for every game category. The speed, color screens, and sound capabilities of the latest Pocket PCs make them great portable game machines. Fortunately, many talented programmers have been hard at work writing games that exploit the capabilities of your Pocket PC.

If you don't find playing games to be relaxing, perhaps lounging on a couch listening to your favorite music is more to your liking. Here too, your Pocket PC is up to the task, thanks to the Windows Media Player, which is capable of playing music stored in digital files that you can download to your Pocket PC or put on storage cards. You can also play audio books using the Windows Media Player or the AudiblePlayer.

Perhaps your favorite way to relax is to curl up in front of a warm fire and read a novel. You can purchase and download electronic books, or eBooks, from the Internet and read them on your Pocket PC using software such as Microsoft Reader.

Perhaps you prefer the complete audio and visual experience of a movie a great form of relaxation. No, you won't be able to play the latest box office hit, but several independent artists make their work available on the Internet that you can download and play on your Pocket PC.

As you can see, your Pocket PC provides many tools to help you relax during a trip. It also lightens your load because you don't have to pack a half dozen CDs or a couple of books. Of course, you don't need to travel to enjoy all these features of your Pocket PC. Anywhere your Pocket PC goes, so goes your favorite music or books. Ready? Let's have some fun!

Play Games on Your Pocket PC

If any one software category represents how well the Pocket PC has sold, it is games. When we wrote the first edition of this book in early 2000, there were not very many games available, but today this is not the case. Right now, http://www.pocketgamer.org/ has 16 different categories of games listed, including Action and Arcade, Board, Role Playing, Simulation, and Strategy, and Games.

Game software evokes a tremendous amount of passion from Pocket PC owners. Go to any online forum and ask which Pocket PC is the best for games, and you are certain to receive many replies promoting one brand over another. The debate over which brand of Pocket PC is best for games centers around three items: processors, screens, and buttons.

Of all the software available for Pocket PCs, games may be the most processor intensive, particularly action and arcade games, as well as simulations. Simply stated, many games run better on faster processors. Of the Pocket PC 2000 devices, processor speeds range from 131 MHz on the Casio E-115 and 133 MHz on the Hewlett Packard Jornada 540 series to 206 MHz on the Compaq iPAQ. Most likely, Pocket PC 2002 devices will also have different processor speeds, with 206 MHhz at the low end. If action and arcade games or simulations are what you like, then you should consider buying the Pocket PC with the fastest processor, however, slower processors are very capable of playing card and board games.

Really good computer games have great graphics, and the Pocket PC's color screens set it above other handhelds for great looking games. Graphics quality doesn't necessarily affect game play, so the differences have more to do with personal preference. You can easily see the differences between Pocket PC screens, so you have to decide whether you want the best or can tolerate something less.

The different types of screens used in Pocket PCs are different types and have different amounts of colors. Two different types of screens are used in Pocket PC 2000 devices. Casio's entire line of Pocket PC 2000 devices has active thin film transistor (TFT) displays, while Hewlett Packard and Compaq Pocket PC 2000 devices use passive color super-twist nematic (CSTN) displays. Active displays have a sharper image and a broader viewing angle than passive displays. Casio's Pocket PCs can display up to 65,536 colors, but the HP and Compaq Pocket PCs are limited to 4,096 colors, and the HP Jornada 525 only displays 256 colors. If you want to see the best graphics in the games you play, pick a Pocket PC that has an active display with the most colors.

Action games not only demand a lot from a computer's processor, they can demand a lot from a player in the form of input. While desktop computers can support a wide array of joy sticks and game pads, the Pocket PC is limited to a few buttons. Casio pioneered the cursor pad on their E-100 Palm-size PCs, and it has become the benchmark for game control on Pocket PCs because it provides complete cursor control.

The iPAQ 3600 and 3100 Pocket PCs from Compaq and the @migo PD-600C from U.R. There's also have a cursor pad, but suffer from what many consider a flaw in not being able to process simultaneous button presses. If you press two buttons at once, one will be ignored, unlike the Casio Pocket PCs, which recognize both button presses. Consequently, you may find it difficult to play action games on Compaq and UR. Both vendors might correct this situation in future devices, so if action games are important to you, then check with the manufacturers before buying their products.

Hewlett Packard includes the HP game buttons setting on their Jornada 520 and 540 series Pocket PCs. The setting enables you to map the buttons on the Jornada to different game functions, such as moving left, right, up, or down, and shooting. By providing this setting, HP compensates for the lack of a cursor pad on these Pocket PCs, but the button layout, even when mapped to game functions, makes it difficult to play action games.

18

How to ... Map Game Buttons on HP Pocket PCs

To use the game buttons setting on HP Jornada 520 and 540 series Pocket PCs, tap Start | Settings | System and tap the HP Game Buttons icon. Tap Select the Enable Mapping check box to turn on button mapping and make sure the Show Status Icon check box is also selected so that you can quickly turn button mapping on or off from the Today screen. When button mapping is enabled, the buttons will not perform their regular functions.

Button mappings are in the middle of the setting screen, with the eight game actions on the left and the corresponding button on the right. The default profile, or mapping definition, already has each action mapped to a button, which you can change by tapping-and-holding on a line in the list and then tapping either Un-map This Action or Un-map All on the pop-up menulist.

You can define six different profiles to correspond with different games. To define a profile, tap the Game Profiles drop-down list and then tap one of the remaining five profiles. Tap the action and then press the button that you want to use for that action. All of the buttons on the Jornada, except the power Power button, can be mapped to a game action. Tap OK to save the profiles and close the settings screen.

To select a profile, or to turn game mappings on or off, tap the HP Game Buttons status icon on the Ccommand bar of the Today screen. Tap the Profiles command in the pop-up menu list and then tap the profile that you want to use. To turn the mapping off, tap Disable Mapping, tap Setup to open the HP Game Buttons Ssetting screen, and tap Exit to close the pop-up list.

Download Games to Play

The best source of Pocket PC games is the Internet, and Table 18-1 lists some of the websites that provide games. Most of the download websites described in Chapter 23 also have categories for games, where you can find many links for games that you can download and install on your device.

Websites	URL
PocketGamer.org	http://www.pocketgamer.org/
Jimmy Software	http://www.jimmysoftware.com/
Rapture Technologies	http://www.rapturetech.com/
Ppcgaming.com	http://www.ppcgaming.com/

TABLE 18-1 Websites on the Internet That Have Pocket PC Games

The process for downloading and installing these games is usually the same. First, download the software to your desktop computer. If the software has been compressed, deuncompress it using one of the many desktop programs, such as WinZip, available for this task. Next, connect your device and run the setup program on the desktop computer.

Use Emulators to Play Games

A game *emulator* is a program designed to run games originally written for other hardware platforms. By using an emulator, you can play games not available for the Pocket PC, however, in many cases the games will not perform as well with an emulator because they were optimized for the hardware. Emulators are available for games that run on the Nintendo GameBoy, Nintendo Entertainment System, Super Nintendo Entertainment System, Sega Master System, Sega GameGear, Sega Genesis, and Atari 2600 VCS. There are also Pocket PC programs that emulate personal computers, such as the Apple II+, Commodore 64, Atari 800, and MS-DOS.

Most of the game programs are written to read-only chips packaged inside cartridges. To legally play most of these games on your Pocket PC, you must own the cartridge, and the program must not be encrypted. A special device is used to download the game off the cartridge, or you can download the ROM images from many international websites on the Internet. There are two websites that provide copyright-free GameBoy images. One website is the Bung Enterprises GameBoy competition page at http://www.bunghk.com, which lists games written by amateurs for a programming competition. The other is the Gambit Studio website at http://www.gambitstudios.com/FreeSoftware.asp. Be sure to check the copyright information at other websites, keeping in mind that if you don't own the game cartridges then that is software piracy.

PocketGamer.org has a complete list of the emulation programs for the Pocket PC at http://www.pocketgamer.org/games/emulators. If you want to try one of these programs, keep in mind that some of them are in various stages of development and could cause problems with your Pocket PC. Before you install any game emulator, you should run a complete backup of your Pocket PC. You will find instructions for performing a backup in Chapter 7.

Play Solitaire on Your Pocket PC

It began as a way to learn a new way of interacting with a computer and quickly became a phenomenon. We all have probably seen people obsessed with clicking-and-dragging until they see cards drop all across their computer screen. Of course, I am talking about the great computer pastime—Solitaire.

Solitaire became part of the computer operating system when it was included with Windows Version 3.1. Since then, every Microsoft operating system, including Windows CE, which is the Pocket PC operating system, has included a version to help teach users how to click-and-drag.

Pocket PC users may not need to learn how to click- and- drag, but some people use Solitaire as a way to compare the speed and feel of different devices. It can also be a great way to kill a little free time.

18

How to ... Track Your Golf Game with Your Pocket PC

This chapter is about playing games on Pocket PCs, but your Pocket PC can also be used while you are playing games, like golf. By using a Pocket PC, you could take a couple of strokes off your golf game!

IntelliGolf Par Edition runs on Pocket PCs and enables up to four players to score analyze, and review the statistics for their golf game. The software also enables players to place *on course* wagers. With this software golfers can do the following:

- Automate golf scoring.
- Calculate an approximate handicap.
- Download courses from the Internet.
- Capture round statistics to help improve their game.

The Birdie Edition of IntelliGolf includes desktop software that will synchronize with the software on the Pocket PC. By using the PC, golfers can review historical trends and evaluate their strengths using over 60 categories of performance statistics. You will find more information about IntelliGolf at http://www.intelligolf.com/.

Play a Game of Solitaire

To start Solitaire, tap Start | Programs | Games | Solitaire, and the game will load as shown in the following image:

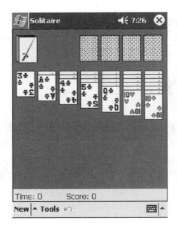

Did you know?

Rules for Playing Solitaire

Solitaire is a term applied to a variety of card games that can be played by one person. Among the most popular of these is Canfield, considered the most challenging game of Solitaire, and Klondike, which is the easiest of the Solitaire games to learn.

Klondike is the Solitaire game included with your Pocket PC. Twenty-eight cards are dealt in seven piles known as a *tableau*. The cards are dealt in rows, starting with one card turned up, followed by six cards dealt face down to the right. The seventh card is turned up and placed on top of the first turned down card in the first row, starting the second pile. Next, five cards are dealt face down to the right, fanned down from the previous row, and the sixth card is turned up and placed on top of the third pile. The remaining cards are dealt in this manner until seven piles have been formed, each with one less card and topped by a card turned up. The remainder of the deck is the *hand*. As they become available, aces form four foundation piles, built up by suit. The objective is to get all 52 cards, or as many possible, into the foundation piles.

The game is played by continuously turning over packets of three cards from the hand, forming the stock. In each turn, the top card is available for play on either any one of the seven tableau piles, in descending order and alternating color, or on a foundation pile, in ascending order and only in the same suite. If the top card is moved to a pile, the next card of the stock is available for play. The top card of each tableau pile is always available for play and can be moved between piles or moved to a foundation pile. Once moved to a foundation pile, a card can no longer be played. When all of the turned-up cards of a tableau pile are removed, the next face-down card is turned over. If all cards are removed from a tableau pile, a new pile can be started with a king. Play stops when cards can no longer be played into the foundation piles.

Pocket PCs break one rule of Klondike by allowing cards from foundation piles to be played into tableau piles. However, when such a play is made, 15 points are deducted from the score.

When you start Solitaire, the cards are dealt and displayed on the computer screen. Four spaces are marked at the top of the screen for building the foundation piles, and the hand is placed face-down in the upper-left corner. Tap the top of the hand to turn over a packet of three cards into the stock. To turn over cards in the tableau piles, tap on them.

18

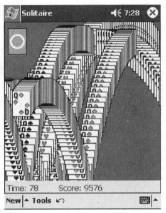

To move a card, tap- and- hold the stylus, drag it to a location on the screen, and then lift up the stylus. If the play is legal, the card will stay on the pile; otherwise, the card returns to its original location. Double-tap a card to move it to a foundation pile, and the card will be placed in the correct pile.

Play continues until you win, exit the game, or deal a new set of cards. When you win, the cards cascade around the screen, as shown here.

To deal cards, tap New.

Configure Solitaire

While the Pocket PC follows the Klondike rules, it does allow for some minor variations. For example, the number of cards played from the hand, which is normally three, can be one. Two levels of scoring, Standard and Vegas, are possible; or scoring can be turned off.

With Standard scoring, points are earned based on time and moves:

- 10 points for each card moved to a foundation pile
- 5 points for each card moved from the hand to a tableau pile
- −15 points for each card moved from a foundation pile to a tableau pile
- −20 points for each pass through the hand after four passes in the Draw Three option.
- −100 points for each pass through the hand after one pass in the Draw One option.

A bonus is given when you complete a timed game, with larger bonuses given for shorter games. With Vegas scoring, the ante is $52.00 to begin playing a game:

- The object is to earn more than you wagered.
- No time penalty or bonus is given.
- If you select the Keep Cumulative Score option, you'll see a running total of the score from game to game.
- You win $5.00 for each card moved to a foundation pile.

How to ... **Deal a Perfect Hand**

You might think I spent all night playing Solitaire in order to capture the screen shot of cascading cards shown in the preceding illustration. Actually, I didn't have to, because you can make Solitaire deal a winning hand every time. (You might want to stop reading the rest of this box if you don't want to know how to cheat at Solitaire.)

Here is what you need to do:

1. Start Solitaire.

2. Open the keyboard version of the software input panel.

3. Tap CTL-SHIFT.

4. Tap New.

Set Solitaire Options

To open the Options dialog box, tap Tools | Options. The following dialog box displays:

To change the draw, select the an option from the Draw drop-down list. Change the scoring by selecting that an option from the Scoring drop-down list. Turn Game Timing off by clearing the Time Game check box. Game Status is turned on or off by checking Display Status. Cumulate Vegas scores by checking Keep Cumulative Score.

The Card Back design can be changed between one of six graphics. Tap a graphic in the Options dialog box to change the card design. Once you finish changing options, tap OK to close the dialog box.

Play Music

Recently, the Internet has become popular for distributing music, thanks to MPEG (Moving Picture Experts Group). MPEG is a family of standards for encoding audio-visual information in a compressed digital format. Part of the standard is the audio-coding format known as MP3, or MPEG Audio Layer 3.

Without compression technology, three minutes of CD-quality sound requires approximately 32MB of storage space, which is too large for distribution over the Internet. MP3 significantly reduces the size of audio filesreduces this storage space to 3MB, making it possible to download sound files from the Internet.

Audio compression enables CD-quality music to be played on personal computers, portable music players, such as the Diamond Rio, and Pocket PCs. The Windows Media Player on your Pocket PC plays music that you can download from thousands of websites on the Internet. With your Pocket PC and a storage card, you can listen to hours of music and not have to carry an extra CD player.

Play Music Using Windows Media Player

Microsoft's Windows Media Player Version 8 from Microsoft plays MP3 and WMA music files and Windows Media Video stored internally on a Pocket PC or on a storage card. It can also play streaming media stored on a network. The player is included in ROM of some Pocket PCs or can be installed on to the Pocket PC and stored in RAM. To start the player, tap Start | Windows Media 8. The following illustration image shows how the program looks when it starts.

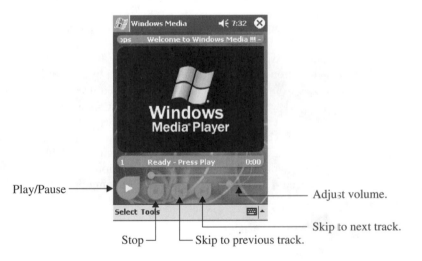

Play/Pause

Adjust volume.

Skip to next track.

Stop

Skip to previous track.

When Media Player starts, it searches internal storage and storage cards for audio and video content. To see a list of the available content, tap Select on the Ccommand bar, and make sure

Did you know?

Audio File Formats

MP3 is one of several different sound file types. Another type is WAV (Waveform), which doesn't compress the size of the file and therefore requires a lot of storage space. It is, however, the simplest sound format and is typically used to create small files, such as the sounds available in Microsoft Themes. As explained in Chapter 13, Voice Recorder creates WAV files that vary in size based on the quality of the sound. Lower quality sound, captured in kilobits per second (Kbps), creates smaller files than higher quality sound. Windows CE, like all versions of Windows, has built-in support for playing WAV files.

Microsoft created the WMA (Windows Media Audio) format. It also compresses audio files, but with half the size of MP3, and with better quality. The file format can be secured to protect sound files from being illegally distributed.

The file formats listed so far, MP3, WAV, and WMA, are called *samples* because they contain the actual recording of the sound. Two other file formats create sound, one is MIDI (Musical Instrument Digital Interface), and the other is MOD (Module). MIDI contains commands that tell the computer how to reproduce sound. Usually, keyboard synthesizers or music generators are used to create these files.

MODs are hybrids of samples and instructions. An explanation of modules is found at http://www.castlex.com/modfaq/index.html:

> Modules are digital music files, made up of a set of samples (the instruments) and sequencing information, telling a mod player when to play which sample on which track at what pitch, optionally performing an effect like vibrato, for example. Thus mods are different from pure sample files such as WAV or AU, which contain no sequencing information, and MIDI files, which do not include any custom samples/instruments.

Local Content is selected from the drop-down list box. You cannot edit the Local Content list, but you can create a new playlist based on it. To create a playlist, follow these steps:

1. Tap Select Playlist on the Ccommand bar to open the Content Selection window, as shown here:

2. Select Organize Playlists from the Select Playlist drop-down list.

3. Tap New and give the playlist a name.

4. Tap the box next to each track you want in the playlist.

5. Tap OK.

Tap here to select and create playlists

After a playlist is created, it can be edited so that tracks move up and down in the list or are removed. To edit a playlist follow these steps:

1. Tap Select Playlist on the Command bar.

2. Select the playlist you want to edit from the Select Playlist drop-down list.

3. Tap the track to edit in the list and perform one of the following edits:

   ■ Tap the up or down arrows on the Command bar to move the track in the list.

   ■ Tap the plus sign (+) on the Command bar to add a track to the list.

   ■ Tap the red X on the Command bar to remove a track from the list.

4. Tap OK to close the playlist, or tap the sideways triangle on the Command bar to start playing the track.

To play music in a playlist, tap Select Playlist on the Ccommand bar, select the playlist from the Select Playlist drop-down list, tap the track you want to start playing in the list, and then tap Play on the Command bar.

To play music or videos stored on a network, tap Tools | Open URL and enter the URL. You can also play music or videos from Internet Explorer. When you tap on a link to the content on a web page, Windows Media Player automatically loads and starts playing the content. To add that content to the Web Favorites, tap Tools | Add Web Favorites, and enter a name in the Favorite Name field. To access Web Favorites, tap Select, and then select Web Favorites from the Select Playlist drop-down list. You can edit the Web Favorites list in the same way as you edit playlists.

The playback quality of music and videos stored on a network depends on the network connection. To specify whether to use an HTTP Proxy server or not, the Internet connection speed, and which protocols to use, tap Tools | Settings | Network.

Personalize Windows Media Player

Tape and CD players have buttons to control music playback. This functionality is provided by on-screen buttons in Windows Media Player. You can program the hardware buttons on your Pocket PC to provide the same playback control. Tap Tools | Settings | Buttons to open the following screen.

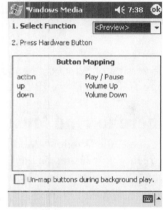

To map a button, first select a function from the drop-down list and then press the hardware button that you want to perform that function. To remove a button mapping, tap-and-hold on the item listed in the middle of the screen, and tap Un-map This Button on the pop-up menu.

The Screen Toggle function is unique to Pocket PCs; and it turns the screen display on or off. Turning the display off saves battery life, which allows you to play more music. All of the button mappings that you program remain in effect while the screen is off so that you can easily adjust music playback.

You should also notice the Un-map Buttons During Background Play check box on the button-mapping screen. If you do not tap this check box, the button mappings will remain in effect when you switch to another program on your Pocket PC. If you are listening to music on your Pocket PC, open Internet Explorer, and find that the navigation hardware button does not move the web page up or down, it's probably because the navigation button has been mapped to something in Windows Media Player.

The Media Player supports *skins,* which you can change to tailor the user interface to your tastes. A Media Player skin consists of a number of bitmap image files and a text file. Files of each skin should be stored in a separate directory on the Pocket PC. The skin directories can be anywhere on the Pocket PC, but keep in mind that if a skin is on a storage card, the card will need to be in the Pocket PC every time you run Media Player so that it can load the skin.

> **NOTE**   *If Windows Media Player cannot find the skin it is configured to use, it will automatically load the Skin Chooser so that you can select another skin.*

To change skins in Windows Media Player, tap Tools | Settings | Skin Chooser. The Skin Chooser dialog box displays with left and right arrows at the bottom of the box. Tap the arrows to scroll through the skins that are available; highlight and tap OK to select the skin. Table 18-2 lists websites on the Internet where you can find Windows Media Player skins to download.

Copy Music to Your Pocket PC

The fastest way to add music to your Pocket PC is to copy the music files from a desktop computer to a storage card using a storage card reader. Chapter 23 provides more information about storage card readers that work with desktop computers. You can also use Windows Explorer, as described in Chapter 7, to copy music files to the Pocket PC.

If you use Windows Media Player Version 7 on your PC, you can use its Portable Device feature to copy music files to a Pocket PC connected to the desktop with a serial or USB cable.

Websites	URL
Microsoft	www.microsoft.com/windowsmedia
Pocket PC Minds	www.pocketpcminds.com
SnoopSoft Inc.	www.snoopsoft.com/PocketPC/WMPSkins.html

TABLE 18-2   Internet Websites Where You Can Find Windows Media Player Skins

The version of Windows Media Player included with Windows XP has a similar feature, called Copy To CD Or Device, that copies music and video to connected Pocket PCs.

Where to Find Music on the Internet

Of course, the Windows Media Player is useless unless you have files to play. Fortunately, there are plenty of websites on the Internet that contain free copies of music files for you to download. In fact, there are so many MP3 websites available that I can't begin to describe them all. The simplest way to find them is to go to a large index website, like Yahoo! or Excite, and perform a search for **MP3**. I assure you, you will find plenty of sites.

Be aware that you won't find legal copies of songs by popular artists in MP3 format because the format does not have provisions to protect against piracy. Most of the music that you'll find at websites like http://www.mp3.com is written and performed by relatively unknown bands and musicians from around the world. This, in itself, makes finding MP3s fun because it gives you a chance to discover music that you have never heard before.

Finding WMA files is a little more challenging because they are not as popular as MP3 files. The best site for WMA files is Microsoft's Windows Media.com at http://windowsmedia.com. At this website, you'll find tracks from popular artists such as 10,000 Maniacs, Berlin, and Indigo Girls. This is because the WMA format supports encryption to prevent music from being played unless it is bought.

Listen To to Books Using Audible Player

Audible Inc. is a leading provider of Internet-delivered spoken content for playback on personal computers and Pocket PCs. The sound files are purchased from the Audible's Web website at http://www.audible.com.

Much of the content you buy is recordings of books, but they also sell special broadcasts, such as *The Wall Street Journal Final & Analysis*. The process of downloading Audible files to a Pocket PC is done in two steps. First, the Audible Manager, which is a program that runs on your desktop computer, logs on to the Audible website and downloads the sound file to the PC. Second, you connect the Pocket PC to the desktop using its serial cable and transfer the sound file to the Audible player.

How to ... Play Audible Content with Microsoft Reader

When you install the Audible Manager, the installation program will configure your Pocket PC, so it must be connected to the desktop. It will install the Audible Player to your Pocket PC, but you can also choose not to download the Player and instead listen to books using Microsoft Reader, which is described in the next section of this chapter. Microsoft Reader lists Audible content along with all other eBooks on the Library page. To play an Audible book, just tap its entry on the Library page. The Reader's playback features are not as robust as the Audible Player, but since Reader is already installed on your Pocket PC, you can save storage space by not installing another program that provides the same functionality.

For every hour of audio programming you will need 2MB of storage space. The recordings will vary in length; for example, *The Wall Street Journal Final & Analysis* broadcast lasts 20 minutes, but you can buy Gregory Peck's narration of the Bible that runs 19 hours and 45 minutes. Fortunately, you can specify where Audible will write the sound files when you download them to the Pocket PC.

The player software contains features optimized for playback of spoken content. You can skip back and forth to sections, which usually are chapters in books. If, during playback, you hear a particular segment that you want to return to, you can create a bookmark that the player is able to skip to during playback.

Read eBooks

For many people, reading a book is the ultimate escape from computers and the Internet. Most people still read books printed on paper, but an increasing number prefer to have their favorite books available on their personal computer or personal digital assistant, which is the idea behind electronic books, or *eBooks*.

Read eBooks Using Microsoft Reader

Microsoft Reader is an eBook-viewing program for the Pocket PC. It uses a font rendering technology called *ClearType* that is designed to make text easier to read on color LCD (liquid crystal display) screens. With Microsoft Reader, you can read eBooks on your Pocket PC that you may have purchased and downloaded from the Internet.

18

Microsoft Reader
Digital Rights Management

Digital Rights Management (DRM) is technology that has the purpose of ensuring that content, such as music and eBooks, is not pirated on the Internet. While this technology is implemented in a variety of ways, it typically involves encrypting the content to prevent it from being copied to multiple computers. The Microsoft's version of DRM has three levels: sealed, inscribed, and owner exclusive. Sealed eBooks are simply encrypted to ensure the authenticity of the content and can be distributed among multiple computers. Inscribed eBooks are sealed and further encrypted to include the purchaser's name on the cover page. They can be distributed amongst multiple computers but will always display the purchaser's information to reinforce honest usage. Owner exclusive eBooks includes additional encryption that requires them to be read only on activated Reader clients. Activation uses the Microsoft's Passport authentication, and you can only activate two computers using a Passport ID.

The Reader program that runs on Pocket PC 2000 devices does not support owner exclusive eBbooks, or what has also been referred to as DRM Level 5. Microsoft does not intended to provide an upgrade for Pocket PC 2000 devices that will support owner exclusive eBooks. You can read sealed (DRM Level 0) and inscribed (DRM Level 3) eBooks on Pocket PC 2000 devices.

The Reader program that runs on Pocket PC 2002 devices does support owner exclusive eBooks, as well as sealed and inscribed eBooks. To read an owner exclusive eBook, you must activate the Reader client. The activation process is explained in a How To section later in this chapter.

To start Microsoft Reader on a Pocket PC, tap Start | Programs | Microsoft Reader, which opens the Microsoft Reader Library page, as shown here.
The Library lists all of the eBbooks that are stored in the My Documents folder on the Pocket PC. eBooks stored in subfolders, or in a My Documents folder on a storage card, are also listed.

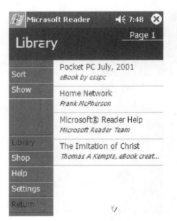

How to ... Activate Microsoft Reader on Pocket PC 2002

Premium eBooks are owner exclusive and can only be read using an activated Reader client. To activate Reader, you'll need a Passport ID, which you can get at http://www.microsoft.com/passport. You'll also need at least ActiveSync Version 3.1 and Internet Explorer Version 4, (Reader cannot be activated on Pocket PC 2000 devices). Your Pocket PC must be connected with a desktop running ActiveSync during activation, and shouldn't have Reader running. You might have activated Reader the very first time you synchronized; if not, then follow these steps:

1. Connect your Pocket PC with the desktop.
2. Start Internet Explorer and open http://das.microsoft.com/activate.
3. Log in to the website using your Passport ID.
4. Click the Activate Your Pocket PC button.

The activation process associates your Passport ID with your Pocket PC. It also downloads files to your Pocket PC that are unique to you, along with an Activation Certificate, which is the key piece of information that enables you to read premium eBooks on your Pocket PC.

The Microsoft Reader Help provides additional information about activation, and you will find a FAQ at the activation website.

To open a book, tap its name on the Library page, and eBook's cover page will open, as shown here.

Along the left side of the cover page are buttons for moving to different parts of the eBook or the Reader program. Tap Go To to open a menu with options for moving to the Table of Contents, Most Recent Page, Begin Reading, Furthest Read, Annotations, About This Title, and Cover Image.

When you tap the Most Recent link, you return to the last page that was open in the eBook; when you tap Furthest Read, you return to the furthest page opened in the ebook. Tap Annotations to open a list of all the annotations added to the eBook, and to quickly move to an annotation, tap its entry in the list.

The easiest way to read an eBook is to tap the First Page link on the cover page and begin reading. Use the Action button

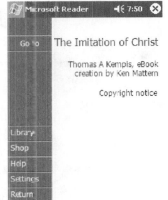

18

on the Pocket PC to move back and forth between pages, or tap the arrows at the upper-right corner of the page. When you tap the title of the eBook at the top of the page, a pop-up menu list appears, as shown here in the following image:

Tap here to return to the previous location.

Tap Settings on the pop-up menu list to change how Reader displays an eBook. There are three pages of settings: the first page is for turning the visual guides on or off, the second page controls annotations, and the third page controls the font size. To select a page, tap Go To, and tap the items on the page to turn them on or off. When you are done making setting changes, tap the Return link at the bottom of the screen.

Text on a page in an eBook can be annotated by selecting the text using the stylus, which causes a pop-up menu list to appear, as shown below.

Tap an entry in the menu to carry out its action. For example, to highlight the text that you selected, tap Add Highlight. When you tap Copy Text, the text is placed on the Pocket PC Clipboard and can be pasted into a Note or Pocket Word document. If you select a word and tap Find, Reader will search through the book for the next occurrence of that word.

Electronic sticky notes can be attached to specific passages of text. To add notes, use the stylus to select text on a page and tap Add Text Note on the pop-up menu. A Note icon appears on the left margin and a notepad displays on the screen. When you are finished writing, tap outside the note to close it. To view notes, tap the Note icon in the left margin; to delete a note, tap-and-hold on the Note icon and tap Delete from the pop-up list. To display a list of notes for an eBbook from the cover page, tap Go To | Annotations.

TIP   *For more information about how to use Microsoft Reader, open the Microsoft Reader Help eBook on your Pocket PC.*

How to ... Create Your Own Reader eBook

Microsoft provides a free Add-In for Word 2000 and Word XP that converts
a document to the .lit format used by Reader. You will find the Add-In at
http://www.microsoft.com/ ebooks/tools/default.asp. OverDrive ReaderWorks is
another eBook creation tool that converts HTML, text, and image files to the .lit format.
ReaderWorks Standard is free; ReaderWorks Publisher costs $69.00 and enables
you to add cover art and marketing data. You can download ReaderWorks from
http://www.overdrive.com/readerworks/.

Download Microsoft Reader eBooks

There are many Internet websites that provide eBooks that you can download and read on your
Pocket PC, some of which are listed in Table 18-3. To read these eBbooks on your Pocket PC,
copy them to the My Documents folder on your device or into a My Documents folder on a
storage card. Tap Shop from the Reader Library, or the cover page of any eBook, to open
Internet Explorer on your Pocket PC and a web page with a link to http://www.microsoft.com/
reader/shop.asp.

Read eBooks Using Other Programs

Microsoft Reader is not the only eBook program available for Pocket PCs. Most of the other
eBook programs are available for Palm OS devices, as well as Pocket PCs, and because of that

Websites	URL
CEWindows.net	http://www.cewindows.net
Elegant Solutions Software and Publishing Company	http://esspc-ebooks.com/default.htm
Pocket PC eBooks Watch	http://cebooks.blogspot.com/
Baen	http://www.baen.com/
University of Virginia	http://etext.virginia.edu/ebooks/
Pocket PC Press	http://www.pocketpcpress.com/
Black Mask Online	http://www.blackmask.com/
Fictionwise	http://www.fictionwise.com/
Memoware	http://www.memoware.com/
Barnes and Noble	http://ebooks.barnesandnoble.com/pocketpc/index.asp

TABLE 18-3 Internet Websites That Have Microsoft Reader eBooks for Download

18

this fact, there are more eBooks available. Ironically, one of the top eBook alternatives for the Pocket PC is the Palm Reader, owned by Palm Digital Media. Originally, the program was the PeanutPress Reader, but became part of Palm Digital Media when Palm Computing purchased PeanutPress during the summer of 2001. Table 18-4 lists the alternative eBook readers for the Pocket PC.

Play Movies

While other handheld computers have games, eBooks, and music software, none are capable of playing video like the Pocket PC. Several video players exist that take advantage of the processing power and colorful screens of Pocket PCs, and the large storage capacity of CompactFlash cards.

Play Movies Using Windows Media Player

The Windows Media Player plays files in the Windows Media Video format and streaming Windows Media on the Internet. Clicking a link to streaming video in Internet Explorer launches the Media Player, which automatically starts to play the video. You can also load a streaming video directly from the Media Player by tapping Tools | Open URL and entering the URL of the video. You select and play video files on storage cards the same way that you play music.

Included in the Internet Explorer favorites is a link to the mobile version of WindowsMedia.com, which is located at http://windowsmedia.com/mobile/. This website has links to streaming video and audio that play on the Pocket PC using the Windows Media Player.

By default, videos display in the small Media Player window, but you can change that so videos display using the entire Pocket PC screen. To display videos at full screen, tap Tools | Settings | Audio & Video, and select All in from the Full Screen drop-down list. Full Screen videos display in landscape on the Pocket PC's screen, and you can flip the display by tapping the Rotate 180° check box on the Audio & Video Settings screen.

Some videos that you play may be designed for a screen larger than the Pocket PC screen. By default, Windows Media Player crops the video to fit the screen. You can change this behavior action so the display is cut in half by selecting the 50% Size option in the Oversized drop-down list on the Audio & Video Settings screen.

Reader	URL
Palm Reader	http://www.peanutpress.com
Mobipocket Reader	http://www.mobipocket.com/en/HomePage/default.asp
TomeRaider	http://www.tomeraider.com/
AportisDoc	http://www.aportis.com/
PeekABook	http://www.oopdreams.com/ce/peekabook/

TABLE 18-4   eBook Reader Programs for Pocket PCs

Play Movies Using PocketTV

The MPEG (Moving Picture Experts Group) is a more popular video file format than Windows Media Video, and you can play MPEG video files on a Pocket PC using PocketTV. PocketTV is free for personal use and can be downloaded from http://www.pockettv.com.

PocketTV is capable of playing streaming video files and can play video in both portrait and landscape. It has a Dither option that uses a special algorithm to improve video playback on devices such as the Compaq iPAQ 3600 and HP Jornada 540 that have only 4,096 colors. PocketTV also has a Microdrive option that reduces the power used when playing videos from the IBM Microdrive.

Encoders are programs that convert audio and video files from one format to another. There are several different encoders for making MPEG video files, which you can use to create your own MPEG files from home videos. You will find several links to encoders at http://www.mpegtv.com/wince/pockettv/encoding.html.

If you don't have the time to make your own MPEG videos, you will find several websites on the Internet that provide files for you to download. Table 18-5 lists websites that have MPEG files optimized for playback on Pocket PCs.

Play Movies Using ActiveSky

The ActiveSky Media Player plays video files in a proprietary format called SKY. The video file format is optimized for playback on Pocket PCs and over wireless networks. There are some unique features in this video player, such as being able to control the playback speed and zooming the display. You can download this free player from http://www.activesky.com.

ActiveSky has partnered with several premier content providers, such as AtomFilms, to develop content for their player. You will find links to these content providers at http://www.activesky.com/content/download.html.

Watch Television Shows Using SnapStream Pocket PVS

The SnapStream Personal Video System (PVS) is the computer equivalent to a VCR. First, you install a TV Tuner card into a desktop computer and connect the card to a TV. Next, you run the SnapStream software to record television shows, which are stored as files on the computer. With the Pocket PVS module, you can have SnapStream synchronize the shows to your Pocket PC, which you can watch at any time.

Websites	URL
PocketMovies.net	http://www.pocketmovies.net
SelfMobile	http://www.selfmobile.com/html/videos.cfm
PocketRocketFX.com	http://www.pocketrocketfx.com

TABLE 18-5   Websites that have MPEG video files optimized for Pocket PCs

18

The Windows Media Player provides the actual video playback on the Pocket PC, and the Pocket PVS module manages the file synchronization. A 30-minute show recorded in standard quality for Pocket PCs requires 29 MB of storage space, while a high quality recording requires 43 MB. The file sizes will vary a little between Pocket PC brands due to optimizations for their screens.

You can buy SnapStream PVS for $49.99, or you can buy it bundled with a Hauppauge WinTV tuner card for $89.99. There is a free version of Pocket PVS that limits video playback on Pocket PCs to files up to 32 MB in size, or you can purchase an unlimited version for $29.99. To find more information about this product go to http://www.snapstream.com.

Wrapping Up

The Pocket PC is a great entertainer. It plays games, stores a library of books, treats you to music, and thrills you with movies. All of these tasks take advantage of the Pocket PC's multimedia features, that which set it apart from the competition. These features also require the additional storage space that CompactFlash cards provide to Pocket PCs. The games, eBooks, music, and movies available on the Pocket PC are available on from the Internet, which can be entertaining on its own. In the next chapter, I will show you how you can connect your Pocket PC to the Internet.

Part III

Go Online with Your Pocket PC

Chapter 19

Connect to the Internet with or without Wires

How To...

- Use the Connection Wizard to configure modem connections
- Use the Connection Manager to configure network connections
- Select a wireless modem
- Use ActiveSync Desktop Pass Through to connect to networks using serial cables
- Connect to local area networks

By all accounts, the number of people who use the Internet has grown at a phenomenal rate. The majority of Internet connections are made using personal computers; but a variety of other devices, such as smart phones, TV/set-top boxes, and handheld computers, are starting to be used to connect to the Internet.

When Microsoft originally designed Pocket PCs, Microsoft recognized the importance of connecting to the Internet; so every Pocket PC has the ability to connect in a variety of different ways. One way is the traditional dial-up method using a modem and telephone line, which is normally called *remote networking* or *dial-up networking*. All Pocket PCs come with the software needed to make this connection, and a number of companies make CompactFlash modems that work with Pocket PCs.

The modem and telephone line combination is the most widely used means of connecting to the Internet, but two alternative methods are emerging. One is *wireless networking,* which provides a connection to the Internet using analog or digital cellular phones, special wireless modems, or wireless Ethernet cards. The second emerging method for Internet access is *broadband*. In the simplest terms, broadband is fast Internet access for consumers. Two implementations of broadband are popular: cable-modem service, using the same cable wire connected to your television set; and Digital Subscriber Line (DSL), which provides high-speed access using regular telephone lines.

For the majority of Pocket PC users, remote networking will be the method used to connect to the Internet; and this chapter provides instructions for making the connection. Wireless networking with cellular phones and wireless modems works the same way as remote networking, which is also covered in this chapter.

You'll find instructions for connecting to the Internet using the device's USB cable and ActiveSync Desktop Pass Through. Finally, instructions are also provided for connecting to local area networks (LANs) using wired and wireless Ethernet cards.

Gather Internet Service Provider Information

Internet Service Providers (ISPs) are companies that provide connections to the Internet. Thousands of ISPs provide telephone numbers that you use to either connect directly to the Internet or, as is the case with America Online (AOL), connect to a private network and then connect to the Internet. Pocket PCs work with the majority of ISPs that connect directly to the Internet, but you cannot connect using AOL.

Before you connect to the Internet, you need to gather some information in order to configure Internet connections. If your ISP provides instructions for connecting to the Internet, then what you need will be provided in those instructions. If your ISP does not provide instructions, you can find the information by opening the Properties of the connection in Windows. You will need the following information to create Internet connections on your Pocket PC:

- Do you provide a username and password in the Dial-Up Connection dialog box, or does a terminal window open after the number has been dialed (in which case you enter a username and password)? If a terminal window is used, you must configure the Pocket PC connection to open one, as explained in the "Modify Internet Connections" section later in this chapter.

- Obtain the maximum baud rate for the connection and the settings for data bits, parity, stop bits, and flow control.

- Find out whether the connection uses Point-to-Point Protocol (PPP) or Serial Line Interface Protocol (SLIP). The most common of these is PPP.

- Does the network access server, or Windows NT remote access server, provide an IP address or is one manually assigned? The most common configuration is server assigned; but if it is manually assigned, you will need the address provided by the ISP.

- Does the connection use software compression and IP header compression? The most common configuration is to use both.

- Does the server assign addresses for name servers or are they manually assigned? If they are manually assigned, you will need the address for Primary DNS, Secondary DNS, Primary WINS, and Secondary WINS.

- Obtain the phone number

Did you know?

Connection Manager Automates Network Connections

In this chapter, you'll learn how to use ISP information to create modem connections and connect to the Internet or corporate networks. Pocket PC 2002 has a new Connection Manager that provides a way to designate modem connections for the Internet and corporate networks, which Connection Manager calls Work. Depending on the type of information you are trying to access, Connection Manager automatically determines which type of connection it needs to make and dials the call.

Use Connection Manager

Your Pocket PC has multiple ways to connect to networks. It can use modems to connect with ISPs or with corporate remote access servers. The USB cable or infrared port that you use to connect a device with a PC creates a small network between the two devices, and can also be used by the Pocket PC to connect with the Internet.

LANs are common in offices today, and are also beginning to be installed in homes to share resources and Internet connections. All Pocket PCs include the necessary software to connect to LANs by using either PC Card or CompactFlash Ethernet network interface cards (NICs).

Connection Manager, as shown in the following image, controls all network connections for Pocket PC 2002.

You can manually establish network connections directly from Connection Manager by tapping the Connect buttons, but the Pocket PC is designed to automatically make network connections. Once you configure Connection Manager, it makes connections based on the type of

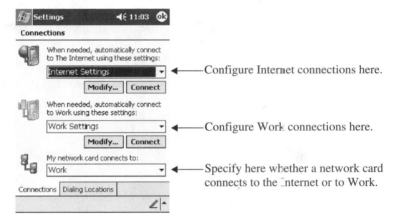

— Configure Internet connections here.

— Configure Work connections here.

— Specify here whether a network card connects to the Internet or to Work.

information that you attempt to retrieve and the peripheral attached to the Pocket PC. Table 19-1

	Internet	Work
Internet Explorer	Enter a URL in a fully qualified domain name form, such as www.pocketpchow2.com.	Enter a one-word URL, such as fmcpherson.
Inbox	All Inbox services connect to the Internet by default.	Configure Inbox services to connect to Work.
MSN Messenger	MSN Messenger is only configured to use a Passport account.	MSN Messenger is configured to use an Exchange account.
ActiveSync	Never connects to the Internet.	Always connects to Work.
Terminal Server Client	Does not directly make a network connection.	Does not directly make a network connection. If you use a modem, you must use Connection Manager.

TABLE 19-1   Scenarios for Which the Pocket PC Will Connect to the Internet or Work Using a Modem

lists the Pocket PC applications that use network connections, along with the connection scenarios when using a modem. If a network card is available instead of a modem, the applications will make a connection based on the network card setting in Connection Manager.

NOTE *If you want to synchronize using a network card, you must configure the card to connect to Work.*

Use the Connection Wizard

Among the first things that you will configure on a new Pocket PC is how it will make network connections. Microsoft makes it easier for you to set up this configuration by providing the Connection Wizard, which you download by clicking the Download link on the following screen of the companion CD-ROM:

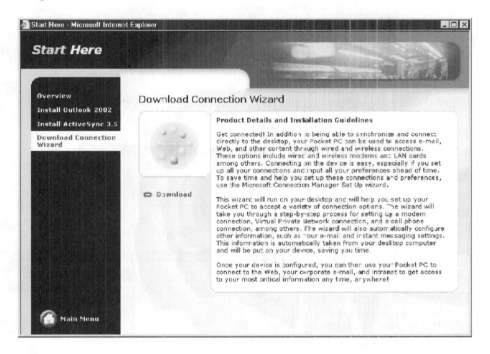

This screen appears when you load the companion CD-ROM into your desktop computer. The companion CD-ROM ships with all Pocket PCs.

The Connection Wizard guides you through the process of configuring connections on your Pocket PC. While it does copy your MSN Messenger User ID from the desktop to the Pocket PC, it does not copy any remote networking or Outlook Mail Services. You will have to enter the ISP and Work network information on the Pocket PC. Before you can begin using the Connection Wizard, you must connect your Pocket PC with a desktop computer.

The following image shows the Connection Wizard reading the settings on the Pocket PC:

Microsoft Pocket PC Connection Wizard

Please wait while your Pocket PC's settings are checked.

This wizard will help you to set up a modem that dials:
    Your work dial-in number
    Your Internet Service Provider (ISP)

You can also set up a network card to:
    Connect directly to your work network
    Connect directly to the Internet

You can set up a proxy server to access the Internet while connected to your work network.

You can also set up a Virtual Private Network (VPN) to access your work network while you're connected to:
    Your ISP with a modem
    The Internet with a network card

Once you have finished this wizard, most programs that need to connect to the Internet or your Work network, such as Inbox and Instant Messenger, will determine the best method to connect and automatically connect for you.

Reading settings from Pocket PC...

        < Back   Next >   Cancel

If you plan to use a modem and it is not attached to the Pocket PC, the following dialog box will display:

Checking For Modems

Are you using an external modem? If so, insert the modem now and click Yes to continue. Otherwise, click No.

    Yes   No

Insert the modem, click Yes, and the Connection Wizard will read the settings again.

On the screen on the right, the Connection Wizard asks you how you will connect to the Internet and to Work networks.

The radio buttons that you select for modem connections will determine which screens you will see in the Connection Wizard. For example, if you select An Internet Service Provider, then you will not see the screens for connecting to Work networks.

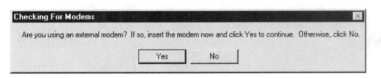

Microsoft Pocket PC Connection Wizard

How do you want to connect?
   Select the methods you want to use to access the Internet and/or your work network.

☑ **I have a modem**
  My modem connects to:
    ○ An Internet Service Provider (ISP)
    ○ My work network
    ◉ Both an ISP and my work network

☑ **I have a network card**
  My network card connects directly to:
    ○ The Internet only
    ○ My work network only
    ◉ Both the Internet and my work network

    < Back   Next >   Cancel

On the next screen, shown on the right, you configure dialing locations.

The Pocket PC uses the dialing locations to determine how to dial a number, and which number to use when multiple connections are available in either the Internet or Work settings. A check mark next to a dialing location indicates that it is the one that the Pocket PC will use when making a call.

Two locations, Home and Work, are available by default on all Pocket PCs, with the locations configured to the 425 area code. You will want to change these area codes to match your home and work phone numbers. You can also create new locations or delete existing locations from this screen.

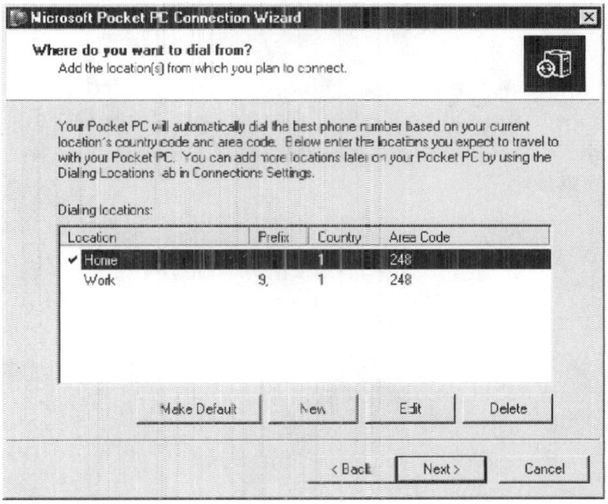

NOTE *You can manually specify dialing patterns for local, long distance, and international calls for dialing locations on the Pocket PC. The Connection Wizard does not provide a way for changing dialing patterns.*

On the screen shown at right, you enter the phone numbers for your ISP. The numbers you enter on this screen are entered in the Internet Settings portion of the Pocket PC Connection Manager.

NOTE *If you did not tell the Connection Wizard that you will use a modem to connect to an ISP, you will not see this screen.*

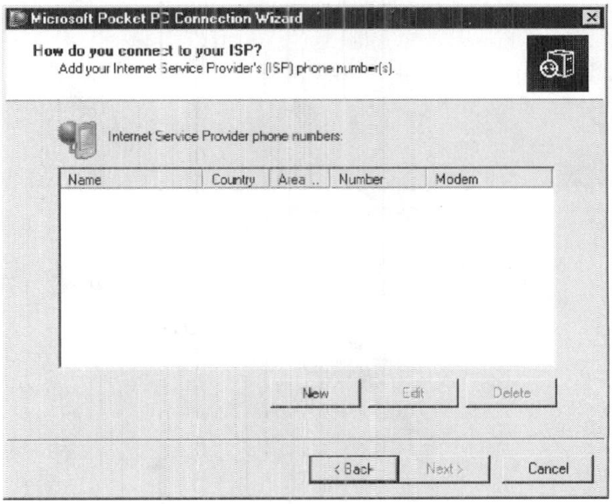

19

To add a number, click New, which opens the dialog box shown on the right.

Enter a name for the connection along with the phone number information, and select a modem. Click OK to save the ISP phone number, or click Cancel to close the dialog box.

ISP Phone Number

Name:	MSN Southfield
Country code:	1	Area code:	248
Phone number:	204-1312
Modem:	PRETEC-CompactModem_3.3V_56K

OK　Cancel

NOTE *An external modem will only appear in the modem drop-down list if the modem is inserted in the Pocket PC and detected by the Connection Wizard.*

You can enter more than one ISP phone number. When multiple ISP numbers are available, Connection Manager will dial the number that has an area code matching the dialing location area code. The one exception is 800 numbers, which will always be used even if there are local ISP phone numbers.

The Work phone numbers, shown on the right, only appear if you tell the Connection Wizard that the modem will connect to a Work network.

The numbers you enter on this screen will be entered in the Work connection portion of Connection Manager on the

Microsoft Pocket PC Connection Wizard

How do you connect to work?
Add the phone numbers you use to dial into work.

Work phone numbers:

Name	Country	Area ...	Number	Modem
Work connection	1	248	555-1212	PRETEC-Compa...

New　Edit　Delete

< Back　Next >　Cancel

Microsoft Pocket PC Connection Wizard

Do you use a VPN server to connect to work?
If you do use a Virtual Private Network server, enter its name or address.

○ No, I do not use a VPN server

● Yes, I use a VPN server

For example, your VPN server may be a host name like vpn.yourcompany.com, or an IP address that looks similar to 157.54.0.1.

< Back　Next >　Cancel

Pocket PC. Multiple phone numbers can also be entered on this screen, and Connection Manager uses them in the same way as multiple ISP phone numbers.

Work connections have two additional settings not available for Internet connections: the VPN (Virtual Private Networking) server and the proxy server. After you enter work phone numbers and click Next, you'll see the screen shown at left for entering VPN information.

If you will use a VPN server to connect to a Work network, select Yes, I Use A VPN Server, enter the host

Virtual Private Networking Provides Secure Connections

VPN is a method for providing a secure connection to Work networks using the public Internet. All information is encrypted and sent to the VPN server, which then decrypts the information and passes it along to the corporate network. There are different methods for implementing VPN, but Pocket PCs only support Microsoft's Point-to-Point Tunneling Protocol (PPTP) by default. Other VPN implementations are supported by third-party software available for Pocket PCs.

name or IP address of the server in the field provided, and then click Next. If you do not use a VPN server, select No, I Do Not Use A VPN Server, and then click Next.

The second setting unique to Work connections is the proxy server. Many companies use proxy servers to provide access to the Internet from the corporate network. If your work network uses a proxy server, select Yes, My Company Requires A Proxy Server To Access The Internet; enter the host name or IP address of the server in the field provided; and then click Next, as shown on the screen at right.

The proxy server setting is the final piece of information that you provide to the Connection Wizard, as indicated in the image on the left.

When you click Next, the Connection Wizard will update your Pocket PC with the connection information.

Connect Using Modems

The Connection Wizard does not provide a way to configure all the possible settings for modem connections. For example, the

How to ...   Buy a Modem for Your Pocket PC

CompactFlash modems are the most common modems for Pocket PCs. All brands
of CompactFlash modems work with Pocket PCs, but you do want to make sure that if
your Pocket PC only has a Type I CompactFlash slot, you buy a Type I CompactFlash
modem. Examples of Type I modems are CompactModem from Pretec; 56K Modem CF
Card from Socket Communications, Inc.; and Pocket Modem from Targus. The CompactCard
Modem 56 Global Access card from Xircom is a Type II CompactFlash modem.

To connect modems such as the 56K Travel Modem from Psion with the Pocket PC
infrared port, select the Generic IrDA modem from the Select A Modem drop-down list
when creating modem connections. You can also connect Pocket PCs to standard external
PC modems by using a serial ActiveSync cable, a null modem adapter, and an RS-232
cable. When using an external PC modem, select the Hayes Compatible on COM1: modem
when creating a modem connection.

Connection Wizard does not provide a way for entering IP addresses for Domain Name Servers
(DNSs). To add these additional settings to modem connections, you must use the Connection
Manager on your Pocket PC.

To create, edit, or delete modem connections for either Internet or Work settings, tap Modify
in either the Internet or Work section of Connection Manager.

Modify Internet Connections

The Internet Settings section of Connection Manager has two tabs, General and Modem, as
shown in the following image:

Tap here to create a
new connection.

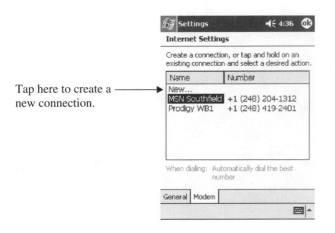

The Modem tab displays by default and lists all of the connections that Connection Manager will use to connect to the Internet. The General tab provides a way for you to change the names of the settings or to delete the settings.

To edit a connection, tap its entry in the Connections list. To delete a connection, tap-and-hold the item, and then tap Delete on the pop-up list. The pop-up list also includes Always Dial and Connect options. If you tap Always Dial, that connection will always be used no matter whether it is a long distance or a local call. An indicator at the bottom of the screen shows which connection is always dialed if one is specified. Tap Connect on the pop-up list to call the ISP and connect to the Internet.

To create a new connection, tap New in the Connections list. The same screens display when you edit existing connections or create new connections, with the first screen looking like the following image shown on the right.

Enter a name for the connection, select the modem and baud rate from the drop-down lists, and then tap Next, unless you want a terminal window to display after dialing or you need to manually assign IP addresses.

To display a terminal window or manually assign addresses, tap Advanced to open the dialog box shown at left.

Select the Use Terminal After Connecting check box to have a terminal window display after the connection completes.

To manually assign the IP address, tap the TCP/IP tab, select the Use Specific IP Address radio button, and enter an IP address in the field provided, as shown in the following image on the right.

Clear the Use Software Compression and the Use IP Header Compression check box if the ISP does not support these settings.

Tap the Name Servers tab to assign the name server addresses, as shown in the dialog box at left.

Select the Use Specific Server Address check box and enter the addresses in the appropriate fields. Tap OK to save the changes and return to the Make New Connection dialog box.

19

In the next dialog box (not shown), enter the area code and telephone number for the dial-up server and then tap Next. Finally, customize the modem settings and tap Finish, as shown in the dialog box on the left.

Modify Work Connections

The Work Settings section of Connection Manager has four tabs, as shown in the image on the right.

General and Modem have the same purpose and work the same way for work connections as they do for Internet connections. VPN and Proxy Settings tabs apply to all modem connections. To add a VPN server to the Work settings, tap the VPN tab and then tap New. Enter a name for the VPN server and the host name or IP address of the server in the fields on the screen shown next.

Companies use VPN to provide access to their private networks via the Internet. It saves them the cost of having to manage hundreds of modems, and it enables people to access the private network by making local calls to ISPs around the world. The modem connection you use to connect to the Internet will have IP address information for the ISP, and a second set of IP addresses are assigned for the private network by the VPN server. If you need to specify IP address information for the private network, tap Advanced on the VPN Connection screen.

To edit the VPN server information, tap its entry in the VPN list. To delete an entry in the VPN list, tap-and-hold the item and then tap Delete.

> NOTE
>
> *You can also use VPN with network cards, which allows you to access private networks using broadband connections. To use VPN with a network card, specify that the network connects to Work in Connection Manager.*

Proxy servers provide access to the Internet from private networks. The proxy settings that you specify on the screen shown at right will be used for modem connections, and will also be used by network cards when they are set to Work in Connection Manager.

Select the check boxes on this screen to specify that the private network connects to the Internet, and that it uses a proxy server. Enter the host name or IP address of the proxy server in the Proxy Server field.

If you need to configure port or Socks settings for the proxy server, tap Advanced on the Proxy Settings tab to open the screen shown next.

The HTTP field and Port setting specify the proxy server and port to be used by Internet Explorer when browsing the Web. The default port for HTTP is 80, and usually shouldn't be changed unless specified by a network administrator.

Wireless Access Protocol (WAP) settings are used to specify a proxy or gateway server and port that enable browsers using WAP to browse the Web. These settings are not commonly used, and they will be blank in most cases.

A Socks proxy server is used by applications that need to access application servers using TCP/IP. If you need to use Socks, enter the proxy server and port number. The default port number for Socks is 1080, and it usually shouldn't be changed unless you are instructed to do so by a network administrator.

There are two versions of the Socks proxy server protocol, Socks 4 and Socks 5. Socks 5 supports authentication; so if you tap the Socks 5 radio button, you must enter a User ID and Password.

Use Dialing Locations

Dialing locations enable you to specify how the modem dials phone numbers. To create a dialing location, tap the Dialing Locations tab of Connection Manager to display the screen shown on the right. In this screen, you configure information about the location you dial from, including the local area code, the local country code, whether you use tone or pulse dialing, and whether or not you need to disable call waiting. You can also control dialing patterns, such as whether the number nine must be dialed to reach an outside line.

19

TIP
Some cities are divided into several area codes, and some require dialing ten digits while others require dialing seven digits. Use dialing locations to specify which area codes require seven- or ten-digit dialing.

By default, there are two dialing locations: home and work. (These locations are set with an area code of 425, which might be OK if you live in Redmond, Washington, but it will cost you a long-distance phone call if you don't modify them to your own area code.)

Dialing patterns are used to control how the modem will dial a phone number from the location you have selected. When you tap Dialing Patterns, you'll see the screen shown at right.

From this screen, you control how local, long-distance, and international calls are dialed. Placeholders—letters and punctuation marks—are used as a type of shorthand so that parts of the phone number that must be dialed each time can be merged into the dialing pattern. For example, suppose that the location you are dialing from uses a nine to place a long-distance phone call. In the field labeled For Long Distance Calls, Dial you should enter **9,1FG**. If the number you are dialing is 248-555-1212, the modem will dial 9,12485551212 because your device will interpret the 9,1FG as dial 9, wait two seconds, and then dial 1, the area code (F), and the number (G). The characters you can use and their corollary interpretations are shown in Table 19-2.

To	Enter
Dial country code	**E,e**
Dial area code	**F,f**
Dial local number	**G,g**
Insert a pause (typically 2 seconds)	**, (comma)**
Wait for credit card tone	**$ (dollar sign)**
Wait for a second tone	**W,w**
Tone-dial the following numbers	**T,t**
Pulse-dial the following numbers	**P,p**
Transfer to another extension (0.5 seconds on hook, 0.5 seconds off hook, sometimes called *hook flash*)	**!**
Wait for *quiet answer* (typically indicated by 6.5 seconds of silence, followed by a ringing tone)	**@**
Use special controls on some systems (tone only)	**ABCD or ＊ or #**

TABLE 19-2 Dialing Patterns Used by the Pocket PC When Dialing Phone Calls

NOTE *You must select a dialing location prior to initiating a call from Pocket PC 2002 devices.*

Use Modem Connections

To manually initiate a modem connection, tap Start | Settings | Connections tab | Connections, and then tap Connect for either the Internet or Work connections. The Network Log On dialog box shown at right appears.

Complete the User Name and Password fields, complete the Domain field if you are connecting to a Windows NT domain, and then tap OK.

TIP *When you tap Connect, the default Internet or Work modem connection dials. To dial a specific modem connection, tap Modify for either the Internet or Work settings, tap-and-hold the modem connection, and tap Connect on the pop-up list.*

After you tap OK, the modem dials the telephone number of the ISP and establishes a connection. If you configured the connection to display a terminal window after a connection is established, the window will display, prompting you to enter a username and password. When the connection completes, you can then use programs such as Inbox or Internet Explorer to connect to the Internet.

Connect Using Wireless Modems

With a wireless modem, you can connect a Pocket PC to the Internet anywhere that the radio of the wireless modem can receive a signal. Wireless modems provide the convenience of not having to locate phone jacks and string phone cable to connect to the Internet; but, currently, they provide slower connections to the Internet than wired modems.

There are two types of wireless modems that work with Pocket PCs. Some mobile phones have built-in modems, and these phones are usually classified as *data capable*. To use the modems in these mobile phones with a Pocket PC, you connect the Pocket PC to the phone by using the infrared port, a serial cable, a CompactFlash card, or Bluetooth. You'll find a list of mobile phones that work with Pocket PCs at http://www.cewindows.net/peripherals/cellular.htm.

NOTE *Some Pocket PCs have an integrated wireless modem that you can use for voice and data communications. To connect these types of Pocket PCs to the Internet, create modem connections, as described in the preceding section, and select the built-in modem.*

The second type of wireless modem is PC Cards that connect to Pocket PCs with PC Card expansion sleeves (such as the Compaq PC Card Expansion Pack) or a PC Card slot. Pocket Spider from Enfora is the only Type I CompactFlash wireless modem. PC Card modems that work with Pocket PCs include the Sierra Wireless Aircard 300 and Aircard 510, and the Novatel Wireless Merlin, Merlin Platinum, Merlin Platinum Special Edition, and Merlin G100.

19

Connect to the Internet with Mobile Phones

Before you can use a mobile-phone modem to connect to the Internet, you need to find out whether or not your mobile-phone service provider supports data communications. Normally, you'll need to sign up for an additional service for data communications that may or may not use the minutes that are part of your regular plan. Contact your mobile-phone service provider and ask whether you can connect to the Internet using their service.

Mobile-phone networks in the United States use a variety of technologies. The maximum data rate for services that use the Global System for Mobile Communications (GSM), such as VoiceStream Wireless, is 9,600 bits per second (bps). Services, such as Verizon Wireless and Sprint PCS, that use Code Division Multiple Access (CDMA) have a maximum data rate of 14,400 bps. CDMA is the most common technology in the United States, and GSM is the standard for mobile communication in Europe.

The data speeds of GSM and CDMA are not optimal for browsing the Web. Fortunately, mobile-phone service providers are upgrading their networks to provide faster data communication. These upgrades are frequently referred to as second-generation (2.5G) and third-generation (3G) upgrades. The current GSM and CDMA technologies are referred to as 2G because they are upgrades of the original analog cellular technology.

The most common 2.5G implementation in the United States is General Packet Radio Service (GPRS), which is being used by Voice Stream Wireless, AT&T Wireless, and Cingular Wireless. These companies began offering GPRS service in limited cities during 2001, and plan to complete implementations in all U.S. cities by the end of 2002. In Europe, there are implementations of GPRS and High-Speed Circuit Switched Data (HSCSD). GPRS and HSCSD will provide data speeds of 19.2 kilobits per second (Kbps) to 115 Kbps.

TIP   *VoiceStream Wireless markets their GPRS service as iStream and they provide a variety of rate plans for Smartphones, PDAs, and laptops. The PDA plan is targeted specifically at the Compaq iPAQ Pocket PC.*

Third-generation upgrades are not planned until some time after 2002. Currently, 3G upgrades are expected to provide data speeds of 38.4 Kbps to 2 Megabits per second (Mbps). The higher speeds promised by 3G are needed to support video transmission.

The method that you use to connect your phone to a Pocket PC will depend on the capabilities of the phone. If the phone has an infrared port, you create a modem connection that uses the Generic IrDA modem and align the infrared ports. Infrared is nice because it is available with all Pocket PCs; but because infrared ports must be lined up, it can be difficult to use.

Alternatives to infrared connections are serial cables; Digital Phone card from Socket Communications, Inc.; and Bluetooth. Most mobile phones have unique ports that require special serial cables, which you can usually purchase from the phone manufacturer. To connect the cable to a Pocket PC, you'll need a null modem adapter and a serial ActiveSync cable for the Pocket PC. Supplynet (http://www.thesupplynet.com) sells cables that connect some mobile phones directly with the Compaq iPAQ Pocket PC, eliminating the need for a null modem adapter or a serial ActiveSync cable.

The Digital Phone card is a Type I CompactFlash card with a cable that connects directly to many popular mobile phones. The card includes a driver that you install on the Pocket PC, which you select when creating a modem connection. You'll find more information about these cards at http://www.digitalphonecard.com.

Bluetooth is a specification for short-range radio links between mobile PCs, mobile telephones, and other portable devices. Its purpose is to eliminate the need to carry and use cables to connect devices, which can multiply like rabbits when you use a lot of different peripherals. Bluetooth provides a function similar to the infrared ports on Pocket PCs, but is better because it does not require a line of sight between devices, and it promises to be supported by a wider range of devices.

To use Bluetooth to connect to the Internet, you need a mobile phone that has a Bluetooth radio and the phone must be able to make connections to the Internet. Examples of phones that support Bluetooth are the Ericsson T68, T39, and R520 phones. The Compaq iPAQ 3870 is the first Pocket PC to have a built-in Bluetooth radio. Socket Communications, Inc., and Anycom sell Type I CompactFlash cards that provide Bluetooth capability to all other Pocket PCs. The cards come with drivers that provide a Bluetooth modem option when creating modem connections.

TIP   *You can also use Bluetooth to connect Pocket PCs to printers and personal computers. However, ActiveSync 3.5 does not support Bluetooth, so Microsoft will have to upgrade ActiveSync before you can synchronize using Bluetooth.*

Connect to the Internet with Wireless PC Card Modems

While mobile-phone modems work with existing mobile-phone service plans, most wireless PC card modems can only be used with wireless Internet service providers (WISPs). Therefore, to use these cards to connect to the Internet, you'll have to pay additional fees for the wireless Internet service.

The one exception is the Sierra Wireless AirCard 510, which is a CDMA PC Card modem that only works with the Sprint PCS network. The AirCard 510 provides data rates up to 14.4 Kbps. You can find more information about this card at http://www.sprintpcs.com.

There has been a considerable amount of change in the WISP market of the Unites States during 2001. Two providers, Metricom, Inc., (with Ricochet Wireless) and OmniSky, have gone out of business and had their assets bought by other companies. The remaining nationwide service providers are GoAmerica (http://www.goamerica.net) and Verizon. Compaq resells the GoAmerica service as iPAQnet.

Data services from GoAmerica and Verizon use Cellular Digital Packet Data (CDPD), which has a maximum speed of 19.2 Kbps. Sierra Wireless and Novatel Wireless sell PC Card CDPD modems that work with service from GoAmerica and Verizon. Pocket Spider CompactFlash CDPD modem also works with GoAmerica and Verizon. The cards come with drivers that make them work like ordinary modems on Pocket PCs

After you install the drivers for CDPD PC Card modems on a Pocket PC, you must configure the driver so that the card works with the network of the service provider. The configuration usually involves entering IP addresses that are provided when you buy the card. You also need to create a modem connection in Connection Manager that uses the CDPD PC Card modem, but you don't enter a complete phone number. Instead, the modem connection turns on the radio of the card, which automatically connects to the network using the addresses you enter in the driver's configuration.

19

Connect Using ActiveSync Desktop Pass Through

Desktop Pass Through is new with ActiveSync 3.5 and it provides network connection sharing between desktop computers and Pocket PC 2002 devices. By using Desktop Pass Through, you can access the Internet or LANs from Pocket PCs while they are connected to desktops using serial, infrared, or USB connections.

NOTE   *Desktop Pass Through is not available for Pocket PC 2000.*

Desktop Pass Through is available by default for all Pocket PC 2002 devices. Once you connect the Pocket PC to the desktop, you can simply use Internet Explorer or Inbox to browse web sites or retrieve e-mail. Desktop Pass Through is always available, but you can control what network the Pocket PC connects to from within ActiveSync. Tap Tools | Options, and then tap the Rules tab to display the following screen:

Internet connectivity is provided when the Pass Through drop-down field (at the bottom of the screen) shows The Internet. Change the drop-down field to Work to enable the Pocket PC to use Pass Through to connect to LANs.

NOTE   *Terminal Server Client, File Explorer network access, and VPN do not work with ActiveSync Desktop Pass Through.*

How to ... Access the Internet Using Desktop Connections with Pocket PC 2000

To access the Internet from a Pocket PC 2000 device using a serial connection, you must install proxy server software on the PC and configure the programs on the device to use the server. You can install one of several proxy server programs, such as WinGate from Deerfield. Foliage Software Systems provides Version 2.1d of WinGate, which includes a free one-user license that you can download from http://www.foliage.com/ce/ibrowser/indexnew.html. A newer version of WinGate is available for purchase from http://wingate.deerfield.com.

Connect to Local Area Networks

Personal-computer industry analysts have been keeping track of the number of homes that have personal computers, and now that analysis is shifting from a count of homes to a count of how many per home. While the kids use one PC upstairs, Dad may use another in the living room, at the same time Mom uses hers in the basement office. In many cases, these multiple home computers are being networked together to share resources such as printers and Internet connections.

In fact, sharing a single high-speed Internet connection may become the number-one reason for installing a local area network (LAN) in a home. The setup works something like this: You subscribe to a broadband service provider, which installs the cable or DSL data service in the home. To use the service with one PC, you install an Ethernet NIC in the PC, and plug a cable into the card and either a cable or a DSL modem.

> **TIP**   *You can also purchase DSL cards for PCs that eliminate the need for installing an Ethernet NIC.*

Sharing a high-speed connection with other PCs on a LAN requires a cable modem or DSL router, which is sometimes called a *residential gateway*. Several different manufacturers sell these devices, and I personally use the Linksys EtherFast Cable/DSL router. You'll find information about the Linksys router at http://www.linksys.com. Practically Networked provides a very complete guide to many of the routers that are available, at http://www.practicallynetworked.com/pg/router_guide_index.asp.

To share a high-speed connection using a router, you connect the Ethernet cable from the cable or DSL modem to the router. Most routers have several ports for connecting PCs, and each connected PC can use the high-speed Internet connection at the same time. You can expand the number of ports available to connect PCs by running an Ethernet cable from the router to a hub.

Personal computers can also share high-speed connections by adding a second Ethernet NIC to the PC and installing software on the PC designated for sharing Internet connections. A cable runs from the second Ethernet NIC to an Ethernet hub to connect the PC to the LAN; the other PCs on the LAN are configured to use the Internet connection–sharing software on the host PC for their Internet access, rather than using a modem.

19

Any device that connects to the LAN can access the Internet using the shared high-speed connection, including your Pocket PC. The following section explains how to use network adapters with your Pocket PC to connect to LANs and to the Internet.

Select a Network Adapter

Several vendors manufacture Ethernet network interface adapters. You can buy wired Ethernet adapters, which usually come in speeds of 10 Mbps or 100 Mbps, or wireless Ethernet adapters. Wireless Ethernet adapters support one of two wireless communication standards: 802.11b or HomeRF. There are several factors to take into consideration when deciding which type of card to buy.

The first decision that you need to make is whether or not you want to buy a wired or wireless Ethernet adapter. To buy a wired Ethernet adapter, you'll need to know the network speed and the type of network cabling that is being used. You can buy adapters that only support 10 Mbps or 100 Mbps, and you can buy adapters that support both speeds. However, if the network speed is only 10 Mbps, you may want to buy a 10 Mbps adapter because they are cheaper. The most common network cable is Category 5 (CAT5) Unshielded Twisted-Pair (UTP), which has a RJ-45 connector. Most Ethernet adapters work with CAT5 UTP.

How to ... Use Wireless Ethernet to Connect to Home Networks

Wireless networking is becoming a popular way to connect computers to home networks where it is difficult to install network cable. There are two ways that you can use wireless Ethernet adapters to connect a Pocket PC to a home network. One way is to use access points in what is usually referred to as *infrastructure mode*. The second way is to create a point-to-point connection between two wireless Ethernet adapters in what is called *ad hoc mode*.

Access points support multiple wireless Ethernet adapters and can be easier to set up than point-to-point connections. You connect an access point to an existing LAN by running a network cable from the access point to an Ethernet hub. This connection allows computers connected to the network with cables to communicate with computers connected to the network with wireless Ethernet adapters. If a cable or DSL modem is connected to the hub, you can access the Internet using the wireless Ethernet adapter.

Wireless Ethernet adapters cost less than access points; so if you only want to connect a Pocket PC to one computer, a point-to-point connection may be desirable. If the computer is connected to a wired network and supports network-connection sharing, the Pocket PC can access the wired network. The downside of point-to-point connections is that when a wireless Ethernet adapter is configured for ad hoc mode, it cannot communicate with access points or other adapters.

Wireless Ethernet adapters have radics that communicate with access points or other wireless adapters. The type of adapter that you need to buy is dictated by the standard used by the access point or wireless adapter that you want to communicate with. If the access point or adapter uses 802.11b, then you must buy an 802.11b card, or likewise for HomeRF. 802.11b is the most popular wireless Ethernet standard because it provides faster speeds.

After you determine whether you need a wired or wireless Ethernet adapter, the next decision is which type of card. You can buy both types of adapters as PC Cards or CompactFlash cards, so you can choose a card based on the type of slot in your Pocket PC. Because CompactFlash cards are smaller and use less battery power, they tend to be the most popular adapters for Pocket PCs.

> TIP *You can also use CompactFlash Ethernet adapters in laptop computers that only have PC Card slots by inserting the CompactFlash card into a PC Card adapter.*

Finally, when buying an Ethernet adapter to use in a Pocket PC, you need to consider whether or not there is a Pocket PC driver that works with the adapter. The card will not work without a driver. Wireless Ethernet adapters require specific Pocket PC drivers, but some wired Ethernet adapters will work with the built-in NE2000 Compatible Ethernet driver that is available on all Pocket PCs. Table 19-3 provides addresses to web sites that list Pocket PC–compatible Ethernet adapters.

Configure Network Interface Adapters

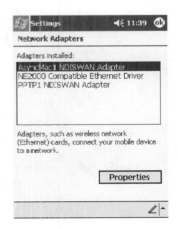

If you purchase a network adapter that has a Pocket PC driver, you must install the driver on your device by following the manufacturer instructions. To see the network drivers installed on a Pocket PC, tap Start | Settings, tap the Connections tab and then tap Network Adapters. The installed network adapter drivers are listed on the screen shown at right.

There can be any number of adapter drivers installed on a Pocket PC. Most Pocket PCs include at least the NE2000 Compatible Ethernet Driver, which is a generic driver that can work with any NE2000-compatible card. Beyond that, each Pocket PC vendor may include any number of additional drivers on their device to support a variety of different types of network

Type of Ethernet Adapter	Websites
Wired PC Card	http://www.cewindows.net/peripherals/pccardethernet.htm
Wired CompactFlash Card	http://www.cewindows.net/peripherals/cfethernet.htm
Wireless PC Card	http://www.cewindows.net/peripherals/pccardwirelesslan.htm
Wireless CompactFlash Card	http://www.cewindows.net/peripherals/cfwirelesslan.htm

TABLE 19-3   Websites That List Pocket PC Ethernet Adapters

19

cards. The configuration screens and process is the same for every driver type, so the following instructions are the same for every brand of network adapter.

To use a network adapter, you need to configure the properties of the driver so that they work in your network environment. To open the Driver Settings dialog box, select the driver and tap Properties. The image at right shows the Settings dialog box for the NE2000 Compatible Ethernet Driver.

The settings that you configure in the TCP/IP and Name Servers tabs are specific to your network. Many residential gateways and cable or DSL routers automatically assign IP addresses; if that is the case for your network, you can select Use Server-Assigned IP Address and tap OK. You will get a message saying that the new settings will take effect the next time you insert the adapter into the Pocket PC.

If you need to use a specific IP address with the adapter, select Use Specific IP address, and complete the IP Address, Subnet Mask, and Default Gateway fields. You may also need to tap the Name Servers tab and complete the DNS and WINS fields, as shown in the image on the left.

Configure Wireless Ethernet Adapters

The network adapter settings are the same for wired and wireless Ethernet adapters, but wireless adapters have additional settings for the wireless portion of the network. The process for configuring these settings will be different for each brand of wireless Ethernet adapter because they use different drivers. Consult the user manual of the adapter for specific instructions on how to configure its driver. The items that you must configure for all wireless Ethernet adapters are described in Table 19-4.

Some brands of wireless Ethernet adapters will have additional settings only found on that adapter. An example of such a setting is a *power-saving mode*, which specifies how power is supplied to the adapter to save battery strength. Read the user manual of your adapter to determine how to change any settings that are unique to the adapter.

Use Network Adapters

After you configure the adapter driver for your network settings, you can insert the card into the Pocket PC CompactFlash slot. You'll need to connect an Ethernet cable to the card and the high-speed router, or an Ethernet hub. Many cards have indicator lights that show whether a connection is available, and most routers and hubs have similar indicators to show connections.

If the network adapter driver is configured correctly for the network, you'll be able to use Internet Explorer, Inbox, MSN Messenger, Terminal Server Client, and File Explorer to access

Item	Description
Extended Service Set Identifier (ESSID)	The ESSID has up to 32 characters and provides a unique identifier for the wireless network. The ESSID assigned to the adapter must be the same as assigned to all access points or other wireless adapters on the network.
Operating Mode	If the wireless adapter communicates with an access point, then it must be set to an infrastructure operating mode. If the wireless adapter communicates with another wireless adapter, then the operating mode must be set to ad hoc. If you use an ad hoc operating mode, then you'll need to specify a channel number, which must be the same for both wireless adapters.
Wireless Equivalency Privacy (WEP) or Encryption	WEP is a special form of encryption designed for wireless Ethernet adapters. There are different versions of WEP depending on the size of the key that the encryption uses. Most adapters today support 40-bit and 128-bit encryption. Some adapter drivers will use ASCII characters for keys, while others will only use hex characters. The WEP key that you enter for the adapter must match the key used by the access point or wireless adapter that the card communicates with.

TABLE 19-4 Common Wireless Ethernet Adapter Settings

resources on the Internet or the LAN. You can also use ActiveSync to synchronize with desktop computers. You may try to use one of these applications and see the dialog box shown on the right.

This message appears when the Connection Manager is not configured to use the network card in the manner in which you are

trying to use it. Tap Settings to open the Connection Manager and change the network card setting, as shown in the image on the left.

To synchronize with desktop computers or access network shares using File Explorer, you must specify that the network card connects to Work in Connection Manager. To browse web pages or retrieve e-mail on the Internet, you must specify that the network card connects to the Internet.

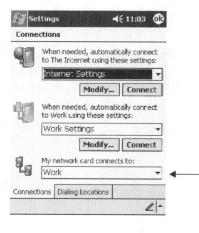

Specify here whether the network card connects to the Internet or Work.

19

How to ... Troubleshoot Network Connections

One of the most important network troubleshooting tools for your Pocket PC is a free program called vxUtil from Cambridge Computer Corporation. You can download this program from http://www.cam.com/vxutil.html. If you have problems connecting to a network, use the Info utility in vxUtil to review the IP address settings of the Pocket PC and make sure they are correct. Use the Ping utility to test network communication between the Pocket PC and a destination computer.

Wrapping Up

Pocket PCs are capable of connecting to the Internet and LANs in a variety of ways. You use Connection Manager to configure all modem connections, and it will automatically connect to the appropriate network based on the type of information you enter. Connection Manager also specifies whether network cards connect to the Internet or Work networks.

Wireless modems and network adapters are becoming the hottest accessories for Pocket PCs. With these accessories, you can use your Pocket PC to connect to the Internet from any location at any time.

Once you get connected to the Internet, you can send and receive e-mail using Inbox on the Pocket PC. In the next chapter, you will learn how to use Inbox to send and receive e-mail using Internet e-mail servers.

Chapter 20

Send and Receive E-Mail

How To...

- Create e-mail services that work with POP3 and IMAP4 servers
- Synchronize e-mail messages with Microsoft Outlook
- Compose, edit, and send new e-mail messages
- Receive e-mail messages and reply to or forward messages
- Manage file attachments

Back in 1992, people did not know much about the Internet unless they were in college, in the military, or computer geeks. My, how things have changed! Today many people, even people who don't consider themselves "into computers," not only know what the Internet is, but use it on a regular basis.

How do you use the Internet? Chances are good that you use e-mail to send messages to friends and loved ones around the world. You probably surf the Web to listen to music, check stock prices or sports scores, buy CDs or books, and follow the news. Perhaps you make friends by interacting with them in an online forum, or keep in touch with other friends by using instant messaging.

Regardless of what you do, chances are also good that the Internet is becoming increasingly important to you. E-mail might be the only way you communicate with coworkers, or perhaps you make a living building websites for companies. As access to the Internet becomes more important, many people are seeking ways to stay connected, wherever they may be.

For that task, Pocket PCs are well suited. The combination of their small size, software, and the communications hardware makes it easy to get connected. Inbox, a program that works with Internet e-mail servers, and Microsoft Outlook is included with every device. In this chapter, you learn how to use Inbox to send and receive e-mail. In Chapter 21, you learn how to send and receive instant messages; and in Chapter 22, you learn how to browse websites.

Use Inbox to Work with E-Mail

One of the first acts of the new United States Congress in 1789 was to authorize a postal service, creating 75 local post offices covering 1,875 miles. The fact that one of the first acts of a new nation was the establishment of a postal service highlights the importance of mail delivery at that time. As the nation grew, mail became more important for communication. For example, the Pony Express is credited with keeping California in the Union by providing rapid communication between the two coasts.

In 1861, the Pony Express gave way to the telegraph, introducing technology as a means of speeding communication. Ever since then, technology—from telephones to satellites—has been used to speed communication around the world. In the 1990s e-mail came into widespread use, reducing the time to deliver messages around the world from days to seconds. Today we are accustomed to writing a message, clicking a button, and expecting it to end up around the world as soon as the button is released.

As e-mail becomes more important, methods for sending and receiving e-mail, no matter where we may be, also become important. Combined with the right communications equipment, small Pocket PCs can be used to send and receive e-mail from your living room or the back seat of a taxi.

One of the reasons why you bought your Pocket PC might have been to send and receive e-mail. In this chapter, I show you how to use Inbox to work with your e-mail. You will learn how to set up Inbox to access Internet mail servers, and then retrieve e-mail from those servers. You'll also learn how to compose and send a message and how to handle file attachments.

Inbox has dual roles: one is as a client to Microsoft Outlook, and the other is as an Internet e-mail client. Unfortunately, while these dual roles provide flexibility, they also add complexity. I will clarify these roles so that you can choose the best method for working with your e-mail.

There are similarities between e-mail and traditional mail. In order for you to receive mail, the post office needs to know your address. When someone sends you a card, they write your address, which includes a postal code, on the envelope. In the United States, the postal, or ZIP, code on the card is used to route it to your state, city, and, finally, post office. Once at the post office, a person determines its final location by using the address.

The equivalent of a post office for e-mail is a mail server, which has a name like mail.acme.com. Just as you must register your address with the post office to receive mail, you need a mailbox registered at a mail server to receive e-mail. Usually, a mailbox is associated with a user ID, such as frank.

Internet e-mail addresses have a defined format, interpreted the same way by all mail servers. The address starts with the user ID, followed by the *at* (@) sign, then followed by a domain name—for example, frank@acme.com. Each of these parts is used by mail servers to send and receive e-mail.

NOTE   *Conceptually, corporate e-mail addresses are similar to Internet e-mail addresses but may have a different format.*

Most post offices have a front and back entrance, with the front being where mail enters the office and the back being where mail leaves the office. E-mail is similar because two servers are involved in the process: one to receive e-mail and the other to send e-mail.

The servers that receive e-mail are called POP3 (Post Office Protocol) or IMAP4 (Internet Mail Access Protocol) hosts because of the protocols that they use. Because mailboxes reside on these servers, they are often simply referred to as mail servers. Servers that send e-mail are called SMTP (Simple Mail Transport Protocol) hosts—again, because they use the SMTP protocol.

E-mail clients, such as the Pocket PC's Inbox, are designed to work with both servers. When you send an e-mail message using Inbox, it transfers the message to an SMTP host. The SMTP host first uses the domain name portion of the e-mail address to contact a Domain Name Server (DNS) and obtain the TCP/IP address of the mail server. Once the SMTP host has the TCP/IP address, it contacts the mail server and tells it that it has a message for the user ID. The mail server determines whether a mailbox exists for the user ID; and if it does, it then accepts the message. If a mailbox does not exist, the SMTP server will return the message to the sender's mail server.

Inbox receives e-mail by logging into the mail server and downloading the messages to the device. As you will see later in this section, Inbox can be configured to download only message headers or entire messages. Downloading message headers provides you with enough information to determine whether you want to download the entire message to your device. With that information, you can decide to skip certain messages that you don't want to read, saving the time it would otherwise take to download the entire contents of that message.

Start Inbox

The process for starting Inbox on a Pocket PC depends on how the Start menu is configured. By default, you start Inbox by tapping Start | Inbox. However, if the menu has been changed, it may be in Programs, in which case you tap Start | Programs | Inbox.

When Inbox starts, the program window shown on the right displays.

At the bottom of the screen is the Command bar, with two menu options and two buttons. Above the Command bar is a status bar that displays the name of the service, the total number of items in the folder, and the number of unread items in the folder.

In the middle of the screen is the list of messages stored in a folder. Use the Show Service drop-down list in the upper left-hand corner, shown below, to select the service and folder that you want to display.

This shows the name of the current service.

Select a service and folder from here.

The name of the open folder displays at the top.

To change the order of the message list, expand the Sort drop-down list in the upper right-hand corner. The items can be sorted on From, Received Date, or Subject, and the field currently used for the sort is displayed at the top. To switch between ascending and descending order, repeat the selection of the sort field. For example, the message list shown on the right is sorted by From in descending order.

To sort the message list in ascending order, select From in the Sort drop-down list a second time.

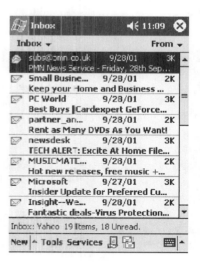

Add Internet E-Mail Services

To send and receive e-mail, Inbox must communicate with POP3 or IMAP4 servers and SMTP servers; and to do that, you must provide Inbox with information about those servers. That information is stored in a *service*.

One of the first things that you need to do in order to use Inbox is add a service. To do that, you will need the following information about your mail servers, which your Internet Service Provider (ISP) can provide:

- The service type, which is the type of mail server that you use to receive e-mail. This will be either IMAP4 or POP3.

- A connection, which is used to connect to your ISP. The process for creating a connection on Pocket PCs is explained in Chapter 19.

- The host or server name, which is the name of the server from which you receive e-mail.

- A user ID, which is used to log in to the mail server. Typically, this is the same user ID that you use to connect to your ISP.

- A password is also used to log into the mail server. This may also be the same password that you use to connect to your ISP.

- If you are connecting to a network that uses Windows NT domain security, you will need the name of the domain. You will not need this for most Internet accounts.

- The SMTP host or server name, which is the name of the server used to send e-mail.

- Your e-mail address, which will look like taz@acme.com.

TIP   *Another source for information about mail servers is Chris De Herrera's ISP FAQ at http://www.cewindows.net/wce/isp.htm.*

After you gather this information, you are ready to start Inbox, create a service, and start sending and receiving e-mail.

How to ... Connect to Multiple E-Mail Services with One Call

When you connect to an ISP from within Inbox, you can only connect with one mail server at a time. If you have multiple e-mail services and want to check e-mail on all of them using Inbox, you must disconnect and end the call before connecting to another service, even if the second service is configured to use the same dial-up connection.

This can be expensive when you are charged for each call that you make. Fortunately, there is a workaround for this problem. The trick is to not use Inbox to connect with the ISP, and instead connect using Connection Manager. Chapter 19 has instructions for creating modem connections in Connection Manager.

To start Connection Manager, tap Start | Programs | Connections, and then tap the Connections icon. To call an ISP, tap the Connect button in the Internet portion of Connection Manager. If you are sending and receiving e-mail from a corporate network, tap the Connect button in the Work portion of Connection Manager.

After the connection is established, switch to Inbox and tap Send And Receive to connect to the mail server and retrieve e-mail. To check other e-mail services, first disconnect by tapping the Connect toolbar button, and this time Inbox will not disconnect the call. Select the second e-mail service, and then tap the Send And Receive toolbar button. If you see a dialog box asking whether you can access the mail server using the current connection, tap Yes, and Inbox will then connect to the service and retrieve the e-mail. To disconnect the call, tap the Connect icon on the Command bar and then tap Disconnect.

While this process works for receiving e-mail, you may experience problems sending e-mail. Some ISPs do not allow you to use their SMTP servers unless you connect to their service. If that is the case, you will need to connect to the ISP in order to send e-mail, or find an SMTP server that can be accessed from any ISP.

To add a service on a Pocket PC, tap Services | New Service. The E-mail Setup screen, shown on the right, will display.

There are five screens for setting up an e-mail service. On this first screen, enter your e-mail address and tap Next.

On the next screen, you see a new feature of Inbox with Pocket PC 2002, Auto configuration. Auto configuration connects to the Internet and then uses the e-mail address you enter to try and retrieve mail server names. The Pocket PC first checks a database on Microsoft's servers for the information; and if there is no match, it attempts to retrieve the information from the e-mail service provider.

Microsoft provides a way for companies to place the e-mail service Auto configuration information on their servers, making it easier to set up access to corporate e-mail servers.

When Auto configuration completes, the screen will look like that shown on the right, and you can tap Next to go to the next step.

Your Pocket PC will need to connect to the Internet for Auto configuration to work. Therefore, if you connect by modem, you will want to plug the modem in before executing this step. If you forget to attach the modem before accessing this screen, you can tap Back to return to the previous screen, attach the modem, and then tap Next.

On the third e-mail setup screen, shown below, enter the name you want displayed on the messages you send, along with your mail server user ID and password:

Tap the Save Password check box if you want Inbox not to prompt you to enter your password each time you retrieve e-mail. Be careful with this; if you save the password, anyone who has access to the Pocket PC may be able to send and receive your e-mail. If you choose to save the password, you might consider password protecting the password by using the Password setting, as described in Chapter 3.

On the fourth e-mail setup screen, select the type of mail server that you will use to receive e-mail in the Service Type drop-down list. The options are POP3 or IMAP4. Enter a name in the Name field and tap Next.

The fifth and final e-mail setup screen, shown on the right, provides fields for entering the names of the incoming (POP3 or IMAP4) mail server and outgoing (SMTP) mail server:

These fields may already be populated if Auto configuration found a match when it connected to the Internet. Otherwise, enter the names for the mail servers in the fields on the screen. If you are connecting to a network that uses Windows NT domain security, enter the domain name in the Domain field. Normally, you will leave this field blank.

TIP — *If you are using MSN's e-mail servers, you must enter **MSN** in the Domain field.*

Tap the Options button to configure additional settings that control how the e-mail service communicates with the mail server. There are three option screens. On the first option screen, shown on the right, you can specify how often Inbox will check for new mail, whether the outgoing (SMTP) server requires authentication, and how the service connects to the Internet.

You should leave the Connection field set to Default Internet Settings, unless the e-mail service is a corporate e-mail server, in which case you should change the field to Default Work Settings.

TIP — *If you are using MSN's e-mail servers, you must check the Outgoing E-mail Server Requires Authentication check box.*

On the second options screen, you can specify whether the e-mail service simply retrieves message headers or entire messages. If you select message headers, you can specify how much of the message the service will retrieve along with the headers. If you are creating an IMAP4 e-mail service, there will be an additional setting on this screen to specify whether the service downloads attachments when getting full copies of messages. You can specify the maximum-size attachment the service will download.

On the third and final options screen, you specify how many days' worth of messages the service displays. Tap Finish to save the e-mail service.

Edit and Remove Services

To change a service that has already been created, tap Tools | Options to display the Options dialog box, shown on the right.

Tap a name in the Services list to open the E-mail Setup screen. To delete a service, tap and hold a name in the Services list and select Delete from the pop-up menu.

Synchronize E-Mail with Outlook

You may have noticed that one of the Inbox services is ActiveSync. It is not listed as a service when you tap Tools | Options, but it is visible in the Services drop-down list of the Inbox list view. This service is built into Inbox and cannot be removed, but you do control whether it is used.

The purpose of the ActiveSync service is to synchronize e-mail messages between the Inbox folder in Outlook and the Pocket PC's Inbox. With this feature, you can download e-mail to your device and then take it with you to read. You can reply to messages offline or create new messages, which will then synchronize to Outlook during the next ActiveSync session. Once in Outlook, the messages are sent using Outlook's e-mail connectivity.

There is one significant limitation to e-mail synchronization. To use it, the Pocket PC must be in only one partnership with a desktop computer. If your device has two partnerships, you will not be able to synchronize e-mail messages.

Inbox synchronization works with serial, infrared, network, and modem connections. It can also be the only way to send e-mail using Microsoft Exchange server, unless you use Exchange's Internet support, or an intermediary server such as XTNDConnect Server from Extended Systems. If the Exchange server is configured to support the Internet mail protocols, you can use an Internet e-mail service with Exchange, which you create as described earlier in this chapter. Chapter 16 has more information about using Pocket PCs with Exchange.

Set Up Inbox Synchronization

To use e-mail synchronization, you must enable the Inbox synchronization option in ActiveSync. Start ActiveSync, and then tap the Options toolbar button, or select Tools | Options. The Options dialog box, shown on the right, will display.

Turn on synchronization by checking the box next to Inbox, as shown in the illustration. Chapter 6 provides instructions for configuring the Inbox synchronization settings.

Use Inbox Synchronization

Inbox synchronization works the same way as it does for calendar, contacts, and tasks. When you connect a Pocket PC to the desktop computer, as described in Chapter 5, ActiveSync compares the contents of the device and the PC and synchronizes the changes. In the end, both have the same items. Of course, if you configure ActiveSync to only synchronize a limited numberof messages, Inbox will not contain everything in Outlook.

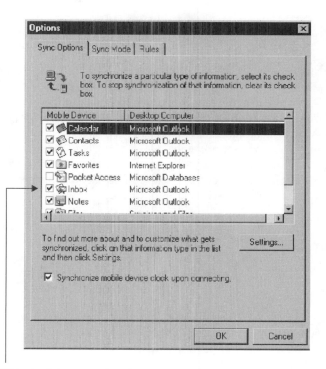

This check box must be selected to enable Inbox synchronization.

Only Outlook's Inbox root folder and subfolders synchronize. Messages that you write and send before synchronizing appear in the Outbox, but are moved to Outlook during synchronization and then removed from the Outbox. Deleted items work in the same way. During synchronization, messages are removed from the Deleted Items folder on the Pocket PC and the message is deleted from Outlook. The contents of the Drafts and Sent Items folders on the Pocket PC do not synchronize with Outlook.

NOTE *Inbox synchronization does not control the number of messages that appear in subfolders. All messages in Outlook Inbox subfolders will synchronize with the Pocket PC, regardless of the setting for the root Inbox folder.*

All Outlook Inbox subfolders appear on the Pocket PC, but you must specify which of those folders synchronize by configuring the ActiveSync options on the desktop computer. Messages that you move to synchronizing subfolders will appear on both the Pocket PC and desktop. However, if you move a message on the Pocket PC to a subfolder that is not synchronizing, the message will be moved to the subfolder on the desktop but not appear in that subfolder on the Pocket PC.

The process of composing, reading, and responding to e-mail is the same for the ActiveSync service as it is for Internet mail services, which is described in the rest of this section.

Send and Receive E-Mail

While you can send and receive e-mail using Inbox synchronization, the only way to update your e-mail is to connect the device with a desktop computer, unless you use remote synchronization. While synchronization works, it may not be very functional. On the other hand, you can use an Internet e-mail service anywhere by using a modem or wireless connection.

Before you send and receive e-mail, you must create an Internet e-mail service, as described earlier in this chapter. If you have more than one Internet e-mail service, select the one you want to use from the Services drop-down list.

How to ... Synchronize with Outlook Express

Many people have asked me how to synchronize their Pocket PC with Microsoft Outlook Express. Most are amazed to learn that ActiveSync does not support this Microsoft product. If you want to synchronize Inbox with Outlook Express, you need SyncExpress, which you will find at http://www.syncdata.it/. SyncExpress adds an Outlook Express information type to ActiveSync, and synchronizes e-mail and addresses. Outlook Express' address book synchronizes with Contacts on the Pocket PC.

To send and receive e-mail, first connect the device to a modem and plug in a phone line. Next, start Inbox and tap the Send and Receive button on the toolbar. The illustration on the right shows the Send And Receive button on a Pocket PC.

Inbox will then display the Network Logon dialog box for the connection that you assigned to the service. Enter a username and password if they are not already provided and tap OK. The modem will then dial the number of the connection and log on to the network. The Connection dialog box will close and you will start to see messages displayed on the status bar.

TIP   *If a network card is plugged into the device, Inbox will use it to communicate with the mail servers, and not open the Network Logon dialog box.*

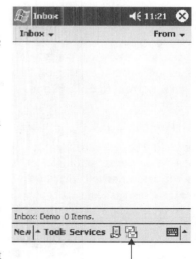

This is the Send And Receive button

First, Inbox will open a transmit port with the SMTP host to send e-mail, and then it will open a receive port with the POP3 or IMAP4 host to receive e-mail. Once these ports are established, Inbox will first send any e-mail waiting to be sent, and then start downloading messages.

While the messages download, you will see the status bar display the message shown on the right.

In a process similar to ActiveSync, explained earlier, Inbox synchronizes messages with the mail server so that they both contain the same items. If a message has already been downloaded, it will not be downloaded again; and if a message on the device is no longer on the server, it will be removed.

By default, Inbox does not automatically delete e-mail from the server. When you delete a message in Inbox, the message moves to the Deleted Items folder. You can open the Deleted Items folder, select the messages, and delete them again, and the messages will then be deleted from the server.

You can simplify this manual deletion process by configuring Inbox to automatically delete messages. Tap Tools | Options and then tap the Message tab, as shown on the right.

Change the selection of the Empty Deleted Items field to either On Connect/Disconnect or Immediately.

You can download a fresh copy of all messages from a server by clearing them from the Pocket PC, by tapping Services | Clear All and then tapping the Send And Receive button.

20

After all of the messages download, the status bar will display the folder name (Inbox) and the total number of items and unread items. Inbox will disconnect the call if you configured the service to do so; otherwise, it will remain connected. If a new message arrives while the device is connected, Inbox will notify you. You will see a notification bubble or hear a sound, unless notification sounds are turned off. If, while connected, you want to force Inbox to check for messages, tap the Send And Receive button.

Compose a New E-Mail Message

An e-mail message can be written at any time, even if the device is not connected to the Internet. When the device is not online, the message is stored in the Outbox folder—where it will stay until the next time you connect with a mail server. Inbox retrieves the e-mail addresses that are stored in Contacts and makes them available for use when creating a message.

To create a new message on a Pocket PC, tap New to open the following dialog box:

Tap here to expand the message header.

Tap here to open the address book.   Tap here to make a voice recording.

The To field is highlighted, ready for you to enter the e-mail address of the person receiving the message. E-mail addresses stored in Contacts can be retrieved for use in this field by either selecting the address or searching for the address.

TIP   *You can also create new e-mail messages directly from Contacts. Tap-and-hold an item in the Contacts list view and then tap Send E-mail To Contact on the pop-up menu. You can also tap a contact's e-mail address on the Contact Summary tab.*

Tap the Address Book button on the Command bar to display a list of all contacts with e-mail addresses. To search for an address, enter the first few letters of the person's name in the search

How to ... Send and Receive E-Mail Using Other Programs

Inbox is a very functional e-mail program, but you may find that it does not meet your needs—or maybe you would prefer to use a different program. The only other e-mail program that works with POP mail servers and runs on Pocket PCs is nPOP by Tomoaki Nakashima. Unlike Inbox, nPOP supports multiple e-mail accounts or a single Internet connection, and it supports signatures. Inbox on Pocket PC 2000 does not support SMTP authentication, so nPOP is a workaround because it supports SMTP authentication and POP after SMTP. Unfortunately, nPOP does not work with Contacts, so you have to enter e-mail addresses in a separate address book. You can download English and Japanese versions of this program at http://www.nakka.com/soft/npop/index_eng.html.

box. As you enter letters, the list is filtered to only display the contacts containing the letters, as shown on the right.

Tap the addresses you want and they will be entered in the To field. If you select multiple addresses, each will be entered in the field, separated by a semicolon. Tap the Address Book button to close the address list.

TIP *Another way to open the address book is to tap the To field.*

Tap here to clear the search box and display all the addresses.

Tap here to collapse the message header.

Enter a subject for the message in the Subj field. To send a carbon copy or a blind carbon copy to another person, expand the message header by tapping the down arrow to the right of the subject line. The message header will then display, as shown to the left.

Enter an e-mail address in either the CC or BCC fields by using one of the methods described earlier.

The last line of the message header shows the e-mail service that will be used to send the message. If you want to select a different service, tap the service name and select one from the drop-down list. When you send the message, it will be stored in the Outbox folder of the service that you select. To collapse the message header, tap the up arrow to the right of the Service field.

TIP *To send a reply to a synchronized e-mail message by using a modem instead of synchronization, change the service for the message from ActiveSync to either a POP3 or a IMAP4 service.*

The body of the message is immediately below the subject line. To compose the message, tap the empty middle pane of the window and begin entering text using the soft input panel or onscreen keyboard. The My Text menu provides a way to quickly insert text into a message. When you tap My Text, a menu expands with ten messages, as shown on the right.

Tap a message to insert the text into the e-mail.

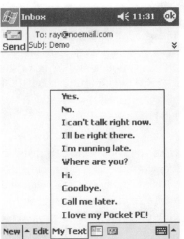

NOTE *The My Text menu contains the same entries for Inbox and MSN Messenger. If you change a My Text menu item in Inbox, that change is available in MSN Messenger.*

You can change the phrases that are in the My Text menu by tapping Edit | Edit My Text Messages, opening the screen shown on the left.

Tap a message in the list and edit in the field at the bottom of the screen.

The Edit menu contains commands—such as Copy, Cut, Paste, Clear, and Select All—that you can use to edit the message. These same options become available when you tap and hold on selected text. The Edit menu also features several items that are new with Pocket PC 2002.

To check the spelling of an e-mail message, tap Edit | Spell Check. To confirm e-mail addresses, tap Edit | Check Names. Check Names will verify e-mail addresses using Contacts and the mail servers that you specify by tapping Tools | Options | Address. You can also address a message by simply entering part of a contact's name in the To, CC, or BCC fields and then tapping Edit | Check Names. You can then select addresses from a list that displays.

TIP *To change the character set for a message, tap Edit | Language and then select the character set.*

If you want to add an attachment to the message, tap Edit | Add Attachment to load the Open dialog box shown on the right.

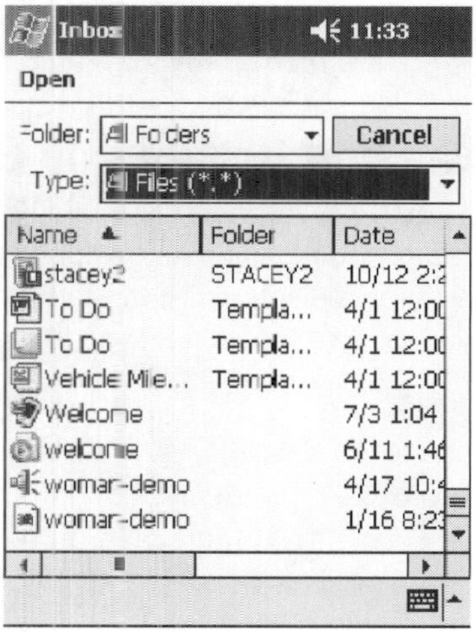

Listed in the dialog box are all the files stored in the My Documents folder. Use the Folder drop-down list to switch to a different folder. While the Type drop-down list is shown in the dialog box, you cannot select anything but All Files. Tap the name of the file to attach and it will be added to the message, as shown below:

The Record command button is a new feature with Pocket PC 2002. It enables you to create voice recordings and automatically attach them to e-mail messages.

If you want to save the message that you are creating without sending it, tap OK and the message will be placed in the Drafts folder. If you want to cancel and delete the message, tap Edit | Cancel Message. When you are ready to send the message, tap Send and the message will be placed in the Outbox folder, as shown on the right.

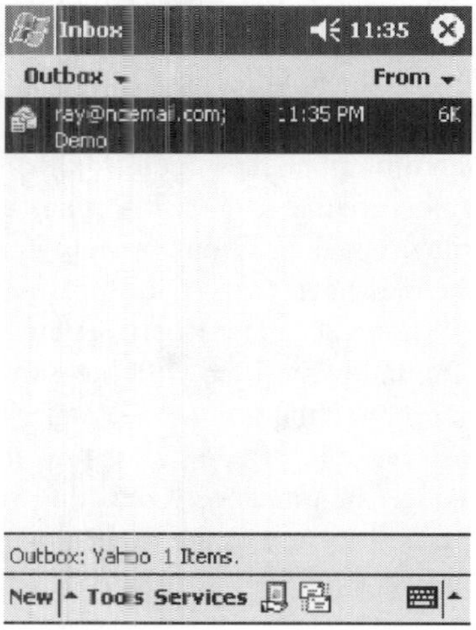

The message will be sent and removed from the Outbox folder the next time you use the service to send and receive e-mail. If the message is composed for the ActiveSync service, during the next synchronization, it will be moved from the Outbox folder on the device to the Outbox folder in Outlook. From there, how the message will be sent depends on how Outlook is configured.

NOTE *The Drafts folder is new with Pocket PC 2002. Pocket PC 2000 stores draft messages in the Inbox folder.*

Read and Respond to E-Mail

New mail is written to the service's Inbox folder and appears in the message list. Messages that have not been read are in bold, and messages that have been read are in a normal typeface. To open a message, tap its entry in the message list, and the message will open, as shown here:

Delete the message.   Forward, Reply All, or Reply

TIP *Inbox opens most HTML e-mail messages as Plain Text. However, some HTML messages may be too complicated and won't appear as designed on the Pocket PC.*

To move to the preceding message in the list, tap the up arrow on the toolbar; tap the down arrow to move to the next message. If the message is at the top or bottom of the list, you will return to the message list. Tap the Delete button to delete the message that is currently open, and the next message will display. Tap the Action button to Forward, Reply All, or Reply to the message.

When you select Reply, a new message is created with the To field already filled with the e-mail address of the person who sent you the original message. The contents of the original message are inserted into the new message and the cursor is placed at the top, as you see on the right.

Enter the text of the reply and tap the Send button.

Reply All also creates a new message and fills the To field with the e-mail address of the person who sent the original message. However, if the original message contained any carbon copies, the additional addresses are added to the carbon copy line of the reply.

You can configure Inbox so that it does not insert the original message in replies. On a Pocket PC, tap Tools | Options, and then the Message tab, shown on the right.

To stop inserting the text, clear the When Replying, Include Body check box. When the text is inserted, it will be indented unless you clear the Indent check box. Each line of the inserted text will contain a leading character that you specify unless you clear the Add Leading Character check box. These options do not affect message forwarding, which will always include the contents of the original message.

Manage Messages

Folders are valuable for organizing and storing many messages, and you can create folders for all e-mail services except ActiveSync. Unfortunately, Inbox does not have the message filter capabilities that you find in Outlook, but you can create folders and manually store messages in them.

Long-time Pocket PC users will be happy to learn that Pocket PC 2002 supports subfolder synchronization. However, Pocket PC 2002 does not allow you to create subfolders for ActiveSync on the device. Instead, you have to create subfolders on a desktop computer, and then set up that folder for synchronization. Pocket PC 2000 does not support subfolder synchronization, but does allow you to create subfolders for the ActiveSync service.

How to ... Use Web-Based E-Mail Services

Web-based e-mail services are another alternative to Inbox. The challenge in using such services with Pocket PCs is finding one that formats e-mail for the Pocket PC's screen. I have found three services that work very well with Pocket PCs. One is Yahoo Mobile, which requires a Yahoo ID. You can access Yahoo Mobile from your desktop at http://mobile.yahoo.com, or from your Pocket PC at http://p5.oa.yahoo.com. MSN Mobile is available at http://mobile.msn.com/pocketpc and provides online access to Hotmail.

The services provided by Yahoo and MSN provide their own e-mail addresses. Gopher King, at http://www.gopherking.com, is different because it only provides access to existing e-mail accounts. It uses SSL to secure communications and assists in setting up e-mail access to many popular ISPs, including AOL. Gopher King supports POP3 and IMAP 4 servers, and also provides many other services, such as newsgroups and instant messaging.

TIP   *If you own a Pocket PC 2000 device and synchronizing folders is important to you, check Intellisync from Puma Technologies. It supports synchronization of e-mail subfolders, as well as Calendar and Contact subfolders. You can find more information at http://www.pumatech.com/intellisync.html.*

Create, Rename, and Delete Folders

Folder management has been simplified to one screen with Pocket PC 2002. To create, rename, or delete folders, tap Tools | Manage Folders to open the screen on the right.

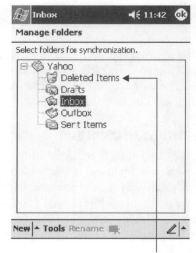

To create a folder, first select a location within the folder hierarchy on the screen, and then tap New. Enter a name for the new folder and tap OK.

To rename a folder, select it in the folder hierarchy, tap Rename, and then enter a new name in the Rename Folder dialog box. Delete a selected folder by tapping the Delete button on the Command bar. The folder and its contents will be deleted.

NOTE   *If you create a folder within Deleted Items and then delete that folder, it will not be removed from the Manage Folders screen immediately. However, if you close Manage Folders and open it again, you will find that the folder is no longer available.*

Tap here to delete a folder.

Move and Copy Messages

Because Inbox does not provide filtering capabilities, you must manually move or copy messages from the main message list to a folder. When you move a message to a subfolder in the ActiveSync service, the message will appear in the destination folder in Outlook. If the destination subfolder is set up for synchronization, you will see the message at both locations. However, if the subfolder does not synchronize, it only appears on the desktop computer. When you move messages associated with Internet services, they are not deleted from mail servers.

To move a message, tap and hold the message and tap Copy To or Move To in the pop-up menu. Select the destination folder and tap OK. To move an open message, tap Edit | Move To, select the destination folder, and tap OK.

Download a Full Copy of a Message

One of the Inbox preferences is only downloading message headers and a specified number of lines. You may decide while reading a truncated message that you want to retrieve a full copy. You can tell Inbox to download a full copy of the message during the next connection with the mail server.

To download a full copy of an open message, tap Edit | Mark For Download. Another way is to select a message in the message list and select Services | Mark For Download. A third way is to tap and hold a message header, and then tap Mark For Download on the pop-up menu.

> **TIP** *If you later decide not to download the entire message, tap Services | Do Not Download, or tap and hold the message header, and then tap Do Not Download.*

Check Inbox Status

Most of the time, you will use Inbox while it is not connected. During that time, you will compose new messages or delete messages. You may also request that Inbox get a full copy of a message. The Status dialog box shows you the actions that are queued up for the next connection.

> **TIP** *The status information is for the current service. To see the status of another service, select it and open the Status dialog box.*

To open the Status dialog box, tap Tools | Status, and the screen on the right displays.

Inbox	11:53 ok
Status	
On next connect	
Messages to be sent:	1
Messages to be copied:	0
Attachments to be copied:	0
Messages to be deleted:	7

Manage Attachments

Attachments are handled differently by POP3 and IMAP4 services. If a POP3 service is configured to only get message headers, it will insert "[Message truncated. Tap Edit->Mark for Download to get remaining portion.]" at the bottom of messages that contain an attachment. To download the attachment to your Pocket PC, you will need to mark the message for download and then reconnect to the mail server. If the POP3 service is configured to get full copies of messages, attachments automatically download to the Pocket PC.

> **NOTE** *Embedded images and OLE objects cannot be received as attachments.*

IMAP4 services always indicate an attachment with an icon at the bottom of the message, in its own window pane, even if the attachment has not been downloaded. The first icon on the right indicates that the attachment still needs to be downloaded. The second icon on the right indicates that the attachment is on the Pocket PC:

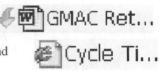

> **TIP** *Both types of e-mail services indicate that a message contains an attachment in the Inbox list view with an icon of an envelope with a paperclip.*

20

IMAP4 services provide two ways to download attachments. One is to configure the service to download attachments when retrieving full copies. Another is to request a specific attachment by tapping its icon.

> **TIP** *Inbox automatically converts Word and Excel documents to the Pocket formats. You can purchase Westtek's ClearVue, which is available from http://www.westtek.com/clearvue.htm, to open Word, Excel, and Power Point attachments in their native formats.*

One of the problems with file attachments is their size, and if you download many messages with attachments, the internal storage space can be quickly used up. Fortunately, you can configure Inbox to put attachments on a storage card. To configure a Pocket PC to write attachments to a storage card, tap Tools | Options and then tap the Storage tab to open the screen on the right.

Select the Store Attachments On Storage Card check box and then tap OK.

Receive Meeting Requests

Pocket Outlook treats appointments, meetings, and events differently. Appointments are activities that you schedule in Calendar that don't involve inviting people. A meeting is an appointment to which you invite someone, and an event is an

How to ... Fix Lost Attachment Folders

If you receive large file attachments, you will probably want to configure Inbox to store those attachments on a storage card. Attachments saved to storage cards are put in a uniquely named folder created in the root of storage cards. When Inbox starts, it looks for that folder; and if it does not find the folder, it displays an error message. The error is most likely caused when you start Inbox while the storage card is not in the Pocket PC. However, if the folder is deleted, your Inbox does not allow you to turn off the attachment storage option.

Fortunately, Marc Zimmermann provides a fix for this problem via a simple program that you can download and run on your Pocket PC. Go to http://www.zimac.de/, click the Selected Software link, and download the Attachment Folder Fix.

activity that lasts 24 hours or longer. Sending and receiving meeting requests involves integration between the Calendar and Inbox programs. The process for sending a meeting request is covered in "Schedule Appointments Using Calendar" in Chapter 8.

If you synchronize Inbox messages with Outlook, you will automatically receive meeting requests. To receive meeting requests using an Internet service, the mail server must be running Microsoft Exchange server. The Exchange server must use Rich Text Format and Transport Neutral Encapsulation Format (TNEF).

TNEF is a Microsoft proprietary method for packaging information to send across the Internet. If it is enabled, you will not receive messages that are included in other messages as attachments, and you will not be able to tell whether a message has an attachment until you get the full copy.

Meeting requests appear on Pocket PCs as attachments, and, therefore, you must either manually or automatically download full copies of the e-mail in order to open them. When you receive a meeting request, tap Appointment and then select Accept, Tentative, or Decline. The response will be sent during the next synchronization, or connection with mail servers, and the appointment is added to the Calendar.

Find Messages

As described earlier, Inbox folders are useful for separating and storing e-mail messages. Unfortunately, Inbox does not provide a way to automatically move messages to folders, which would make the process for finding messages easier. However, you can search for messages; and if you search on the same sending address, they will all appear in one list.

To search for a message on a Pocket PC, use the Find utility, which is used to search for any information on the device. Tap Start | Find to open the screen on the right.

Enter a name, e-mail address, or phrase in the Find field, select Inbox from the Type drop-down list, and then tap Go. The results are displayed in the dialog box. To open a message, tap it in the list.

Wrapping Up

Your Pocket PC has all the tools for sending and receiving e-mail to family, friends, and coworkers. Inbox works with standard POP3 and IMAP4 e-mail servers and synchronizes with Microsoft Outlook. Instant Messaging is another popular form of communicating over the Internet; and in the next chapter, you will learn how to use Pocket PC programs to chat via MSN, Yahoo, or AOL.

Chapter 21

Send and Receive Instant Messages

How To...

- Send and receive instant messages using MSN Messenger
- Send and receive instant messages using Yahoo Messenger
- Send and receive instant messages using AOL Instant Messenger
- Send and receive instant messages using ICQ

Instant messaging is the CB radio of the Internet. If you are too young to remember, CB (citizens band) radios provide two-way voice communication, and they were very popular in the mid '70s. The pop song "Convoy" by C.W. McCall shows how CB radios were popular among truck drivers at the time.

CB radios were popular because you could use them to communicate with other people who had the same radios whether you were at home, in a truck, or walking around. The radios use airwave frequencies that are unlicensed; so, unlike phone calls, you did not have to pay for the conversations. Today, CB radios have been replaced by mobile phones; however, the spirit of free, two-way conversation lives on in the form of instant messaging on the Internet.

In 1996, a small Israeli company called Mirabilis Ltd. created ICQ, which stands for "*I Seek You*". It was the first of what is now called *instant messaging software*. With an instant messaging program you can see whether your friends are connected to the Internet; and if so, you can send them text messages. Instant messaging is faster than e-mail, because you know the recipient is online to receive your message.

All of the popular instant messaging programs are available for free; so, like CB radios, you can use them to communicate with people across great distances for free. As CB radios provided mobile communication, so do Pocket PCs, which run all the popular instant messaging programs; and they can connect to the Internet nearly anywhere. In this chapter, you'll learn how to use instant messaging programs on Pocket PCs.

Send and Receive Instant Messages Using MSN Messenger

The Microsoft Network (MSN) Instant Messenger only runs on Pocket PC 2002. It is installed in ROM on most Pocket PC 2002 devices, or it can be installed in RAM on Pocket PCs upgraded to Pocket PC 2002 when it becomes available for download at http://www.pocketpc.com. As of this writing, Microsoft plans to provide a version for download during 2002.

> **TIP**   *If you have a Pocket PC 2000 device, you can send instant messages using the MSN Messenger Service by using MSN Messenger Force by Ruksun. You will find this program at http://www.ruksun.com/mobile_computing/windowsce/index.html.*

Before you can use MSN Messenger, you'll need to create a Hotmail or Passport account. Hotmail is a free web-based e-mail system; you can create a new account at http://www.hotmail.com. If you don't want to use the Hotmail e-mail service, you can create a Passport account at http://www.passport.com.

After you create either a Hotmail or Passport account, configure MSN Messenger to use the account by tapping Tools | Options and then tapping the Accounts tab, as shown in the image on the right.

Select the Enable Passport Account check box, even if you are using a Hotmail account. In the Sign In Name field, enter the full e-mail address, such as **johndoe@hotmail.com**, and enter the password in the Password field. Tap OK to close the dialog box and save the account information.

NOTE *Microsoft Exchange Server provides an Exchange Instant Messaging service that supports instant messages using the MSN Messenger client. Some corporations use this service to provide instant messaging within their private network. Pocket PCs can also work with Exchange Instant Messaging if you select the Enable Exchange Account check box and provide the required login information.*

Send and Receive Messages

To use MSN Messenger, you must connect your Pocket PC to the Internet. MSN Messenger automatically uses the default Internet modem connection that you set up in Connection Manager, or a network card if one is available. Chapter 19 provides the instructions for creating modem connections in Connection Manager.

TIP *MSN Messenger also works with ActiveSync Desktop Pass Through, which is described in Chapter 19.*

When you start MSN Messenger, you'll see the screen shown on the right.

Tap the middle of the screen to sign in to the MSN Messenger server. Another way

Tap here to sign in to MSN Messenger Server. ➔ Tap here to sign in

to sign in is to tap Tools | Sign In. When you do, you'll see the sign-in screen shown at right.

If you configured MSN Messenger with a Hotmail or Passport account, that information will already be on the screen, or you can enter it on the screen and tap Save Password to save the account and password. Tap Sign In to connect to the server.

TIP   *To sign out from MSN Messenger, tap Tools | Sign Out.*

All of your MSN Messenger contacts are stored on the Messenger server, and you will see all of your contacts that are Online or Not Online in the main program window, as shown in the following:

These contacts are online.

This contact is away from his desk.

These contacts are not online.

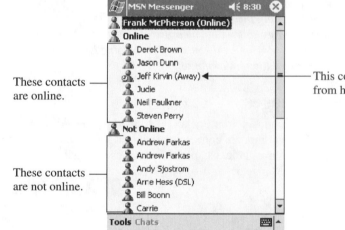

To send a message to a contact that is online, tap the contact name to open the screen on the right.

Enter a message and tap Send. The message that you enter moves to the top of the screen, which is where you will also see any replies from the person you are chatting with.

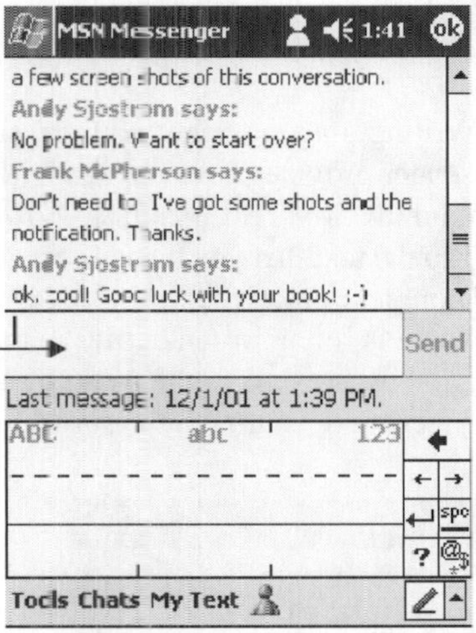

TIP *You can also tap-and-hold on the contact name and then tap Send An Instant Message on the pop-up list. To send an e-mail message, tap-and-hold on the contact name and tap Send Mail on the pop-up list. You can send e-mail to online and offline contacts.*

Enter messages here.

You can chat with more than one person by using the Chat menu to switch between people. However, each chat is in a separate window and you cannot participate in conference chats. If you receive a message from a person with whom you are not chatting with, or for whom you don't have the chat window open, their message will appear in a Notification bubble, such as shown in the image on the right.

The Notification bubble displays for about 30 seconds, and if it closes before being acknowledged, the indicator shown here appears at the top of the Pocket PC screen:

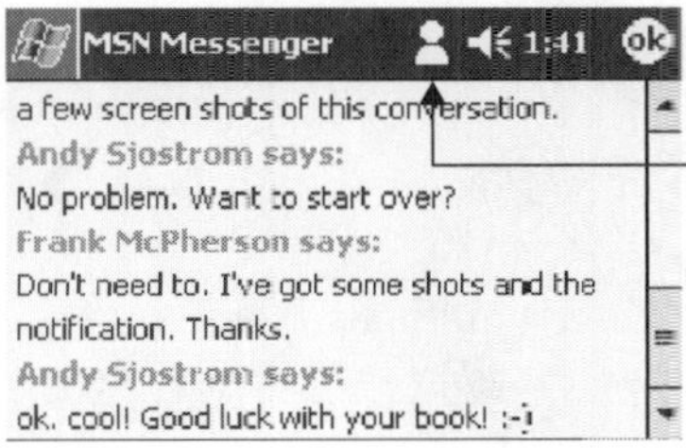

Chat notification indicator

The Notification bubble and indicator will also appear if you have another program open on your Pocket PC while MSN Messenger is running. When you tap Chat on the Notification bubble while another program is running, the Pocket PC switches programs so that you can enter a response.

If you do not want to chat, tap Ignore on the Notification bubble. To change your status to indicate that you do not want to chat, tap Tools | My Status.

Writing long messages with the stylus can be tedious, so MSN Messenger provides a way to send predefined messages; these are 4listed in the My Text menu, as shown in the image to the right.

Tap the text that you want inserted in the message, and then either add more text or tap Send.

There is room for ten entries in the My Text menu, and you can change what appears in the menu by tapping Tools | Edit My Text Messages, to open the screen shown next.

```
Yes.
No.
I can't talk right now.
I'll be right there.
I'm running late.
Where are you?
Hi.
Goodbye.
Call me later.
I love my Pocket PC!
My Text
```

To change text, first tap the item you want to change in the scroll list at the top of the screen; then highlight the text in the field under the scroll list and enter the new text. When you tap a different text item or tap OK, the text you enter is saved.

Change the text here.

MSN Messenger and Inbox both have My Text menus that contain the same items. When you change an item in one program, it also changes for the other program.

Manage Contacts

MSN Messenger Contacts are not the same as Pocket Outlook Contacts; MSN Messenger Contacts are stored on the MSN Messenger server. Because the contacts are on the server, the same contacts appear in versions of MSN Messenger running on desktop PCs or Pocket PCs. Before you can add a contact, you must be online with the MSN Messenger server.

To add a contact using a Pocket PC, tap Tools | Add A Contact, and enter the contact's MSN Messenger sign-in name in the Sign-in Name field on the screen on the right.

Tap Next, and if the sign-in name is found on the server, you'll see a message indicating that the contact has been added to your list. If the sign-in name is not found, you'll see a message saying that the operation has failed, and you'll return to the Add a Contact screen.

To delete a contact, tap-and-hold on its entry on the MSN Messenger screen, and tap Delete Contact on the pop-up list. A message box appears to confirm whether or not you do want to delete the contact. Tap Yes to delete or No to cancel.

If you want to prevent a contact from ever sending a message to you, tap-and-hold its entry on the MSN Messenger screen and tap Block on the pop-up list. When you block a contact, you'll always appear offline to that person. Blocked contacts have a cross-out indicator on the MSN Messenger screen, as shown below.

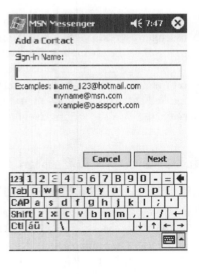

To unblock a contact, tap-and-hold on its entry, and tap Unblock on the pop-up list.

Change MSN Messenger Options

If you want to block multiple contacts, the simplest way is to tap Tools | Options, and then tap the Privacy tab, which displays the screen here:

Tap the contact that you want to block from the My Allow List, and then tap the arrow in the middle of the screen pointing toward the My Block List. To unblock contacts, tap entries in the My Block List and tap the arrow pointing toward the My Allow List.

At the bottom of the Privacy tab there is a check box to alert you when another MSN Messenger user ads you to their Contact list. If you want to receive these notifications, make sure to select the check box. To see who has you in their Contact list, tap View.

To change your name as it appears to other MSN Messenger users, tap Tools | Options and enter the new name in the Name field of the General tab. To change the MSN Messenger sign-in name and password, or to configure MSN Messenger to work with the Exchange Instant Messaging service, tap Tools | Options, and then tap the Accounts tab.

Send and Receive Instant Messages Using Yahoo Messenger

Yahoo Messenger is an instant messaging client for Pocket PCs and desktop computers that works with the Yahoo Messaging service. The program runs on Pocket PC 2000 and 2002 devices, and you can use it to send instant messages with other people that use the Yahoo Messaging service.

Before you can use Yahoo Messenger, you need to create a free Yahoo account. Open http://messenger.yahoo.com on a PC, click the Acct Info link, and then click the Sign Up Now link. Remember your Yahoo User ID and Password because you will need to enter that information on your Pocket PC.

Download and Install Yahoo Messenger

To download a free copy of Yahoo Messenger, open http://messenger.yahoo.com on a PC, click the Windows CE link, and then click the Download For Windows Pocket PC link. The setup program will download to a directory that you specify on the hard disk of the PC. Connect the Pocket PC to the desktop computer, use Windows Explorer to open the folder on the desktop where you downloaded the setup program, and run ymsgr-ppc.exe.

To start Yahoo Messenger, tap Start | Programs | Yahoo Messenger. To sign on to the Yahoo Messenger server, you'll need to enter your Yahoo User ID and Password by tapping Sign In | Change User/Sign In. Enter your Yahoo User ID and Password on the screen and tap Sign In. If you want Yahoo Messenger to remember your User ID and Password, tap the Remember My ID And Password check box. To sign off from the Yahoo Messenger server and exit the program, tap Sign In | Exit.

TIP   *If you want to sign in to Yahoo Messenger, but not let other Yahoo Messenger users know that you are connected, tap the Sign In Using Invisible Mode check box on the Sign In screen.*

Send and Receive Messages

After you sign in to Yahoo Messenger, you'll see a listing of all your Yahoo friends on the main program window (friends that are online appear in bold on the screen). To send a message to a friend, double-tap a name on the screen, enter the message, and tap Send. Sent messages appear at the top of the screen, which is where you also see messages sent to you.

You can exchange messages with more than one friend at a time by using the tabs at the top of the screen to switch between conversations. The Pocket PC version of Yahoo Messenger does not support conferences with multiple users.

When someone sends you an instant message, the program automatically displays the message window. The window automatically displays if you are currently in Yahoo Messenger or another program on your Pocket PC. You will also hear a sound when you receive a message, which you can change or turn off by tapping Edit | Preferences | Sounds.

Yahoo Messenger provides a way to quickly enter text into a message by enabling you to select text from a drop-down list in the message window. However, there is no way for you to edit the text in the list.

Manage Friends

To add a friend to Yahoo Messenger, tap Friends | Add A Friend Group, enter your friend's Yahoo User ID, and specify the group you want your friend to be listed under. You can also specify how your name will appear in your friend's Yahoo Messenger list, as well as provide a message that will be sent to your friends when they are notified that you added them to your list.

To delete a friend from Yahoo Messenger, tap Friends | Remove A Friend. Enter the Yahoo User ID to be deleted, select the group that contained the User ID, and tap Delete. Tap OK on the confirmation message box that appears, or tap Cancel to cancel the deletion.

If you want to ignore Yahoo Messenger users so that they cannot tell whether you are online or they cannot send you messages, tap Edit | Ignore List. Tap Add and then enter the Yahoo User ID of the person you want to ignore. To remove a person from the list, first select their User ID and then tap Remove. You can also automatically ignore all Yahoo Messenger users that are not in your Friends list by selecting the Ignore If Not On My Friend List check box.

Change Preferences

Yahoo Messenger provides preference settings to specify how you connect to the Internet, what alerts you see, and what sounds you hear. To change the Preference settings, tap Edit | Preferences.

The Connection tab provides a way for you to specify which modem connection to use when you connect to the Internet. If you tap the Auto-Dial check box and select a modem connection, Yahoo Messenger will automatically dial that connection when you sign on to the server. If you use a proxy server to connect to Internet, you can also provide the proxy server information on the Connection tab.

Yahoo provides free e-mail and a calendar, and Yahoo Messenger can notify you when you receive e-mail or when an appointment is due. Yahoo Messenger provides a hyperlink to a text-only My Yahoo page with links to e-mail and calendar, which opens in Pocket Internet Explorer. To turn these alerts on or off, tap the Alerts tab on the Preferences screen and select or clear the check boxes.

Yahoo Messenger can play different sounds when you receive a message, when a friend comes online, or when you get an alert. Specify what you hear on the Sounds tab of the Preferences screen by selecting a sound for each option from drop-down lists on the screen. To turn the sounds off, select None from each drop-down list.

Send and Receive Instant Messages Using AOL Instant Messenger

The America Online Instant Messenger (AIM) is one of most popular messaging services on the Internet. Fortunately, there is version of this program that runs on Pocket PC 2000 and 2002 devices. Before you can use AIM, you need to create a free screen name. Open http://www.aol.com/aim/aim4wince.html on a PC, click the Register link, and complete the forms. Remember your screen name and password because you will need to enter that information on your Pocket PC.

> **NOTE** *Even though a version of AIM for Pocket PCs is still available, AOL has stopped supporting this program, so AOL may not release new versions of the program in the future.*

Download and Install AOL Instant Messenger

To download a free copy of AIM, open http://www.aol.com/aim/aim4wince.html on a PC, and click the Get It Now link. The setup program will download to a directory that you specify on the PC hard disk. Connect the Pocket PC to the desktop computer, use Windows Explorer to open the folder on the desktop where you downloaded the setup program, and run aim.exe.

The installation program adds a shortcut to the Pocket PC Start menu. To start the program, tap Start | AIM. To sign on to AIM, tap Sign On on the Command bar, and then enter your screen name and password on the Sign On screen. To exit from AIM and disconnect from the server, tap File | Exit.

> **TIP** *If you want AIM to automatically log in, tap the Auto-Login check box in the sign-on window.*

Send and Receive Messages

When you start AIM, you'll see a program window with two tabs: one for showing buddies that are online, and one for managing your buddy list. AIM provides four default categories for grouping buddies, and you can create additional categories as well.

To send a message to a buddy, either double-tap the buddy's name on the screen, or single-tap the buddy and then tap Send Message at the bottom of the screen. You'll see the Instant Message screen where you enter messages and receive replies.

AIM does not provide a shortcut for entering text, but it does provide a window for selecting *emoticons.* Emoticons are a clever way of using standard punctuation to express emotion. For example, a smiley face is made with a colon and right parenthesis like :). On desktop computers, AIM displays emoticons as graphics; but while you can select a graphic on a Pocket PC, you will see the punctuation marks in the message area.

When you receive a message from someone that you are not chatting with, AIM flashes a Notification icon at the bottom right of the screen. Tap the icon to open the message window and send a reply.

To start a new message session with another buddy from the message window, tap Start A Session. End a message session by tapping End Session. You can be chatting with more than one buddy at a time, but the Pocket PC version of AIM does not support conferences. To switch between conversations, expand the drop-down list at the top right of the screen, and then tap the buddy's name.

Manage Buddies

To add and delete buddies, create buddy groups, and rename buddies, tap the List Setup tab of the Buddy List screen. To add a buddy or group, tap the appropriate buttons and enter the buddy's screen name or a group name.

AIM provides a way for you to rename a buddy in your buddy list, but you need to be careful with this feature. If your buddy does not change their name, you will not be able to send messages to that buddy, nor will you be able to see whether they are online. To rename a buddy, tap Rename Buddy and then enter a new name.

To delete a buddy or a group, first tap the buddy or group name, and then tap Delete.

Change Preferences

AIM provides preference settings for privacy, instant messaging, news headlines, stock quotes, and general settings. To change the preferences, tap Edit | Preferences. The privacy settings enable you to control who can send you a message. The options include Allow All Users, Allow Only Users On Your Buddy List, Block All Users, Allow Only The Users You List, and Block The Users That You List.

On the instant messaging, or IM tab, you specify whether AIM plays a sound when you receive a message, and whether AIM shows an Accept Message dialog box when you receive messages from people not on your buddy list. You can also create a customized message that is automatically sent when you receive a message while you are away from your Pocket PC.

AIM displays general news headlines, business, sports, and entertainment news. You can specify which of these items you want to see by selecting a check box for each on the Preferences News tab. Likewise, the Stocks tab provides check boxes for displaying market indices, and a field for you to enter stock tickers of the companies for which you want to see stock quotes.

The General tab provides a way to remove all the screen names on your buddy list and to reset all the preferences. Be careful using this feature because the process cannot be reversed; AIM will display two confirmation messages to make sure you really want to delete screen names.

Send and Receive Instant Messages Using ICQ

ICQ was released in November 1996 by the Israeli company Mirabilis Ltd., and later sold to AOL in 1998. Despite little advertising or marketing, there are now over 100 million people who use ICQ to send instant messages across the Internet.

With the success of ICQ, it is not surprising that Pocket PC users have long sought a version of the program for Pocket PCs. If you use ICQ on your desktop, you'll be happy to know that an alpha version of the Pocket PC program is now available.

If you already use ICQ on your desktop PC, you'll want to upgrade the program to version 2001b because it now uploads all your ICQ contacts to a server. Putting your contacts on a server makes it easier to use those same contacts on Pocket PCs or other desktop computers.

If you have never used ICQ, you'll need to first download and install the software for your desktop PC in order to create an ICQ ID, otherwise known as a *Universal Internet Number*. The Pocket PC version of ICQ does not provide a way to create an ID, and there is not a web-based method for registration. To download the software, go to http://www.icq.com and click the Download ICQ link. During the installation process, you'll register yourself with ICQ and receive your ID, which you'll need in order use ICQ on your Pocket PC.

Download and Install ICQ

To download ICQ for the Pocket PC, go to http://www.icq.com and click the PDA/Handhelds link, which you'll find on the right side of the page under the heading ICQ Anywhere. The direct link to the program is http://www.icq.com/pda/pocketpc/alpha/, but this may change in the future.

Download the setup program to the hard disk in your PC, connect your Pocket PC with the desktop, and then run the setup program. The installation program automatically adds an ICQ link to the Pocket PC Start menu, and you start the program by tapping Start | ICQ.

When you first start ICQ, you'll see the Sign On screen where you enter your ICQ ID number and password. There are check boxes available to save the password and to auto-login, which bypasses the Sign On screen and connects directly to the ICQ server. To exit ICQ and disconnect from the server, tap File | Exit.

Send and Receive Messages

After ICQ connects to the server, you'll see the main program window. In the middle of the window are all of your ICQ contacts, categorized into different groups. You can double-tap the categories to contract or expand the listing of contact names.

Along the right side of the screen are buttons for performing all of the program functions: send an instant message, send a Short Message Service (SMS) message, display information about a contact, delete a contact, display your information, change preferences, and display stock quotes. SMS is a text messaging service that works with mobile phones, so you can send a text message from your Pocket PC using ICQ to a mobile phone.

To send a message to a contact, either double-tap the contact name on the screen, or tap a contact once and then tap Instant Message. Enter your message and then tap Message. After a message is sent, you'll see it at the top of the screen, which is where you also see messages that the contact sends to you. ICQ also provides an emoticon menu to easily select and send various emoticons in your messages.

When you receive a message from someone that you are not chatting with, ICQ flashes a Notification icon at the bottom right of the screen. Tap the icon to open the message window and send a reply.

To close the messaging window and return to your Contact list, either tap Back at the bottom of the screen, or tap the drop-down list at the top left of the screen and then tap Contact List.

Manage Contacts

To add a contact to your Contact list, tap Add/Invite Users at the bottom of the screen. ICQ will search for a contact by first and last name, e-mail address, or ICQ ID. To delete a contact from your Contact list, tap the contact name and then tap Delete.

Change Preferences

ICQ has general preference settings, along with settings for stock quotes and privacy. To change the preferences, tap Edit | Preferences. On the General tab, you specify whether or not you want ICQ to play sounds when receiving messages, whether or not you want to only receive messages from people on your Contact list, and whether or not you want to see a confirmation message when you sign off.

The Stocks tab provides check boxes for selecting stock market indices to display when ICQ retrieves stock information. You can also add and remove the display of a company's stock market ticker in ICQ. You change your ICQ password on the Privacy tab.

Wrapping Up

You can use your Pocket PC to chat with friends, family, and coworkers using the MSN, Yahoo, AOL, and ICQ instant messaging services. All you need is the free software provided by these companies and a connection to the Internet, and you can chat whenever and wherever there is a need. E-mail and instant messaging are two of the popular ways people use the Internet, while everyone browses the Web for information. In the next chapter, you'll learn how you can use Internet Explorer on the Pocket PC to open web sites and download content to read when you are not connected to the Internet.

Chapter 22

Browse the Web

How To...

- ■ Browse websites using Pocket Internet Explorer
- ■ Save shortcuts to your favorite websites
- ■ Synchronize web pages to your Pocket PC
- ■ Subscribe to and view AvantGo channels

In 1989, the World Wide Web was nothing more than a project for British physicist and computer scientist Timothy Berners-Lee. In 1993, when the first major browser, Mosaic, was developed, the Web was still not used for much more than research. All of that has changed dramatically—today some companies exist with nothing more than a web page as their storefront.

The Web has become the graphical user interface for the Internet—the method by which the majority of people use it. When you access the Internet to check stock quotes, buy a book, find a phone number, or read a magazine, you probably do so on the Web with a web browser.

Because of the importance of the Web, a web browser is now perhaps the most important program on your computer. Go to any computer store, look at any computer, and you'll find a web browser. Pocket PCs are no different; they, too, have a web browser, called Pocket Internet Explorer.

Like all the Pocket PC applications, Pocket Internet Explorer; is not designed to be your full-time browser. However, it provides enough functionality to perform the majority of tasks necessary when you don't have access to a browser on a desktop computer. In fact, the combination of a Pocket PC, Pocket Internet Explorer, and wireless networking may represent the future of the Internet, a future in which the Internet is used for communication wherever one may be, whether at home or the grocery store, or while traveling.

NOTE   *The web browser software on Pocket PCs has the name Internet Explorer; but because it is different from web browsers for desktop computers, I prefer to call it by its original name—Pocket Internet Explorer. The smaller screen on Pocket PCs means that most pages will not look the same as on a PC, and Pocket PCs cannot display graphics at the same resolution and color density as a PC.*

Pocket Internet Explorer is based on Internet Explorer Version 3.1, but does not support all of its features. The following is a summary of the features that are *not* supported:

- ■ Java applets designed to run within a web browser
- ■ Microsoft Visual Basic Script
- ■ Several multimedia file formats, such as AVI and MPEG
- ■ The HTML tags APPLET, BLINK, ISINDEX, LINK, MARQUEE, OBJECT, and STYLE

Pocket Internet Explorer supports all of the basic security types, including the 128-bit encryption used by some websites. Pocket PC 2000 does not have built-in support for 128-bit encryption, but you can add it by downloading and installing the Microsoft High Encryption Pack for Pocket PCs from http://www.microsoft.com/mobile/pocketpc/downloads/ssl128.asp.

Did you know?

New Protocols for Pocket PC 2002 Release

The Pocket PC 2002 release of Internet Explorer includes support for several protocols that are not available for Pocket PC 2000. Included among those protocols is WAP 1.2.1, which is used to provide content for mobile phones. If you would like to view WAP content with Pocket PC 2000, you can use the EZOS EzWAP browser, which you can download from http://www.ezos.com. Pocket PC 2002 also supports cHTML, which is used by the i-mode devices that are popular in Japan, and it has limited support for dHTML. Both the Pocket PC 2000 and 2002 versions of Internet Explorer support XML. To view content available in any of these protocols, simply enter the URL for the site in the Internet Explorer address bar.

Start Pocket Internet Explorer

To start Pocket Internet Explorer on a Pocket PC, tap Start | Internet Explorer, or Start | Programs | Internet Explorer, depending on how the Start menu is configured. The program window looks like the following image:

Address bar

The Address bar is at the top of the program window, and the Command bar menu options and buttons are at the bottom. To turn the Address bar on or off, tap View | Address Bar. You cannot move the Address bar to another location on the screen.

Browse Websites

The process for browsing websites in Pocket Internet Explorer is the same as with Internet Explorer. First, you must connect to the Internet, which requires a dial-up or LAN (Local Area Network) connection. Chapter 19 provides the instructions for using Connection Manager to configure Internet connections. Connection Manager automatically connects to the Internet based on how it is configured and the URL you request in Internet Explorer.

> **TIP** *You can also browse websites while your Pocket PC is in its cradle by using the ActiveSync Desktop Pass Through. You will find more information about Desktop Pass Through in Chapter 19.*

Use the Address Bar and History

Access a website by using the Address bar or Favorites. To use the Address bar, enter an address in the bar, and then tap the button to the right of the Address bar, as shown in the following image:

Tap here to
retrieve web pages.

How to ... Use a Proxy Server

Proxy servers are often used when connecting to the Internet through a LAN, such as a corporate network. They allow multiple users to share the same connection to the Internet, and provide added security by masking the TCP/IP address of the client PC.

On Pocket PC 2000 devices, Pocket Internet Explorer must be configured to access the Internet via a proxy server. Tap Tools | Options and then the Connections tab. Select Use Proxy Server, and enter an address in the Proxy Server HTTP field (the Address field on a Pocket PC), and a number in the Port field. Ask your network administrator for the address and port number of the proxy server if you do not know them. If you also access an intranet website, you must select Bypass Proxy For Local Addresses so that the browser does not try to use the proxy server to access intranet sites.

Pocket PC 2002 moves the proxy server settings from Pocket Internet Explorer to the Work Settings portion of Connection Manager. To configure the proxy server, start Connection Manager by tapping Start | Settings | Connections | Connections. Tap Modify in the Work Settings portion of the screen, and then tap the Proxy Settings tab. Tap the two check boxes on the screen and enter the host name or IP address of the proxy server on the screen. You will find more instructions for using Connection Manager in Chapter 19.

The Address bar keeps a history of the websites that you visit. The most recent ones are available from the drop-down list, as shown in the following image:

To open one of these websites, select the address, and Pocket Internet Explorer will load the page.

Pocket Internet Explorer also keeps a history of each web page that you visit, which you can use later to return to a page. To view the web page history, tap View | History to open the following screen:

Tap here to display Page ⟶ Titles or Addresses.

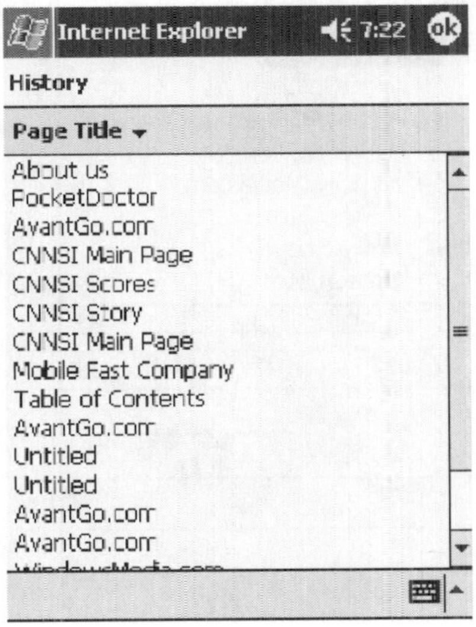

Open a page by tapping an entry in the list.

Use Favorites

The second way to access a web page is by selecting a shortcut in Favorites. To access a web page by using its Favorites shortcut, tap the Favorites Command bar button, shown in the following image, and then tap a shortcut listed in the Favorites dialog box.

Tap this button to open a list of Favorite shortcuts.

Keep Track of Your Favorite Pages

Web addresses can be difficult to remember and tedious to enter, particularly on a Pocket PC. Pocket Internet Explorer solves these problems by providing a place to store the address of your favorite websites. Whenever you want to return to a site, all you need to do is select the site name from the Favorites menu, as described in the Use Favorites section.

Add to Favorites

The first step to store a favorite site on either device is to open the website in Pocket Internet Explorer. To store a favorite website, tap the Favorites button, and then tap the Add/Delete tab to open the following screen:

Tap Add to open the Add Favorite dialog box, and tap OK to store the site in the Mobile Favorites folder. If you want to change the name of the website, delete the contents of the Name field and enter the new name before tapping OK.

> **TIP**
> *A quick way to add the current page to Favorites is to tap-and-hold on the page, and then tap the Add To Favorites option in the pop-up list.*

You can group your favorite shortcuts into folders, but you must create the folder first. To create a folder, tap New Folder, enter a name for the folder, and then tap Add. Shortcuts cannot be moved to folders.

Synchronize Favorites

If Microsoft Internet Explorer 4 or later is installed on your desktop computer, you can synchronize favorite links. If Internet Explorer 5 or later is installed, you can also download offline favorites, which is described in the upcoming "Store Web Pages on Your Pocket PC" section. When you install ActiveSync on your PC, it will add a Mobile Favorites folder to Favorites in Internet Explorer.

To synchronize the links, you must enable the Favorites information type in ActiveSync. Start ActiveSync and select Tools | Options, and then select the check box next to Favorites as shown in the following image:

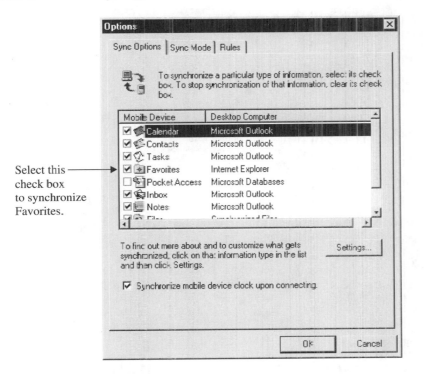

Select this
check box
to synchronize
Favorites.

During the next synchronization, the contents of the Mobile Favorites folder in Internet Explorer will synchronize with Favorites on the Pocket PC. You can then add a link to either the desktop computer or the Pocket PC; when you synchronize, the link will appear on both.

Configure Security Options

Pocket Internet Explorer supports the security protocols used by secure sites. To determine whether a web page is secure, tap View | Properties.

The security settings on a Pocket PC are not sophisticated. The Pocket PC supports all of the standard security protocols, but does not provide you with the option for turning them on or off.

A warning message will display when Pocket Internet Explorer moves from a secure page to an insecure page. To turn that message on or off, tap Tools | Options, and then select the Advanced tab to display the following screen:

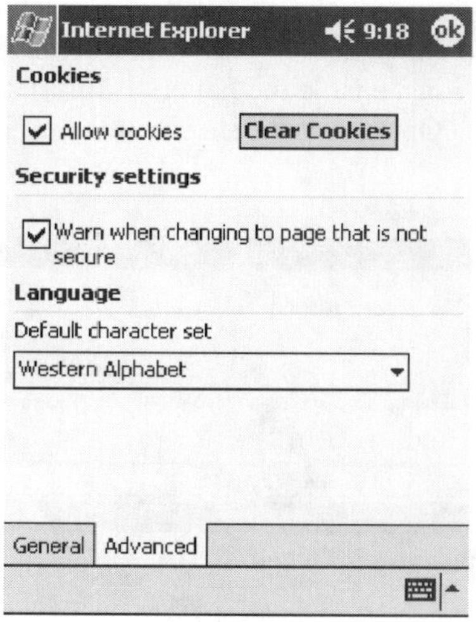

Tap here to turn the security-warning message on or off. →

Cookies

☑ Allow cookies   **Clear Cookies**

Security settings

☑ Warn when changing to page that is not secure

Language

Default character set

Western Alphabet ▼

General | Advanced

Control Cookies

Cookies are files stored on the device that contain information about your identity and preferences. They are written by a web page, and retrieved the next time you open the web page so that information can be tailored to your needs.

To prevent Pocket Internet Explorer from accepting cookies, tap Tools | Options, and then select the Advanced tab; clear the Allow Cookies check box and tap OK. To clear the cookies already on a Pocket PC, tap Clear Cookies.

Change the Display

Unfortunately, the small screen size of Pocket PCs affects the way Pocket Internet Explorer displays a web page. Another problem is that the browser does not support as many colors as desktop computers; therefore, graphics may not look the same. Fortunately, you can make changes to help compensate for these problems.

Control How Pages Display

Changing the font size of text on a web page enables more text to appear in the program window. To change the font size, tap View | Text Size and select a size.

Web pages designed for higher-resolution screens may require scrolling unless Pocket Internet Explorer changes the display so that it fits completely in the program window. Pages will display within the program window when you tap View | Fit To Screen.

While graphics make web pages visually appealing, they can take a long time to download to your device. Often, the words on the web page are all you need. To prevent Pocket Internet Explorer from downloading graphics, tap the Show Pictures button on the Command bar, as shown here:

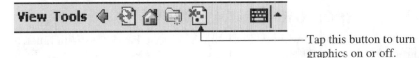

Tap this button to turn graphics on or off.

When graphics are turned off, you'll see the locations on the page where they would appear. To select individual images for display, tap-and-hold on the location, and tap Show Picture in the pop-up list.

People all around the world create web pages, and some use alphabets other than the Roman alphabet (which Pocket Internet Explorer calls the Western Alphabet) used in many countries around the world. To display characters of different alphabets, tap Tools | Options | Advanced and select an alphabet from the Default Character Set drop-down list.

Change the Home Page

The home page is the web page that opens whenever you start Pocket Internet Explorer. At first, this will be set to the default page, which is stored on the device. You may prefer a different home page to open whenever you start the browser.

To change the home page, first open the new page in Pocket Internet Explorer, and then tap Tools | Options to open the following screen:

Tap Use Current to set the new home page. If you later decide to reset the home page to the default, open the Options screen and tap Use Default.

TIP *As you open web pages on your Pocket PC, they are written to internal storage; and over time, they can take up a significant amount of storage space. You can free-up space by tapping Delete Files on the General tab of Internet Explorer options.*

Store Web Pages on Your Pocket PC

A new feature introduced with the Pocket PC is Mobile Favorites. With this feature, you can synchronize Internet Explorer favorite links to your Pocket PC. If you use Internet Explorer Version 5, you can also download web pages to your Pocket PC by synchronizing offline favorites.

When you install ActiveSync, the installation program adds a Mobile Favorites button to the Internet Explorer toolbar. A Mobile Favorites folder is also added to Internet Explorer Favorites, as shown here:

NOTE *If Favorites is not listed as an information type for your Pocket PC in ActiveSync, open the Options dialog box, click the check box next to Favorites, and then click OK.*

Synchronize Mobile Favorites Content

The process of adding a Mobile Favorite is the same as adding Internet Explorer Favorites. When you have a page open that you want to add to Mobile Favorites, click the Mobile Favorites toolbar button, or click Tools | Create Mobile Favorite. The Create Mobile Favorite dialog box will display, as shown in the next imag.

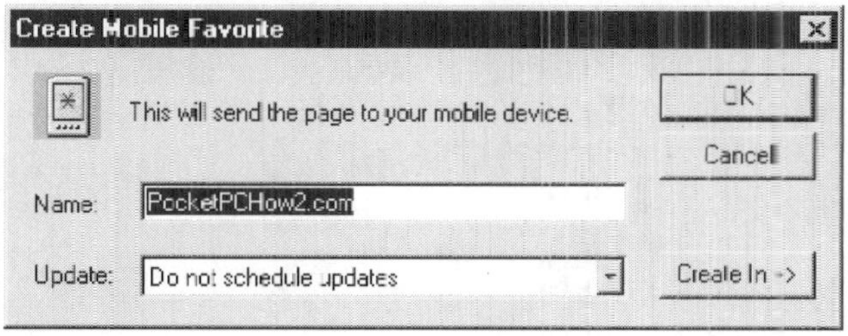

Create Mobile Favorite

This will send the page to your mobile device.

OK

Cancel

Name: PocketPCHow2.com

Update: Do not schedule updates

Create In ->

If you are running Internet Explorer Version 5, the website content will download to your PC, and the page will be added to the ActiveSync list of pages to synchronize to your Pocket PC. The next time you connect the Pocket PC to the desktop computer, the content will download. To see the list of pages that will synchronize, double-click the Favorites information type in ActiveSync on your PC. The Favorite Synchronization Options dialog box will display, as shown in the following image:

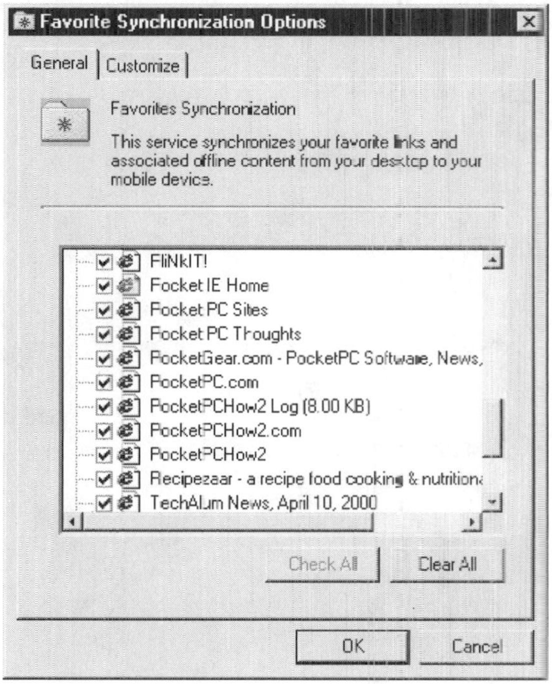

Favorite Synchronization Options

General | Customize

Favorites Synchronization

This service synchronizes your favorite links and associated offline content from your desktop to your mobile device.

- ☑ FliNkIT!
- ☑ Pocket IE Home
- ☑ Pocket PC Sites
- ☑ Pocket PC Thoughts
- ☑ PocketGear.com - PocketPC Software, News,
- ☑ PocketPC.com
- ☑ PocketPCHow2 Log (8.00 KB)
- ☑ PocketPCHow2.com
- ☑ PocketPCHow2
- ☑ Recipezaar - a recipe food cooking & nutritiona
- ☑ TechALm News, April 10, 2000

Check All   Clear All

OK   Cancel

To stop synchronizing a page, clear the check box next to its name in the Favorite Synchronization Options dialog box. If you want to stop synchronizing all of the pages, click Clear All. Any content on the Pocket PC associated with the page that you stop synchronizing will be removed during the next synchronization. The link, however, will remain in Mobile Favorites.

To remove a Mobile Favorite from Pocket Internet Explorer, tap Favorites to open the Favorites dialog box; and then tap the Add/Delete tab, as shown in the following image:

Select an item, tap Delete, and then tap OK to close the dialog box. The link and any offline content will be deleted. During the next synchronization, the item will be removed from the Favorite Synchronization Options dialog box in ActiveSync, and the link will also be removed from the Mobile Favorites folder in Internet Explorer.

How to ... Fix Mobile Favorites Synchronization Problems

One of the problems Pocket PC users frequently experience is that they try to set up a web page to synchronize, and find that it never appears on their Pocket PC. This problem is typically caused by the fact that the web page has not been downloaded to their desktop computer. Offline Mobile Favorites takes advantage of the synchronization features available with Internet Explorer 5 and later, which downloads web pages to desktop computers. When ActiveSync synchronizes favorites, it simply copies the pages from the desktop to the Pocket PC. So, the pages must already be on the PC or they will not be available for ActiveSync.

The most common reason why the web page is not on the PC is that Internet Explorer is not set up to automatically download the page. When you create a Mobile Favorite, the default setting to is not schedule updates. This means that until you either schedule an update or manually force Internet Explorer to synchronize pages, there will be nothing available to download to your Pocket PC.

To manually synchronize pages in Internet Explorer on your desktop computer, click Tools | Synchronize, and then click Synchronize on the Items To Synchronize dialog box. To fix a page so that it automatically downloads on your desktop computer at a specified time, click Tools | Synchronize, select the page, and then click Properties. Click the Schedule tab, and make sure that a date and time is selected for synchronization.

View Mobile Favorites

The process for viewing Mobile Favorites that have been downloaded to a Pocket PC is the same as browsing web pages online. Start Pocket Internet Explorer and tap Favorites. The items not available for offline viewing are grayed out, as shown in the following dialog box:

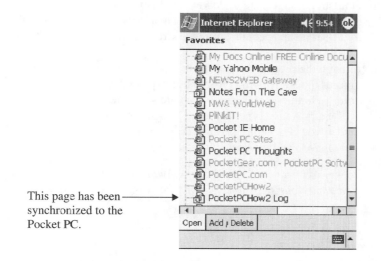

This page has been synchronized to the Pocket PC.

To view an offline page, tap one that is not grayed out in the Favorites list.

> **NOTE** *Some pages are not grayed out, yet do not synchronize to your Pocket PC. Those pages were previously viewed on the Pocket PC, and the pages are still stored on the Pocket PC and can be opened. You can clear those pages by deleting temporary Internet files from the Pocket Internet Explorer Options screen.*

Synchronize AvantGo Content

AvantGo.com is a web-based information service for handheld devices. Hundreds of channels designed specifically for the devices are available from name-brand content providers such as *USA Today,* the *Wall Street Journal,* The Weather Channel, and MapQuest. Some channels are interactive; for example, you can submit a FedEx tracking number and have information about the package sent back to you during synchronization.

The most common way to use AvantGo.com is to synchronize content to your device using ActiveSync. Your PC must be connected to the Internet during synchronization in order to download content. Synchronization can also be achieved by using a modem or LAN connection to the Internet, and AvantGo.com even provides content specifically designed for wireless connections.

AvantGo.com is integrated into Pocket Internet Explorer on Pocket PCs, which includes the software needed to communicate with the AvantGo.com servers. The AvantGo information type is also part of ActiveSync, so every Pocket PC includes all that is needed to download AvantGo.com content right out of the box. All you need to do is browse to the AvantGo.com website and sign up for the service.

Sign Up with AvantGo.com

Before you can use the AvantGo.com client on a Pocket PC, you must create an account on the AvantGo.com server by opening http://avantgo.com/setup/ on a desktop computer. Because your Pocket PC already has the client software, you just need to set up an account. Click the link on the AvantGo.com setup page to set up an account without downloading software.

The next step is to specify that you will be using AvantGo.com with a Pocket PC. Accomplish this by clicking the Pocket PC link. To set up an account, fill in the Create Account page, and then click I Accept.

The next two pages step you through the process of configuring the AvantGo.com client and synchronizing. The first page configures the ActiveSync information type and tests the network communication to the AvantGo servers. On the second screen, you are instructed to manually initiate synchronization by clicking Sync in ActiveSync. If AvantGo is listed in the ActiveSync details, then content will synchronize to your Pocket PC. However, if AvantGo is not listed, you will need to add it by tapping Tools | Options and then selecting the AvantGo check box.

> **TIP** *You can select channels to view on your Pocket PC on the AvantGo website from your desktop computer. After you make your selections, simply synchronize and the new channels will appear on your Pocket PC.*

Configure AvantGo Connect

The Pocket PC and ActiveSync include all of the software that you need to connect with the AvantGo.com server. Most of the time, you'll configure AvantGo from your desktop computer using their web-based configuration tools. However, you can also configure AvantGo synchronization from your Pocket PC. The process involves configuring AvantGo Connect on your Pocket PC, and then synchronizing the device with the desktop computer.

To configure AvantGo Connect on a Pocket PC, tap Start | Settings, and then tap the Connections tab to open the Settings screen, as shown in the following image:

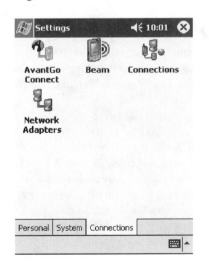

Next, tap AvantGo Connect to open this screen:

The screen should include a server setting for the AvantGo.com server, as shown in the image. If the server is not listed, tap Add and complete the fields in the dialog box as described in Table 22-1.

If the AvantGo.com server is listed in the dialog box, select it and tap Properties to open the Server Settings dialog box. Complete the Username and Password fields as described in Table 22-1, and then tap OK.

After you configure AvantGo Connect on the Pocket PC, the next step is to synchronize the device and desktop computer. Before synchronizing the two, connect the PC to the Internet so that communication with the AvantGo.com server can be established. During synchronization, the settings that you enter on the Pocket PC will be copied to the desktop.

During synchronization, the AvantGo Connect software on the PC will contact the AvantGo.com server and transfer information to your device. You will see the status line change to show the synchronization progress. When synchronization is complete, the status will change to Synchronized. From this point, every time you synchronize the device and PC, the AvantGo Connect software will update the content on your device.

Field	Value
Hostname	sync.avantgo.com
Port	80
Username	Enter the username you created on AvantGo.com.
Set password	Tap Set Password and enter the password you created on AvantGo.com.
Connect to this server	Leave checked
Refresh all content on next sync	Leave checked

TABLE 22-1   AvantGo.com Server Settings

How to ... Retrieve AvantGo Content Using Network Connections

AvantGo content can be downloaded from the Internet using a modem or LAN connection, which is valuable for retrieving information when you are away from a desktop PC. To retrieve content using a modem, you must create a modem connection to the Internet, as described in Chapter 19.

Connect your Pocket PC to the Internet using the modem connection, and then open the AvantGo channels page in Internet Explorer. Tap the Tools link at the bottom of the page, and then tap Modem Sync. While the page suggests that you are performing modem synchronization, the process also works for LAN connections and ActiveSync Desktop Pass Through.

On occasion, a problem may occur during synchronization, which causes the AvantGo channels page to disappear on the Pocket PC. You can recover this page by either synchronizing the Pocket PC with a partner desktop computer, or starting synchronization from the AvantGo Connect settings on the Pocket PC. In this case, to start synchronization, follow these steps:

1. Tap Start | Settings.
2. Tap the Connections tab.
3. Tap AvantGo Connect.
4. Tap Sync All.

The AvantGo Connect program will connect with the AvantGo.com server and update the content on your Pocket PC. After the update is complete, tap OK to close the AvantGo Connect program window, and then open Pocket Internet Explorer to view the AvantGo content.

View AvantGo Channels

To view the AvantGo channels on your Pocket PC, start Pocket Internet Explorer and tap Favorites. As you can see in the following dialog box, AvantGo Channels is listed in Mobile Favorites.

Tap here to open the AvantGo Channels home page.

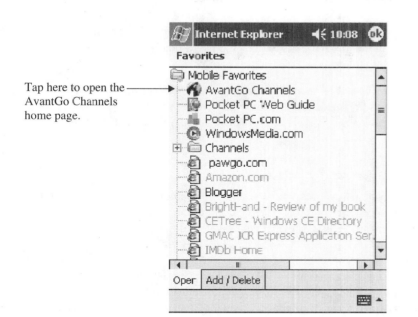

When you tap AvantGo Channels, the AvantGo home page will display a listing of your channels, as shown in the following image:

A link to the AvantGo home page is also available from the Internet Explorer default home page. To display your AvantGo channels, tap the AvantGo image on the default home page.

AvantGo Channels contain links just like ordinary web pages. To open a channel listed on the home page, tap its link; continue tapping links to open the pages that belong to the channel. You can also tap the Pocket Internet Explorer Back button to move backward through the pages.

> **TIP** *To make the AvantGo home page the default home page for Pocket Internet Explorer, open the page, tap Tools | Options, tap Use Current, and then tap OK. After you make this change, tapping the Pocket Internet Explorer Home button displays the AvantGo home page.*

Subscribe to Channels

Included among the AvantGo pages on your device is a listing of recommended channels. You can subscribe to any of the channels listed on that page by tapping the Add link on the AvantGo home page. Tap the check box next to any of the channels listed, and then tap Finish. During the next synchronization, the channels that you selected will be added to your AvantGo.com account and downloaded to the device.

AvantGo.com has hundreds of channels that are not listed on your device. To subscribe to any of those channels, go to the AvantGo.com website at http://avantgo.com/frontdoor/index.html. Enter your username and password to log on to your account, and then select from the channels listed on the website. The next time you synchronize your device and PC, the new channels will download to your device.

How to ... Move AvantGo Channels to Storage Cards

By default, AvantGo channels are stored in internal storage, which can be used up if you have too many subscriptions. You can move channels to a storage card, but it requires making a change to the Pocket PC registry. Keep in mind that if you make this change, the storage card must be in the Pocket PC during synchronization, and you may not be able to synchronize using modem connections with CompactFlash modems.

Information Appliance Associates provides a free tool called RegKing that makes the registry changes needed to synchronize AvantGo channels to storage cards. Go to http://www.doctorce.com/regking.htm and download RegKing to your Pocket PC. Run RegKing and apply the *Store AvantGo Channels on Flash Cards* registry hack. If you determine to move the channels back from the storage card to internal storage, you can use RegKing to undo this registry change.

Next, you need to move the AvantGo channels to the storage card. First, close Pocket Internet Explorer by using either a program task manager or the Running Programs tab of the Memory settings (Start | Settings | System | Memory). Second, use File Explorer to move the contents of the \Windows\AvantGo folder and subfolders to the \Storage card folder.

Finally, you need to refresh the AvantGo channels or your Pocket PC. You can force a refresh either from a partner desktop computer, or directly from the Pocket PC. From a desktop computer, double-click the AvantGo information type in the ActiveSync details section, and then click Properties and select Refresh All Content At Next Sync. Synchronize the Pocket PC to refresh the content.

To refresh AvantGo content from a Pocket PC, tap Start | Settings | Connections | AvantGo Connect, and then tap Properties. Select Refresh All Content At Next Sync and tap OK. Finally, tap Sync All on the AvantGo Connect screen.

Synchronize Content Using Mazingo

Mazingo is similar to AvantGo in that it provides offline viewing of web content on your Pocket PC. However, it also provides the distribution of audio and video content to Pocket PCs. Like AvantGo, you need to register with the Mazingo service before you can select channels. To register and download the Mazingo software, go to http://www.mazingo.net.

Unlike AvantGo, Mazingo is not integrated with ActiveSync or Pocket Internet Explorer. The software has two parts, one that runs on desktop computers, and the other that runs on Pocket PCs. You can configure the Mazingo desktop software to automatically synchronize whenever a Pocket PC connects, so you don't have to do any extra work to synchronize Mazingo content.

Another feature that sets Mazingo apart from AvantGo is its built-in support for storage cards. When you set up a Mazingo account, you can specify whether content should be written to internal storage or a storage card. You can also configure the desktop software to download content directly to a storage card if you have a storage card reader attached to the computer.

Wrapping Up

Pocket Internet Explorer enables you to access websites when you are away from a desktop computer. It has most of the features that you use to view web pages while connected to the Internet, and with Offline Mobile Favorites and AvantGo, you can also view pages while not connected to the Internet. One of the top reasons that people access the Internet is to download software; the next chapter provides information about the top Pocket PC software download sites and the programs they make available.

Part IV

Customize Your Pocket PC

Chapter 23

Expand Your Pocket PC with Software and Hardware

How To...

■ Find Pocket PC software on the Internet
■ Try some of the best software for Pocket PCs
■ Add storage space to your Pocket PC

Right out of the box, a Pocket PC is useful for the majority of people. However, you might want to explore beyond what is built-in and use your Pocket PC for tasks other than word processing or managing appointments. One way to increase the functionality of your Pocket PC is to install software. This chapter describes some of the greatest Pocket PC programs that are available for download, where to find them, and how to get them.

The number of programs you can install on your Pocket PC is limited by the amount of available storage space. Even though your device has limited built-in storage memory, you can increase the total storage available by adding storage cards. In this chapter, you'll find information about the different storage card options available for Pocket PCs.

Find Pocket PC Software

In this chapter, we'll look at some of the places to find Pocket PC software on the Internet. Software is basically distributed in two ways, either commercially through stores, or downloaded as a shareware or freeware product. Shareware is software that you download and install, and if you find that you like it, you pay the author of the program. After a trial period, you are expected to either purchase the software or remove it from your computer. Freeware is software that is free.

The majority of Pocket PC software is available only on the Internet, whether it's shareware, freeware, or the more traditional retail shrink-wrapped products. In many cases, you'll find demonstration copies of commercial software online so that you can download and try it before buying it. Usually, the demonstration software will lack some of its functionality or quit working after a period of time. Shareware is different because it includes all functionality and will probably work even after the trial period. We all benefit from this method of distribution because we can try software before spending our money on something we find does not meet our needs.

Download Free Software from Microsoft

Microsoft provides support for Pocket PCs through their website at http://www.pocketpc.com. At this site, you'll find tips and news about Pocket PCs, support, and software downloads. The Downloads page at http://www.microsoft.com/mobile/pocketpc/downloads/default.asp contains links to all of the Pocket PC software updates and applications that you can download from their site.

Microsoft sells three Pocket PC software titles: the Pocket PC Entertainment PocketPak, the Arcade PocketPak, and the Games PocketPak. The Arcade PocketPak includes three of the most popular arcade games: Pac-Man, Ms. Pac-Man, and Dig Dug. The Games PocketPak includes five games made only for the Pocket PC by Rapture Technologies. One of these games, Cubicle Chaos, is available for free.

Also available at the Downloads site are a number of files that fix Pocket PC problems. Among these is Service Pack 1 for Pocket PC 2000, which you should only install on Pocket PC 2000 devices. Also only available for Pocket PC 2000 is the Microsoft High Encryption Pack, which adds 128-bit encryption to Pocket Internet Explorer.

Download Software from CNET

CNET's Download.com is a very large website with software downloads for many different computing platforms, including Pocket PCs. The site is located at http://www.download.com and has a link to the Handheld Downloads page. Software at this site is categorized into seven areas, and the top-level page lists featured downloads and the most popular downloads.

The software listings at the CNET site include the application name, operating system version, licensing type, and a brief description. Also included is the date the software was added to the list, how many times it was downloaded, and its file size. The application name is a link to a page that provides a more detailed description of the application, along with the company's name and website link, the approximate time to download, and minimum system requirements.

Nice features at this site are the Most Popular, New Releases, and Our Picks categories. The Most Popular category lists software ranked by number of downloads, giving you an indication of what other Pocket PC users are downloading. The New Releases category lists software added in the last two weeks. The Our Picks category is a listing of what CNET believes is the best software at their site.

Download Software from TUCOWS PDA

In 1994, Scott Swedorski started TUCOWS (The Ultimate Collection of Winsock Software), a website with a reputation of being one of the best for Internet-related software. Since then, the site has expanded to a network of 500 affiliate sites in over 70 countries worldwide, making it the number one Internet software site. TUCOWS PDA is part of the TUCOWS network, and its Pocket PC software can be found at http://interworld.pda.tucows.com/pocketpc.html.

When I am looking for Pocket PC software, TUCOWS PDA is the first site I visit because it is easy to use. You'll only find software downloads at this site. The software is grouped into ten categories, each of which has additional subcategories. Each software listing includes the version of the software, the latest revision date, file size, how it is licensed (commercial, shareware, or freeware), a link to the software author's website, operating system version, and a brief description. Links to the software files are provided by processor type, which is important because some software will only run on a specific processor.

The site includes a search page that you use to search through the software listings. Each entry in the listing includes a graphical rating indicating the popularity of the program.

Download Software from HPC.net

HPC.net is found at http://www.hpc.net and claims to be the original online community for Windows CE and Pocket PC users. In addition to software downloads, it also has news, discussion boards, classified ads, and an online store for buying commercial applications. The top-level page of the website lists the latest software additions and a link to the Software Directory, which groups software into 19 categories.

Each software entry includes the software title, a brief description, and a link to the software author's website. None of the software listed in HPC.net directory is actually stored on their server. Searches can be done across the entire site or just on the software directory.

The HPC.net online store categorizes software into five categories. You also find three special sections titled Hits, Deals, and Hot New Titles. Once you purchase the software by entering a credit card number on their secure web page, it is available for download. Product support is provided through an 800 number.

Download Games from PocketGamer.org

If games are what you want, then go to http://www.pocketgamer.org for the most complete listing of Pocket PC games anywhere on the Internet. The games are grouped into 17 categories such as Action/Arcade, Board, and Adventure/Role Playing Games. You'll also find dozens of game reviews on the website to help you decide which game to try. There is an online forum for you to post questions about games and receive answers from other Pocket PC users.

Download Skins and Themes

As you saw in Chapter 3, you can use skins and themes to change the appearance of your Pocket PC. Fortunately, for those of us who are artistically challenged, we can benefit from the work of several people who create skins and themes and make them available to download. The following is a list of some of the websites on the Internet that provide skins and themes:

Pocket PC 2002 Themes

Here are some places you can find themes online.

- Pocket Themes   http://www.pocketthemes.com/
- PocketNow.com   http://skins.pocketnow.com/
- InfoSync   http://www.infosync.no/resources/skins/
- MobileViews.com   http://mobileviews.com/merlin/themes/

Dashboard/Gigabar/WISBar Skins

If skins are more your style, the following sites may be useful to you.

- CESkins   http://ceskins.com/skins/neilskins.html
- Web McDeb   http://www.mcdeb.com/
- Ojster's World   http://www.ojster.com/
- WinCustomize   http://www.wincustomize.com/

Buy Pocket PC Software

Most Pocket PC software is sold as shareware. Prior to the Internet, buying shareware involved paying the software developer directly through the mail. Today, we expect to be able to buy on the Internet using credit cards at online stores. Many software developers cannot process credit card payments, so they turn to other companies who sell their product for them in online stores.

Two of the most popular online stores of Pocket PC software are PocketGear and Handango. You'll find 104 different categories of software at PocketGear, which is at http://www.pocketgear.com. Handango, at http://www.handango.com, has fewer categories, but bundles some software together at a significant savings. Some of these Handango software *suites* are also available at retail stores like CompUSA.

The Top Ten Pocket PC Downloads

What you choose to install on your Pocket PC depends on your needs. You might want a better personal information manager than Pocket Outlook, or you may want to play games, view images, or play music. I have found a number of downloads to be very valuable for use on my Pocket PC, and I've included a personal Top Ten list of favorites, although by no means am I suggesting that these programs are the best of what's out there. Rather, what's presented here is a small sample of the type of software available for Pocket PCs and programs that I think will appeal to a wide variety of users.

PowerToys

Shortly after Windows 95 was released, Microsoft made available on their website a bundle of programs they call PowerToys. At the time of its initial release, PowerToys was billed as items that the Microsoft Windows Shell Development Team would have included in Windows 95 if they had had the time. Even though Microsoft makes the programs available, they do not provide technical support for them.

PowerToys is also available for Pocket PCs, and you can download the bundle of programs from http://www.microsoft.com/mobile/pocketpc/downloads/powertoys.asp. Make sure you download the correct PowerToys for your Pocket PC, because some of the programs are designed for specific versions of the Pocket PC software.

There are seven PowerToys for the Pocket PC, and you can download each one individually. Table 23-1 summarizes the PowerToys available for Pocket PCs.

NOTE   *All PowerToys only run on English Pocket PCs.*

Create Lists with ListPro

Do you find yourself making lists on all sorts of scrap paper? Many people create shopping lists to identify what they need to buy when they are at a store, or lists of Tasks to Do, Toys to Buy, Movies to Rent, and so on. Some lists are in numerical order, while others may be indented like

Program	Description
Theme Generator for Pocket PC 2002	This PowerToy is a desktop program that only runs on PCs with Windows 2000 or Windows XP. With the Theme Generator, you can easily create your own themes.
Remote Display Control	With this PowerToy, you can display the Pocket PC screen and user input on desktop computers. This tool is useful for demonstrating Pocket PCs to large audiences by using a PC monitor or a projector. You can use the PowerToy with an Ethernet network or ActiveSync connections.
Microsoft Password	This PowerToy only works on Pocket PC 2000 devices. It replaces the Pocket PC 2000 Password application and adds support for lowercase letters, numbers, and some symbols. The functionality that this PowerToy provides is built into the Pocket PC 2002 Password application.
Microsoft Power Contacts	This PowerToy adds options to the Contacts pop-up list. You can Create Appointments that use the contact as the attendee and subject, Create Tasks with the contact as the subject, or Open web pages associated with contacts. There is a bug in Create Appointments and Pocket PC 2002 that prevents this PowerToy from creating meeting notifications.
Microsoft Internet Explorer Tools	This PowerToy only works with Pocket PC 2000. It enables you to adjust the Internet Explorer settings. You can turn JScript support on or off, and set the amount of storage space available for temporary Internet files.
Microsoft Today Screen Image Tool	This PowerToy enables you to add an image to the Today Screen. You can also configure the image so that when it is tapped, a program launches. While the toy allows you to add multiple images to the Today screen, it does not provide a way to remove the image items—but you can turn them off.
Windows Media Skin Chooser	This PowerToy is needed to change skins for the original Windows Media Player bundled with Pocket PC 2000. Versions 7 and 8 of Windows Media Player include this functionality, so you will not need this toy for Pocket PC 2002 devices.

TABLE 23-1   Pocket PC PowerToys

an outline. The Pocket PC Tasks application is good for unordered lists, but does not support numbered lists or indentation. To overcome these deficiencies, download ListPro from Ilium Software. With ListPro, you can create and re-use any type of list that you need.

You can find this program at any of the download websites listed in this chapter, and also at the Ilium Software website at http://www.iliumsoft.com. A 30-day trial version of this program is also available; and after the trial period, it will stop functioning unless you purchase a registration code. You buy the code at the Ilium Software website.

23

Versions of the program exist for all Windows CE platforms, including Pocket PC 2000 and 2002. Also, you'll need to download and buy the Windows 95/98/NT version if you want to synchronize lists between your device and a desktop computer.

Lists are stored in a single file and can be organized into folders. Once you create a file, you then create a list by defining how you want the list to work and what should display. By default, a list item displays a check box and description in columns. Additional columns can be added to the display. Certain columns are associated with special actions; for example, when you select an item, its color can change.

List items can be sorted by any column and filtered so that only certain items display. If a list has an amount column, those amounts can be totaled at the tap of a button. Resetting a list clears all item check boxes, enabling you to re-use lists. If you find yourself writing the same shopping list over and over, create it using ListPro; and when you have finished shopping, just reset the list to use it another day.

Read the Bible with PocketBible

Your Pocket PC is as handy as a book; wouldn't it be great to be able to read a book on it? Bible readers will appreciate PocketBible, a version of the Bible for Pocket PCs from Laridian Electronic Publishing, because, with it, verses are only a tap away. PocketBible consists of two parts, the reader program and any number of Bibles. Each piece is sold separately and six different translations of the Bible are available, including the popular New International Version. A demo is available from Laridian at http://www.laridian.com/.

What makes this program particularly useful is its Go To Verse keypad. With a couple of taps of the keypad, you select the book, chapter, and verse to read. You can also search for verses using the PocketBible Find command and Boolean logic (AND, OR, NOT, and XOR). The Find dialog box even auto-completes popular search phrases.

Each Bible requires 2 to 3MB of storage space on the device, which can be on a storage card. If you store a Bible on a storage card, the software will run a little slower than if the file were stored internally. The PocketBible reader program can be stored internally, enabling you to store different translations on more than one storage card.

Test Network Connections with vxUtil

One of the more frustrating things about Pocket PCs is that while they provide a number of different ways to connect to networks, they don't include the basic tools for troubleshooting network connectivity problems. For example, Pocket PCs do not have a way to display IP addresses. Pocket PCs also do not have a *Ping utility*, which you normally use to test network connectivity between two devices. Without these very basic tools, it is impossible to determine what causes a network connectivity problem.

Fortunately, Cambridge Computer Corporation provides vxUtil, which is a free program that provides 12 network utilities. The program displays the current IP address of the Pocket PC and has a standard Ping utility. It also includes DNS Lookup, Finger, Get HTML, IP Subnet Calculator, Password Generator, Port Scanner, Quote, Time Service, Trace Route, and Whois utilities.

If you connect your Pocket PC to a network, you should download and install vxUtil. You'll find the download file at http://www.cam.com/vxutil.html.

Create Outlines with OutALine

When I write magazine articles or chapters for this book, I first create an outline using Outline view in Microsoft Word. I find that outlines help me write about a subject thoroughly by identifying main points and related topics. Unfortunately, Pocket Word does not provide a way to create outlines. To create outlines on my Pocket PC, I use OutALine from DeveloperOne, which you can download from http://www.developerone.com/pocketpc/outaline/.

OutALine provides all the basic functions for creating outlines, such as Expand and Collapse, and Indent. You can move items by using Command bar buttons or drag-and-drop. Each outline level can appear in different colors, and can include check boxes and notes. OutALine is not integrated with Pocket Word, but you can export outlines to a text file and then open the text file in Pocket Word.

Secure Information in eWallet

If you are like me, you probably have a number of different User IDs and passwords for websites on the Internet. User IDs, passwords, and account numbers are the type of information that you want secure. To store and secure all of this type of information on my Pocket PC, I use eWallet from Ilium Software.

With eWallet, you store information on cards, for which there are 30 different templates. For example, you can store credit card numbers on a card with a background that looks like a credit card. Information is organized in six categories: Accounts, Information, Internet, Memberships, Passwords, and Software Registration Codes; each category can be protected with a password.

The eWallet data file is secured with RC4 128-bit encryption, and you can configure eWallet to prompt for a password in order to open a file. You can also configure eWallet to lock and close after a set period of inactivity, as well as lock access for a period of time after a certain number of incorrect password attempts. There is a desktop version of eWallet so that you can access information if your Pocket PC is lost or stolen.

eWallet is the most important program on my Pocket PC. You can download this program from http://www.iliumsoft.com/wallet.htm.

Explore the Pocket PC Registry

Besides their similarities in user interfaces, Pocket PCs have another thing in common with Windows, which is the registry. The registry contains many of the settings that control how the Pocket PC operates. Incorrect changes to the registry can lead to severe problems that you only can fix by doing a *hard reset* of your Pocket PC. A hard reset restores a Pocket PC to its original state when it shipped from the factory, and deletes all data and user-installed applications. You should not edit the registry without first performing a full backup of your Pocket PC.

The safest way to make changes to your Pocket PC is through the various settings available when you tap Start | Settings. However, there are some changes that you may want to make to your Pocket PC that are not available as settings. A safe way to make these changes is to use RegKing from Information Appliance Associates or PalmTweak from Tillanosoft. You will find RegKing at http://www.doctorce.com/regking.htm. PalmTweak is available at http://tillanosoft.com/ce/ptweak.html.

If you are comfortable with editing the Pocket PC registry directly, I recommend PHM Registry Editor by Philippe Majerus, available at http://www.phm.lu/products/regedit.asp. This free program provides all the functions you need to explore the registry. Philippe Majerus also provides instructions for implementing changes to the registry at http://www.phm.lu/PocketPC/RegTweaks/.

> **TIP** *If you are interested in seeing what DLLs are currently in use or what processes are running on your Pocket PC, check out PocketTools from Citadel Development Corporation at http://www.citadeldevelopment.com/products/pockettools.asp.*

Capture Screenshots with Pocket ScreenSnap

As you have read this book, you have seen a number of screenshots that I captured using Pocket ScreenSnap from DeveloperOne. Pocket ScreenSnap creates bitmap image files (BMPs) that are written to a folder you specify, which can be on storage cards. This program is available at http://www.developerone.com/pocketpc/screensnap/.

You can specify a filename prefix for the images, and assign a hardware button for capturing screenshots. Some Pocket PC dialog boxes disappear when you press a hardware button, so the Pocket ScreenSnap time delay feature is handy. Before you can use the time delay feature, you have to enable it by tapping Options | Time-Delayed Snapshots in Pocket ScreenSnap. To use the time delay feature, you start Pocket ScreenSnap, switch to the program for which you are capturing the screenshot, and open the dialog box that you want to capture. After the time elapses, Pocket ScreenSnap automatically creates a screenshot.

Print Pocket Word Documents and E-Mail

One of the features available on all desktop computers, but not available with Pocket PCs, is printing. To print a Pocket Word document, you have to first transfer the document to a desktop computer, and then print the document from the desktop. With PrintPocketCE from Field Software Products, you can print Pocket Word documents and e-mail directly from a Pocket PC to a number of different printers.

PrintPocketCE supports color printing, and it can print across networks. It even supports the Bluetooth CompactFlash cards from Socket Communications, Inc., and Anycom for printing to Bluetooth-compatible printers. To print a document, start PrintPocketCE, and select the document or e-mail from List view. You can change the font size of a document prior to printing without editing the document, and you can specify a font and font size when printing plain text documents.

You will find PrintPocketCE, along with a list of printers that it supports, at http://www.fieldsoftware.com/PrintPocketCE.htm.

View Flash Content

One of the most popular forms of multimedia content on the Internet is Flash. Websites built with Flash appear and sound like programs that run on desktop computers. Macromedia sells the

How to ...   Develop Pocket PC Programs

If you are interested in writing your own Pocket PC programs, you will be happy to know that Microsoft provides the development tools as a free download or, for a nominal cost, on CD-ROM. You can find the Embedded Visual Tools, along with several tutorial articles, at http://www.microsoft.com/mobile/developer/default.asp. There are several websites and newsgroups on the Internet that provide information about writing programs for Pocket PCs. You'll find a list of these resources at http://www.microsoft.com/mobile/developer/onlinecommunity.asp.

toolkits for making Flash content, and provides Flash players for free from their website. You can download the Flash player for Pocket PCs from http://www.macromedia.com/software/flashplayer/pocketpc/download/.

The Pocket PC Flash player is integrated with Pocket Internet Explorer, and you normally will play Flash content by opening a web page on the Internet. However, Flash content can also be downloaded as individual files, which have the file extension .swf. You cannot open an SWF file on a Pocket PC; instead you must open an HTML file that is designed to display the Flash file. To open the file, use File Explorer to locate the HTML file, and then tap to open the file in Pocket Internet Explorer.

Examples of the type of Flash content available for Pocket PCs include a Tetris game, New York City subway map, and a Hewlett-Packard Scientific Calculator. You will find Flash files that you can download and play on your Pocket PC at http://www.flashenabled.com/mobile/ and at http://www.pocketpcflash.net/homefs.htm.

Add Storage Space with Peripheral Cards

To install the programs described in this chapter, you'll need storage space on your Pocket PC. As you install more programs, there will be less built-in storage space, so you will need to either remove programs from your Pocket PC to make room or add more storage space by using peripheral cards.

Over the years, several different peripheral card formats have been developed for mobile devices. Unlike Palm Computing and Handspring devices, Pocket PCs have always supported industry-standard card slots. In this section, you'll learn about the PC Card, CompactFlash, and Secure Digital card formats that can be used to expand Pocket PCs.

Expand with PC Cards

Standardization of PC Card technology began with the Japan Electronic Industry Development Association (JEIDA) in 1985. The organization promoted memory cards, personal computers, and other portable devices. In 1989, the Personal Computer Memory Card International

Association (PCMCIA) was formed by a group of small companies to develop standards for memory cards. The creation of such a standard enables cards to be created by multiple sources for use with multiple devices.

The first mission of the PCMCIA was to create removable memory cards that could be used for storage and software distribution for small devices. Later, I/O capabilities were added to the standards to support more types of PC Cards than just memory cards. In June 1990, the first PCMCIA standard was released, defining a 63-pin interface for Type I and Type II form factors. There have since been five releases of the standards, with the most recent release in February 1995. Prior to 1995, compliant products were called PCMCIA cards; but since 1995, the products have been simply called PC Cards.

Today, the PC Card standard defines a 68-pin interface between the card and a PC Card slot, into which the PC Card is inserted. There are three different PC Card sizes: Type I, Type II, and Type III. Each card has the same width and length, but they have different thicknesses. Type I cards are the thinnest at a thickness of 3.3mm, and are often used for memory cards. Type II cards are often used for I/O peripherals, which require more components and hence a thickness of 5mm. Type III cards are the thickest at 10.5mm and support small rotating disks.

The type of card that they can support defines PC Card slots. A Type II slot holds Type I and Type II size cards, but cannot hold a Type III card. Type III slots support all three card sizes.

Another difference among PC Cards is power requirements. Older PC Cards use 5 volts of power, which is provided by the batteries of the device. The 1995 PC Card standard provides for low-voltage cards that work with 3.3 volts, which contributes to longer battery life for the device. Low-power PC Cards are preferred because they contribute to longer battery life for the device.

A number of different types of PC Cards can be used with Pocket PCs. However, in order for the card to work, there must be a Pocket PC driver for the card. The driver provides the instructions to the operating system about how to use the PC Card, and cards specifically designed for Pocket PCs include the necessary drivers that you install onto the device. Pocket PCs include a set of generic drivers that work with standard storage and network interface cards. PC card modems have built-in drivers that, in most cases, are recognized by Pocket PCs

Expand with CompactFlash Cards

In 1994, SanDisk introduced the CompactFlash (CF) card, which is about the size of a matchbook. CF cards provide the same functionality as PC Cards, at about one-half the thickness of Type II PC Cards. Unlike their PC Card counterparts, CF slots only have 50 pins; but CF cards can be inserted into adapters that, in turn, can be inserted into PC Card slots. By using such an adapter, any CF card can be used in a Type II PC Card slot.

Most CF cards support dual 3.3- and 5-volt operation, which means that the card can operate with either voltage. Cards using only 3.3 volts are preferred because they contribute to longer battery life in the device.

The CompactFlash Association is the standards body that defines the CompactFlash standard; and, in 1998, they approved the Type II CF and CF+ specifications. Type II CF cards are 5mm thick, allowing them to contain more components than Type I cards, which are 3.3mm thick. The CF+ specification defines how magnetic disk drives and other I/O devices, such as modems and network interface cards, can be used in Type I or Type II CF card slots.

Unlike PC Cards, Type I and Type II CF cards simply define card thickness, while CF+ adds I/O functionality. This means that CF+ I/O devices can be found in both slot sizes, which is good because some Pocket PCs only have Type I slots. The most popular CF+ cards are the CompactFlash modems and network cards described in Chapter 19.

> **NOTE** *The Hewlett-Packard Jornada 560 series supports Type Ie CompactFlash cards, which are thicker than Type I card, but not as thick as Type II cards. No other Pocket PC supports Type Ie cards.*

All Pocket PCs support CF+ cards, but you should determine the CF slot type in your device before you buy a CF+ card. The user manual for your device should provide the information about which slot type is in your device.

Expand with Secure Digital Cards

Secure Digital cards are the newest type of mobile device cards. The cards weigh less than 2 grams and are about the size of a postage stamp. Secure Digital cards have the same physical characteristics as MultiMedia Cards, but include built-in support for encryption.

> **NOTE** *Pocket PCs with Secure Digital slots can read and write data to MultiMedia and Secure Digital cards.*

Data written to Secure Digital cards is not automatically encrypted. Special software uses the information on the card to encrypt data as it is written to the card. Once the encrypted content is stored on the card, it cannot be copied intact to any other location.

Currently, Secure Digital cards are only used for storage, though there are plans for making I/O devices in the Secure Digital form. Data is written and read to Secure Digital cards one bit at a time, so file transfer rates are slower than with CompactFlash cards. The current maximum size of a Secure Digital storage card is 128MB, and they are more expensive than comparable CompactFlash cards.

Increase Storage Space

Random access memory (RAM) is used in Pocket PCs for storage and program memory. As you read in Chapter 2, you can configure the amount of RAM used for each type of memory, but there is a limited amount available. Most devices come with a maximum of 32MB of RAM, and manufacturers do not provide internal memory upgrades for Pocket PCs.

You can add storage space by using CompactFlash or Secure Digital flash memory storage cards. *Flash memory* is a type of constantly powered, nonvolatile memory that can be erased and reprogrammed in units called *blocks*. Nonvolatile memory has a continuous source of power so that the contents are not lost when the memory is removed from a computing device. Flash memory gets its name from the fact that the chip is organized in such a manner that the memory cells can be erased in a single action, or a *flash*.

Because flash memory stores information in blocks, it cannot be used for program memory, like RAM, which needs to access information in bytes. Flash storage cards use the same specifications as those used to access hard disks, and therefore are treated like hard disks by computer operating systems.

If you are trying to decide which storage card to buy for your Pocket PC, there are two items for you to consider. First, what type of card you buy depends on the type of slot in your Pocket PC. If your Pocket PC only has a Type I CompactFlash slot, you don't want to buy a Type II CompactFlash storage card because it won't fit in the Pocket PC slot. Likewise, a CompactFlash card will not fit in a Secure Digital slot.

The second consideration is cost. There are several different brands of storage cards to choose from that all work equally well, so price is what distinguishes between storage card brands. As a rule, larger capacity storage cards are more expensive.

> **TIP**   *Another consideration in the future may be speed, as SanDisk recently announced the Ultra CompactFlash format that allows transfer speeds up to 2.8MB per second.*

Flash storage cards are available in the PC Card, CompactFlash, and Secure Digital form factors. Flash storage PC Cards are not popular because they are limited in storage size and more expensive. However, there are hard drives available in the PC Card form that will work in some Pocket PCs. PC Card hard drives can provide more storage space at a lower cost than flash storage.

The storage capacities of CompactFlash storage cards continue to increase; and, as of the time this book was written, the largest announced CompactFlash card is 1GB. Currently, the largest available Secure Digital storage card is 128MB.

CompactFlash storage cards are the most popular and can be used in some digital cameras, as well as Pocket PCs. Adapters are available to plug CompactFlash cards into Type II PC Card slots, enabling them to be used with notebook computers and desktop computers that have PC Card readers.

Store More Files for Less Money

Flash storage cards are like hard drives, but are better because they have no moving parts and retrieve data faster. Unfortunately, their maximum size of 1GB is small compared to the multi-gigabyte sizes of personal computer hard drives. A 1GB CompactFlash card can cost as much as $800.00.

The IBM Microdrive can store 1GB of files for half the price of CompactFlash. *Microdrives* are mechanical disks in the CompactFlash size, currently sold in 1GB, 500MB, and 340MB sizes. IBM plans to sell larger microdrives in the future.

If you need more than 1GB of storage space, and you own a PC Card sleeve for your Pocket PC, you can buy PC Card hard drives with capacities up to 5GB. There are two companies that sell PC Card hard drives for Pocket PCs. One of these is CMS Peripheral, which sells the Fire & Forget 5GB drive, and the other is Kingston Techonology, which sells the DataPak 5GB drive.

When you plug the drives into a Type II CompactFlash or PC Card slot of a Pocket PC, the disk is recognized like any other storage card, and does not require any special drivers.

> **NOTE**   *Because microdrives and PC Card hard drives have moving parts, they use more power and drain batteries faster than flash storage cards.*

Wrapping Up

The success of any computing platform is measured by the amount of software available for that platform. Thousands of people have downloaded the free development tools that Microsoft provides, resulting in hundreds of programs that you can download and install on your Pocket PC. Every day, more and more programs are becoming available for you to expand the functionality of your Pocket PC. The expansion capabilities of Pocket PCs ensure that you will be able to continue enjoying new software on your Pocket PC for many years to come

Index

INTERNATIONAL CONTACT INFORMATION

AUSTRALIA
McGraw-Hill Book Company Australia Pty. Ltd.
TEL +61-2-9417-9899
FAX +61-2-9417-5687
http://www.mcgraw-hill.com.au
books-it_sydney@mcgraw-hill.com

CANADA
McGraw-Hill Ryerson Ltd.
TEL +905-430-5000
FAX +905-430-5020
http://www.mcgrawhill.ca

GREECE, MIDDLE EAST,
NORTHERN AFRICA
McGraw-Hill Hellas
TEL +30-1-656-0990-3-4
FAX +30-1-654-5525

MEXICO (Also serving Latin America)
McGraw-Hill Interamericana Editores S.A. de C.V.
TEL +525-117-1583
FAX +525-117-1589
http://www.mcgraw-hill.com.mx
fernando_castellanos@mcgraw-hill.com

SINGAPORE (Serving Asia)
McGraw-Hill Book Company
TEL +65-863-1580
FAX +65-862-3354
http://www.mcgraw-hill.com.sg
mghasia@mcgraw-hill.com

SOUTH AFRICA
McGraw-Hill South Africa
TEL +27-11-622-7512
FAX +27-11-622-9045
robyn_swanepoel@mcgraw-hill.com

UNITED KINGDOM & EUROPE
(Excluding Southern Europe)
McGraw-Hill Education Europe
TEL +44-1-628-502500
FAX +44-1-628-770224
http://www.mcgraw-hill.co.uk
computing_neurope@mcgraw-hill.com

ALL OTHER INQUIRIES Contact:
Osborne/McGraw-Hill
TEL +1-510-549-6600
FAX +1-510-883-7600
http://www.osborne.com
omg_international@mcgraw-hill.com